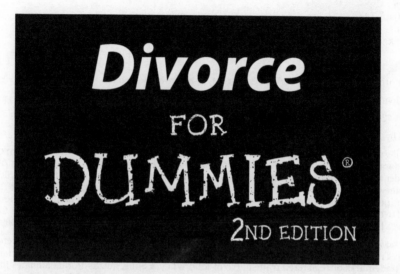

Divorce FOR DUMMIES®

2ND EDITION

by Elizabeth Walsh, Thelma Fisher, Hilary Woodward, John Ventura and Mary Reed

WILEY

A John Wiley and Sons, Ltd, Publication

Divorce For Dummies® 2nd Edition

Published by
John Wiley & Sons, Ltd
The Atrium
Southern Gate
Chichester
West Sussex
PO19 8SQ
England

E-mail (for orders and customer service enquires): cs-books@wiley.co.uk

Visit our Home Page on www.wiley.com

For general information on our other products and services, please contact our Customer Care Department within the U.S. at 800-762-2974, outside the U.S. at 317-572-3993, or fax 317-572-4002.

For technical support, please visit www.wiley.com/techsupport.

Wiley also publishes its books in a variety of electronic formats. Some content that appears in print may not be available in electronic books.

British Library Cataloguing in Publication Data: A catalogue record for this book is available from the British Library

ISBN: 978-0-470-74128-3

10 9 8 7 6 5 4 3 2 1

WILEY

About the Authors

Elizabeth Walsh graduated from Manchester University with a Law degree and was one of the first solicitors to be articled to a Clerk to the Justices in the Magistrates Courts. After qualifying, she moved to private practice as a family law advocate and then into publishing so that she could spend more time with her young and growing family. Elizabeth is now the editor of Family Law, the leading journal for practitioners in family law. She is also editor of International Family Law, the journal for family law practitioners worldwide. In 1993 she trained as a family mediator at the Institute of Family Therapy in London and in 1996 set up a mediation service in Buckinghamshire under the auspices of National Family Mediation, where she still practices. She was Chief Executive of the UK College of Family Mediators from 1997 to 1999. She became a Magistrate in 1990 and now heads up the Central Buckinghamshire Family Proceedings Panel. She is a member of the Thames Valley Family Mediation Council and in 1997 wrote *Working in the Family Justice System: the Official Handbook of the Family Justice Council,* now in its third edition. She has contributed to many other publications including *Family Mediation: Past Present and Future.*

Thelma Fisher was one of the first practitioners in the UK to apply the process of family mediation to divorcing couples. She had previously qualified and worked as a social worker and couple counsellor after graduating in English Literature and Language at King's College London. From 1981 she pioneered both the professional practice of mediation and its place in the Family Justice System, setting up one of the first family mediation services in Swindon before moving on to help create family mediation's early literature and training while a social work lecturer at the University of Bath. Her special interests included the effects of separation and divorce on children. From 1989 to 1999 she was appointed the first director of the national network of services that later became known as National Family Mediation and was Chair of the UK College of Family Mediators from 2000 to 2003.

Thelma has lectured on mediation in many countries, including Canada, Norway, France, Bosnia, Croatia, Serbia and the Republic of Macedonia. In the UK, she has regularly addressed national and international conferences and frequently appeared in the national media. She has published articles on family mediation in the *British Journal of Social Work, Family Mediation and Family Law.* She edited two editions of a standard textbook on family mediation, *Family Conciliation within the UK* and a UK edition of the influential American textbook by John Haynes, *The Fundamentals of Family Mediation.* She is also the author of *National Family Mediation Guide to Separation and Divorce: The complete handbook for managing a fair and amicable divorce.* Thelma was awarded the OBE in 1997and made a Fellow of Kings' College London in 2000. She and her husband had three children and she has two grandchildren.

Hilary Woodward did her first degree in Sociology and Anthropology at the London School of Economics and Political Science and worked on a variety of research projects with the Institute of Education, Medical Research Council and Institute of Psychiatry. In 1973 she started work for a London firm of solicitors where she made the decision to train as a solicitor. She was admitted to the Law Society's Roll of Solicitors in January 1982 and specialised in family law for over twenty years. She was a partner and then consultant in private practice in Bristol with Henriques Griffiths until her retirement from private practice in June 2003. Hilary trained and practices as a family mediator with Bristol Family Mediation. She was a governor and honorary treasurer for the UK College of Family Mediators from 2002 to 2008. Since 2002 she has worked as an associate on various socio-legal research studies, initially with Bristol University and now with Cardiff School of Law. She is the co-author of a number of articles on family law including, with Gillian Douglas and Julia Pearce, *A Failure of Trust: Resolving Property Disputes on Cohabitation Breakdown*.

John Ventura is an authority on consumer advocate law and financial issues. He earned degrees in both law and journalism from the University of Houston. He currently operates three law offices specialising in bankruptcy, consumer law, and personal injury in the Rio Grande Valley. He has written eight books on consumer and small-business legal and financial matters, and is the author of *Law For Dummies*. In addition, he writes a regular column for a Texas business journal and hosts a weekly radio program on legal issues. John has been a frequent network TV show guest on CNN, CNN-fn, and CNBC, and has done numerous national and local radio programs. He has provided expert opinion for publications including *Money, Kiplinger's Personal Finance Magazine, Black Enterprise, Inc., Martha Stewart's Living, The Wall Street Journal,* and *Newsweek*.

Mary Reed has ghost-written numerous books on money and legal matters and has been a regular contributor to *Home Office Computing* and *Small Business Computing* magazines. She is the owner of MR_PR, a public relations and special events firm based in Austin, Texas. Prior to starting her own business, Mary was vice-president of marketing for a national market research firm, public affairs and marketing director for a women's health-care organization, and public relations manager for an award-winning regional magazine. She holds a bachelor's degree in political science from Trinity College in Washington, D.C., and a master's degree in Business from Boston University.

Sandy Cartwright, a family lawyer in Austin, Texas, acted as a Special Contributor to the US edition of this title.

Dedication

This book is dedicated to The Rt Hon the Baroness Hale of Richmond, DBE, Justice of the Supreme Court, otherwise known as Brenda Hale, the first female Law Lord, who has made a remarkable contribution to the development of family law and family mediation over the last twenty years.

Acknowledgements

We are grateful for the help of the following people in contributing their specialised knowledge and experience to this book:

Fiona Garwood, who contributed much of the original material on divorce law in Scotland, was a family mediator for 20 years with Family Mediation Lothian and also worked as an Assistant Director for Family Mediation Scotland where she was responsible for mediation training and standards.

Rhona Adams, who updated Scottish Law for this edition, is a partner in the family law team at Morton Fraser, one of Scotland's leading law firms. She has extensive experience in the field of family law and is accredited by the Law Society of Scotland as a Specialist in Family Law. Rhona also practices as a solicitor mediator in family cases with CALM. She is a member of Scotland's Family Law Association.

Sheena Bell was a member of the Northern Ireland Family Mediation Service which operated between 1987 and 2000. She held all the professional posts within the service during the ensuing years – mediator, intake worker, co-ordinator, supervisor and trainer. She is the lead practitioner and professional practice consultant of the charity Family Mediation Northern Ireland, which was formed in 2004. She also mediates workplace disputes, mediates for the Disability Conciliation Service and has a private counselling practice.

Gregg Taffs has been a financial adviser for 17 years. Gregg started with the insurance division of Barclays Bank before leaving to become an independent financial adviser for Solace Associates and is now Investment Manager with Moore Stephens Financial Services, providing specialist advice to high net worth clients focusing mainly on investments and pensions.

Publisher's Acknowledgements

We're proud of this book; please send us your comments through our Dummies online registration form located at www.dummies.com/register/.

Some of the people who helped bring this book to market include the following:

Acquisitions, Editorial, and Media Development

Project Editor: Steve Edwards

(Previous Edition: Amie Jackowski Tibble, Daniel Mersey)

Content Editor: Jo Theedom

Commissioning Editor: Nicole Hermitage

Publishing Assistant: Jennifer Prytherch

Copy Editor: Andy Finch

Proofreader: David Price

Technical Editor: Hilary Woodward

Publisher: Jason Dunne

Executive Editor: Samantha Spickernell

Executive Project Editor: Daniel Mersey

Cover Photos: © Grant V. Faint/GettyImages

Cartoons: Ed McLachlan

Composition Services

Project Coordinator: Lynsey Stanford

Layout and Graphics: Reuben W. Davis, Sarah Philippart

Proofreader: Jessica Kramer

Indexer: Cheryl Duksta

Contents at a Glance

Introduction **1**

Part 1: Trouble in Paradise **7**

Chapter 1: Checking Out Your Divorce Roadmap 9

Chapter 2: Deciding What to Do First When Things Start to Go Wrong 21

Chapter 3: Wising Up to Your Family's Money Matters 33

Chapter 4: Finding Out about Family Law Basics 53

Chapter 5: Discovering the Basics of Divorce Law 67

Chapter 6: Considering Separation: A Healthy Breather or
a Prelude to Divorce? 93

Part 11: Divorce Preliminaries **103**

Chapter 7: Setting Your Divorce in Motion 105

Chapter 8: Helping Your Children Get Through Your Divorce 123

Chapter 9: Taking Care of Your Emotional Self 137

Part 111: Decisions, Decisions **145**

Chapter 10: Deciding Who Cares for Your Children 147

Chapter 11: Dividing Up What You Own 173

Chapter 12: Looking at Maintenance for You or Your Spouse 197

Chapter 13: Providing Financially for Your Children 207

*Part 1V: Working Out the Terms of Your
Divorce Agreement* **221**

Chapter 14: Doing Some of the Negotiating Yourself 223

Chapter 15: Choosing a Family Solicitor 239

Chapter 16: Using a Mediator to Help You Work Things Out Together 261

Chapter 17: Helping Your Solicitor Get the Best Results Possible 281

Chapter 18: Putting the Decisions in the Hands of a Judge 295

Part V: After Your Divorce 1s Finalised **313**

Chapter 19: Handling the Practical Matters of Life after Your Divorce 315

Chapter 20: Solving the Toughest Post-divorce Problems 329

Chapter 21: Thinking Ahead: Pre-marital Agreements 341

Part VI: The Part of Tens 349

Chapter 22: Ten Ways to Help Make Everything Okay for Your Children.............. 351
Chapter 23: Ten Tips for Putting Your Divorce Behind You and Moving On 355
Chapter 24: Ten Strategies for Next Time 361

Part VII: Appendixes 367

Appendix A: Glossary of Terms 369
Appendix B: Useful Divorce Websites... 381

Index 389

Table of Contents

Introduction 1

Why You Need This Book 1
Foolish Assumptions 2
How This Book Is Organised 3
    Part I: Trouble in Paradise 3
    Part II: Divorce Preliminaries 3
    Part III: Decisions, Decisions 3
    Part IV: Working Out the Terms of Your Divorce Agreement 4
    Part V: After Your Divorce Is Finalised 4
    Part VI: The Part of Tens 4
    Part VII: Appendixes 4
Icons Used in This Book 5
Where to Go from Here 5

Part 1: Trouble in Paradise 7

Chapter 1: Checking Out Your Divorce Roadmap 9

Divorcing Is a Process 10
Getting to the Bottom Line: The Law 10
    Grasping the basis of divorce law 10
    Changing the focus on children 11
    Understanding the differences in UK law 12
Starting the Divorce Process 12
Finding Your Way Through Your Divorce 13
    Looking at your financial picture 14
    Caring for your children 15
    Getting the help you need 16
    Going it alone 18
Moving On to Pastures New 18
Gearing Up for Your Divorce 19

Chapter 2: Deciding What to Do First When Things Start to Go Wrong 21

Recognising the Signs of Trouble 21
Should I Stay or Should I Go? 22
Trying to Work Things Out 23
    Taking a relationship mini-break 23
    Going for relationship counselling 24

When Staying Isn't an Option...25
    Separating before making a final decision................................26
    Separating permanently with no intention to divorce...................27
    Getting your marriage annulled 27
    Getting a divorce...28
What to Do if Things Become Abusive or Violent...............................29
    Understanding what is meant by domestic abuse 29
    Calling the police 29
    Getting an injunction against your spouse................................30
    Filing criminal charges 31
    Going to a refuge 31
    Considering other safety measures you can take.....................32

Chapter 3: Wising Up to Your Family's Money Matters **33**
It Takes Two to Manage (Or Mismanage) Money................................34
Financial Fundamentals: What You Must Do First 36
    Finding out what you have and what you owe............................36
    Drawing up a spending plan and sticking to it.........................37
    Creating a Household Income Sheet 41
    Owning a house...42
    Deciding what is fair 45
Finding Out What You Need to Know 46
Maintaining Your Employability...47
Building a Positive Credit Record 48
Establishing Your Own Credit Record...49

Chapter 4: Finding Out about Family Law Basics **53**
Changing Laws for Changing Times 53
    Ending the blame game...54
    Recognising children's rights...54
    Managing child support 54
    Supporting your spouse...55
    Living together without being married 55
Tying the Knot 56
    Carrying a licence to marry...56
    Understanding your marital rights and responsibilities 58
    Agreeing to the terms before you marry 59
    Marrying in a religious ceremony...59
    Uniting in a civil partnership...60
Knowing What the Law Says About Children 61
    Understanding parental responsibility 61
    Agreeing that there's no place like home –
        determining residence...62
    Keeping contact with your children..62
    Putting the children first..63

Distinguishing One Lawyer from Another 63
Courting Justice 64
Looking at Foreign Marriage and Divorce 66

Chapter 5: Discovering the Basics of Divorce Law **67**
Not Just Anyone Can Get Divorced 68
Understanding irretrievable breakdown 68
Resolving Basic Divorce Issues 70
The Ground Rules of the Divorce Court 72
One Objective (But Many Ways to Get There) 72
The co-operative divorce 74
The difficult divorce 75
The fully contested divorce 75
Initiating the Divorce Proceedings 76
Remembering your marriage certificate 77
Including a Statement of Arrangements for the children 77
Serving and receiving the papers 78
Signing the affidavit in support of petition 80
Getting Through the First Stage: The Decree Nisi 80
Finalising Your Divorce with the Decree Absolute 81
Agreeing to Disagree: What Happens After You Decide to Litigate 82
Formal Applications to the Court: Financial Issues 83
Powers of the court 84
Statements to file 84
First directions appointment – or FDA 86
Financial dispute resolution appointment – or FDR 86
Disclosure 87
Full hearings 90
Judge's decision – the order or judgement 90
Formal Applications to the Court: Issues Regarding Your Children 91
Role of the Cafcass officer or Family Court Adviser 91
Final hearing in children matters 92

**Chapter 6: Considering Separation: A Healthy Breather
or a Prelude to Divorce?** **93**
You're Married, but Only Sort Of 93
Considering why you need to separate 94
Knowing the drawbacks of separating 94
Talking things over before you separate 95
Initiating a Separation 96
Protecting Yourself When You Separate Informally 96
Formalising Your Separation Agreement 97
Trying the art of compromise 99
Deciding what to put in a separation agreement 100
Safeguarding your liquid assets 100
Being careful about what you sign 100

Not Quite Divorce: Judicial Separation.......................................101
If You Kiss and Make up 101
  Reconciling for the right reasons 102
  Fortifying your relationship with counselling.....................102

Part II: Divorce Preliminaries 103

Chapter 7: Setting Your Divorce in Motion 105
Breaking the News to Your Spouse...105
  Maintaining your composure 106
  Making sure that your spouse hears the news from you first 106
  Waiting until your spouse is ready to begin negotiations...........107
Gathering Your Financial Information 108
  Listing what you own 109
  Listing what you owe..112
  Gathering miscellaneous financial documents together 113
  Creating income and expenditure worksheets 113
Planning for Your Life After Divorce..114
  Deciding on your goals and priorities.................................114
How Much Do You Have to Spend to End Your Marriage? 116
  Hoping for the best: The least it costs 117
  Fearing the worst: The most it costs...................................117
  Getting help from public funding (Legal aid) 118
  Receiving state benefits and tax credits 119
Anticipating a Hostile Divorce 120
  Opening a bank account in your own name........................120
  Closing or freezing your joint accounts..............................121
  Finding a safe place for your important personal property........121
  Protecting your mutual assets from being wasted
    by your spouse 122
  Identifying sources of ready funds 122

Chapter 8: Helping Your Children Get Through Your Divorce 123
Remaining Sensitive to Your Children's Feelings......................123
When, What and How to Tell Your Children What's Happening...........125
  Finding help with telling your children...............................126
  Keeping your children out of the argument 128
  Deciding when to tell your children 129
  Telling your children individually or all together 130
Anticipating Your Children's Responses....................................131
  Listening to your children 132
  Recognising signs that your children are finding
    it hard to cope 133
  Handling your children's questions 134
  Understanding how children vary with age 135
  'No one tells us anything'...136

Chapter 9: Taking Care of Your Emotional Self...................137

Preparing for the Emotional Ups and Downs............................137
Understanding the Stages of Grief..138
Keeping Your Emotions in Check..140
How your emotions can affect you.......................................140
Ways of getting through the tough times 140
Dealing with the Response of Your Family and Friends.............141
Meeting with disapproval...141
Keeping grandparents..142
Coping if friends become more distant...............................142
Sorting out tensions 143

Part III: Decisions, Decisions..................................... **145**

Chapter 10: Deciding Who Cares for Your Children..............147

Deciding for Yourselves..148
Understanding Parental Responsibility – Much More
than Just 'Custody' 149
Deciding Where Your Children Are Going to Live.....................150
Staying primarily with one parent.......................................150
Good Relationships Make Good Contact....................................152
Living in two households...153
Consulting your children...155
Keeping in Contact with Your Children....................................158
Making your arrangements work for your children 159
Tackling potential contact problems 161
Going the Extra Mile with a 'Parenting Plan'............................164
Putting it all into the plan...165
Improving your living arrangements with a parenting plan........166
Making the plan flexible..166
Satisfying the Judge about Your Arrangements 167
Finding a Way Forward When You Can't Agree.........................167
Preparing for a court hearing..169
Questions you can expect a judge to ask 170
Orders a judge can make 170
Neither of you may get the children....................................171
Children divorcing their parents 172

Chapter 11: Dividing Up What You Own........................173

Getting to Grips with Property Basics 173
Distinguishing between tangible property
and intangible property..174
Identifying your marital property..174
Understanding matrimonial property in Scotland 175
Valuing Your Assets..176

Following the Legal Guidelines 177
Working Out Your Money Matters When You Divorce in Scotland 179
    Financial principles of Scottish family law 179
    Financial orders in Scotland 180
Getting Up-front Advice 181
Deciding What to Do With Your Home 181
    Finding out what your home is worth 181
    Evaluating your options 182
    Hearing some good news about capital gains tax 185
Dividing Up Your Retirement Benefits 185
    Finding out the value of your pension 187
    Evaluating the options for dealing with your pension 188
    Knowing your pension options 189
Getting Down to Business: How to Deal with Your Joint Enterprise 191
    Understanding your options, in a nutshell 192
    Assigning a value to your business 193
Endowment and Other Insurance Policies 194
Dealing With Your Debts 195
    Tips for avoiding trouble 195
    Where the law stands on your debts 196

Chapter 12: Looking at Maintenance for You or Your Spouse 197

What Is Maintenance and When Is It Paid? 198
How the Courts View Maintenance 200
    Knowing the factors that a judge considers 201
Taking Capital Instead of Maintenance 203
Seeking a Change in Maintenance 204
Preparing for Life without Maintenance 205
Maintenance and Tax 206

Chapter 13: Providing Financially for Your Children 207

Supporting Your Children 208
    Caring for your children all the time 209
    Sharing your children's care 209
Working Out What You Pay or Receive 210
    Getting state benefits and tax credits 211
    Applying to the court: Special circumstances
        a judge may consider 213
Agreeing on Extra Expenses 214
    Purchasing life insurance for the benefit of your children 214
    Providing private medical cover 214
    Purchasing disability insurance 215
    Providing 'extras' for your children 215
Negotiating Your Own Child Support Agreement 216
    Understanding child support and contact 217
    Changing the agreement as your lives change 218

Making Sure the Child Support Gets Paid 218
Getting a court order 218
Using automatic deductions from wages 219
Knowing when child support obligations cease 220
Understanding Child Support and Tax 220

Part IV: Working Out the Terms of Your Divorce Agreement 221

Chapter 14: Doing Some of the Negotiating Yourself 223

First, a Word of Caution 223
Remaining on Your Best Behaviour 224
Starting Off on the Right Foot: The Preliminaries 225
Planning a Method of Negotiation 225
Choosing the Right Setting 226
Scheduling the Time 227
Deciding on the Order of Business 227
Acquiring (and Paying for) Expert Advice 229
Bringing in a Solicitor to Help You 230
Getting some basic information 230
Asking your solicitors to review and draft your
final agreement 231
Creating a Parenting Plan that Works for Everyone 232
Working Out Child Support 232
Determining a reasonable standard of living 233
Getting a court order, even if you agree 233
Discussing Spousal Maintenance 234
Dividing Up Your Property and Debts 235
Splitting it down the middle – or not 235
Dividing up the big stuff 236
Sharing out smaller items 237
Working Out What to Do With the House 237
Remembering Your Taxes 238
Getting to a Solution 238

Chapter 15: Choosing a Family Solicitor 239

When to Engage a Solicitor 239
What to Look for in a Solicitor 240
Appropriate skills and experience 241
Personal style 242
Affordability 242
Knowing What You Can (and Should) Expect from Your Solicitor 243
Finding the Right Solicitor 243
Locating a Specialist 244

Avoiding Certain Solicitors...245
Meeting Potential Solicitors 245
    Requesting a free consultation 245
    Questioning the solicitor, and responses you need to hear 246
    Producing the documents you need 248
    Finding out what a solicitor wants to know about you.................249
Getting the Terms and Conditions of Business in Writing.....................250
Changing Your Solicitor if You're a Private Client 250
Changing Your Solicitor if You're Publicly Funded............................251
Discovering What to Do if You Can't Afford Your Solicitor's Fees........251
    Qualifying for public funding: legal aid 251
    Qualifying for public funding: the Family Help scheme.............253
    Finding alternative ways to pay 258
Considering a DIY Divorce 259

Chapter 16: Using a Mediator to Help You Work Things Out Together. 261

What is Mediation?...261
    When do you start mediation?..262
    What do mediators do?..263
    Who are mediators?...263
Reaping the Benefits of Mediation..265
Finding Family Mediators 266
Taking Your First Mediation Step..268
Understanding How Mediation Works...269
    Identifying the issues and making an agenda........................270
    Exploring the issues in detail 270
    Verifying the details..272
    Negotiating your future budgets...273
    Consulting your children during mediation 274
    Including other family members in a mediation session............275
The Memorandum of Understanding..276
    Including your financial details in an Open Statement 276
    Making your Memorandum of Understanding legally binding.....277
Asking for Mediation Help from Your Solicitor 277
Getting Help with the Cost of Mediation 278
Going to Your Solicitors if You Can't Agree in Mediation.....................279

Chapter 17: Helping Your Solicitor Get the Best Results Possible 281

What to Expect from Your Solicitor 281
What Your Solicitor Expects from You..283
    Speaking your mind and not being afraid to ask questions 283
    Paying your bills on time 284
    Keeping your solicitor up to date with any changes
        in your life 284
    Avoiding using your solicitor as a therapist 285

First Things First: Seeking Urgent or Interim Orders 285
Providing Your Solicitor with Essential Information 286
    Personal information 287
    Legal and financial information 288
    Other important information 289
Hammering Out the Details of Your Settlement 289
Evaluating the Proposal 290
Making a Deal: The Final Settlement 291
Changing the Agreement Later 292
Applying for the Final Decree 292
Using the Collaborative Law Process 293
    How does the collaborative process work? 293
    How long does the collaborative process take? 294
    How expensive is the collaborative process? 294

Chapter 18: Putting the Decisions in the Hands of a Judge 295
Making Certain You Want to Go to Court 296
Settling Out of Court 297
    Receiving the offer 297
    Deciding on the offer 297
Settling Issues through a Pre-trial Hearing 298
Preparing for the Final Hearing 300
    Setting the stage 300
    Understanding the disclosure process 301
    Producing evidence 302
    Calling witnesses 302
    Preparing the court bundle 304
    Rehearsing for your big day (or days) 304
    Dressing the part 305
    Acting the part 305
Understanding the Judge's Role 306
Having Your Day in Court 307
Finally, the Judgement 308
Appealing the Decision 309
Preparing for the New Family Procedure Rules 311

Part V: After Your Divorce Is Finalised 313

**Chapter 19: Handling the Practical Matters of Life
after Your Divorce 315**
Tying Up the Loose Ends of Your Final Court Order 316
    Transferring real property 316
    Transferring other property 317
    Paying off debts 317
    Collecting state benefits and tax credits 318
    Protecting your pension rights 318
    Changing your final order 318

Rethinking Your Estate Planning..319
   If you don't have a will, now's the time to write one 319
   Estate planning tools to help you 320
Assessing Your Financial Situation 321
Finding a Job or Landing a Better One..323
   Acquiring the education you need 323
   Searching for the right job..324
Dealing with Personal and Family Issues 325
   Being easy on yourself 325
   Taking time to reflect on what happened.......................................326
   Finding a support group 326
   Becoming handy around the house..326
   Focusing more attention on your children......................................327
   Finding activities you and your children enjoy 327
   Working at rebuilding a sense of family..327
Making New Friends 328

Chapter 20: Solving the Toughest Post-divorce Problems 329

Your Ex-spouse Interferes with Your Child Contact Arrangements 329
   Avoiding retaliation by withholding payments...............................330
   Making an application to the court 330
Child Support Payments Don't Arrive...331
   Enforcing a child support agreement..331
   Fulfilling an order for child support 332
   Enforcing a CSA assessment..333
Your Ex-spouse Leaves the Country 334
Your Ex-spouse Disappears with Your Children 335
Your Ex-spouse Owes You Maintenance 336
Your Ex-spouse Fails or Refuses to Sign Property Over to You 336
You Want to Change Some Terms of Your Divorce Settlement 337
   Demonstrating a change in your circumstances 337
   Securing a court order if you change the
      agreement yourselves 338
Your Ex-spouse Files a Bankruptcy Petition 339
   Support obligations – theory and practice....................................339
   Capital and property orders...340

Chapter 21: Thinking Ahead: Pre-marital Agreements 341

Accepting that PMAs Aren't Just for the Wealthy Anymore..................342
Broaching the Subject With Your Spouse (Delicately)...........................343
Deciding What Goes in Your Agreement 344
Making Your Pre-marital Agreement Fit for Court 345
Getting Legal Help with Your Agreement 347
Drafting a Post-marital Agreement 347
   Understanding how to use a post-marital agreement..................348
   Doing your best to make your post-marital agreement
      stand up in court..348

Part VI: The Part of Tens 349

Chapter 22: Ten Ways to Help Make Everything Okay for Your Children 351

Showing Your Children that You Still Love Them.................................351
Encouraging Your Children to Respect and Love their
    Other Parent 352
Keeping Your Burdens from Your Children..................................352
Trying to Agree with Your Ex-spouse on the Ground
    Rules for Parenting 352
Making Your Children Feel at Home in Your New Place 353
Avoiding Manipulation...353
Keeping Your Promises 353
Waiting to Date 354
Creating Stable and Predictable Lives for Your Children 354
Avoiding Becoming a 'Super Parent'..354

Chapter 23: Ten Tips for Putting Your Divorce Behind You and Moving On 355

Finding an (Adult) Shoulder to Lean On....................................355
Starting to Keep a Diary...356
Seeking Help If You Need It 356
Fighting the Urge to Return to Your Ex 356
Focusing on Your Work...357
Getting in Touch with Your Spiritual Side....................................357
Cleaning Up Your Debts..357
Trying Something Entirely New 358
Sharing Your Space to Save Money...358
Re-starting Your Social Life 359

Chapter 24: Ten Strategies for Next Time .361

Communicating, Not Just Talking..361
Making Time for Each Other 362
Fighting Fair...363
Trying New Ways of Resolving Old Problems................................363
Maintaining Your Sense of Humour 364
Forgiving and Forgetting...364
Resolving Problems Quickly 364
Attending Pre-marriage Counselling to Avoid Surprises....................365
Attending a Marriage Enrichment Course.....................................365
Supporting Your Spouse's Outside Interests.................................366

Part VII: Appendixes.................................. *367*

Appendix A: Glossary of Terms 369

Appendix B: Useful Divorce Websites........................381
Divorce and Procedure...381
Advice, Information, and Support 382
Solicitors and Mediators..383
Five Government Help Websites 383
Four Websites for You and Your Children....................384
Children's Commissioners Websites 385
Ten Websites in Scotland 385
Ten Websites in Northern Ireland................................386

Index *389*

Introduction

Welcome to the second edition of *Divorce For Dummies*. Divorce is commonplace now but it is not only married couples who split up. Since 2005, same-sex couples in the UK can enter into civil partnerships and although the ending of a partnership is called dissolution rather than divorce, the process is much the same. In addition, the number of couples who live together without marrying increases dramatically year by year and their separation, although not governed by the laws of divorce or dissolution, will have financial and emotional consequences for those couples and their children.

Most people are almost completely at a loss over what to do if *their* relationships are breaking up. Overwhelmed by confusion, anger, fear and resentment, many couples panic over the changes occurring in their lives (and the lives of their children) and end up making emotionally and financially costly mistakes that could have been avoided if they'd had more information. Others turn what may have been an amicable break-up into a cut-throat battle. They end their relationships bitter, angry and a whole lot poorer at a time when this isn't necessary at all.

But divorce (and we include dissolution in that term) isn't about winners and losers, and it doesn't have to include huge legal bills either. This book is about what to do before, during and after your divorce (and we include dissolution in that term) and much of it applies to cohabiting couples as well, particularly as regards your children. With the right information, tools and advice (and the proper attitude), you and your partner can work out the terms of your parting with a minimum of expense, stress and emotional upheaval. In this book, we tell you how it can be done.

Why You Need This Book

Dip into this book and you can discover the following:

- What to do first before you file a divorce petition.
- Family law and divorce law basics, including how divorce laws may vary throughout the UK (though you must always defer to your solicitor).

- Facts to consider when you're deciding on how you'll care for your children, including maintenance, child support and the division of your assets.

- Mistakes to avoid and insights into effective negotiating.

- Tips for finding a solicitor who's competent *and* affordable.

- Advice for keeping your emotions as well as your legal expenses under control, including tips for using mediation and other non-confrontational methods for getting through your divorce as amicably as possible.

- For the small percentage of you who are involved in hostile divorces and have to sort out your differences through a court, this book can prepare you for your experience in a courtroom.

- Advice for minimising the potential negative effect divorce may have on your children, and suggested ways to rebuild a new life for yourself after divorce.

Foolish Assumptions

Because you've picked up this book, we're assuming that you've come to the realisation that your marriage has what may be insurmountable problems and you're seriously considering a divorce. Or perhaps you're already separated and are ready to take legal steps to end your marriage. We're not going to give you reasons for why you should or shouldn't get divorced – you need to make those decisions yourself. However, we do give you advice on how to start and get through the whole divorce process while handling its ups and downs as gracefully as possible.

The law is known for having very specific, impenetrable language – often it's impossible to understand unless you're a lawyer (and sometimes, even if you are). Divorce law is littered with obscure words, so we always give you a definition and you can find most of them in the glossary at the end of the book. We don't save you from them altogether, however, as you'll meet up with them at times. Someone recently wrote how when you travel by ship you may be initially embarrassed to use words like 'stern' and 'starboard' but may end up casually saying them because no one seems to be astonished or impressed when you do. You may acquire some of that ease yourself, and thankfully, many lawyers belong to the 'plain-speaking' brigade and we definitely approve of that.

How This Book Is Organised

You can use this book in one of two ways. You can read it cover to cover, and never skip a beat on the subject of divorce, or you can pick it up when you need an answer to a particular question or want to know more about a certain subject. For even easier reading, it's organised into six parts.

Part 1: Trouble in Paradise

This part of the book helps prepare you for dealing with a seriously troubled marriage and reviews your options if you're in a failing relationship. It provides information on gathering facts about your family's finances and honing your money management skills before you get divorced. This part also offers you an overview of family and divorce law and the responsibilities that parents have towards their non-adult children. We close this part with a chapter on separation – to save your marriage, or as a prelude to divorce.

Part 11: Divorce Preliminaries

The second part of *Divorce For Dummies* tells you how to prepare yourself for the divorce process and has specific advice for the spouse who initiates a divorce and for the spouse who gets the bad news. It devotes a full chapter to telling your children that mum and dad won't be living together any more and helping them get through your divorce as painlessly as possible. Lastly, this part provides advice on coping with the emotions you inevitably feel and dealing with the reaction of your friends and family.

Part 111: Decisions, Decisions

When your divorce or separation has begun, you have to make some important and sometimes tough decisions: Will you pay or receive spousal support? Where will your children live, and if not with you both in your separate households, how will you make sure that they stay in touch with both parents? What about child support? How will your marital property be divided up? These questions aren't to be taken lightly, but their answers should be easier to reach after you read the chapters in this part of the book.

Part IV: Working Out the Terms of Your Divorce Agreement

This part of the book is a must-read whether you and your spouse negotiate most of your divorce yourselves or you each hire solicitors to do most of the negotiating for you. You find out about the benefits and drawbacks of negotiating yourselves, and discover the many benefits of using mediation to help settle your divorce. We tell you where and how to find affordable solicitors and what you must expect from them, and what your solicitor expects from you. For those of you heading for divorce court, the final chapter in this part tells you what to expect before, during and after a judge decides your divorce terms.

Part V: After Your Divorce Is Finalised

After your divorce is wrapped up, you still have paperwork to deal with and money matters to handle. Plus, you now face the prospect of getting by on your own. You may also face problems with your divorce agreement or with your spouse failing to adhere to court orders or the plans you made for your children or spousal maintenance. This part provides advice for these and other common post-divorce problems. Finally, we include a chapter that explains the value of pre- and post-marital agreements if you marry again.

Part VI: The Part of Tens

The first chapter in this part offers advice for helping your children cope in the aftermath of your divorce. In the second chapter, you can find practical tips for how to put your divorce behind you and move forward with your life. The final chapter offers help on building and sustaining a mutually fulfilling relationship in the future.

Part VII: Appendixes

You may hear some unfamiliar words and terms in this book as you read through it, so we give you a handy glossary in this part for quick reference. We also give you a list of helpful websites that you can turn to for help in finding information and support.

Icons Used in This Book

 This icon lets you know about something especially useful that can save you time, money or energy while you're going through your divorce.

 Make a note when you see this icon – it indicates something that you must keep in mind as you make your way through the divorce process.

 Stop and read this information to steer clear of mistakes and pitfalls that are common in divorce.

 For those of you who like as much in-depth information on a subject as possible, you may want to make a point of reading this material.

 This icon highlights scenarios we've seen (or heard about in the news) that may help you realise you're not alone as you go through your divorce.

 If you lizve in Scotland or Northern Ireland, pay close attention when you see this icon. The laws in these two countries are slightly different from those in England and Wales and we've highlighted the major differences with this icon. Many of the laws are the same throughout the UK, however, so don't depend on these icons for the whole picture.

Where to Go from Here

The divorce process is never an easy one, but we do our best to give you the information you need to make it as smooth as possible. However, as with any legal issue, make sure that you talk things over with your solicitor before making any major decisions, because the laws evolve over time and you need the most up-to-date information possible.

Part I
Trouble in Paradise

'It's my wife calling — she wants a divorce.'

In this part . . .

If your marriage is rocky and you think that you're heading for a breakup, this part of the book provides information to prepare you for the divorce process. (Because divorce may not be an option for some of you, we also talk about marriage as well as divorce issues.) We also offer information on what to do if you're a victim of domestic violence.

We provide you with some solid advice for getting your finances together (whether or not you're divorcing), an overview of your legal rights and obligations during the divorce process, plus some basic information on family law in general and divorce law and procedure in particular. This part ends with a chapter on separation, which you may opt for as a last-ditch effort to save your marriage or use as a prelude to – or instead of – divorce.

Chapter 1

Checking Out Your Divorce Roadmap

In This Chapter

▶ Understanding the basic requirements of the law

▶ Caring for your children

▶ Making decisions about home, money, pensions and possessions

▶ Locating who is out there to help you

▶ Getting ready for life after divorce

*T*he word 'divorce' literally means 'turned aside'. You may be contemplating 'turning aside' from your spouse or facing the effects of your spouse 'turning aside' from you. You can be forgiven for thinking of divorce as a negative mirror image of your marriage. Getting a divorce means taking apart, bit by bit, all the things you and your spouse put together over the years. A divorce is like watching your married actions in reverse – unmaking the promises, telling your families an unwelcome story, enacting the end not the start of your relationship, perhaps selling the home you struggled to buy and sharing out the care of any children you were thrilled to conceive together.

You can, however, look at your situation in a more positive light. Think of it as holding up a mirror to yourself during a major life crisis. With this mirror in front of you and this book in your hand, we hope you can watch the expression on your face change from uncertainty to determination to self-confidence. To get through your divorce with as little difficulty as possible, you need good information and an optimistic outlook. This approach, we hope, sums up what we've written. We don't deny, though, that divorce takes its toll on you, and therefore in Chapter 9 we give you ways to look after yourself as you work your way through the process.

Divorcing Is a Process

Like most crises, your divorce is a process not an event. It has a beginning, a middle, and – yes, eventually – an end. In this book we give you a map of the whole process of divorce – from the moment you decide that your relationship is in serious trouble to the moment your divorce is finalised – and we offer tips for dealing with the changes in your life afterwards. Because everyone is different, we give you a variety of routes. This chapter is a bird's-eye view of the whole landscape to help you choose where to start.

We don't always spare you hard words (check the Glossary at the back if you come across a word you're unsure of), and neither do we always spare you hard problems to overcome and hard decisions to take. We do, however, provide ways to avoid creating unnecessary problems, and we warn you when difficult decisions lie ahead. No matter how hard you try to dodge them, when you come across decisions that must be made, you need to be prepared.

If at all possible, we recommend you go for a co-operative divorce, but we know it can be difficult and you may end up in court with a fully contested divorce (see Chapter 5). One of our favourite solicitors is a wonderful mediator, but if she's representing someone in a full hearing, she is very, very tough. So when it comes to your divorce, we're not bland – we're not cynical. However, we are realistic about what divorce means for you.

Getting to the Bottom Line: The Law

The legal effects of both marriage and divorce are to change your legal status. In the eyes of the State, you changed once from a single person to a married person and divorce changes you back again. However, only a judge in a county court or high court can change your status back to being single. That is the bottom line of divorce law. Because you collect responsibilities by being married, the law is accompanied by a stack of documents and a series of routine court procedures to make sure that you give the judge the information required for your divorce to be granted with the minimum of unfairness to you or your spouse. If you have children, the law exists to protect them – and so divorce law has links to family law.

Grasping the basis of divorce law

The Matrimonial Causes Act 1973 is the law governing divorce if you live in England and Wales. In Scotland, the relevant law is the Divorce (Scotland) Act 1976 and in Northern Ireland it's the Matrimonial Causes (Northern

Ireland) Order 1978. In all cases, the only ground for divorce is the irretrievable breakdown of your marriage, but you must establish that by one of the five following facts:

- ✔ Your spouse has committed adultery and you find it intolerable to live with him.

- ✔ Your spouse has behaved in such a way that you can't reasonably be expected to live with him.

- ✔ Your spouse has deserted you – for a minimum of two years (no longer applicable in Scotland).

- ✔ You have been separated for at least two years (one year in Scotland) and your spouse consents to a divorce.

- ✔ You have been separated for at least five years (two years in Scotland).

Chapters 4 and 5 spell out the legal aspects of marriage and divorce in detail.

Since the early 1980s, the divorce rate has stabilised, largely due to the decline in marriage and the increasing proportion of couples cohabiting, particularly since 1990. The number of divorces in the UK fell by 2.6 per cent in 2007 to 144,220, compared with 148,141 divorces in 2006. The number of divorces in Scotland fell by 1.9 per cent from 13,014 in 2006 to 12,773 in 2007. However, the number of divorces in Northern Ireland increased – in 2007, 2,913 divorces took place, 14 per cent more than the 2,565 divorces in 2006.

Changing the focus on children

The law about children was changed radically when the Children Act 1989 was passed. This law shifted the focus away from deciding 'parental rights' to the notion of 'parental responsibilities'. You no longer have rights over your children, which you can fight about at divorce; rather you have responsibilities for your children, which you don't shed when you divorce. Accordingly, the law stops talking about *custody*, which the court granted to one parent, and *access*, which was granted to the parent who doesn't 'get' the children. Instead, the law now encourages parents to decide for themselves what's in the best interests of their children, where they live (their *residence*) and how they're going to have *contact* with the parent they aren't living with.

Divorced or separated parents now have more flexibility in working out their arrangements and many children now live with both parents at different times according to whatever works best for them. Of course, if you and your spouse can't agree, the court decides and the law spells out what factors the judge must consider in making his decisions.

Chapter 4 goes into more detail about the Children Act 1989 and what it means for your family, and Chapter 10 covers the ways you can plan for your children's care.

Civil partnership

Since December 2005 couples of the same sex who live together can register as civil partners. If you sign a civil partnership registration document you commit yourselves to a range of rights and responsibilities, essentially the same as those associated with marriage. Civil partnership is not precisely the same as gay marriage but the legal rules and consequences are more or less the same. If the relationship breaks down you can end your civil partnership through the courts just like a divorce. Take a look at Chapter 4 to see whether this applies to you.

Understanding the differences in UK law

Divorce law, procedures and courts differ in some respects in England and Wales from those in Northern Ireland and even more so from those in Scotland. The divorce laws themselves are relatively similar but the Scottish laws about children and property are significantly different. We have given you the main legal differences where they occur but we don't have sufficient space to spell out the minor – but important – differences in the law and procedures in detail. Therefore, if you live in Scotland or Northern Ireland, we recommend that you consult a solicitor for those further details.

Starting the Divorce Process

The chances are that if you'd been able to prevent your marriage from breaking down you'd have done so. If you're still not 100 per cent sure that divorce or separation is what you want (or have to accept), you may be better starting at Chapter 2. Here, we give you suggestions for trying to improve your relationship if a chance remains of saving it, or at least for thoroughly testing the inevitability of its end. We suggest alternatives to divorce, such as separation, but emphasise that you shouldn't leave your home without first thinking through the consequences that we spell out in Chapter 6.

If you've decided that your relationship is over, no turning back is possible and you're ready to take legal steps to end your marriage, have a look at Chapter 7. Although, Chapters 4 and 5 give you the legal background, Chapter 7 starts you on the path, with tips on everything from telling your spouse it's over to working out your family's financial situation and how that's affected by your separation.

Separating when you never married

You may have picked up this book thinking that you're in a *common law* marriage: that although you never married, when you live with someone for a period of time, and especially have children, that's as good as marriage and when you separate the outcome is also the same. The law doesn't look at it this way – legally you don't have the rights and responsibilities that married couples do (although the position in Scotland is different). For example, you can't claim ongoing financial support from your ex-partner and, unless your name is on the deeds to your home, you may not be able to claim a share of it. But you can still find much of this book useful and children are treated the same whether you're married or not. Chapter 4 may be the place to start finding out about cohabitation. A solicitor specialising in this area can give you more advice.

We urge you to make sure that everyone stays safe. A relationship breaking down can be the result of abuse or can be the trigger for abuse. In either case, your safety, your spouse's safety and your children's safety are paramount. Chapter 2 tells you how and where to find help when abuse is a risk in your household. Gone are the days when what went on in people's homes was treated as their business alone. Nowadays the police treat all domestic violence as a crime and take it very seriously.

The end of your relationship can trigger overwhelming feelings, including grievances and fear that your security is ebbing away, and emotions can get out of control. Your children are likely to sense what's going on around them even if your outbursts of anger don't land directly on them. You can find crucial information about the steps to take to protect yourselves in Chapter 2.

Finding Your Way Through Your Divorce

After you've started the divorce ball rolling by informing your spouse, getting a full picture of your financial situation, and ascertaining what both your expectations are for your lives after the divorce, you and your spouse need to work out how you want to handle extricating your lives from each other. The serious stuff that you have to sort out falls broadly into these categories:

✔ **Your money,** including salaries and pensions – and your debts

✔ **Your house,** if you have one

✔ **Your possessions,** including everything from your car to your CDs

✔ **Your children,** if you have them

We go into detail on how to handle all these issues, though we don't spend as much time on possessions (such as pictures and CDs). Dividing these items can feel like a sword in your soul but in the long run they are replaceable. You may also have other things of value, such as cars, a business or other properties. For the most part, anything owned by either or both of you before, during, or after your marriage (even an inheritance) can be viewed by the court as belonging to both of you and open to claim, so everything needs to be entered into the calculations. Chapter 3 helps you work out what you have and what you owe, and you can find advice on dividing possessions in Chapter 11.

Looking at your financial picture

When you come to sorting out your finances, you mustn't look at each item in isolation. We discuss your salaries, pensions, houses, mortgages, assets, and debts under separate headings because differences apply to the options you have for sorting them out. But they aren't actually separate issues when you look at them within your total financial situation. As you collect information about what you earn, own and owe, you're going to build up a big picture of what comes in and what goes out and how that looks when you try to divide it. The information you find in Chapter 11 can help you understand your whole financial picture. Chapter 12 covers the issue of financial support for you and your spouse, including whether it's an option in your situation and if so, who's likely to pay it, and who's likely to receive it (and how much).

Until 1995 divorcing spouses were unable to divide up their pension benefits. Your pension was your own, you earned it, and it didn't belong to your spouse. The tables were most probably turned by the efforts of wives who had no pension in their own right (often because they gave up work to look after their children) and lost any future share of their husband's pension on divorce. Since 1995, pensions could be 'earmarked' or 'attached' (a lump sum or income can be paid from your spouse's pension, when in payment, to you) and from 2000 pensions can be calculated and shared at the time of your divorce. We describe your options in Chapter 11.

Keep these issues in mind when thinking about dividing up your finances:

- ✔ Think about your future ability to pay for your house before deciding what to do with it.

- ✔ Think about your future earning capacities before you do a deal over your pensions.

- ✔ Remember to take your debts and commitments into consideration when you think about your current income.

- ✔ Take time to weigh up the impact of your decisions on each other, on how much money you have coming in and on how much will be going out when you're apart.

Chapters 7, 11, 14, 16, and 17 all have things to say about gathering up the different parts of your financial information and fitting them together to give you a clear picture of your situation – before and after your divorce.

 If you end up with little money to live on after your divorce, you may be able to get government financial support in the form of welfare benefits and tax credits (see Chapters 7 and 15). You may also be eligible for public funding (previously known as *legal aid*) during your divorce. Chapter 15 tells you what it covers and how you qualify for it.

Caring for your children

If you have non-adult children, the end of your marriage is not the end of your family. Your young children may think of your 'family' as it was before you parted and may dream that you're all still together even if they know that you aren't. In the 1970s, most commentators thought that every divorce harmed a child. Since then hundreds of reputable pieces of research into the effects of divorce and separation on children have revealed that 'it all depends'.

In essence, research suggests that your children are most at risk of lasting damage to their well-being, self-esteem, happiness and future prospects if you subject them to a lot of conflict – especially if you don't resolve the conflict and your children think that it's about them. If you and your spouse can co-operate, both keep in loving touch with your children, keep them informed appropriately about what's happening, listen to them and continue to support them as well as you can financially and practically – despite your own distress – your children should do well. They aren't going to be happy while things are changing – none of us likes change that's out of our control – but they'll grow through your divorce.

 If you're worried that your children are very confused, unhappy and torn between you and your spouse, you can suggest that they talk through your divorce with someone outside the home. Have a look at Chapter 8 for ways to help your children through your divorce. You can also find out about counselling and support groups for children by contacting your local Relate (www.relate.org.uk) or a local Family Mediation Service (www.nfm.org.uk).

Chapters 8, 10, and 13 give you lots of information to help you make decisions where your children are concerned. They also cover what you can do when you and your spouse aren't able to manage things as you'd like to for your children and you end up going to court. In such circumstances, a Cafcass officer (the Children and Family Court Advisory and Support Service) can help you and the judge to reach decisions about your children. (See Chapter 18 for how to handle taking your divorce through the court process.)

Children talking

As we say, how your children fare depends a lot on how you manage your divorce. Here are two contrasting examples of what children said about their new lives when asked about them in a study led by Carol Smart at the University of Manchester:

- A 15-year-old girl living with her mother after her divorce said, 'I have this image of really nice parents . . . but our family definitely isn't like that. It's stressful because nobody really gets on. . . .' When describing that she lives with her mother and her mother's new partner and their new baby,

she says, 'She doesn't listen . . . he gets at me,' and concludes, 'it's just like I'm a person who lives here . . . sort of like a tenant.'

- In contrast, a boy of 8 said of his separated family: 'Good fun . . . we laugh at quite a lot of things. We've got a new cat and a garden . . . Mum laughs more . . . it's quite an ordinary family . . . it was good when they split up because they used to argue a lot . . . it's better now, lots better . . . it's nice to be with Mum and Mel and I get to see Daddy Pete in London and he phones us.'

Raising your children is expensive. Chapter 13 talks specifically about child support – but all the factors concerned with money and property have an impact on your children. Work to maximise what resources you have for their benefit instead of spending everything on fighting each other. Keeping their interests in mind throughout your divorce protects your children, as far as you can, from poverty.

Getting the help you need

You can choose to go through your divorce alone (see the section 'Going it alone' later in this chapter), but you don't have to. Heaps of people are out there who can help you negotiate your way through it, including:

- **Relationship and other counsellors:** Relationship counsellors don't set out to 'put you back together' unless that's what you both want. Accredited counsellors are very well trained and can guide and support you while you work out what you want to do individually about your relationship, work with you together to improve it, or support you after it's ended. If you're interested in trying counselling, or just finding out how a counsellor can help you, Chapter 2 tells you how.

- **Solicitors and barristers:** Most family solicitors work to the Resolution (formerly the Solicitors Family Law Association) Code of Practice and are also guided by a Law Society protocol that strongly encourages a conciliatory approach. Furthermore, specialist family judges don't appreciate combative solicitors and barristers in their courts. Chapters 15 and 17 help you to choose and work with your solicitor to achieve a fair and – as far as possible – even-tempered divorce and, if you have children, focusing on their needs. Chapter 15 also sets out the role of the Community Legal Service in helping you gain access to legal services and, if you're eligible, fund your legal bills.

TIP

Your solicitor's job is to be your personal legal adviser, and so you and your spouse need to have different solicitors representing you. He should also guide you through the steps you need to take, keeping in mind how you want to play things during your divorce. Your solicitor should give you the advice and information you need to make decisions about your future – but you make the decisions. He also acts as a sign-post to other forms of help if you need it and, if necessary, prepares and supports you if your case comes to a full hearing. Chapter 18 talks you through what happens if you take your case to court.

✔ **Family mediators:** A mediator's job is to work with you together as a couple. The unique characteristic of mediation is that it can keep the lines of communication open between you. If you can still communicate with each other, you can then problem-solve together. You're able to part on better terms if you work together than if you pull up the draw-bridge and prepare the boiling oil.

Joint problem-solving not only cuts down your legal costs but, if you have children, it helps you continue to talk to each other as their parents. Bitter disputes about children can often be resolved in a single media-tion session because you may hear your worst fears, such as 'I'm afraid I'll lose the children', replicated in the words of your spouse. Chapter 16 tells you how mediators work, how they can help you, and when using them isn't such a good idea. Mediation is effective in helping divorcing couples reach an agreement quickly and with a minimum of conflict.

✔ **Children and Family Court Advisory and Support Service (Cafcass) officers:** If you have children and your divorce goes to court, you may well come across a Cafcass officer. These officers of the court are trained to focus on the needs of your children and to report to the judge to help him decide what order to make. You may be referred to a Cafcass officer by the judge if he wants to know more about you and your children before making a decision. Chapter 18 tells you more about this stage of your divorce.

Cafcass doesn't exist in Northern Ireland but instead you may be referred to a Court Welfare Officer, who has a similar, specialised train-ing and function and who, if possible, assists you in making a joint deci-sion and conveys this to the court.

✔ **Judges and magistrates:** Family judges who work in the county or high courts, and magistrates who work in family proceedings courts, all now have specialist family training. Your imagination may run riot when you think of judges and magistrates, but you usually find that they are sym-pathetic as well as experienced and knowledgeable. At the same time they can be clear and stern when faced with abuse or violence. Chapter 18 describes what role a judge plays in your divorce.

Going it alone

Although you can get a divorce without any legal help, we don't recommend it unless everything is straightforward and you're both in absolute agreement and fully trust each other's grasp of the issues, or when you haven't been married long enough to acquire many assets and you have no children. Before you go down the route of a do-it-yourself divorce, look at Chapters 3 and 7, which set out the factors that you need to consider. Chapter 14 also gives you guidance on how you can sensibly negotiate with each other to cut down on the cost of professional help. Remember that in England and Wales, with your solicitor's help you can still get a divorce without attending court in person and we think (we would, wouldn't we!) that family solicitors and family mediators are too good these days to disregard.

Moving On to Pastures New

After you have your final decree, you can begin a new phase of your life. Chapter 19 starts you thinking about ways to get back in the swing of things – perhaps with a new job, or a rediscovered hobby, or spending more time with your children. However, even after your divorce is final, you may need to take action to implement your decisions. Chapter 20 spells out this situation, including help with solving persistent post-divorce problems.

Because your life doesn't end when your marriage does, at some point you may think about getting into a new relationship. You may be scared that because this relationship didn't work out you can't make any relationship work. However, this just isn't true. Part V is the place to start when you're ready to think about moving on. Chapter 22 can help you ensure that things are as easy as possible for your children. For tips about moving on after your divorce and ways to avoid divorce the next time around, have a look at Chapters 23 and 24. When you're ready to think about marriage again, we offer guidelines for putting your expectations on paper (in the form of pre- and post-marital agreements) in Chapter 21.

Fitting together your family life after divorce can be an awe-inspiring challenge, especially if your new household collects children from two (or more) previous families. Even finding words for your new life can be difficult – 'single again', 'stepfamily', 'one-parent family' or even 'blended family'. None of these labels reflects all the possibilities. However, your new lives will gradually fall into shape and you'll look back and say 'How did I ever get through all that?' – because you have!

Gearing Up for Your Divorce

Now – what's your most immediate concern? Do you need to ask your spouse to leave the family home? Are you desperate for someone to talk to? Is money, or the lack of it, your biggest worry? Are you still unsure whether divorce is the only road ahead? Take some time out from your daily routine to have a good think about your situation. Whatever issue you come up with – that's your starting point. The Cheat Sheet at the front of this book provides you with details of a range of organisations that can help you, from finding a solicitor to providing a counsellor to talk to you or your children. Alternatively, you can use this book to help you decide what to do first. You're going to survive your divorce, but you'll need help along the way.

Chapter 2

Deciding What to Do First When Things Start to Go Wrong

In This Chapter

▶ Determining if you have cause for concern

▶ Staying put or getting out

▶ Taking steps to improve your marriage and avoid a divorce

▶ Deciding whether to separate or divorce

▶ Dealing with violence and abuse

Marriages rarely die overnight. Almost always, the breaking up of a marriage happens little by little, over time. If your marriage is in really serious trouble, any discussion, co-operation, or compromise may be impossible, and you may have no option but to end it yourself, possibly against your spouse's wishes.

To help bring some objectivity and common sense to your situation, so that you can gain a true appreciation of how bad (or not so bad) things really are, this chapter reviews some of the common signs of a marriage in crisis and highlights your options for dealing with relationship problems. We also address the steps you can take if the pressures in your troubled relationship cause your spouse to turn abusive or violent.

Recognising the Signs of Trouble

When your marriage is going through a tough time, you may find yourself wondering whether it's an instance of the 'for better or for worse' alluded to in your marriage vows, or whether your relationship is truly on the rocks.

Although no test exists that can tell you whether your problems are typical reactions to the stress and strain most marriages experience at one time or another, or whether they point to more serious issues, troubled marriages do tend to exhibit many of the same characteristics. Do any of the following statements apply to your marriage?

- ✔ Your spouse just can't do anything right anymore in your view.
- ✔ You argue or fight constantly.
- ✔ You've lost the ability or the willingness to resolve your marital problems.
- ✔ You've replaced patience and love with resentment and contempt.
- ✔ You've turned from lovers into flatmates.
- ✔ You, your spouse, or both of you are having an affair.
- ✔ You go out of your way to avoid being together and, when you are together, you have nothing to talk about.

Don't panic if you find that your marriage exhibits some of these characteristics – you're not necessarily heading for a divorce. However, you do have cause for concern and you and your spouse, first separately and then together, have to assess your options and decide what to do next.

Marital problems can trigger depression, feelings of vulnerability and powerlessness, anger and sleep problems, any of which can impede clear thinking and sound decision-making. A counsellor or therapist can help you deal with these disturbances so that you can move forward. The British Association for Counselling and Psychotherapy (www.bacp.co.uk) can help you locate someone in your area.

Should I Stay or Should I Go?

Many couples opt to stay married after their relationships have failed – perhaps you fall into this category. Maybe you feel that raising your young children in a two-parent household is important, or you can't afford a divorce straight away. Or you're feeling pressure from family and friends to stay together. Maybe your religious faith forbids divorce, or possibly you've come to an understanding that allows you and your spouse to lead separate lives but remain under the same roof. Perhaps you're still together because you're afraid of what life will be like if you're single again. Fear of the unknown may motivate you to tolerate a situation that would be unbearable to others.

If your home is full of tension and anger because of your marital problems, you may be doing yourselves and your children more harm than good by staying together. Under new law, children who see or even overhear domestic violence are harmed and this experience is taken into account in both criminal and family courts.

Never stay in a marriage if your spouse has or is threatening to harm you or your children physically. At the very least, separate and give your spouse an opportunity to get professional help. If you're afraid that leaving may trigger violent behaviour in your spouse, contact the Women's Aid Helpline (0808 2000 247, www.womensaid.org.uk), the Scottish Women's Aid (0800 027 1234, www.scottishwomensaid.co.uk), Women's Aid in Northern Ireland (0800 917 1414, www.niwaf.org), the Muslim Women's Helpline (0208 904 8193 or 6715), or MALE (Men's Advice Line Enquiries) Helpline (0845 064 6800). All these groups provide information in several languages as well as English. Also, take a look at 'What to Do if Things Become Abusive or Violent' later in this chapter for more information.

Trying to Work Things Out

If you decide to stay in your marriage, you have two basic options: you can try to improve your relationship; or you can grit your teeth, shut down your feelings, and put up with things the way they are. The first alternative is almost always the better choice. To give your relationship a chance, try taking a short break from one another or going for marriage counselling. Neither of these options is mutually exclusive, so you may want to try both.

Taking a relationship mini-break

When you just can't get on and your emotions are running high, sometimes what you really need is a short time apart – a day or two, a long weekend, maybe even a holiday on your own. At the end of your time apart, you may have a whole new attitude towards your relationship and a renewed commitment to it.

Use the time apart to calm your emotions, assess your situation, and put your marital problems in perspective. Think about whether you're giving your spouse adequate attention and affection. Try to assess why you aren't getting on and your own role in those difficulties. Analyse the kind of arguments you're having – what you tend to argue about, how often you argue, and when – to determine whether any patterns emerge.

If you spend your time apart with a close friend or family member, choose that person carefully. Avoid anyone who doesn't like your spouse or resents your marriage. If you're looking for advice from the person you're going to be spending time with, the friend or family member should be impartial and someone whose judgement you trust.

Going for relationship counselling

Unfortunately, saving your marriage may require more than just taking a break from your spouse (if only solving the problem was always that easy!) You may need to re-establish or improve communication between the two of you, so that you can begin a productive dialogue about what has gone wrong in your relationship and why, and what you can both do to improve things.

Timing is everything when your marriage is falling apart. Don't wait until your marriage is damaged beyond repair to get professional help.

Finding a qualified relationship counsellor

Working with the right counsellor can help save your marriage; doing so can save you and your spouse months or even years of anguish while you try to decide what to do about the problems in your relationship.

Choose your counsellor carefully. Several national relationship counselling agencies exist and can tell you how to find a counsellor in your area. These agencies are not-for-profit organisations that offer counselling on a sliding-fee scale for couples, families, and individuals. Just knowing that a way out of your situation may be available, without having to resort to divorce, can take some of the pressure off and make addressing your marital problems easier. Here are some places to start when you begin looking for a qualified relationship counsellor:

- ✔ **The British Association for Counselling and Psychotherapy** (www. bacp.co.uk): This organisation can give you a list of accredited counsellors in your area, along with details about their qualifications, background and specialisms.

- ✔ **Relate:** Relate offices provide all sorts of help for relationship problems, including sex therapy. Find your nearest office at www.relate.org.uk, www.relatescotland.org.uk or www.relateni.org.

✔ **Your faith community:** Counselling services can be found within many different faiths, for example for Catholics at www.marriagecare.org.uk.

✔ **Local counselling resources:** Try contacting one of the following – Relationship Counselling for London (www.counselling4london.com) or Scottish Marriage Care (www.scottishmarriagecare.org), or find counsellors through your GP or local mediation service (www.familymediationhelpline.co.uk).

✔ **Referral from a friend or relative:** Lots of people have been through relationship counselling and can recommend a professional who helped them through their difficulties.

Make sure that both you and your spouse feel comfortable with the person you choose. You may have to share intimate and painful information about yourselves with the counsellor.

If your spouse refuses to go with you to talk to a relationship counsellor, go by yourself. You may find out things about yourself as well as new relationship skills that can help improve your current marriage or prepare you for a happier relationship or marriage in the future.

Getting comfortable on the counsellor's couch

Remember that everything you say in counselling is confidential – a situation in which you can feel comfortable talking about your problems. When your marriage derails, stepping back, objectively assessing what's going on and determining what changes to make can be difficult. A trusted and experienced counsellor can provide invaluable assistance and the right counsellor can help promote discussion and mutual understanding. She can also offer insights into your problems, help you both come to an agreement about what to do about those problems and even show you new marriage skills.

Your spouse's unwillingness to attend counselling sessions with you may signal that she isn't willing to change or is no longer committed to your marriage.

When Staying Isn't an Option

Living together while you try to resolve your marital differences and save your marriage may be an unrealistic option for you. Instead, you may decide to separate or live apart for a while.

Separating before making a final decision

Separating can provide you with an opportunity to find out what living in separate residences is really like. Meanwhile, the door is still open for getting back together. However, separation can also be a prelude to divorce.

Before you separate, protect yourself by talking with a family solicitor beforehand, especially if you want spousal or child support during your separation. The solicitor can warn you about anything that may jeopardise your standing in a divorce if you both decide to end your marriage.

You can opt for one of two types of temporary separation – with or without a separation agreement:

- ✔ **Separating without an agreement means that you simply begin living apart.** When you and your spouse clearly anticipate that your separation is temporary and that you're going to reconcile eventually, separating without an agreement may be your best option.

- ✔ **Separating with an agreement is recommended if you view your separation as the first step towards a divorce and have no plans for reconciliation.** Your solicitors work with you both to formalise your separation and put the agreed terms in writing. Remember that in the UK the same solicitor can't advise both of you.

A separation agreement is often preferable for many financial and legal reasons:

- ✔ You can formalise the terms of your separation including whether one of you intends to help support the other financially while you're living apart, how to deal with the arrangements for where your children will live, how they're going to see the parent not living in the home and how to work out child support. If you plan to change your financial or housing situation, the agreement can cover these changes as well.

- ✔ You can spell everything out to minimise the potential for conflict while you're separated. An agreement can also protect against either of you acting independently to the long-term disadvantage of the other – by selling valuables you own together or taking an unfair disadvantage of a joint bank account, for example.

- ✔ You can get the court to help enforce the agreement under contract law if one of you breaks the terms of your separation agreement – the agreement is a contract between you and your spouse.

- ✔ You can find that fewer issues need to be decided on if you end up eventually getting a divorce. A judge always has the final discretion but is more likely to enforce your agreement if you can each show that you've had independent legal advice and fully and frankly disclosed your financial positions to each other.

Legal annulments do not equal religious annulments

Legal annulments and religious annulments are two different animals. In some religions, if you divorce and want to remarry, your religion doesn't recognise your new marriage unless your old marriage is religiously annulled.

Religious annulments are most commonly associated with the Roman Catholic faith. For religious purposes, you may need a religious annulment as well as a civil divorce.

Chapter 6 gives you more information about separation agreements. If you and your spouse agree to divorce on the basis of your separation, you need to live apart from one another for at least two years. Check out Chapter 5 for more about the grounds for divorce.

Dating others while you're separated isn't usually a good idea because your spouse may then be able to divorce you more quickly on the grounds of adultery or unreasonable behaviour.

Separating permanently with no intention to divorce

If divorce isn't an option for you, you can opt for a permanent separation called a *judicial separation*. People very rarely use judicial separations these days and even more rarely for financial reasons. The process for getting a decree of judicial separation is similar to the process for getting a divorce. You and your spouse can still work together to negotiate the terms of your separation and work out, as appropriate, the division of your marital property, arrangements for the children, child support and maintenance for one of you by the other. You can use solicitors to help you negotiate such an agreement within the judicial separation proceedings and take this agreement to court. The key difference between a judicial separation and a divorce is that, when all is said and done, if you only separate you're still married. You can't therefore remarry but you would still be entitled to widows'/widowers' death in service benefits or pension. Judicial separation simply releases you from the duty to cohabit.

Getting your marriage annulled

A *nullity decree* is a court action that either voids your marriage or proclaims that it was never legally valid in the first place – as if the marriage had never taken place – or declares that the marriage is voidable – in other words, the marriage is treated as void from the date of the nullity decree. If you have young children from that relationship, a nullity decree doesn't modify or cancel your parental responsibilities to your children. To get a nullity decree you have to prove to the court that your marriage is void or voidable.

The most common criteria for nullity include:

- ✔ You or your spouse was already married at the time of your marriage.

- ✔ Your spouse was under 16 when you got married.

- ✔ You weren't respectively male and female.

- ✔ You didn't comply with certain formal requirements, such as filling out marriage forms properly, or getting married in a licensed venue (see Chapter 4 for the requirements you need to meet).

- ✔ You or your spouse is incapable of consummating the marriage (by having sex) or refuses to do so.

- ✔ You didn't give your valid consent to the marriage.

- ✔ Your spouse was suffering from a sexually transmitted disease in a communicable form at the time of your marriage.

- ✔ Your spouse was pregnant with another man's child at the time of your marriage ceremony. You can't be granted a nullity decree if, for example, you knew about the pregnancy beforehand and you still went ahead with the marriage.

If you want a religious annulment, you must apply to your church's authorities. Remember that this doesn't, in itself, count as a legal divorce or judicial separation. Chapter 5 can tell you more about religious annulments and Jewish Gets.

Getting a divorce

Your final option when your marriage is failing is to get divorced, ending your marriage and many of your associated rights and responsibilities regarding your spouse. Every chapter of this book provides information that can help you get through the divorce process as painlessly as possible.

What to Do if Things Become Abusive or Violent

Sometimes when a marriage is falling apart one spouse begins to be abusive, threatening the other with violence or becoming physically violent. If this happens in your marriage, take the threats or the violence very seriously. Ignoring them can literally be a matter of life or death!

Understanding what is meant by domestic abuse

Domestic abuse or domestic violence is often thought of as involving only physical harm. Nowadays, however, abuse is understood to include more than physical harm. If you've experienced emotional or verbal abuse and felt seriously undermined or threatened as a result, you know the personal costs. In addition, your children are also affected.

Calling the police

Domestic abuse is a crime. If your spouse harms you or threatens to harm you, call your local police station. One or more police officers will be sent to talk with you and prepare a police report. If you've obviously been abused, the police may arrest your spouse on the spot, persuade your spouse to leave, or at least help to defuse the situation.

Although they're in a very small minority, some police officers believe that domestic violence is not a police matter – they think that it's a private matter between a husband and wife. However, the police themselves can now be dismissed if they're found guilty of domestic violence. Therefore, if you call the police for help and the responding officers seem reluctant to prepare a police report, calmly request that one be prepared and get the officers' names and numbers. If the officers continue to refuse, having this information is helpful when you contact their superiors. Official police policy is to treat domestic violence just as seriously as, if not more seriously than, any other crime.

Getting an injunction against your spouse

Injunctions are a form of court order. An *occupation order* (also known as an injunction or ouster order, or *interdict* or exclusion order in Scotland) is a court order that can force your spouse to leave your home, or forbid your spouse to enter or come within a certain distance of your home, or restrict your spouse's rights within the home. The court may attach a power of arrest that allows a police officer to arrest your spouse if he breaches the terms of the order.

The court very rarely makes an occupation order without giving your spouse an opportunity to speak, which may mean going back for a second hearing. During the hearing, the judge decides whether to grant you an occupation order by reading your statements and hearing your evidence on oath and by reviewing any police or medical reports relating to your situation. The judge has to weigh up the harm to each of you, or your children, when deciding whether to make an order.

If you get an injunction prohibiting your spouse from entering your home, don't be tempted to let him back in again. A judge doesn't take kindly to you allowing your spouse to breach the order, and may even think twice about giving you further protection if you do allow him back in and trouble ensues.

You can also ask the court for a *non-molestation order*, which means that your spouse must not harm you, or trouble you, or use violence towards you or your children. If your spouse breaks the order he can be arrested by the police and brought before the criminal courts. Sometimes the court recommends a violent or abusive spouse to enter an alcohol or drug addiction rehabilitation programme or to attend an anger management course. A Cafcass Officer (Children and Family Court Adviser) may be asked to arrange this if the abusive spouse agrees.

Getting a protective order against your spouse can be easier if police reports are on file. The reports can also help if you file criminal charges against your spouse. If the court attaches a power of arrest to any part of the order, you or your solicitor have to make sure that a copy of the order and power of arrest are lodged with your local police station. The order is not effective until your spouse has had proper notice of it.

If you need immediate protection and the courts are closed at a weekend, during the evening or a holiday, your solicitor can get an order from a local judge that the police can act upon. It stays in effect for just a few days until you can go back to court again.

If you get an occupation or non-molestation order, or both, but your spouse refuses to obey them, call the police and your solicitor immediately. Your spouse may then be arrested and criminally prosecuted, or your solicitor may apply to the court for your spouse to be sent to prison. To make certain that the police arrest your spouse if the situation requires it, keep a certified copy of the court order with you at all times.

You can ask a judge or magistrate for an anti-stalking order that helps protect you if your spouse is following you, waiting for you outside your home, making threatening or harassing phone calls, or displaying other sorts of behaviour in order to intimidate and frighten you.

Certain circumstances apply when it may be appropriate for you to accept an *undertaking*, or solemn promise to the court, from your spouse to do something, such as to leave the home or not use violence, instead of having a court order against him. An undertaking has the same force as an order, except that you can't have a power of arrest attached to it. But if your spouse breaches his undertaking to the court, or fails to comply with an order, he is in contempt of court. The remedies for contempt of court include a fine or, more seriously, committal to prison. Always consult your solicitor about the pros and cons for you of an order or an undertaking, especially if your spouse is in breach.

Filing criminal charges

If your spouse has already been physically violent to you, in addition to getting a non-molestation order from the court you can file criminal assault charges against him. Taking both actions provides you with different and overlapping protections. The police also have the power to charge your spouse if he is persistently harassing you.

Going to a refuge

If you're afraid to remain in your home despite an occupation or non-molestation order against your spouse, consider going to your local refuge. You can take your young children with you. Refuges don't publish their addresses for safety reasons, but you can find your local refuge's phone number from the police, the telephone directory, your local Housing Department, your local Social Services Department or the Samaritans (08457 909090).

If you're in a crisis situation (your spouse has just beaten you or is threatening to do so) and you can get to a phone or use your mobile, call the Women's Aid Helpline (0808 200 0247, www.womensaid.org.uk), Scottish Women's Aid (0800 027 1234, www.scottishwomensaid.co.uk), Women's Aid in Northern Ireland (0800 917 1414, www.niwaf.org), the Muslim Women's Helpline (0208 904 8193 or 6715) or MALE (Men's Advice Line Enquiries) Helpline (0845 064 6800). The person answering the phone will help calm you down, advise you on how to handle the situation, and call the police for you. Finding and keeping their number handy in case you need it is a good idea.

The Women's Aid website is a very good source of information and includes guidance on how to remove any evidence that you ever contacted the website. The Women's Aid Helpline tells you how to find out about resources in your area for victims of domestic abuse and for individuals who are afraid that their spouses may become abusive.

Considering other safety measures you can take

In addition to keeping the phone number of your local refuge, here are some other things you can do to protect yourself if your spouse has been abusive in the past and you're afraid you may be harmed again, or if your spouse is threatening you with violence for the first time:

✔ Hide an extra set of keys, some money, and some clothes in a safe place in case you need to get out of your home quickly.

✔ Always have in mind a safe place to go that your spouse doesn't know about.

✔ Tell your children (if they're old enough to understand) that if you say a certain 'code word' they should run to a neighbour's house or call the police.

✔ Tell friends and family about the abuse. Sharing this information with others diminishes the power of some abusers.

✔ Join a support group. The people on the other end of the Women's Aid Helpline can help you find a group in your area or you can call your local refuge for information. Joining a group may give you the resolve you need to deal with your situation in a decisive manner.

✔ Testify in court against your spouse.

Chapter 3

Wising Up to Your Family's Money Matters

In This Chapter

▶ Knowing what your family owns and owes

▶ Getting educated about money management issues

▶ Finding out about pensions

▶ Understanding the importance of having your own credit record

▶ Staying employable

*W*e'd all like to believe that the till-death-do-us-part wedding vows guarantee that every marriage is going to last forever. But these days the reality is that more than one in three marriages ends in divorce. So it makes sense for every married and about-to-be-married person to be prepared not only for the possibility that his or her marriage may end in divorce but also for the financial consequences that can follow. At a minimum, your preparation needs to include the following:

✔ Becoming familiar with your family's finances

✔ Discovering how to manage your money

✔ Working to maintain a positive credit record in your own name

✔ Building and maintaining marketable job skills

Understandably, you may view marrying with the possibility of divorce looming over your happy union as pretty cynical. But when you understand how *not* being prepared for the end of your marriage can affect you and your children, you'll be convinced that the advice we give you on what you can do to minimise the impact of divorce on your life is wise (albeit unromantic).

Consider this point: Your lack of preparation may force you to stay in a bad marriage because you can't support yourself or because you don't have the financial resources to live on your own. And, without the right preparation, you may be at a disadvantage when the time comes to work out the financial details of your split. Plus, when you're single again, you may have a hard time building a financially secure life for yourself.

This chapter offers advice about protecting yourself from the financial fallout of divorce and preparing to earn your own living or make more money after a divorce. If you're a stay-at-home spouse or if you put your career on the back burner during your marriage, pay special attention to this information.

If you think a divorce may be in your future, the sooner you can put the advice in this chapter into action, the better prepared you are, financially and legally, for life on your own.

Here are some facts that should motivate you to take action. A wife's lack of financial know-how can cost her dearly when she gets divorced. In 2008, the Institute for Social and Economic Research (ISER) showed that mothers who separate from their partners still experience a significant drop in their incomes (although the fall is significantly lower than it was ten years ago). Despite the improvement in the circumstances of women with children, because of better employment prospects and tax credits, large gaps remain on average between the short-term income positions of separating husbands and separating wives.

The report also looked at the longer-term consequences of marital splits and found that, although women's family incomes do recover, they don't return to their pre-separation levels. In the fifth year after a split, incomes remain about 10 per cent below pre-split levels on average. Women who do find a job or a new partner (or both) see their incomes recover the most. But if not, women typically don't see much recovery of income. They may also lack the financial know-how, confidence or credit record that they need to build a good life for themselves after they are divorced.

It Takes Two to Manage (Or Mismanage) Money

Don't rely entirely on your spouse to pay your household bills, reconcile your chequebook, make investment decisions, and so on. You need to share these responsibilities. At the very least, you must know what bills need payment, how much is in your bank accounts, and where your money is invested. Here's why:

- ✔ **Your spouse may resent having to shoulder all the responsibility for managing your family's finances.** This resentment can cause trouble in your marriage.

- ✔ **Your spouse may not be a good money manager.** You and your children may be harmed by your spouse's bad decisions. In addition, your spouse's financial mismanagement may damage *your* credit record – not just his own.

- ✔ **You or your spouse may become incapacitated by a serious illness or accident, in which case the other may be unprepared to manage your family's finances.** As a result, you may make costly financial mistakes.

- ✔ **You have fewer arguments over money.** If you're both fully aware of your financial situation, you have less to argue over.

- ✔ **You're more apt to notice a drain on your resources.** In a worst-case scenario, if your spouse is having an extramarital affair or has a problem with gambling, drinking, drugs or the use of Internet chat rooms – all of which cost money – the money has to come from somewhere. If you're aware of your financial situation, you're more likely to see exactly where the loss is coming from.

- ✔ **You're prepared to make good decisions if you and your spouse negotiate your own divorce agreement.**

- ✔ **Your divorce is more expensive if you don't know your financial situation.** If your divorce is not co-operative and your solicitor lacks the information he needs to handle it, that information has to be acquired through the time-consuming and potentially expensive *disclosure process*. The formal disclosure process helps the parties of a divorce get the facts in preparation for a legal action so that neither side takes the other by surprise. To find out more about the disclosure process, see Chapter 5.

- ✔ **Your spouse has free reign over the family finances, which may harm you.** For example, your spouse can waste your cash and assets or hide them from you so that they aren't included in your divorce negotiations.

- ✔ **You may be without the financial resources and information after your divorce that you need to build a new life.** Keeping track of your family's finances helps you to keep track of your own.

Financial Fundamentals: What You Must Do First

To play an active, informed role in the management of your family's finances, you must have certain information about your household finances, as well as basic money management skills and other resources important to your financial life and wellbeing. Check out Chapters 7 and 11 for more tips on understanding and managing your financial situation after your divorce.

Finding out what you have and what you owe

You don't have to be a chartered accountant to work out your family's financial worth. You just need to discover your family's debts and assets. A *debt* is something that you owe, such as your mortgage, your credit card bill, or your car payments, not to mention the 20 quid you borrowed from your best friend. An *asset* is a thing of value. Depending on the type of asset, you can use it to purchase something else, you can sell it, or you can use the asset as collateral for a loan. An asset can be tangible – such as cash, property, vehicles, antiques, fine jewellery or art – or intangible – such as stocks, bonds, or pension benefits. Any assets should be registered in both of your names. Get a notebook and make a list of the following:

- ✔ Your total household income and the source(s) of that income.

- ✔ The cheque and savings account numbers that you and your spouse use and the bank(s) in which those accounts are held.

- ✔ Your family's significant assets and the approximate value of each. Your home and your pensions are often the biggest (See Chapter 7 for a worksheet to help you work out your assets.)

- ✔ How your *joint assets* are titled or deeded – joint tenancy with right of survivorship or tenancy in common (See the Glossary of Terms in Appendix A.)

- ✔ Your family's debts – whom you owe and how much.

- ✔ Where financial and legal documents important to your family are stored, including bank records, tax returns, wills, titles and deeds, mortgages, loan agreements, insurance policies and documentation pertaining to any investments, stocks, shares, bonds and mutual funds you or your spouse may own, as well as paperwork relating to the pension plans in which either of you participate (See Chapter 11 for more details.)

✔ What your credit record says about you and your spouse.

✔ The names, addresses and phone numbers of your solicitor, bank, accountant, financial adviser and stockbroker, if you have them.

✔ Basic information about your spouse's business, if your spouse is self-employed, including its legal form, assets and liabilities.

Have an understanding with your spouse that you share fully all your household's financial information with each other and that all financial records are kept in a place that is readily accessible to both of you.

Drawing up a spending plan and sticking to it

Knowing how to manage your debts and assets is essential so that you have enough money to pay your bills each month, don't take on too much debt, and accomplish as much as you can with any money you may have left over. Being a good money manager means knowing how to do the following:

✔ **Develop and manage a household spending plan.** See the later sidebar 'Budgeting basics' to understand more about spending plans, and use the sample form in Table 3-1, which is designed to help you keep track of your finances.

✔ **Manage your chequebook and your balance statements.** When you don't keep track of how much money is in your account by recording each cheque you write, all account deposits and withdrawals, and then reconciling your account balance with your monthly bank statements, you can lose money in bounced cheques.

✔ **Use credit wisely.** Although credit helps you to purchase necessities you can't afford otherwise, using credit too often or not understanding the terms of credit before you apply for a credit card or get a loan from a bank, credit union or finance company can land you in trouble.

✔ **Make sound investment decisions with stocks, bonds, mutual funds, property, and so on.** Even if you use professional stockbrokers, financial advisers, and estate agents to help you manage important investments, you need to know enough about your investments so that you can intelligently evaluate their advice.

Using the following forms, total how much you spend in a month. For help developing and using a budget, you can also check household budget sites on the Internet.

Pensions: A thumbnail sketch

In the UK, many different types of pension schemes are available. If you're divorcing you need to know exactly what type of pension(s) you and your spouse have so that you can work out how to share them – or not – as part of your negotiations. If you're separating without a divorce, your pension entitlement as a spouse, widow or widower remains the same. If you're separating after cohabitation, you have no right to a share of your partner's pension at all. You can find more information about pension division in Chapter 11. Pensions and the laws associated with them are complicated, and the following is only a simplified guide.

You're entitled to a basic *State Retirement Pension* if you've paid, or been credited with, National Insurance contributions. The amount that you're entitled to depends on your contributions. Depending on your employment history, you may have also accrued credits in one or more of the additional state pensions available over the years, such as SERPS (now known as the State Second Pension or simply as S2P). You can obtain a forecast of your state pension entitlement by completing form BR19, available from the Post Office or the Pensions Service website (www.thepension service.gov.uk).

A variety of non-government pension schemes are also available; the Pension Simplification legislation introduced on 6 April 2006 removed a lot of the complications around administering pensions and they're all now known as Registered Pension Schemes. However, using the old group names is still easier and pensions generally fall into two main categories:

Occupational pension schemes:

- ✔ The *final salary scheme*, or *defined benefit scheme*, is the traditional type of retirement plan that you imagine receiving along with a gold watch after 50 years of loyal service to an employer. In these pensions, you build up a fraction of your final salary for each year's service (usually 1/60th or 1/80th). You therefore know broadly what your entitlement is going to be at retirement and are not exposed to the risks associated with investments. However, over the last few years the majority of schemes in the private sector have closed due to the increased contributions required by the employer to honour the promise made and the administrative costs involved. The main public sector schemes (teachers, police, firemen, and so on) remain in place, although even here employers are looking to reduce benefits to help reduce their costs.

- ✔ A *money purchase*, or *defined contribution scheme*, is the type of retirement scheme that many employees are offered these days. Your employer, and/or you, the employee, contribute money to your scheme. The level of pension available at retirement is dependent on the fund value at that time and *annuity* rates applicable (you have to use the fund to buy an annuity – an annual income). The member rather than the employer therefore takes on board the investment risk.

Personal pension schemes:

- ✔ *Retirement annuity contracts* are a form of pension available up to July 1988.

- ✔ *Personal pension schemes* replaced retirement annuity contracts in 1988 and are available to both the employed and self-employed. Many employers now offer Group Personal pension schemes instead of occupational schemes because they are flexible and have a reduced regulatory regime and so have lower administration costs.

✔ *Stakeholder plans*, introduced in April 2001, are low-cost portable personal pensions plans that comply with government restrictions on charges, access and terms. They are designed to encourage greater participation in pensions by people who weren't previously eligible to participate in a pension scheme, such as part-time and lower paid employees or people who aren't earning but who can afford to contribute.

Specialist arrangements

Investment Regulated Pension schemes are available for people who want to retain direct control over their pension investments.

✔ *Small self-administered schemes* (SSASs) are occupational pension schemes and are usually only available for company directors. They are able to invest in a broad range of assets including commercial property.

✔ *Self-invested personal pensions* (SIPPs) are used by both employees and the self-employed. As with SSASs, they offer the member greater control over how his funds are invested.

✔ *Additional voluntary contributions* are arrangements available to enable members of occupational schemes to top up their benefits. In the main, these arrangements have been replaced by personal pensions because the restrictions on membership of personal and occupational scheme membership at the same time have been removed.

✔ *Section 32 buy-out policy* is a special single premium arrangement designed to accept the transfer in of benefits from an occupational scheme. Scheme trustees often use them to wind up an occupational pension and distribute the funds to the members.

Table 3-1	Sample Form for a Household Spending and Savings Plan
Fixed Monthly Expenses	**Amount (£)**
Rent or mortgage	
House and contents insurance	
Ground rent	
Car purchase payments	
Other finance agreements	
Other insurance	
Children's allowances/activities	
Childcare	
TV licence, satellite and broadband subscriptions	
Other monthly commitments	
Total	£

(continued)

Table 3-1 *(continued)*

Variable Monthly Expenses*	Amount (£)
Groceries	_____
Utilities (for example, gas, electric, council tax)	_____
Telephone (including mobiles)	_____
Petrol/diesel	_____
Clothing	_____
Credit card payments	_____
Dental, optician or medical costs	_____
Magazines and books	_____
Church or charitable donations	_____
Personal expenses (haircuts, and so on)	_____
Recreation (including sports and meals out)	_____
Miscellaneous	_____
Total	£ _____
Periodic Expenses*	**Amount (£)**
Education	_____
Car tax and insurance	_____
Other insurance	_____
Taxes	_____
Household repairs	_____
Birthday and holiday gifts	_____
Entertaining	_____
Subscriptions	_____
Total	£ _____
Estimate the entire year's periodic expenses and divide by 12 for the monthly amount.	
Total monthly household expenses (the three previous totals from this table combined)	£ _____
Net monthly household income	£ _____
Surplus or deficit (net household income minus total monthly expenses)	£ _____
Surplus allotted for savings	£ _____
Surplus allotted for investments	£ _____

Creating a Household Income Sheet

Counting up your income from all sources for both of you is a good idea, so that you can check that your spending plan isn't over-spending your income. Any money you have left over in the month also helps to decrease your debts as you approach the possibility of divorce. You need to list everything on the form shown in Table 3-2. See Chapter 7 for help with checking the values of your assets and liabilities.

Table 3-2	Sample Household Income Sheet
Your gross salary/wages for the year:	
Full-time employment	£ _____
Part-time employment	£ _____
Subtotal (A)	£ _____
Your deductions for the year	
National insurance	£ _____
Income tax	£ _____
Pension contributions	£ _____
Other deductions (union subscriptions, charitable donations, health insurance)	£ _____
Any share save schemes or similar that you're paying into (Remember that these are usually optional and you may not be able to afford to continue with them after your divorce)	£ _____
Subtotal (B)	£ _____
Calculate your net available income	
Subtotal (A)	£ _____
Less Subtotal (B)	£ _____
Net available income	£ _____
Additional employment-related income	
Bonus/commission (not included above)	£ _____
Other fringe benefits from your employment such as car allowances or contributions towards a computer or office at home	£ _____

(continued)

Table 3-2 (continued)

State benefits and tax credits	
Child benefit	£ _____
Working tax credit	£ _____
Child tax credit	£ _____
Pension credit	£ _____
Disability benefits	£ _____
Rent or council tax rebates	£ _____
Other sources of income	
Rental income from property	£ _____
Trusts	£ _____
Dividends	£ _____
Fees	£ _____
Casual payments	£ _____
Maintenance or child support from a previous spouse	£ _____
Total*	£ _____

Divide the total by 12 to work out your monthly income

Owning a house

When you get divorced, the law in England, Wales and Northern Ireland (unlike in Scotland – see Chapter 11 for why this is) views everything that you owned before you entered the marriage, plus all that you acquired during the marriage, as potentially open to claim by both of you. This means that the judge has to take all assets into account, regardless of whose name they are in or when they were acquired. If you have children, the judge also views your house as your home – it's still a home for you and your children instead of simply a financial asset. Have a look at Chapter 11 for help in working out what to do with your house when you divorce.

Registering your interest in your home

Check whether the deeds to your home, and to any other property that you own, are in both of your names. You need to register formally your interest in the property if your name is not on the deeds. You can get most of the information and forms that you need from the Land Registry website: www.landregisteronline.gov.uk. Here's a step-by-step guide to what you need to do to register the deeds:

1. **Find out whether the property is registered at the Land Registry (most properties are) and in which district it's registered.** You can find this out from the deeds or paperwork relating to the property. If you don't have access to the deeds, contact the Land Registry for a SIM form (an application for an official search of the index map), then complete and return it with your fee to the Land Registry. The reply tells you whether the property is registered or not and, if it is, the title number.

2. **Add your name to a registered property by asking the Land Registry for an HR1 form (an application to register rights in a home).** Complete and return the form to your district Land Registry (no fee applies).

Budgeting basics

Developing a spending plan isn't difficult; it's simply a matter of recording your monthly household expenses, tallying them up, and then comparing them to your monthly household income. To get a comprehensive picture of your monthly expenses, review your chequebook stubs, your bank statements, including direct debits and standing orders, your current account withdrawals and your cash receipts. To get a true picture of your expenses, look at several months' worth of information.

Some expenses are fixed, whereas others change every month and other expenses occur periodically throughout the year. To budget for periodic expenses, divide the total annual cost of each periodic item by 12. That gives you a monthly cost to include in your budget. To budget for variable expenses, tally up a few months' worth of what you're spending – on groceries, for example – or preferably a year's worth for the utilities, and divide by the number of months you kept track to get an average.

Your total *net* monthly household income is the actual amount of money available to spend (*gross* income less taxes and other deductions).

That income can include wages and salaries, investment income or child support. If you're paid weekly, remember to multiply that figure by 52 and then divide by 12 to get an accurate monthly amount.

Try using the forms in Tables 3-1 and 3-2 to record your income and expenses. If the total amount of your monthly expenses exceeds your total household income each month, you need to reduce your expenses or increase your income to avoid serious financial trouble.

If your budget shows that you have a surplus of cash at the end of the month, you can pay off your debts more quickly, put more money into savings and investments, or spend some of the money on things you or your family really want or need.

One final comment about spending plans: developing one may not be difficult, but living with one can be really tough if you don't exercise self-control. In the end, a spending plan is only as good and as useful as the discipline you put behind it!

3. **Register your interest in the property if you find it's not already registered by using a K2 form (application for registration) from the Land Charges Department of the Land Registry.** Complete and return the form to the Land Charges Department with your fee of £1 payable to HM Land Registry.

Keep a copy of all your applications and any replies with the deeds. In both these cases you're registering your rights of occupation in the matrimonial home, but you're also preventing your spouse from dealing with the property without any reference to you.

4. **Register your interest in a property other than the matrimonial home in the same way as in step 2, although the process is slightly more expensive.** You just need different forms: a CT2 form if the property is already registered (and the £40 fee to register), and a K3 form (fee is £1). You also need to have a legitimate claim to the property. Contact your solicitor for help in proving that you do.

Joint property and your rights to it

You can own joint real estate or property in two ways. How you own that joint property affects your rights when the time comes to split it up.

🗸 *Joint tenancy* **with the right of survivorship.** Under a joint tenancy, each owner owns all the property. If your spouse dies, his share automatically goes to you, no matter what your spouse's will says, and vice versa. A property held under a joint tenancy bypasses a will. Most married people own property in this way.

🗸 *Tenancy in common.* In this sort of joint ownership, often used by cohabiting couples, each of you has a distinct share. If the size of your share is not defined, it is likely to be assumed to be 50 per cent unless you can prove otherwise. The important point to remember is that either of you can leave your share by will or intestacy (when no will exists). Your spouse can do what he wants with his share of the property – give it away, sell it, trade it, use it to collateralise or secure a loan, or encumber it with some sort of claim.

If you don't want your spouse to have your share of your house on your death, you need to make sure that you own your house under a tenancy in common and that you leave a will naming the person who's to receive your share. To change your ownership from a joint tenancy to a tenancy in common, you send a notice to your spouse telling him that this is what you're doing. If your property is registered, you must then register the change at your district Land Registry by means of Form 75, known as *a restriction*. If your property isn't registered, you need to put a copy of the notice with the title deeds. This process is known as 'severing the joint tenancy'. If you're a cohabitant who owns more than a half-share of the house, take advice before you do this.

Finding out about your mortgage

You probably have one or more mortgages on your home. The type of mortgage (for example, repayment or interest only) doesn't really matter when it comes to working out what to do with your house. However, you do need to know how much you owe, what the payments are, and how much longer they need to be paid. If the information isn't to hand, check with your lender.

If one of you is keeping the house, the other must try to remove his name from the mortgage so that he isn't liable and is eligible for another. Your lender is likely to agree to remove your name from the existing mortgage when you have a good track record and the person remaining has enough income, or when enough equity exists in the property to cover the mortgage. Chapter 11 tells you more about dealing with your mortgage when you divorce.

Deciding what is fair

During your divorce, you can decide for yourselves what is a fair distribution of your assets and income (Chapter 14 offers help on how to do this); or use the assistance of a mediator in working out the financial terms of your divorce (see Chapter 16 for info on mediation); or your solicitors can negotiate this issue on your behalf (Chapter 17 has the scoop on dealing with your solicitor). As a last resort, you can leave it to a judge to decide (read Chapter 18 for a taste of what happens when you go to court).

When making a decision, a judge must give priority to the needs of any children of the family and in addition may weigh up a whole range of factors. Fairness is relative and varies from divorce to divorce. The most common criteria for working out who gets what include:

- ✔ How much each of you earns or may earn in the future, and your other financial resources
- ✔ Your financial needs, obligations and responsibilities now or in the future
- ✔ Your current standard of living
- ✔ The value of your property
- ✔ The contribution each of you made to your marriage – and, as it should, being a full-time homemaker or stay-at-home parent counts
- ✔ The pension benefits to which each of you may be entitled
- ✔ The length of your marriage
- ✔ Your age and your health

In extremely rare instances, the judge may weigh up how either of you have behaved in the marriage.

The law may treat inheritances and gifts to a spouse during marriage as joint property, including any future inheritances that are certain and foreseeable. Any personal injury settlement may also not be beyond claim by your spouse.

Finding Out What You Need to Know

If you review the list of 'financial-ought-to-knows' earlier in this chapter and realise you're the one who doesn't know the answers, don't panic. You can get up to speed in several ways. Start with your spouse. Ask him to sit down and describe your family's finances in as much detail as possible, show you where key documents and other important records are kept, and answer your questions.

If your spouse seems threatened by your sudden interest in the family finances, try alleviating that concern with an explanation of why you want to know. Explain that if you know more about your family's finances, your spouse won't have to shoulder all the burden for managing your money. Also, you'll be better able to make wise decisions for the family if your spouse becomes incapacitated or dies.

Review your family's financial records and documents, including information stored on your home computer (many households use personal finance software to help them manage their money). If you don't know where your tax returns are filed and your spouse refuses to tell you, you can obtain copies by writing to the Inland Revenue.

Money management and personal finance courses are a good resource for increasing your financial skills and knowledge. Your local community college or university may offer classes for little cost. Also, many investment companies and financial advisers offer investment seminars as a way to attract new clients or develop additional business from their current client base. These seminars are usually free, and no purchase is required. However, these advisers often assume that their audience has a better-than-average knowledge of investing, not to mention better-than-average money to invest! Another possible source of financial education is the Citizens Advice Bureau (CAB) office in your area.

If you, or you and your spouse, owe a lot of money and are having trouble paying your bills, your local CAB advisers may be able to help you work out more affordable payment plans with your creditors so that you can get out of debt. The less debt you have going into a divorce, the less potential for problems after your divorce. Look for your local CAB in the telephone directory. Alternatively, several helplines are available:

✔ **Citizens Advice Bureau:** www.adviceguide.org.uk

✔ **National Debtline:** 0808 808 4000, www.nationaldebtline.co.uk

✔ **Consumer Credit Counselling Service:** 0800 138 1111, www.cccs.co.uk

✔ **Payplan:** 0800 917 7823, www.payplan.com

✔ **Money Advice Scotland:** 0141 572 0237, www.moneyadvicescotland.org.uk

Bookshops stock many titles about personal finance and investing. Even if you're a financial novice, you can find many books written for people just like you. The Amazon website (www.amazon.co.uk) is full of them. The Open University (www.open.ac.uk) runs a course on personal finance, as does the IFS School of Finance (www.ifslearning.ac.uk) at a basic level.

Although a financial seminar or adviser can certainly inform you of the pros and cons of different money management ideas, you and your spouse may not agree about things such as how much to spend and how much to save and what is an acceptable amount of credit card debt. A marriage counsellor may be able to help you resolve those disagreements. Or this may become an item to negotiate about in mediation. Chapter 16 tells you more about mediation. Differences about money can affect the quality and financial stability of your marriage and can impact your life long after your divorce.

Maintaining Your Employability

Even though two-income families are becoming the norm in today's society, many women, and a growing number of men, choose to be full-time homemakers and stay-at-home parents for at least some point during their marriage. If you're one of them, be aware that in today's fast-changing work world your job skills can quickly become rusty or even obsolete and you may lose many of your work or professional contacts as well.

To protect yourself while you're out of the job market, try to do what you can to keep your job skills up-to-date, and also develop new ones, if possible, even if you have no immediate plans to work outside the home. You may also want to begin preparing for a new career. Your local school, community further education college, or university continuing education department are all potential sources of training and education. At the very least, discover how to use a computer, if you're not already computer literate. Most jobs these days assume or require that you have at least some computer skills.

Don't lose yourself in your marriage by always making your needs secondary to those of your family. Taking care of and developing yourself is not necessarily selfish. By doing so, you gain the confidence and the resources – both inner and financial – to rescue a failing marriage, end a bad marriage, or take care of yourself if you're widowed. In other words, hope for the best but be prepared for the worst.

Working part-time is another option for building and retaining your job skills and professional contacts. A part-time job helps you build a CV. Plus the money you earn can fund a savings account in your own name, provide extra income to help pay your family's bills, or help finance your children's education.

Being prepared to enter the work world as quickly as possible, perhaps when your children have started school, is important now that life-long spousal support is rare. The more quickly you can land a good job and earn a good living, the better off you're going to be.

Building a Positive Credit Record

Your *credit record* is a record of how you manage the credit accounts that you maintain in your name or that you share with your spouse. Those accounts may include bank credit cards, bank loans, store cards, and so on.

One or both of the 'big two' credit reference agencies, Equifax or Experian, or a third, CallCredit, has your credit history stored in a computerised database. (See the later sidebar 'Contacting the credit reference agencies'.)When you apply for a bank loan, credit card or some other form of credit, the creditor reviews your credit record to make sure that you aren't likely to be a risk. If problems do exist, obtaining credit at reasonable terms – or any credit at all – may be difficult.

Creditors look not only at how much credit you're servicing but also at your credit limits. In other words, if you have a credit card with a limit of £1,000, even if you're not carrying a balance on that card, the fact that you're able to run one up is something that creditors consider when evaluating whether or not to extend credit.

Having good credit in your own name (not just *joint credit* that you share with your spouse) plus your own trouble-free credit record are essential in preparing for the possibility of divorce. Here are some of the most important reasons why:

✔ Without your own credit record, obtaining a bank loan or a credit card, purchasing a home or renting a car can be difficult for you – maybe even impossible – if you get divorced. Also, because some employers and insurance companies review credit records as part of their decision-making process, you may even find getting the insurance or job you need tough! Although you can build your own credit record after your divorce, the process takes several years.

✔ When you and your spouse share joint credit, both of you are legally responsible for those accounts. Therefore, if your spouse mismanages that credit, your credit record, as well as that of your spouse, is damaged.

✔ If your divorce agreement requires that your spouse pay off certain debts for which you were both liable, and if your ex-spouse fails to meet that obligation, the creditor can still try to collect the money from you.

If, prior to your divorce, you or your spouse close all your joint accounts and you later tell those creditors that you would like credit with them in your own name, they can require that you re-apply for credit if the joint accounts were based on your spouse's income. If you don't already have a credit record that reflects credit in your own name, you're likely to be denied the credit you want.

Some single men and women with their own credit and bank accounts close them when they marry, open joint bank accounts with their spouses, and apply for joint credit. If your spouse fails to pay one of his individual debts, therefore, the creditor can try to get paid by coming after *your* share of the marital property, not just your spouse's share.

No law insists that when you get married you and your spouse must merge your finances!

Establishing Your Own Credit Record

Before you begin the credit-record process, request a copy of your credit report from one of the credit reference agencies (Equifax, Experian or CallCredit). It would also be good to know what's in your spouse's credit report, but your spouse has to agree to order it. However, your own credit reports provide you with information on most of your joint debts as well as your individual ones; they just don't tell you about your spouse's individual or separate debts.

Contacting the credit reference agencies

You can obtain a copy of your credit record from any of the credit reference agencies below. Go to their websites or phone for details of how to apply.

Equifax	Experian	CallCredit
Credit File Advice Centre	Consumer Help Service	Consumer Services Team
PO Box 1140	PO Box 8000	PO Box 491
Bradford	Nottingham	Leeds
BD1 5US	NG80 7WF	LS3 1WZ
Tel: 0870 010 0583	Tel: 0844 481 8000	Tel: 0870 060 1414
www.equifax.co.uk	www.experian.com	www.callcredit.co.uk

If you find any errors on the report, you can apply to have them removed. If for instance a county court judgement is registered but has been satisfied, apply to the county court for a Certificate of Satisfaction (called a Scottish Decree in Scotland), or send proof of payment from the individual or organisation that took the case to court (called 'the pursuer' in Scotland) to the Registry Trust with a £4.50 search fee. All rating agencies receive notification of the change within four weeks and adjust their records. If a credit account has been settled but this has not been recorded, you need to contact the company in question and ask them to notify the rating agencies.

Check to make sure that any jointly held credit is recorded in your individual names instead of, for example, Mr and Mrs R. Smith. Ask the creditors to begin reporting information on these accounts in your name as well as your spouse's. Assuming that these accounts have positive payment histories, having them in your credit file may help you build your own credit history.

Review your credit reports carefully for errors and omissions. If you find any problems, write to the agency informing them of the correct situation. If you used to have credit in your maiden name, make sure that this credit is a part of your credit history. If it's not, ask the credit reference agency to add that information.

If some of the joint accounts in your credit history reflect late payments or even defaults due to your spouse's mismanagement of those accounts, you may be able to distance yourself from that negative information by preparing a 'Notice of Correction'. This can be an explanation of up to 200 words on what has occurred and why. Any future lender sees the notice when they search your report. Send the notice to each of the main credit reference agencies (see the sidebar 'Contacting the credit reference agencies'). The notice you provide becomes a permanent part of your credit record.

Avoid using any of the agencies that offer to rebuild your credit, especially those stating that, for a fee, they can remove detrimental information from your record. If they sound too good to be true, they most likely are.

When you've resolved any difficulties in your credit record, continue to build a solid credit history. You can do this by applying for a small unsecured loan (£500) from your bank/building society and repaying it over a reasonable period (12 months). Let the degree of crisis in your marriage guide how quickly you pay back what you borrow.

If the bank refuses to loan you money without a co-signer, don't ask your spouse – you end up linking your credit to your spouse's. Ask a relative or close friend to co-sign instead.

After you pay off a loan, you must take a few more steps to secure a good credit history:

- ✔ Take out another small loan – this time not co-signed – in your own name.

- ✔ Order a copy of your credit report from each of the credit reference agencies to make sure that they reflect your loan payments. If they don't, ask the bank to report your payment history to the credit reference agencies it works with.

- ✔ Apply for one or more store cards, because they tend to have a more relaxed application process. Beware, though – interest rates are high: don't overspend and repay the debt quickly.

- ✔ Apply for a credit card, preferably with a zero per cent interest rate, and ensure that you make regular payments within the grace period.

- ✔ Always proceed with caution, because too many applications for credit in a short period can temporarily damage your credit file.

Being an *authorised user* on your spouse's accounts doesn't help you build your own credit history. That's because being an authorised user means that you get to use the credit but you have no legal responsibility for the account.

Chapter 4

Finding Out about Family Law Basics

. . . .

In This Chapter

▶ Following the evolution of family law

▶ Understanding the legal side of marriage obligations

▶ Finding out about the role of family courts and family lawyers

▶ Examining your parental responsibilities

. . . .

he rules of the game for marriage, separation and divorce, as well as those that apply to parent-child relationships, fall under the heading of *family law*. Among other things, family law establishes the ground rules for what makes a marriage or divorce legal, sets out the obligations of one spouse to another, and defines the basic responsibilities that you as parents have towards your children, such as supporting them financially even after your marriage has ended.

This chapter provides an overview of the laws that apply to beginning and ending your marriage. It also offers a brief historical perspective on how those laws have evolved to accommodate and reflect society's changing values.

Check out www.divorceaid.co.uk for easy-to-understand advice and information on a variety of divorce-related legal and emotional issues.

Changing Laws for Changing Times

The past few decades have seen dramatic changes in our society's lifestyles, values and attitudes, not least in the introduction of civil partnership and the spread of cohabitation. The movement of women out of the house and into the work world was one of the most significant of those changes. In turn, fathers began playing a more active role in the care and bringing up of their children. As a result, lawmakers and family courts began to re-evaluate their attitudes towards arrangements for children and financial support between spouses (including civil partners).

Ending the blame game

You can obtain a divorce without blaming your spouse if you're willing and able to wait until you've been separated for two years – if your spouse consents to the divorce. (You need to wait five years if your spouse doesn't consent.) In Scotland, those periods have recently been reduced to one year with your spouse's consent and two years without.

Nearly all the professionals who work with divorcing couples want the law to change so that 'fault' can't be used as a ground for divorce (as it now can): they want to take the blame element out of all divorces. Parliament tried to reform the law in the 1990s but the Government dropped the changes and politicians are unlikely to try again in the near future.

Recognising children's rights

The Children Act 1989 and the Children Order (Northern Ireland) 1995 radically shifted the emphasis from parents' *rights* in respect of their children to parents' *responsibilities* towards them. This shift was partly in response to an increasing awareness of the damage being done to children caught up in the bitter disputes of their parents, or who lost touch with one parent. The Children Act emphasised the rights of the children rather than the rights of the parents and improved considerably the way caring for children is handled in divorce cases.

Managing child support

As the number of single parent families grew in the latter half of the last century, so did the demands on the state for financial support. As a result, the government introduced the Child Support Act 1991 and the Child Support (Northern Ireland) Order 1991, devising a formula for the calculation of child support payable by each parent and shifting most of the power for deciding child support issues from the family courts to an administrative agency known as the Child Support Agency (CSA). The main aim was to make parents more responsible for the financial support of their children following divorce or separation, and also to reduce the costs of litigation. The formula was simplified in 2003 – partly to minimise the scope for the administrative errors and delay that have dogged the Agency since its inception. The Government is phasing out the CSA and has introduced 'son of CSA' called the Child Maintenance and Enforcement Commission (CMEC) in order to simplify procedures and reduce costs. Have a look at Chapter 13 for more on child support, the CSA and CMEC.

Supporting your spouse

Attitudes towards spousal support have also changed over the past few decades, with a growing number of women earning their own money. Orders for spousal maintenance are less common, and judges are now expressly required by statute to consider whether or not to dismiss such claims on divorce. Nominal maintenance orders – such as 5p a year – may still feature, mainly to leave open the possibility for claim by a spouse while dependent children are involved. Spousal support and maintenance are fully explained in Chapter 12.

Living together without being married

According to the Office of National Statistics, as many as one in six couples in the UK live together and don't marry – also known as cohabiting or 'common law marriage' – and they predict this to rise to one in four couples by 2031. You may often hear about this in the same context as marriage. However, under UK law, no such thing as a common law marriage exists, no matter how long you've been together, although over half of those people who cohabit believe, falsely, in the existence of common law marriage. These couples living together think that they have similar rights, obligations and protections to married couples if they separate, but this is not the case – except with regard to their children. As parents, your responsibilities in the eyes of the court are the exact same towards your children regardless of marriage. If you're not married and you separate, you don't have to go through a legal divorce process. Some other big differences for cohabitants are the following:

- ✔ You have no obligation to share any part of your estate (that is, everything you own) with your cohabitant when you die, unless you have been living together for at least two years up to the date of your death, or your cohabitant can prove that she was financially dependent upon you. (In Scotland, no two-year provision applies – you can go to court to establish 'widow's' or 'widower's' rights to your unmarried partner's assets after living together for any length of time.)

- ✔ You aren't automatically entitled to your cohabitant's pension. Some pension schemes, however, do allow claims from cohabitants.

- ✔ Your property ownership rights, if you share a property together, are governed by trust and property law, not by family law. Therefore, if you don't have your name on the deeds, you may not be entitled to anything, even if you have children together. (Your dependent children, however, may have a claim.)

> ✔ You have no legal right to claim maintenance or ongoing financial support for yourself.
>
> ✔ As a father, you don't have legal parental responsibility for your children unless you have a court order, or a written agreement registered at the Principal Registry of the Family Division, or – since 1 December 2003 – you've registered the birth of your child with the mother. Otherwise, only the natural mother has parental responsibility (see the section 'Understanding parental responsibility' later in this chapter).

In Scotland, a new law was introduced in 2006 that enables a separated cohabitant, in certain limited circumstances, to make a claim against her former partner for payment of a capital sum. In order to qualify for such an award, you must demonstrate that you were financially disadvantaged in some way during the relationship to the corresponding financial advantage of your partner. Such a claim must be raised in court no later than one year from the date of separation. Although rare, establishing a common law marriage is possible in Scotland if you're both free to marry, have lived together for a reasonable time prior to May 2006, and can show that almost no one realised you weren't married. You're then treated as legally man and wife. However, proving a common law marriage isn't easy, and depends on showing consent to marriage – if your partner for instance didn't believe in marriage, you wouldn't have a common law marriage. This legal status can be important for inheritance as well as for the financial consequences of divorce. This type of common law marriage has been abolished in Scotland for cohabiting relationships that commenced after the new law came into effect there in May 2006.

Tying the Knot

People typically think of marriage as a romantic relationship and most marriages do start out that way. However, marriage is also a financial and legal relationship. In fact, the financial and legal aspects of marriage last long after the romance fades and those aspects of marriage become paramount if you decide to separate legally or get divorced.

Carrying a licence to marry

If you're reading this book, you're likely to be already married and considering divorce, and you may not care what your responsibilities should have been when married – you want us to cut to the chase! But knowing what you're responsible for *during* marriage helps you better understand your responsibilities after divorce.

You're required by the state to give notice of your intention to marry in order to ensure that no legal objections are in place, such as a previous marriage that hasn't been dissolved. (So if you want to remarry, make sure that your divorce is finalised first!) Your notice can take any of the following forms, depending on where you want to get married:

- **A register office wedding:** If you're planning a marriage in a register office, you must give prior notice of your intention to the Registrar.

- **A religious wedding ceremony:** The person conducting your wedding ceremony can tell you whether or not she is also licensed to act as Registrar, in which case you don't need to contact the register office. (If you get married in the Church of England, your Banns, announcing your marriage and giving the opportunity for objection, are then called in the parish churches where you each live.) If the person conducting your religious ceremony isn't licensed for civil marriages, you must also inform the Registrar and additionally arrange a register office marriage.

- **Another approved marriage venue:** If you plan to marry in a secular venue other than the register office (for instance, an approved hotel) the organiser tells you how to inform the Registrar.

In all these situations, you need to show proof of your age, identity and address. If either of you have been married before, you need to give evidence that the marriage has ended – by showing proof of your divorce or your former spouse's death.

You can't legally marry under the following circumstances:

- You're under 16 years old. You also need to have your parents' consent if you're under 18 – unless you live in Scotland.

- You're planning to marry a close relative such as your parent, sibling, grandparent, child or grandchild.

- You're already married to someone else – that's called *bigamy*.

- You aren't respectively male and female (see the sidebar 'Same-sex relationships').

After you're married, you receive a certified copy of your marriage certificate to show that you're legally married. If you don't have a copy and need one for your divorce, the original marriage certificate is kept at the church or register office and they should be able to give you a copy.

Many couples these days choose to live together without marrying. The law relating to cohabiting couples is very different to that relating to married couples. You can read more about living together in the earlier section 'Living together without being married'.

Same-sex relationships

Same-sex marriages are not currently allowed in the UK but same-sex couples can register their partnerships and gain rights and obligations very similar to those of married couples – called civil partnerships. See the section 'Uniting in civil partnership' later in this chapter.

Understanding your marital rights and responsibilities

After your marriage ceremony, you and your spouse have a legally binding marital contract with one another. With that contract you've agreed to assume a number of important financial and legal obligations to one another. The contract also entitles you to certain legal rights as spouses. Some of those obligations and rights include the following:

- ✔ **You have an obligation to support each other financially.**

  The law doesn't say how you must provide the financial support or how much support you have to provide. Furthermore, if you're a spouse based at home, the courts view the work you perform in taking care of your home, bringing up your children or supporting your spouse's career as just as much a contribution to your marriage as your spouse's financial contribution.

- ✔ **You have an obligation to provide financial and other support for your children.**

- ✔ **You have the right to choose where, when and how you fulfil your legal obligations to your children, within limits.**

  For example, the authorities don't mind if you raise your children as vegetarians, but they intervene if they have reason to believe you're starving them – in fact you may lose care of your children as a result. And although you're free to choose your own doctor, if the authorities decide that you're withholding lifesaving medical treatment from your child, the authorities may intervene.

- ✔ **You have an obligation to provide for your spouse on your death.** If you don't make provision, your spouse can make a claim against your estate.

- ✔ **You're exempt from testifying against each other in court.**

> ✔ **You have a right to certain retirement and state benefits.**
>
> ✔ **You have a right to register your spouse's death and to claim bereavement benefits and fatal accident damages.**
>
> ✔ **You have a right to succeed to the tenancy of a house.**

Agreeing to the terms before you marry

You may attempt to limit or extend your marital obligations towards one another by signing a *pre-marital* or (sometimes called a *pre-nuptial*) agreement before you marry. For example, before you marry you may agree that you don't have any financial rights to a business that your future spouse owned for some years before you knew each other. The courts in England, Wales and Northern Ireland aren't necessarily bound by such agreements if a later disagreement arises between you, but judges are now taking such agreements into account more often, especially in a short or childless marriage. Agreements in Scotland are likely to be upheld. Pre-marital agreements are especially popular with mature people entering into second marriages. Chapter 21 covers pre-marital agreements in more detail.

Marrying in a religious ceremony

Although a religious ceremony is not a requirement for a legal marriage, it is customary in all faith communities. However, a religious marriage ceremony is only also a legal marriage if the minister who performs the ceremony and the place where it is being held is registered for marriage. If it isn't, you must also have a civil marriage in a register office. Therefore, if you only had a religious ceremony in an unlicensed venue, you may not be considered legally married!

If you get married abroad, your marriage is generally legally recognised in the UK as long as your marriage complies with the laws of the country in which you're married. (For more details on marriage abroad, see the later section 'Looking at Foreign Marriage and Divorce'.)

Mick Jagger contested Jerry Hall's divorce application on the grounds that their Hindu wedding was a ceremony and not a marriage. In the end an English judge ruled that their 'marriage' in Bali was not valid in Indonesia or under English law. The judge granted a decree of nullity and a private financial settlement was reached. In Scotland, provided that they both believed themselves to have been validly married at the time, Jerry Hall would have been able to ask the court to make a finding to the effect that they had a common law marriage. She could then have asked the court to make orders for financial provision in the same way as though they had been validly married.

Uniting in a civil partnership

Since 5 December 2005, same-sex couples have been able to get legal recognition of their relationships. Couples who form a civil partnership have a new legal status, that of 'civil partner', and have equal treatment as married couples in a wide range of legal matters, including:

- ✔ Tax, including inheritance tax
- ✔ Employment benefits
- ✔ Most state and occupational pension benefits
- ✔ Income-related benefits, tax credits and child support
- ✔ Providing financial support for your civil partners and any children of the family
- ✔ Applying for parental responsibility for your civil partner's child
- ✔ Inheritance of a tenancy agreement
- ✔ Recognition under intestacy rules (dying without making a will)
- ✔ Protection from domestic violence

Two people of the same sex and over the age of 18 (or 16 with consent from their parents, or 16 without parental consent in Scotland) can enter into a civil partnership by giving notice. As with marriage, both must sign the partnership register in the presence of a civil partnership registration officer and two witnesses at the local register office and the basic ceremony can be livened up with music and readings. A ceremony can be held in any venue already approved for civil marriages. People can change their names when they've formed a civil partnership by deed poll.

Dissolution is the term used to describe the end of a civil partnership – a procedure similar to divorce – and a dissolution can be obtained after one year of civil partnership. One partner applies for a 'petition', which states why the civil partnership has 'irretrievably broken down'. Just as in divorce, if children of the family are involved, a court has to approve a 'statement of arrangements' concerning plans you've made for the children when the dissolution is final – just like divorce.The main difference from divorce for civil partners is that you can't use adultery to prove the irretrievable breakdown of the partnership. All the rest is the same. So in this book anything related to 'spouses' or 'husbands and wives' generally applies also to civil partners. We point out anything specific you need to know as we go along. For more information about civil partnerships see Chapter 5 and also the Government website www.direct.gov.uk.

Knowing What the Law Says About Children

The Children Act 1989 and the Children (Northern Ireland) Order 1995 concentrate on *children's* rights, requiring a change in the language we use to refer to their care. The phrases 'custody', 'care and control' and 'access' are no longer used because they imply that children are possessions to be shared (or fought over) by their parents. Instead the legal system, and gradually the media and general public, are using the terms 'parental responsibility', 'residence' and 'contact', which encourages divorcing parents to think of their children as people, rather than possessions to be fought over. Read on for full explanations of these terms.

Understanding parental responsibility

If you're married, the law says that both of you have parental responsibility – meaning that you both have a responsibility to provide for the moral, physical and emotional health of your children. This responsibility includes:

- ✔ Providing your children with food, clothing, medical care and a place to live

- ✔ Disciplining your children

- ✔ Ensuring that your children receive at least minimal education (college isn't required) in a state or private school or at home

- ✔ Choosing your children's names and religions

Child abduction

Taking a child from the person who has care of her without that person's consent is a criminal offence. Consult a solicitor immediately if your child is abducted, especially if you believe your ex or soon-to-be-ex is the culprit and may take your child to a country outside England and Wales.

The Hague Convention, the European Convention and European Union regulations all say that decisions about custody must be made in the country where the child resided before the abduction. Therefore, if you and your children live in England but your ex-spouse abducts your son to Morocco, the residence and childcare decisions made in England take priority.

The law in Scotland presumes that, after your divorce, you and your ex-spouse consult each other on what's best for your children, just as you were presumed to do when you were married. Your responsibilities as parents in Scotland are to:

- ✔ Safeguard and promote your child's health and wellbeing

- ✔ Provide direction and guidance for your child

- ✔ Maintain direct contact and personal relations with your child if you're not living together

- ✔ Act as your child's legal representative

- ✔ Consult your child about her living arrangements to the extent that she can understand, particularly if the child is over the age of 12

Throughout the UK, these obligations remain yours regardless of whether you and your spouse separate or divorce. Usually your parental obligations remain until your child becomes a legal adult at the age of 18. See Chapter 10 for more about parental responsibility.

Agreeing that there's no place like home – determining residence

As parents, during the divorce process you need to settle your children's *residence* – the arrangements about where and with whom the children are going to live. You have two options:

- ✔ **Sole residence:** The children live with one parent. For example, they are based with their mum.

- ✔ **Joint (also known as shared) residence:** The children split their time between both parents' households. For example, they may spend one week living with their dad and the next week with their mum. Joint residence can also mean that children live with two people together, for example, they live with their mum and stepdad.

Research has shown that children are usually better off living with both of their parents in one way or another.

Keeping contact with your children

If your children live with you and you're separated from their other parent, you're expected to allow your children to have some degree of contact with her. Most parents have *direct contact*, spending time with their children. However, in some cases, such as where allegations of abuse have been made, the children don't have physical contact but may have *indirect contact*, exchanging letters or phone calls instead. Studies show that, for their emotional development and wellbeing, children shouldn't lose touch with either parent, and so direct contact with both mum and dad is optimal.

Putting the children first

The law says that – whether you're married or not – you have to give priority to your children's needs when you make any major decisions concerning them. Their welfare must always be your paramount consideration.

When a judge looks at the residence and contact arrangements you and your spouse are recommending to see if they're satisfactory, her highest priority is the child's best interests. The judge has to consider a checklist of factors when asked to make such decisions, including:

✔ The wishes and feelings of the child concerned, in light of age and understanding

✔ The child's physical, emotional and educational needs

✔ The likely effect on the child of any change in circumstances

✔ The child's age, sex, background and any characteristic that the court considers relevant

✔ The harm, if any, which the child has suffered or is at risk of suffering

✔ The capability of the parents to meet the child's needs

✔ The range of powers available to the court

During your divorce proceedings, a court doesn't make an order about your child (for example, about residence or contact) unless the judge thinks it is in your child's interest for the court to do so. This *no order principle* is based on the view that you know your children better than anyone else and are therefore better placed than the court to make a decision on your child's best interests.

Distinguishing One Lawyer from Another

If you're involved in a family law dispute, at some point you're likely to have dealings with lawyers, whether they're representing your spouse or yourself. The two main sorts of lawyer that you come across in England and Wales are *solicitors* and *barristers*. Chapters 15 and 17 have advice on finding and working with your solicitors and barristers, but following are brief descriptions of the differences between the two kinds of lawyers:

✔ **Solicitors:** Your first point of contact with a lawyer is almost certainly with a solicitor. Solicitors are legally qualified and trained professionals who advise and represent you in all non-court matters. They can write letters on your behalf to your spouse or her solicitor and they can negotiate and help prepare your case for court if necessary. Solicitors have many capable and educated people working with them, including legal executives, trainee solicitors and paralegals. You may encounter some of these key players when working with your solicitor.

We strongly recommend that if you're considering divorce, you choose a solicitor who specialises in family law and preferably is a member of Resolution (check out their website for a list of solicitors in your area: www.resolution.org.uk).

✔ **Barristers:** With your permission, your solicitor may instruct a barrister, often referred to as counsel, to give an opinion on your case or to represent you in court. Barristers aren't usually involved with the day-to-day running of your case – that's left to you or your solicitor – but their job is to keep particularly up to date with developments in the law and to act as skilled advocates. Experienced solicitors sometimes perform both roles.

Barristers are called *advocates* in Scotland.

Courting Justice

When you're getting legally separated or divorced, or if you're in a family law dispute of another kind, your legal issue falls under the jurisdiction of the family courts that are 'civil' courts. If some aspect of your separation or divorce ends up in court, the judge decides on the issue after a hearing. Although sometimes called a trial, a hearing isn't like a criminal trial; no jury is present and most family proceedings take place in private. Your solicitor can advise which level of the family courts is the most appropriate for you, or on whether the proceedings need to be transferred from one court to another:

✔ **The Family Proceedings Court:** This court is the family wing of the Magistrates Court. Proceedings for the protection of children brought by local authorities always start in the Family Proceedings Court. All other proceedings concerning children start in the County Court and can be transferred to the Family Proceedings Court. As divorces always start in the County Court, those children cases always stay there. A magistrate in the Family Proceedings Court also has power to grant limited financial relief if you're separating from your spouse but not yet planning to divorce.

✔ **The County Court:** This court deals with almost all divorce or separation proceedings, but it must be designated as a divorce County Court. You don't have to issue the divorce proceedings at the County Court in the area where you live, although it's usually more convenient. However, issues regarding children must be dealt with in the jurisdiction where the children currently live. A district or circuit judge of the County Court hears your case. The equivalent court in London is called the Principal Registry.

✔ **The High Court:** Your divorce or separation proceedings go to the High Court only if an awful lot of money is involved or your case involves a particularly complex issue, such as a foreign marriage. A judge who's authorised to sit in the High Court hears your case.

✔ **Criminal Courts (Magistrates and Crown Courts):** These courts are not part of the family court system. If you pursue criminal charges against your spouse for harassment or physical abuse, those charges are heard in the criminal courts. In most cases that's the Magistrates Court but in very serious cases it may be the Crown Court where people can be tried by a jury. If found guilty of serious violence or abuse by the court, your spouse is sent to prison.

The Scottish and Northern Irish court systems

The court system in Scotland is very different from the one in England and Wales. Scotland doesn't have County or Magistrates Courts. Most divorce and family actions are handled by the *Sheriff Courts*: the local courts found in major towns and all cities throughout Scotland. The Sheriff Courts handle both civil law actions, which include family, divorce and public law cases, and criminal law cases. If your case goes to court, you need to instruct a local solicitor to act for you and an advocate to represent you in court.

Some divorces are heard in the highest civil court: the *Court of Session* in Edinburgh. Cases usually go to the Court of Session when a lot of money is involved or an unusual point of law needs to be decided. You need an advocate to represent you in the Court of Session and cases take longer and cost more than actions in the Sheriff Courts.

In Northern Ireland the court system is more like the English and Welsh one, but with some differences. For example, the Magistrates' family courts deal regularly with cases aimed at preventing domestic abuse, such as removing a spouse from the family home. Another big difference is that magistrates are legally qualified and are advised by members of a lay panel – one male and one female. The County Courts deal with private family cases, such as simple undefended divorces and children applications, but separate courts called Family Care Centres deal with public law proceedings such as complicated applications for care orders. However, the High Court deals with the bulk of applications for divorce and financial orders linked to divorce proceedings.

Looking at Foreign Marriage and Divorce

Many marriages in the UK now have an international element to them – not least because the EU has opened its borders and immigration from all corners of the world together with increasing globalisation has had an impact on marriage and divorce. British citizens not only marry people from other countries, but also they can marry overseas and live in the UK or marry in the UK and then live overseas. This situation can lead to complications when divorcing as well as complications with children. In 2006, according to the Office for National Statistics, over one fifth of all children born in the UK had a foreign mother. In addition international considerations can apply not only to divorce and separation, but also to child abduction, taking children out of the UK, pre-marital agreements, civil partnerships and cohabitation.

For example, if an international aspect is involved, as soon as you're thinking of separating you must also think about where a divorce should take place. Divorce procedure and the grounds for divorce differ from country to country and so do financial settlements. England has been called the 'divorce capital of the world' because of the courts' recent generous awards to women married to wealthy men. But even for the not so rich, where you divorce can have an effect on the outcome, including arrangements for your children.

If you find yourself in this position, getting advice from a specialist international solicitor is essential. To find one, contact Resolution on 01689 820272 (www.resolution.org.uk).

Chapter 5

Discovering the Basics of Divorce Law

- -

In This Chapter

▶ Meeting the minimum requirements for a divorce

▶ Waiting two years or blaming your spouse

▶ Examining the three basic kinds of divorce

▶ Finding out what happens if your divorce ends up in court

▶ Finalising a divorce

- -

*Y*our divorce may be your first encounter with the legal system (except for that appearance in court for the odd traffic offence). Understandably, the prospect of dealing with solicitorss, courts and legal jargon can be fairly intimidating.

One of the best ways to steel yourself for what's to come and boost your self-confidence is to find out about the laws that apply to divorce and the legal processes involved in getting a divorce. With that in mind, this chapter provides an overview of the basics of divorce law and some of the key decisions you need to make to comply with the requirements of the legal system.

So, the first thing you need to know is that the main Act dealing with divorce in England and Wales is the Matrimonial Causes Act 1973. This Act is the basic framework for divorce, and deals with whether or not you can get divorced and provides guidelines for you, your solicitor, your mediator and the courts to follow. In Scotland and Northern Ireland, the key pieces of legislation are the Divorce (Scotland) Act 1976 and the Matrimonial Causes (Northern Ireland) Order 1978, respectively.

Not Just Anyone Can Get Divorced

To get a divorce in England and Wales, you have to meet some minimum requirements:

✔ You, your spouse or both of you must be habitually resident in England and Wales for a minimum of one year. However, if you can show that England or Wales is your country of *domicile* (you have sufficient connection with the country – for example, it's your usual home, even though you're working abroad), you can get a divorce in England or Wales without being in the country.

✔ You or your spouse must not have initiated similar proceedings in any other country anywhere in the world.

✔ You've been married for a minimum of one year.

In Northern Ireland, the minimum period is two years. No minimum period applies in Scotland. The rules in Scotland relating to domicile and habitual residence are broadly similar to those in England and Wales.

✔ Your marriage has irretrievably broken down.

Understanding irretrievable breakdown

The court accepts that your marriage has irretrievably broken down if you can establish that any one of the following five facts applies to you:

✔ **Your spouse has committed adultery and you find it intolerable to live with him.**

Adultery means sexual intercourse between a man and a woman, one or both of whom are married and not to each other. You can't petition on the basis of your own adultery. Adultery is easier to prove if your spouse is prepared to admit to it. Sometimes a spouse is prepared to admit to adultery if you promise not to pursue any claim for costs. You don't have to name the third party, but if you do, that third party has to be given notice and allowed to respond. You can't rely on adultery as a basis for divorce if you and your spouse live together for more than six months after you first find out about the adultery, unless the adultery is continuing. (Note that this fact doesn't apply to civil partners.)

✔ **Your spouse has behaved in such a way that you can't reasonably be expected to live with him.**

To cite behaviour as your basis for divorce, you need to provide the court with at least three examples of behaviour by your spouse that you've found unacceptable, and preferably give dates. If the behaviour is extreme, such as serious violence, one incident may be enough. Other examples of behaviour include drinking or gambling to excess; constant verbal abuse; refusal to have, or excessive demands for, sexual intercourse; or complete lack of financial or other support.

The test is whether the court thinks that expecting you to continue living together is unreasonable. Living together for more than six months since the last incident of behaviour isn't an absolute bar to divorce, but the court takes account of this fact, and it may undermine your claim that the marriage has irretrievably broken down.

✔ **Your spouse has deserted you for a minimum of two years.**

Divorces based on desertion are relatively rare. You have to prove that your spouse has refused to live with you for at least two years without good cause. Any attempt at reconciliation for up to six months doesn't count against you, but you have to add any periods of reconciliation onto the two-year period leading up to your petition. This basis for divorce no longer applies in Scotland.

✔ **You've been separated for at least two years and your spouse consents to a divorce.**

You have to establish not only that you haven't lived together for the two years leading up to your petition, but also that you believed that the marriage was over at the time you separated. You can live under the same roof as your spouse for part of or all this time, but you need to satisfy the judge that you lived as separate households. Just stopping sleeping together is not enough; you need to prove that you no longer eat meals together, do chores for each other or generally function as a couple. You also need written confirmation of your spouse's consent to divorce.

A reconciliation for up to six months doesn't prevent you from getting a divorce on this basis, but you have to add the period of reconciliation onto the two-year period leading up to the divorce petition. For example, if you and your spouse separate in January 2007 and hope to divorce two years later, but then you have an unsuccessful reconciliation for three months, you can't petition for divorce until April 2009 – two years and three months after your original separation.

You don't have to blame your spouse for the breakdown of your marriage if you can wait for two years before filing your petition. You do still need to try and agree all the key issues between you, namely the arrangements for your children and finance, preferably before you separate.

In Scotland, and provided that your spouse consents to divorce, you need to have been separated for a period of only one year.

✔ **You've been separated for at least five years.**

The same conditions apply to a divorce on this basis as they do to a divorce based on two years' separation, except that you don't need your spouse's consent.

In Scotland the period of separation required where your spouse doesn't consent is two years.

The Office for National Statistics records that in 1991, nearly a third of divorces were granted on the grounds of adultery, whereas in 2006 that proportion had dropped to 20 per cent. The Office attributed this change to the rise in the use of mediation, whereby couples are more likely to choose the no-fault basis for divorce of two years' separation.

Nearly all petitions for divorce go through on an undefended basis, even when they're based on adultery or behaviour – allegations made in a petition rarely affect the outcome of the other key issues in your divorce. Keep in mind, however, that allegations of fault increase the potential for bad feeling between you.

Resolving Basic Divorce Issues

You and your spouse need to decide on several fundamental issues during your divorce. Although finalising your divorce before you resolve all children and financial issues is technically possible, you're wiser to wait until all such issues have been resolved. Some of the reasons for this advice are as follows:

✓ **Your children need to know what the arrangements are going to be for them.**

✓ **You and your spouse are next of kin until your divorce is finalised.** If your divorce is finalised before you sort out the benefits you have as next of kin, such as retirement or insurance rights, you may lose these important benefits.

✓ **You may lose any matrimonial rights you've registered if you don't have your name on the title deeds to your home.** See Chapter 3 for how to register your interest in a property that isn't in your name.

✓ **You or your ex-spouse may pursue financial claims against the other many years after the divorce itself has been finalised, unless and until a final financial order is made in the divorce proceedings.** Your ex-spouse may also claim against your estate on your death, if he has not remarried and believes that you haven't made reasonable provision for him. If you want to avoid those possibilities, you must have a final order settling all financial and property matters between you and dismissing all future claims, including those on death.

✓ **You can't make any financial claims against your ex-spouse, if you remarry following your divorce, unless you've reserved those claims in your petition for divorce.** This situation is known as the *remarriage trap*, and is a particular risk if your spouse started the divorce proceedings and you agreed to them going through on an undefended basis. If you subsequently remarry without having secured from the court a final order with regard to all financial and property matters, you're prohibited from pursuing your claims at a later date. You're also at a severe disadvantage should your ex-spouse decide to pursue his financial claims against you.

Your decisions must include answers to the following questions:

- **How are your property, pensions and debts going to be divided up?** If you're unable to agree on a division, complex laws, plus a wide discretion on the part of the judge in applying those laws to your case, can make deciding who gets what a complicated undertaking, especially if you and your spouse have managed to amass a considerable amount of assets. (See Chapter 11 to help you work out how to divide up your assets.)

- **Is one of you going to pay spousal support or maintenance to the other?** If so, how much are the payments going to be and for how long will they continue?

  If you're an older woman who has never worked outside the home during your marriage or has not done so in many years, you may have difficulty finding a well-paid job after you're divorced. Therefore, getting an adequate amount of maintenance for a long enough period of time – possibly the rest of your life – is essential to maintaining an acceptable post-divorce lifestyle. However, if your divorce is rancorous, your spouse may fight against paying you the maintenance you think you need. (See Chapter 12 for more on maintenance.)

- **How are residence and contact issues going to be handled (if you and your spouse have dependent children)?** These issues can be some of the most emotional in a divorce. Some spouses fear that if they don't become the resident parent, they'll no longer play a meaningful role in the lives of their children; others may view fighting for the children as a way to get back at their spouses. See Chapter 10 for more about making decisions on the arrangements for your children.

- **What arrangements are you going to make for child support?** Since 1993, the Child Support Agency (CSA) and its replacement – the Child Maintenance and Enforcement Commission (CMEC) – has taken over most of the powers with regard to child support from the courts. CMEC calculates child support according to a formula, which is described in Chapter 13. You don't have to wait for divorce proceedings to apply to the CMEC; you just have to be separated. Even if you and your spouse agree the question of child support without going to the CMEC, make sure that you're aware of the formula.

If you and your spouse can work together to resolve these issues, your divorce can be relatively quick and inexpensive. If you can't work together, or if your divorce has complicating factors (your property or debt is substantial, for example), bringing your marriage to an end can take time and money. In a worst-case scenario, you must look to the courts for help.

The Ground Rules of the Divorce Court

The divorce laws and statutory guidelines provide a framework and set boundaries for resolving the basic issues that you need to decide when you separate. In other words, those laws and guidelines are actually quite flexible, within certain limits:

- As you work your way through the divorce process, you and your spouse have a considerable amount of leeway when you decide on most of these issues, as long as you're both *in agreement*.

- As you address the division of your family property, spousal support and child residence and contact, assume that a *family law judge* is looking over your shoulder. This means that whatever you decide about these matters must give priority to the needs of your children and be fair to you both. Your decisions must reflect an appreciation of what the judge might decide if your divorce issues were to end in a full hearing. You can find more on the guidelines used by judges when they decide about money and property division in Chapter 11 and on children in Chapter 4.

Second-guessing family law judges can be tricky because judges have considerable discretion in how they interpret the law and the weight that they give to the various statutory guidelines in each case. As a result, approaches may vary somewhat from one court to another or even from one judge to another in the same court.

You can appeal a judge's decision, but an appeal can be hard to justify legally and may be risky. Plus, appealing means more delay and legal fees.

Divorce law helps resolve legal and financial issues. The law doesn't resolve the anger, guilt, fear or sadness you may feel. Don't look to the legal system to do that for you or you're going to be left feeling disappointed and frustrated when your divorce is over.

One Objective (But Many Ways to Get There)

The goal of any divorce is to end a marriage. That goal can be achieved in many ways, however. You can work together to make your divorce process as easy and inexpensive as possible, or you can turn it into an expensive battle full of anger, unreasonable demands and uncompromising behaviour.

Divorce is a process, not an event. Just what path your divorce process takes is up to you and your spouse. Here are your basic options, all of which are described in more detail in the sections that follow:

✔ **Option 1 – the co-operative divorce.** You and your spouse work out the terms of all the key issues of your divorce together. One of you files an agreed divorce petition and you ask the court for a consent order regarding your property. You can also use a mediator or engage solicitors, or even hire both a mediator and solicitors, to help you work out the details and formalities, but you still keep things friendly.

✔ **Option 2 – the difficult divorce.** You and your spouse can't agree on all the key issues in your divorce. You may be able to avoid a full hearing by resolving your differences with the help of solicitors or through mediation (see Chapter 16).

✔ **Option 3 – the fully contested divorce.** At this point, you lose control of one or more of the key issues in your divorce. They are now in the hands of a divorce court judge. Luckily, only the minority of cases end up this way.

Your divorce can be a combination of two or even all three divorce options we just listed. For example, you and your spouse may work some things out together, engage solicitors to negotiate other aspects of your divorce, and then have a judge resolve the issues on which you're deadlocked.

Using collaborative law

Another option for working out the terms of your divorce outside of court in a friendly manner is available through a process called *collaborative law*. You, your spouse and your respective solicitors (who must be trained in the collaborative law process) sit down together to reach a settlement on all the issues of your divorce. Unlike mediation, no neutral third party is involved. After you hammer out an agreement, your divorce petition and agreed order is filed with the court. The benefits of this approach include:

✔ Lower costs

✔ Less stress for you, your spouse, and your solicitors

✔ Creative solutions to divorce issues

✔ Increased co-operation between spouses

✔ A positive foundation from which to build a post-divorce relationship if you and your spouse share young children

The drawback to using collaborative law to negotiate your divorce is that if you and your spouse are unable to come to an agreement and need the court's involvement, the solicitors you've been working with must withdraw from your case and you have to find new solicitors. That does not mean that you begin the divorce process all over again however, as you can take the information you collect with you for use by your next solicitor. To find out more, visit www.resolution.org.uk and click on Alternatives to Court.

Many couples committed to working things out themselves with minimal help from solicitors also use *mediation* as a way to help them structure their divorce negotiations and reduce the opportunity for emotions to get in the way of reason. (See Chapter 16 if you feel that you and your spouse can benefit from mediation.)

The co-operative divorce

A *co-operative divorce* is the easiest divorce option on your chequebook (and on your emotions). With co-operation, filing a *divorce petition* (the legal paperwork that initiates a divorce) is little more than a formality, because your spouse doesn't object to the petition. A straightforward uncontested divorce should be completed within three to six months.

When is a divorce not a divorce?

A civil divorce that is valid according to UK law may still not be enough for the purposes of your church or faith community if you want to remarry according to your faith. For example, a divorced Catholic who wants to remarry in the Catholic Church must obtain a religious annulment first. If you're Jewish, you remain married according to Jewish religious law unless you also have a religious divorce, known as a Get. A Muslim needs a religious divorce under the Islamic law of Sharia in order to remarry. Check the requirements for divorce with your own religious authorities if you want to end your marriage according to your faith.

(The newspapers early in 2008 were full of stories about the Archbishop of Canterbury and his view that Sharia law can co-exist with the legal system in the UK. In fact, the Jewish community has operated separate religious courts (called Beth Din) in the UK for over 300 years. Those courts deal with various issues, including family disputes and particularly divorce.

What the Archbishop was talking about was widening our legal system to include laws that are not 'one size fits all'. But in reality any such changes are extremely unlikely.)

So, a divorce that takes place in the UK must comply with UK law to be valid. A divorce that takes place outside the UK is generally regarded as valid in the UK if it complies with the divorce laws of the country in which it has taken place and if some proceedings giving both spouses adequate notice and an opportunity to respond are involved. A Muslim divorce, for example, by a *bare talaq* (a single unilateral declaration of divorce by a husband) isn't regarded as valid in the UK; but an application by a wife to a judge of the Sharia Court, or a divorce that otherwise complies with Islamic law, is regarded as valid as long as both parties have consented or have had proper notice and an opportunity to respond. Check with your solicitor if you're not sure whether your divorce is legally valid in the UK.

You and your spouse work together to structure agreements relating to your children and to your finances that you both think are fair. If you reach an agreement about your children that is clearly in their interests, the court is unlikely to interfere, and no further formalities are involved. After you agree on the terms of your final financial settlement, you or your solicitors file the agreement with the court as a draft consent order for the approval of the judge. Providing the judge approves the draft order, neither you nor your spouse should need to attend court. Everything can be done by post. Judges approve most draft orders as long as you've both had some independent legal advice, you've been open and honest about your finances, and on the face of it the agreement appears to be fair.

The difficult divorce

If any of the key issues in your divorce are contested, solicitors are almost always involved. For example, you may have a hard time accepting that your spouse is blaming you for the breakdown of your marriage when you know that you're both equally responsible. You may ask your solicitors to negotiate on the contents of the petition or on the question of costs. Most solicitors tell you that arguing over the divorce itself is rarely worthwhile (that is, over the *reason* for the end of your marriage) if you both agree that the marriage has broken down; the reason for the divorce rarely affects the way the judge deals with any of the other issues such as the children or money. These days only a tiny number of divorce petitions are fully defended.

If you and your spouse can't agree over the arrangements for your children or for your finances, you can go to mediation to resolve the issues or ask your solicitors to try to negotiate a solution for you. More correspondence and paperwork mean that the difficult divorce takes longer to complete than the co-operative divorce and is more stressful for you – and costs more.

The fully contested divorce

The fully contested divorce is more emotional, time-consuming and expensive, and involves more paperwork and legal red tape than your other options. It can exhaust both your emotional and financial resources. Also, the animosity between you and your spouse probably isn't going to go away and you may have difficulty even carrying on a polite conversation when everything is over.

The main issues that you may contest are the following:

- The basis of the divorce petition itself (see the section on 'Understanding irretrievable breakdown' earlier in this chapter). These days, a fully contested petition is rare.
- The arrangements for your children
- The arrangements for your money and property
- The short-term occupation of your home and your personal protection, if your safety, or that of your children, is under threat.

If any aspect of your divorce ends with a full hearing, you're more likely to end up revisiting the terms later on. Doing so not only takes money and time but may also mean that you can never really put your divorce and your failed marriage behind you.

Initiating the Divorce Proceedings

Every divorce starts the same way – one spouse sends or *files* a *petition* with the court. If you do the filing, you're called the *petitioner* and your spouse is the *respondent*. (The legal rules governing divorce are soon going to change the words simply to *husband* or *wife*.) In Scotland, the divorcing parties are known as the *pursuer* and the *defender*. If your petition is based on your spouse's adultery, you don't have to name a third party, but if you do, he becomes known as the *co-respondent*.

In your petition, you establish the facts and the issues of the divorce as you see them, and indicate what you may want financially from your spouse. This *ancillary relief* may include maintenance (or *periodical payments*), lump sums, property and pensions for you, and maintenance or lump sums for your children. You can also claim costs. If you want to activate these claims, you must make a separate formal application to the court.

Even if you think you're unlikely to want to make a formal application, preserving all your possible claims in the petition is still a good idea. Otherwise, if you change your mind later, you have to get the permission of the court first to make the application, and that costs you extra time and money, especially if your spouse objects.

When you file a divorce petition, you're actually initiating matrimonial proceedings against your spouse. As the *petitioner*, you pay at least the initial court costs of your divorce. If you also make a formal application and your case ends up in court, you present your side first.

Unless your divorce is based on fault, you both probably pay your own legal and court costs. However, you can try to agree between you a provision that your spouse reimburse you for all or part of your costs. You need to include the claim for costs in your petition. If you're publicly funded, you don't have to pay any costs up front, but you may be liable for them in the long run because public funding usually takes the form of a loan rather than a gift. For more about costs and public funding, see Chapter 7.

 New procedures in all family cases are due to come into force after 2010 in England and Wales. As well as changing the procedure, the rules are due to change some of the terminology. Have a look at the end of Chapter 18 for more info.

Remembering your marriage certificate

When you file a petition for divorce, you're required to file a certified copy of your marriage certificate at the same time. If your divorce goes through, the marriage certificate remains on your divorce file with the court. If you can't find your marriage certificate, you can apply for another certified copy from the church or register office where you married. You need to provide your full names, the date of your marriage ceremony and a fee (currently £7.00).

Including a Statement of Arrangements for the children

If you have any children in your family, you must file a statement detailing the current and proposed arrangements for them, including:

- ✔ Where they now live and are going to live

- ✔ Where they now, and are going to, attend school

- ✔ What child support is in place and proposed

- ✔ What contact is in place and proposed

- ✔ Whether they have special health or educational needs

'Children of the family' includes not only the children of you and your spouse, but also any children of either of you, or of anyone else, if the children have lived with you and been treated as children of the family. The statement has to be filed with the court at the same time as the petition.

Serving and receiving the papers

After a petition is filed, your spouse must be formally notified. The notification can be accomplished in a number of ways:

- ✔ **Ask the court to post a copy of the papers to your spouse.** This is the most common way. The court sends a copy of the petition and any statement of arrangements to your spouse with an explanation of the proceedings and a form of acknowledgment for your spouse to return.

- ✔ **Ask the court bailiff to serve the papers personally.** This is a rarer alternative. You need a special form for this request (Divorce 96), a description or recent photograph of your spouse, and a court fee. This option is best if you anticipate difficulties in proving that your spouse has received the papers.

- ✔ **Hire your own private process server to serve the papers personally on your spouse.** This is more expensive and only necessary if your spouse fails to acknowledge receipt of the papers, or you have to make an urgent application.

- ✔ **Use substituted service.** If you have real difficulty in proving 'service' (formally presenting the documents) upon your spouse, the court sometimes allows *substituted service* – the papers are delivered to a particular address from which the judge thinks the respondent is likely to receive mail. The judge may even *dispense* with service if he is satisfied that you've made every possible effort to trace your spouse and failed.

When your spouse has received the papers, he has eight days within which to return the *acknowledgement of service* to the court detailing whether he:

- ✔ Consents to the divorce
- ✔ Intends to defend it
- ✔ Objects to any claim for costs in the petition
- ✔ Agrees with the arrangements for your children

The form also gives the details of any solicitor engaged by your spouse.

Your spouse has 21 days to file an *answer* if he intends to defend the divorce, and also needs to file a cross-petition if he agrees that the marriage has broken down but not for the reasons you've stated. In addition, when adultery is the basis for your petition, your spouse needs to admit to the adultery on the acknowledgement of service, or you need some other strong evidence.

You need your spouse's signed consent on the acknowledgement of service if you're basing your petition on having been separated for two years. Your spouse can defend a petition based on two or five years' separation on the grounds that financial matters need to be resolved first, or that he is going to suffer hardship if the divorce is granted. The court then deals with those issues before the divorce can be finalised.

Divorcing in Scotland

Scotland has two kinds of divorce actions: the simplified procedure and the ordinary procedure.

✔ **The simplified procedure is sometimes known as the 'do-it-yourself divorce'.** To qualify to use the simplified procedure, you must have no children of the marriage under 16 years old or any financial claims between you and your spouse. Also, no other ongoing actions can exist between you.

You can ask for the forms for the simplified procedure from the local sheriff clerk's office or from the Citizens' Advice Bureau (CAB) or from your own solicitor. The forms and guidance on filling them in can be downloaded from the Scottish Courts website: www.scotcourts.gov.uk. A fee applies for using the simplified procedure, which is explained on the forms. Doing your divorce yourself is a lot cheaper than using the ordinary procedure, but you must still seek legal advice at the outset, because you may lose rights to which you're entitled only on or before the divorce is granted.

✔ **The ordinary procedure is for divorces where you have children under 16 years old, financial claims between you and your spouse, or both.** The person who raises a divorce action is called the *pursuer*. You can be a *party litigant* (someone who brings or defends a court action without a solicitor).

However, using a solicitor is wise – to act on your behalf to raise a divorce action under the ordinary procedure. You can find a solicitor to act for you from the Law Society of Scotland: www.lawscot.org.uk. Also, considering a solicitor who specialises in family law matters is a good idea. Some of these solicitors are members of the Scottish Family Law Association: www.fla-scotland.co.uk.

Under the ordinary procedure, actions can be defended or undefended. In a defended action, the *defender* (the person against whom the action is raised) opposes the pursuer's claims and/or raises his own counter-claim against the case or parts of the case raised by the pursuer. Although grounds for the divorce to be defended are unusual, you may come across defended actions relating to arrangements for children and financial matters.

In an undefended action, the defender doesn't oppose the pursuer's claims or raise counter-claims, and the action can be dealt with by affidavit evidence – by a statement, sworn on oath in front of a notary public (an official authorised to certify documents). For this type of action, you need a witness. If you and your spouse have an undefended divorce, you may have matters on which you disagree. These matters can often be negotiated by your solicitors through correspondence.

Signing the affidavit in support of petition

The court forwards a copy of the acknowledgement or statement of service to you or your solicitor. You then need to sign a statement on oath confirming the contents of your petition and statement of arrangements, and saying whether you're pursuing any claim for costs. This statement is known as the *affidavit in support of petition*, a term which may change to *statement in support of application* after 2010. Attach a copy of your spouse's acknowledgement of service or the bailiffs' certificate of service to your affidavit.

An affidavit is a statement that's signed on oath in front of a solicitor or an officer of the court. You can't sign the affidavit in front of your own solicitor – you must pay a fee to a solicitor for witnessing your signature (about £5 per document and £2 per attachment) but the officer of the court doesn't charge you for this service. Send your sworn affidavit to the court for the judge to check. The judge then certifies whether you're entitled to a divorce, and whether the arrangements for your children are satisfactory.

The initial writ or summons in Scotland is simply a formal statement of the reasons for your divorce, your financial claims, and requests for orders in relation to your children. A writ is served by recorded delivery post or personally by Sheriff Officers in the Sheriff Court or Messengers at Arms in the Court of Session. No acknowledgement of service is required. In Northern Ireland, the petitioner is not permitted to give evidence by written statement alone: He has to attend court personally to give evidence to the judge.

If you and your spouse aren't already legally separated but are going to start living apart now that your divorce has begun, obtain a written agreement that details your living and financial arrangements and how you intend to handle child-related issues during the divorce process. (See Chapter 6 for more about separation.)

Getting Through the First Stage: The Decree Nisi

After the judge has granted the certificate confirming that you're entitled to a divorce and that the arrangements for your children (if any) are satisfactory, the court fixes a date for the *decree nisi*. On that date, a judge reads out in open court the names of the couples who are to be divorced and the basis of their divorces. That completes the first stage of your divorce. You don't need to attend court, and the court sends a copy of the decree and any agreed order for costs to you and your spouse or your solicitors.

If an argument occurs between you and your spouse over who should pay the costs of the divorce, either of you can make written representations to the court or request a short appointment with the judge. The judge usually orders the respondent to pay the costs of the petitioner if he is satisfied that the petitioner has proved the adultery, behaviour or desertion alleged.

On the rare occasions the judge identifies a major problem over the arrangements for the children or over the basis for the divorce, he may direct that further evidence be filed, or that the parties attend before the court.

Finalising Your Divorce with the Decree Absolute

You can apply to the court for your final decree of divorce, known as the *decree absolute,* not less than six weeks and one day from the date of your decree nisi. The court doesn't grant the decree absolute before then unless exceptional circumstances apply. If you wait more than 12 months to apply for the decree absolute, you have to file a statement giving the reasons for the delay. You must keep your decree absolute in a safe place because you may need it in the future (to remarry or apply for a passport, for example).

The effect of your decree absolute is that you and your spouse are no longer next of kin and you're free to remarry. If you've made a will naming each other as an executor or beneficiary, the will becomes invalid in those respects. You need to make or review your will at that stage, if you haven't already done so. See Chapter 19 for more about wills and estate planning.

Negotiating your way out of a stalemate

At any time during your divorce, you and your spouse can reach an agreement about the issues being contested. In fact, good solicitors should be actively trying to help you reach a negotiated divorce settlement. Every key issue you can resolve outside of court saves you money and time.

Alternatively, you and your spouse can attend a mediation session together to try and resolve the issues. The good news is that mediation works: In an estimated 70 per cent of all divorces that go to mediation, at least some of the issues are resolved through the out-of-court dispute resolution process. Chapter 16 has more information about mediation.

You may want to delay the application for your decree absolute until you've resolved all financial issues. See the section 'Resolving Basic Divorce Issues' earlier in this chapter for the reasons why this approach may be a sensible decision for you.

If you're the respondent and your spouse hasn't applied for the decree absolute within three months, you may apply to the court instead, giving your reasons for making the application. The judge grants the application if he is satisfied that no good reason for the delay exists.

Remember that, if you're the petitioner, you can stop the divorce at any time, even up to the date of the decree absolute. If you and your spouse reconcile, or you start having doubts about whether a divorce is really what you want, you can simply do nothing further, so that the divorce doesn't progress, or you can apply to the court to dismiss the petition. If you reconcile after the decree nisi has been pronounced, you can ask the court to rescind the decree. However, by then, if only you're having second thoughts, and your spouse still wants a divorce, he can apply to the court for the decree absolute as described in the section above.

In Scotland, no decree nisi exists. If you're granted a divorce by a judge, you're divorced from that date.

Agreeing to Disagree: What Happens After You Decide to Litigate

When your divorce is not co-operative and you're in dispute with one another, you, your spouse and your solicitors work through a very specific legal process. At its most extreme, the process culminates with a court-ordered judgement after a fully contested hearing. However, at any point during the process, you and your spouse can reach an agreement regarding all the issues in your divorce and therefore avoid a full hearing.

So that you understand some of what's to come, the following information offers a brief overview of each stage in the divorce process if any issue goes all the way to court. Chapter 18 goes into more detail about the conduct of the final hearing if you get to that point.

Emergency applications

If you're in urgent need of an order from the court because you have reason to believe that your spouse is disposing of assets in order to defeat or reduce your claims, you can apply to the court for emergency relief. You must provide evidence to support your claims in the form of a written statement. Depending on the urgency and merits of your application, the judge may either grant an immediate order to protect your assets, or insist on notice first being given to your spouse or to a third party who's going to be directly affected. You and your spouse then have to argue the application in front of the judge.

If you or your children need protection from the court because you're suffering abuse or violence from your spouse, and are at real and immediate risk of harm, you can ask the court to grant you a non-molestation or occupation order. This order may forbid your spouse to threaten, harass or use violence towards you or your children and may require your spouse to leave the home or allow you to return. Such an order usually lasts for about six months. A judge rarely orders anyone to leave his home without hearing both sides of the story first (see Chapter 2).

Formal Applications to the Court: Financial Issues

Family law protocol requires solicitors to make every effort to help you resolve the issues between you. But if you and your spouse are unable to agree on the financial arrangements during or after your divorce, either of you may issue a formal application to the court, known as an application for *ancillary relief*. Your application must state briefly what you're applying for, such as maintenance – or *periodical payments* – for yourself, lump sums for yourself or your children, a property adjustment, or pension order. This application is known as the *Form A*. Applications for child support are not now usually included on the Form A. (For more on child support, see Chapter 13.)

If you live in Scotland or Northern Ireland, check with your solicitors how financial applications are made, because the laws have subtle – but very important – differences from those in England and Wales.

On receiving your application and court fee, the court fixes a timetable and a date for your first appointment with a judge, usually three to four months ahead. With regard to the timing of applications for ancillary relief, you need to bear in mind a few points:

✔ You can't apply for ancillary relief until after the divorce petition has been issued.

✔ The court can't make any final orders for capital, property or pensions until after the decree nisi has been granted.

✔ The order can't take effect until after the decree absolute has been granted (although your solicitor may be able to find a way round this restriction for you).

✔ In Scotland, capital and property orders have to be made before the divorce decree is issued.

When the court issues the application, you and your spouse, or your solicitors, are sent a copy of the application and the timetable. You or your solicitors are responsible for promptly sending a copy of the application to the landlord or mortgage lenders of any property, and to the administrators of any pension fund from which you're claiming.

Powers of the court

Following is a list of the main financial orders that a court can make:

✔ **Maintenance pending suit:** Regular financial spousal support until the final decree of divorce.

✔ **Periodical payments:** Regular spousal support after your divorce.

✔ **Lump sum:** A fixed sum, in one or more instalments, for you, your spouse, or your children.

✔ **Periodical payments for a child:** Regular payments of child support (although these are more often dealt with through the CMEC, previously known as the CSA).

✔ **Property adjustment:** The sale, transfer or adjustment of an interest in property.

✔ **Pension provision:** Dividing between you or attaching an interest to a pension fund.

Statements to file

You and your spouse must complete a statement of means on a standard form known as the *Form E,* including the following details:

✔ Background – including your full name and address, date of birth and occupation, your children's names and dates of birth, and details of any other court proceedings between you and your spouse or about the children

✔ Assets – listing everything you own, including your property, savings, income, valuables and pensions

✔ Liabilities – listing everything you owe, including mortgages, credit card debts and outgoings

✔ Income – listing everything you earn, plus income from tax credits, state benefits, dividends, interest on savings and maintenance from a former partner or any other source

✔ Needs – for income, capital, property or pensions

✔ Contributions to the family – whether financial or otherwise

✔ Orders that you're seeking

✔ Special factors, if any

You also have to attach proof of your means including copies of valuations; mortgage, pension and bank statements; payslips and P60; business accounts; and so on. You must send one copy of everything to the court and one to your spouse or solicitor by the date specified by the court, usually about six weeks before your first court appointment.

If you're in urgent need of maintenance, you can apply to the court for an earlier *interim* appointment. You don't have to file a full Form E for this, but you do need to give the court enough information to make a decision. That decision usually lasts until your divorce has been finalised or until the final financial order has been made.

Two weeks before the first court appointment, your solicitors must file with the court and exchange with each other the following:

✔ A chronology, or timeline of events

✔ A concise statement summarising what you see as the main issues in the case

✔ A questionnaire saying what further information or documents you believe your spouse should disclose

✔ A *Form G* to say whether you want the judge to give some informal guidance on the case at the first appointment, or at a later appointment

Form E isn't in use in Northern Ireland. Instead, the court usually asks for the same information at a preliminary hearing. Any other information is usually contained in the affidavits exchanged between spouses.

First directions appointment – or FDA

About two weeks after filing the paperwork with the court, you and your spouse attend your first court appointment with your lawyers (your solicitor or a barrister your solicitor has chosen to represent you in court) also known as the first directions appointment (FDA). This appointment is a good opportunity for you to discuss all the issues and the steps needed to resolve them. In court, each lawyer has a chance to address the district judge; if you made the application, your lawyer goes first. The judge may ask questions to clarify the issues. You don't have to say anything; usually your lawyers do the talking for you.

The judge then makes *directions* about the future conduct of your case, and sets dates for compliance, either as agreed or as he thinks best. These directions are geared towards identifying and resolving the main issues as quickly and cost-effectively as possible, and may relate to any or all the following:

- Valuations of property
- Questions and requests for documents to which you must reply
- Further evidence or reports (such as a pension actuary report) that are required
- The next court appointment

The court allows about 15 minutes for each appointment unless your case is complex and your lawyers have asked for longer. At the end of the appointment, your lawyers have to give the judge a written estimate of your costs.

Financial dispute resolution appointment – or FDR

You and your spouse must comply with all the judge's directions before you return to court a second time. In addition, you must each send to the court copies of any offers of settlement that you've made. The main aim of the second appointment, known as the *financial dispute resolution appointment* or FDR, is to help the two of you settle and avoid a full hearing. The judge gives some guidance on the likely outcome based on the court papers and offers, but without hearing any oral evidence from either of you. Again, your solicitors must give the judge a written estimate of your costs.

The judge who deals with this appointment can't deal with the final hearing, if one is to be held, because he has been privy to offers made between you on a *without prejudice* basis – that is, offers made without prejudicing any claims in your Form Es.

In more straightforward cases, such as one where you and your spouse have agreed on all or most of the relevant factual information before the first appointment, you can ask the judge on a Form G to combine the first appointment with the FDR appointment. This can save you both time and money. The court doesn't allow you to postpone any of these appointments without a good reason.

Disclosure

Solicitors use the *disclosure* process to help you determine the facts of a case. Depending on what you want to discover through disclosure, the solicitors may use a variety of formal legal tools, some of which are described in this section.

The disclosure process can take a short time, especially if the facts of your divorce are clear and undisputed and all the important documents are attached to your Forms E; or it can last many months. Some form of disclosure takes place no matter whether your divorce is co-operative, difficult or fully contested.

Protocol requires that you and your solicitors co-operate over all reasonable requests for disclosure in order to minimise costs and the risk of a contested hearing. If you disregard such protocol, and your case goes to court, you may be penalised on the question of costs.

Disclosure can be dealt with directly between you, through your mediator or through your solicitor. What follows is a description of the process as usually dealt with through solicitors.

Voluntarily providing your spouse's solicitor with the information he requests is less painful than going through the formal disclosure process. Plus, this way you save time and money. Disclosure can be formal or voluntary depending on whether:

- ✔ Your solicitor has to force your spouse's solicitor to provide certain information relating to your issue through a court order (or if your spouse's solicitor has to do the same).

- ✔ The two solicitors agree in writing to willingly exchange all the information you need to work out the terms of your settlement.

- ✔ Your solicitors need formally to acquire additional information relating to your case from other sources.

- ✔ Your divorce is amicable (in which case less need exists for formal disclosure) or contentious.

Voluntary disclosure

Voluntary disclosure occurs when your solicitor asks your spouse's solicitor (or vice versa) for financial, legal, medical or other information and the information is provided voluntarily without the need for a court order. The particular types of information your solicitor asks for depend on the issues involved in your divorce.

Ideally, most of the disclosure in your divorce is voluntary, because formal disclosure can be time-consuming and expensive, depending on just how much formal disclosure either solicitor wants. Your solicitor may have to complete extra paperwork, formulate questions to ask your spouse or others, and then review and analyse all this information.

Formal disclosure

Witness summonses, statements, questionnaires, and notices for the production of documents are all formal disclosure tools. The following list tells you what each of these terms means:

- ✔ **Witness summons:** A legal document requiring someone to attend a court hearing or trial. Anyone who ignores a summons faces legal penalties.

- ✔ **Statement:** A statement by a witness, made out of court and filed with the court. Witnesses are under oath or have to confirm in their statements that they believe that everything they're saying is true, and that they're aware that the statement is going to be used in the proceedings.

- ✔ **Questionnaires and notices to produce documents and other information:** Written questions for the respondent prepared by the applicant's solicitor or vice versa, seeking information or documentation on a relevant issue. Questionnaires deal specifically with issues that are being disputed in the case, and the costs involved in producing the information must be proportionate to the benefits being sought.

  Depending on the issues that have to be resolved before your application can be determined, any number of individuals may be involved in the disclosure process. For example, the information provided by accountants, valuers, actuaries, employers, business associates, bankers and so on may be used to help resolve questions regarding the value of your marital property, spousal support, business or pension.

After orders are made for the various forms of disclosure, you may not ask your spouse for any further disclosure, and vice versa, without the prior permission of the judge. The Form E and ancillary relief procedure described in the previous sections are designed to make the disclosure process as efficient and cost-effective as possible.

Giving evidence

Although you may not want to give evidence, you're almost certainly going to have to do so if you want any chance of persuading the judge to make the order that you want. Here are some tips on how to manage the situation:

✔ Tell the truth, even if it hurts.

✔ Ask for any question that you don't understand to be repeated.

✔ Give your answer and nothing more – no extra facts and no elaboration. Providing more information than you're asked for may hurt your case.

✔ Be polite and don't argue with your spouse's lawyer.

✔ Direct your responses towards the judge. The judge records your evidence, and he or she decides the issues.

Your lawyer listens when you give your evidence. If your lawyer objects to a question, and the judge accepts the objection, don't answer it. A tactical and legitimate reason for your remaining silent probably exists.

Such formal disclosure is most common in divorces involving spouses who are unwilling to co-operate with one another. However, even if your divorce is amicable, you may be required to do a limited amount of formal disclosure in order to:

✔ Narrow the scope of your negotiations by identifying exactly where you and your spouse disagree, and the particulars of your disagreements. The more that you know you agree on, the less you have to negotiate or litigate later, and the less your divorce costs.

✔ Assess the strengths and weaknesses of your position versus your spouse's.

✔ Assess how well your spouse is likely to perform on the stand if your case goes to a full hearing and your spouse is called to give evidence.

✔ Get your spouse to admit to certain activities or to establish certain facts. If your case goes to a full hearing and your spouse gives evidence that differs from what he said during the disclosure process, your solicitor can use the discrepancy to undermine your spouse's credibility.

The court doesn't allow you to go on a fishing exercise just for the sake of it. You and your spouse have to justify the information that you're seeking and demonstrate that it's essential for the judge to determine the issues in your case.

Full hearings

If you and your spouse can't agree a final settlement, you have to go to court with your lawyers (your solicitor or a barrister your solicitor has chosen to represent you in court) and any witnesses to enable a judge to make a final decision on the issues between you. (Only about 10 per cent of all financial divorce cases get to this stage.) Your lawyers outline the facts and the arguments, and you must give evidence on oath. The lawyer representing the applicant has the first and the last say. All the relevant applications, orders, statements, reports, and documents are usually agreed upon and filed with the court in advance, for the use of all concerned at the hearing.

Judge's decision – the order or judgement

After listening to your lawyers' opening and closing statements; hearing evidence from you and your spouse and from any witnesses involved in your case; and reviewing any reports, documents and other written information entered as evidence, the judge makes an order or *gives judgement* on the issues in your case.

The judge may announce the decision immediately at the end of the hearing, or, more rarely, he may take time to consider all the evidence and announce the decision at a later date.

The judge also has to decide who's to be responsible for the costs of the case. New rules introduced in 2006 mean that couples have to foot their own legal bills rather than hoping to be able to push them all onto the other side.

Under the new rules, the judge is aware of offers made in correspondence and costs are part of the main court hearing, not as previously a separate issue to be decided when the judge had ruled on the financial issues between the parties. The general rule is that no order for costs applies: both parties pay their own costs out of their share of the assets. The judge can still take into account bad conduct if he so desires. Regardless of offers made during the course of proceedings, the court can penalise a party who refused to negotiate in the early stages, or at all, or who is difficult, is obstructive or pursues issues with little or no merit or supporting evidence.

If you and your lawyers strongly disagree with the order or judgement made, you can appeal the decision. You have a limited amount of time to file your appeal, usually 14 days for financial decisions and seven days for decisions about your children. Remember that appeals are risky, and involve yet more time, money and stress for both of you. They also almost certainly reduce the financial resources that you're seeking to share between you.

Formal Applications to the Court: Issues Regarding Your Children

Private disputes about children follow a different procedure from those about money and property. If you and your spouse can't agree on the arrangements for your children, such as where they're going to live, how much they're going to see of the other parent, or where they'll go to school (Chapter 10 gives you advice on how to make these decisions), one of you files a formal application with the court known as a C1 (or C2 if you've already started divorce proceedings). The forms give basic details for yourself, your spouse and your children, and the reasons why you're making the application.

The court sends a copy of the application to your spouse, or to his solicitor, and your spouse has 14 days to acknowledge it, saying whether he wants to oppose the application or make any other application.

The court arranges an initial appointment at which the judge tries to clarify the issues between you, see if any agreement can be reached, and, if not, make any necessary directions for the conduct of the case.

Role of the Cafcass officer or Family Court Adviser

Cafcass stands for *Children and Family Court Advisory Support Service*. In Wales the organisation is called *Cafcass Cymru.* No equivalent of Cafcass exists in Scotland and the procedures differ quite a bit (flip to Chapter 10 for more details). A professional social worker who works as a Cafcass officer (called sometimes a Family Court Adviser (FCA) or in Wales a Family Proceedings Officer (FPO)) and specialises in children matters, is usually available at the first court appointment to see you and your spouse in a private 'conciliation' meeting, to try to help sort out any disagreements. The Cafcass officer (FCA or FPO) reports back to the judge on what you've agreed. About 80 per cent of children cases are now settled in this way at court without a full hearing. Conciliation is more pressurised than out-of-court mediation, which is why trying mediation first is better.

If you and your spouse can't agree on a suitable arrangement, the judge usually directs each of you to file with the court and exchange with each other a written statement by a certain date, usually 14 to 28 days hence. This statement sets out in more detail what you're asking the judge to decide and why.

The judge may order a Cafcass officer to investigate and file a report on the issues in dispute. This process can take at least three months – usually a great deal longer. Social workers, psychiatrists, your friends or your spouse's friends, the police, grandparents and others may be included in the disclosure process in children cases. (Refer to the section 'Disclosure' earlier in this chapter.)

Final hearing in children matters

The final hearing in children matters follows a similar pattern to that for financial matters, with your lawyers (your solicitor or a barrister your solicitor has chosen to represent you in court) presenting the facts and arguments to the judge, and evidence being given on oath by you, your spouse, and any witnesses. If a Cafcass officer has filed a report, he or she may be called to answer questions that your or your spouse's lawyer may have. At the end of all that, the judge makes a decision.

An order for costs is rarely made against either party in children matters. In most cases, both parties take responsibility for their own costs.

Cases involving children are always heard in private and all statements and reports are confidential to you and your legal representatives. If either of you disclose the contents of such statements or reports to anyone else, apart from certain people such as your MP, a CAB adviser or a mediator, you may be in contempt of court and liable to be committed to prison. The courts take very seriously the need to protect children from any outside interference with their well-being, and they expect you to do so, too. However, note that this privacy doesn't apply in Scotland, where the procedures are in any event very different, although the court may grant orders preventing publication in the media.

Chapter 6

Considering Separation: A Healthy Breather or a Prelude to Divorce?

In This Chapter
▶ Understanding what being separated means
▶ Exploring the pros and cons of separation
▶ Reviewing your separation options
▶ Making reconciliation work

Separation is more than just a matter of living apart from your spouse. It is an important step with legal, financial and emotional ramifications that requires plenty of advance planning. Separation can be the beginning of the end to your marriage, or the start of a better-than-ever union. Either way, don't take the decision to separate casually.

Before separating, you need to understand the pros and cons of such a change in your living arrangements. You and your spouse or civil partner must also be clear about the direction in which you anticipate your separation is going to take you – towards reconciliation or to a divorce court. Otherwise, you may be setting yourself up for disappointment and more heartache.

You're Married, but Only Sort Of

Separation is the equivalent of marital limbo. You don't live with your spouse and you may even feel single again – but you're *still married*. All the formal 'benefits' of being married, such as spousal inheritance, pension rights and death benefits remain intact during a separation. However, your relationship has changed. When you live apart, you see one another less frequently and are less accountable to one another for your comings and goings, and what you do and don't do at home. After separating, you and your spouse may try 'dating' each other in an effort to put the spark back in your marriage, or you may avoid any contact unless absolutely necessary.

Dating your spouse, and especially having sex with your spouse, while separated can jeopardise your grounds for divorce. The courts understandably question the credibility of a divorce based on allegations of adultery or behaviour when you're still dating your spouse. Consult your solicitor before going on that hot date. However, if you're informally separated with the intention of reconciling, no real danger lies in dating your spouse.

Considering why you need to separate

Couples separate for many reasons. Sometimes these reasons are well thought through and logical; other times they are based on fear or misguided hope. Sometimes, you and your spouse have no other option. Among the most common reasons for separating are the following:

- ✔ You want to find out what living on your own feels like.

- ✔ You need time to assess your commitment to your marriage away from the day-to-day stress and responsibilities of the relationship.

- ✔ You want to send your spouse a strong message that things have to change if you're going to stay married. (For example, your spouse has a substance abuse problem and has been unwilling to deal with it.)

- ✔ Your spouse wants a divorce but you don't. By agreeing to separate you hope to delay or even prevent the end of your marriage.

- ✔ You've agreed to divorce but must separate for two years (see Chapter 5).

- ✔ You anticipate an amicable divorce but living with your spouse until your divorce is official is emotionally impossible.

- ✔ You and your spouse are estranged and can no longer continue living under the same roof.

- ✔ Your spouse has become physically violent and you're afraid for your or your children's safety.

- ✔ You can't afford to get divorced yet.

- ✔ You have religious objections to divorce.

Knowing the drawbacks of separating

Although separating certainly has its pluses, living apart from your spouse can have its drawbacks, too. So before you agree to separate, consult a family law solicitor experienced at handling divorces and separations (see Chapter 15 for advice on how to find a solicitor). In addition, try to determine if any of the following situations apply to you:

✔ Your individual living expenses are going to increase after you and your spouse separate.

✔ Your new place – if you're moving out – may not be nearly as plush as your former home.

✔ Your children may have a hard time understanding that 'daddy and mummy are spending some time apart'.

✔ You may not have enough money to live on if you don't have your own source of income.

✔ You may end up paying for certain expenses twice if you separate legally and then later get divorced.

✔ You may give your spouse grounds for a divorce based on your behaviour or desertion if you separate against your spouse's wishes.

✔ You may still be treated as a married couple with regard to pensions, life insurance and contractual obligations. A carefully worded separation agreement written by a family law solicitor can help address these issues.

If your spouse agrees to pay certain debts while you're separated and fails to do so, your creditors may have a legal right to come after both of you for payment. Furthermore, if your spouse gets into debt while you're separated you can be held responsible for the debt even if you have a written agreement to the contrary. If you end up paying that debt, you may be able to claim reimbursement from your spouse later.

Any assets that you acquire following your separation may still be taken into account as assets on your divorce – that is to say, your spouse can still make a claim on them even though she may not have contributed in any way. Consult a family law solicitor first in order to gain a clear understanding of the pros and cons of separating given the particulars of your situation.

Talking things over before you separate

Both of you together must discuss the reasons for your separation (assuming that you can have a calm and productive conversation) and make it clear why you're separating – as a prelude to a divorce or as a last-ditch effort to save your marriage. Try not to harbour any illusions about the final outcome of your separation. That way, you can focus on achieving your goals for the separation. If you and your spouse are uncertain whether separating is your best move, a relationship counsellor (see Chapter 2 for how to find a relationship counsellor) may be able to help you decide what is best for you both, and a family law solicitor can help with the legal issues.

Initiating a Separation

Whether you're drawing up a formal separation deed (see the section 'Protecting Yourself When You Separate Informally' later in this chapter), or just separating informally, always try to agree on the terms of your separation before you move out. Make a note of the date that you or your spouse moves out of the home. Even if you decide to live separately under the same roof, you need to note the date that you start the new arrangements. This date may be important later, particularly if your separation is going to form the basis of your divorce. Check this out further in Chapter 5.

Often, the spouse who wants the separation is the one to move out of the couple's home. However, if your spouse is the primary carer of your young children, you must consider being the one to move so that the lives of your children are disrupted as little as possible.

Protecting Yourself When You Separate Informally

You can separate on an informal basis, or you may be able to agree the terms of separation in writing between you through a formal *separation deed*. A separation deed is usually best in that it's contractually binding, but if the following statements apply to you, an informal separation may be all you need:

- ✔ You and your spouse both earn a good living and can comfortably support yourselves.

- ✔ You have no dependent children from your marriage.

- ✔ You don't share joint bank accounts or jointly owe a great deal of money.

- ✔ You're confident that your separation is going to be relatively brief and amicable.

If you opt for an informal separation, you must nevertheless set ground rules for your time apart and make them part of a written agreement that you both sign and date. (Ensure that you both keep a copy of your final signed agreement.) An informal separation agreement can help protect you from the potential repercussions of a civilised separation that turns sour.

Identify any issues that may disrupt the peacefulness of your time apart and determine ahead of time the best way to deal with them. Working out solutions to possible disruptive conflicts in advance minimises the potential for disagreements and misunderstandings during your separation.

Here are a few practical steps that you may want to take when one of you leaves the home, to save you both some time, cost and inconvenience later:

- ✔ **Get your gas, electricity and phone meters read so that you can apportion the bills at a later date if necessary.** If you think that the separation may go on for a while, have the bills put into the name of the spouse who's remaining in the home.

- ✔ **Let your council tax authority know the date on which you or your spouse leave.** The remaining spouse may then be able to claim a 25 per cent reduction in the council tax bill as a sole adult occupier, and the one who's leaving doesn't retain liability.

- ✔ **Take your personal valuable documents with you.** Don't forget your medical card and passport.

- ✔ **Take details or copies of financial documents that may become important if any claims arise between you.** For example, you need your mortgage account number and copies of joint policies (see Chapter 7 for a list of important documents you may need during your divorce process).

- ✔ **Decide how you're going to manage any joint bank accounts between you.** Consider asking the bank to freeze the account if the risk of misuse is possible, so that you can only draw on it with joint signatures. Make sure that any important direct debits and standing orders are covered first.

- ✔ **Make an agreed inventory of the main contents of your home.** You can't remember everything and you may have to agree how to divide up your possessions at some point. Also, a record is handy in case anything goes missing.

- ✔ **Notify HM Revenue and Customs (www.hmrc.gov.uk) if you aren't planning on getting back together.** They're likely to treat you as a single person for income tax purposes.

- ✔ **Talk to your solicitor to find out if you need to take any other steps to protect yourself.** Everyone's circumstances are different.

If your spouse mismanages your finances while you're separated, your credit rating (and not just your spouse's) may be damaged. You must be sure that your separation agreement states that your spouse will *not* include your name on any new financial or bank accounts and will *not* sign your name on any documents – especially financial documents – during your separation.

Formalising Your Separation Agreement

If you're separating permanently as an alternative to divorce, you absolutely must have a written statement, such as a formal separation agreement, which spells out the terms of your separation. Make sure that all the terms of your separation are in black and white and enforceable by law – you need to protect yourself from miscommunication or future disagreement on what the terms of the agreement are. Your solicitor can draw up the agreement for you, and you don't need to go to court.

Having a legal separation deed or agreement is always a good idea, even when your separation is amicable and you both hope to reconcile: If either of you fails to live up to the terms of the agreement you can ask the court to help enforce it. Any of the following situations can be made easier when the terms of your separation are stated in a formal separation agreement:

✔ You and your spouse are so estranged from one another that communication and co-operation are impossible.

✔ You don't trust your spouse to live up to her verbal promises.

✔ You want financial help from your spouse while you're living apart.

✔ You have dependent children.

The longer you live apart, the greater the chance that your relationship with your spouse may deteriorate. Your spouse may become involved in a new romantic relationship and abandon your reconciliation plans. Or you may find it harder to co-operate with one another as time goes on. At times like these, having a written separation agreement can help prevent the total breakdown of your relationship.

You may have to ask a judge to decide the terms of your separation if you and your spouse can't come to an agreement. If any major financial matters remain that you can't agree on, such as what happens with the house, you may have to resort to divorce or judicial separation proceedings (see 'Not Quite Divorce: Judicial Separation' later in this chapter). A legal separation agreement can serve some very practical purposes especially in regard to your finances:

✔ A well-written separation agreement can help limit your liability for any debts that your spouse may rack up during your separation.

✔ A separation agreement can provide for the continuance of certain spousal benefits including health insurance and continued access to credit on a shared account.

A judge is more likely to enforce your agreement if you can each show that you've had independent legal advice on the terms of your agreement, and that you've fully and frankly disclosed your financial positions to each other.

Trying the art of compromise

You may find that give and take works better than strong-arm tactics when working out the terms of your separation. In other words, don't expect to get everything you ask for. Refusing to compromise is likely to backfire – you may end up in court where the judge has the final word and you have no control. That said, you need to be aware of the sort of provisions that are worth including in your separation agreement and the sort that you need to avoid if possible.

Men – and women – behaving badly

If rules of proper behaviour existed for separated spouses they'd include the following do's and don'ts. Ignoring these ground rules can turn an amicable split into a hostile one, derail any plans for reconciliation, and even weaken your position when the time comes to negotiate your divorce. To avoid such problems, take heed of these separation don'ts:

✔ **Don't get involved in a serious relationship** – especially if the result is that you spend less time with your young children. And don't bring a romantic interest home for the night when the children are staying with you. If your spouse finds out about your love affair, it's likely to increase any hostility she may already be feeling towards you.

✔ **Don't bad-mouth your spouse, ever!** – you're likely to upset your children if they hear you. Plus, nothing short of spousal abuse annoys a judge more quickly than discovering that you've been saying disparaging things to your children about your spouse.

✔ **Don't do things that you know are going to be hurtful to your spouse** – ultimately, the person you hurt most may be yourself!

✔ **Don't engage in sexual relations with your spouse without first understanding the potential ramifications of doing so** – after you've filed the petition for divorce, you may weaken your grounds for divorce if you're sleeping together. Furthermore, you may mislead your spouse into thinking you want to reconcile.

And, while you're at it, keep in mind these separation etiquette musts:

✔ **Keep the lines of communication open between you and your spouse.** Even if you can't agree about anything, you're more likely to sort things out quickly if you know where you both stand on the big issues.

✔ **Allow your spouse to spend plenty of time with your children if they live with you (unless your spouse has been abusive).** If you have a separation deed, the chances are that it states when and where your spouse can see the children.

✔ **Meet all your obligations to your spouse and children without fail.** They're depending on you, and may not trust you in the future if you don't.

Deciding what to put in a separation agreement

A legal separation agreement can address most, if not all, of the same issues that a divorce agreement covers, including child support, child residence and contact, spousal support and division of marital property and debts. If you separate and then decide to divorce, all or some of what you include in your separation agreement can be converted into your divorce agreement, subject to the final discretion of the judge.

As long as you're still married, you should be able to claim any rights as a spouse that you may have to your spouse's pension, and your spouse can also nominate you for the death in service benefits.

Safeguarding your liquid assets

A *liquid asset* is cash or something that can be quickly converted to cash. That includes the cash advance on your credit card, a bank account overdraft, as well as investments that allow you to write cheques against them. Be sure that your agreement gives you ready access to the liquid assets that you and your spouse own. You may need them during your separation to help pay bills, put food on the table or cover unexpected expenses – especially if your income is low and you're receiving little or no spousal support.

Liquid assets can work both for you and against you. If you can draw on these assets, your spouse probably can too, and you may end up being liable for your spouse's overdraft.

Being careful about what you sign

Question anything in a separation agreement that you don't understand. Don't agree to any provision in your agreement because 'it's good enough for now' or because you 'can live with the arrangement for a while'. Separation agreements often become the basis for divorce agreements. When something is in a separation agreement, voiding or modifying that provision can be difficult, if not impossible. Unless the problems caused by your separation agreement are obvious and significant, you and your spouse must abide by the agreement.

Think about whether you need to give yourself some room to manoeuvre by clearly indicating in writing whether the separation agreement binds you to the same terms in your final divorce agreement.

Not Quite Divorce: Judicial Separation

If you live in England or Wales, you can ask the court for a decree of judicial separation instead of having a formal separation deed or applying for a divorce. A decree of judicial separation releases you and your spouse from living together, but doesn't allow you to remarry.

You may want to apply for a decree of judicial separation if you have religious objections to divorce or want the financial remedies without freeing your spouse to remarry. However, decrees of judicial separation are increasingly rare these days. Chapter 5 tells you about the financial remedies that are available to you on divorce and judicial separation.

The procedure for judicial separation is exactly the same as with a divorce, with three exceptions:

- ✔ **You don't have to prove that the marriage has irretrievably broken down.** If you don't want to say that it has, judicial separation is for you.

- ✔ **Only one decree applies, not two.** The decree of judicial separation is the only decree, instead of the decree nisi and decree absolute of divorce.

- ✔ **The court has slightly different powers to make financial orders than it does for divorce.** The powers include orders for maintenance, capital and property. In most cases you preserve your claims against your spouse's pension, unlike divorce, but you're treated as if you're divorced for inheritance purposes.

If you decide to go for a divorce at a later date, you can use the basis of your judicial separation petition as the basis of your divorce petition – but, be warned, you end up *paying twice* for almost the same work.

If You Kiss and Make up

You may possibly breathe a huge sigh of relief after you've separated but, conversely, you may begin to miss certain aspects of married life. When you're now living in a smaller place surrounded by rented furniture and just a few items from your home, you may long for the old familiar comforts. You may miss your children if they're not living with you, or want your spouse's help when you're overwhelmed with all the responsibility of caring for them if they are with you. Or you may realise that you truly love your spouse and are willing to do what's necessary to repair your marriage. For any or all these reasons, you and your spouse may decide that living together is better than living apart. And, like many couples who reach that conclusion, you can reconcile and end your separation.

Stuart and Sarah separated when Stuart had an affair and Sarah began an affair in retaliation. However, they found themselves meeting every day to sort out things about their children. They eventually realised, in discussion with a mediator and when they got over their hurt pride, that they were contriving to be together because that was exactly what they both wanted.

Reconciling for the right reasons

Make sure that you're reconciling because you both really want to – not because you feel guilty, are scared to be alone, or are tired of doing your own laundry. Initially after you've reconciled you may feel a sense of exhilaration and renewed hope for your future as a couple. But sooner or later the old problems in your relationship are likely to resurface and you may respond to them in the very ways that contributed to your marital troubles in the first place. So take a positive step to address the problems before they get out of hand. Have a look at Chapter 24 for tips on making your relationship work.

Fortifying your relationship with counselling

Despite your happiness at being together again, both of you may be harbouring anger, hurt, doubt and distrust toward one another as a result of your separation. Although these feelings are quite natural under the circumstances, they can get in the way of rebuilding your marriage. Therefore, if you're really serious about staying together and repairing your marriage, see a therapist or relationship counsellor if you aren't already doing so. (See Chapter 2 for help with finding a relationship counsellor.)

You're more apt to make your marriage work the second time around if you begin therapy or counselling while still in the honeymoon phase of your reconciliation. Working things out is a lot easier when you're more motivated to make your marriage a success.

Part II
Divorce Preliminaries

'I haven't seen my husband since the divorce,
but there's always something around that
reminds me of him.'

In this part . . .

Your marriage is definitely over and the time is right to take action. Chapter 7 gives you advice on breaking the news to your spouse, help in determining what you want out of your divorce, and practical ways of estimating and preparing for what divorce is going to cost you (both personally and financially). Chapter 8 tells you how to help your children cope with the changes that your divorce brings to their lives. And, finally, to ease some of the stress and pain, Chapter 9 provides suggestions on how to deal with your emotions.

Chapter 7

Setting Your Divorce in Motion

. . . .

In This Chapter

▶ Telling your spouse that you want to call it quits

▶ Working out your financial situation

▶ Determining what you want from your divorce

▶ Estimating the cost of your divorce

▶ Protecting your assets in case your divorce gets hostile

. . . .

*W*hen you definitely know that you're heading for a split, you can't begin preparing for the divorce process too soon. You need at least a general idea of what's to come in order to negotiate a fair divorce agreement intelligently. If you head into your divorce unprepared, you're likely to feel overwhelmed and panicky. Taking a proactive stance helps alleviate some of the natural anxiety you feel about your divorce.

Conducting your divorce amicably benefits everyone. Therefore we offer practical advice for talking about divorce with your spouse to give yourselves the best chance of a fair divorce process. We also provide tips for getting your money matters in order and ensuring that you have the info you need to get a fair and adequate divorce settlement. (Chapter 3 has more information on general financial preparedness.) If you can co-operate in collecting financial information and making joint financial decisions, including covering the cost of your divorce, you can maximise your resources to meet your needs in the future. Although not panicking about money can be difficult, staying calm and working it out with cool heads pays off.

Breaking the News to Your Spouse

You and your spouse may have tried just about everything to resolve your problems. Maybe you've decided to call it quits because things are simply not going to get better. Or perhaps only one of you is ready to end the marriage. If you're the one who wants to end your marriage, the way you break the news to your spouse can have a big influence on whether your divorce is going to be amicable or contentious. It can also help set the tone for your post-divorce relationship, an important consideration if you have dependent children.

Maintaining your composure

Telling your spouse that you want a divorce isn't easy, particularly if the news comes as a shock or if your spouse has been hoping that somehow, some way, you can work out your marital problems and stay together. The following suggestions may help you to ease into that conversation and help your spouse accept the news as calmly as possible:

- **Tell your spouse, quietly and slowly, your reasons for wanting to end your marriage.** Review what you consider to be the problems in your marriage, what you may have done to try to fix them, and why you feel that your efforts haven't worked. Even if you've covered this same ground many, many times before, go over it again.

- **Avoid blaming your spouse for the end of your marriage (as difficult as that may be).** Avoid accusatory or derogatory language and try to steer clear of starting an argument.

- **Speak in terms of how *you* feel as much as possible.** Arguing with someone about his feelings is difficult. If your spouse does try to argue with you, reiterate your feelings and intentions, over and over again if necessary.

If a calm conversation is impossible because your spouse is simply too upset about the idea of divorce, tell him that you would like to talk again later. Your next conversation may well be a little easier to take. You may need to have a few conversations concerning your intention to divorce before your spouse finally accepts the news.

Making sure that your spouse hears the news from you first

Your spouse must find out about your divorce plans from you first and not through the rumour mill (from mutual friends, relatives or even your children). Second-hand news is a cruel way for your spouse to find out that his marriage is ending and a sure way to make for a bitter divorce.

If you've already filed a petition for divorce, tell your spouse that you've done so before he receives the divorce papers. If you can't tell your spouse in person or with a phone call, write a letter (compose it yourself and not through your solicitor). A solicitor's letter is too impersonal and your spouse may be angry that you didn't bother to write it yourself. If your spouse holds a grudge, it can make your divorce negotiations even more difficult.

Waiting until your spouse is ready to begin negotiations

Don't expect to begin negotiating your divorce agreement as soon as you tell your spouse the news. It may take weeks or even months before negotiations can begin. Be patient and move slowly. Remember, you've probably been thinking seriously for some time about divorce and may have even begun preparing for that change. Therefore, you're probably much more prepared to end your marriage than your spouse is.

Your spouse's initial reaction is more likely to be anger, shock and disbelief rather than the desire to get cracking on the divorce proceedings. Give your spouse a chance to let the news sink in and time to do some preparation before you set your divorce in motion.

If you move too fast, feelings of guilt or remorse, or anger or abandonment, may result in bad decisions that you both regret later. You may concede too much to your spouse or be too willing to compromise. Your spouse may make unreasonable demands out of anger and spite. Feeling pressure from you, your spouse may panic, engage a solicitor straight away, and turn your divorce into a hostile battle when that wasn't necessary.

However, waiting for the right time may not be possible or practical. You may not be able to hold off until your spouse is ready to co-operate. Your spouse may never be ready, or you as a couple may be so estranged that being civil and working co-operatively is impossible.

If and when you're both ready, have a general discussion about the issues in your divorce – particularly whether you want to negotiate yourselves, use mediation or use solicitors to negotiate for you – and try to develop a timetable for beginning the process. Unless you both feel in control of your emotions and ready to talk, don't push him to iron out the details of your divorce straight away. For example, if you can wait for your divorce until after two years of separation (see Chapter 4), the process can more easily be co-operative because neither of you need blame the other.

Jane was so shocked and hurt by her husband's attempts to end their marriage that they clung to each other for several days, allowing the reality to dawn. Their reaction gave them time to get onto a more even keel, and led to their co-operating over telling their children and working out the practical and financial consequences for the family.

Keeping cool if your spouse initiates the divorce

Even if the writing has been on the wall for months or even years, finding out that your spouse wants a divorce can send you into an emotional tailspin of shock and disbelief. As time goes on, you may vacillate between feelings of anger and sadness, or anger and depression.

The sooner you can face facts and move forward, the better off you're both going to be. Although feeling sorry for yourself is an understandable response to finding out that your marriage is ending, especially if you didn't want it to end, thinking of yourself as a victim doesn't help you face up to your situation. Allowing yourself to become obsessed about 'the unfairness of it all', how you've 'been wronged' and 'what could have been' prevents you from working out a reasonable divorce agreement. Feeling sorry for yourself for too long may even drive away your friends and family members at the time when you may need them the most. If keeping cool seems impossible, find a good counsellor (see Chapters 2 and 9 for tips on locating one).

As you work through your emotions and begin dealing with the practical realities of your divorce, avoid angry recriminations and don't insult your spouse. And don't force yourself to spend time together or to remain apart; do what makes you feel most comfortable.

Gathering Your Financial Information

From the law's perspective, your divorce, in practical terms, is about arrangements for your children and an equitable sorting out of your finances. Ideally, these issues should be resolved before your divorce is finalised.

To finalise a divorce in Scotland, all the arrangements must be made ahead of time! All matters of capital and spousal maintenance must be dealt with by the time the divorce is granted.

Complete and accurate financial information is essential to obtaining an equitable divorce settlement. You need this information whether your divorce is amicable or rancorous, and whether you negotiate a settlement with your spouse or place your family's future in the hands of a judge.

Without adequate financial information you may not get your fair share of assets or a reasonable amount of spousal or child support. If your spouse holds all the financial cards, deciding when to raise the stakes, when to hold steady, and when to close is a guessing game. If you guess wrongly, you may end up with less than you deserve.

Listing what you own

One of the first things to do in preparation for your divorce is develop a comprehensive picture of your financial situation. Determine exactly what you and your spouse own, and what your assets are worth. To create a full portrait of your finances, make a list of all your household assets and note a current market value for each. *Current market value* is the amount you can get if you sell an asset at the present time.

You may have already prepared a list of your assets, but that list may need updating when your divorce becomes a reality. You or your spouse may have sold assets or purchased new ones, the value of your assets may have changed, and you may have paid off debts or acquired new ones.

If you have a family accountant, financial adviser or stockbroker, he can help you pull together the information and documentation you need for a full list of your assets. Have a look at the Asset Worksheet in Table 7-1 to help make sure that you aren't forgetting anything.

Table 7-1	Asset Worksheet
Family home	
Joint or sole ownership?	
Current value	
Type of mortgage(s) (for example, repayment or interest only)	
Less mortgage(s)	
Gross equity	
Other properties	
Joint or sole ownership	
Current value	
Type of mortgage	
Less mortgage	
Gross equity	
Any savings scheme linked to your mortgage	
Type of scheme (for example, endowment policy, pension collective investments such as unit trusts, open ended investment companies (OEICs), investment trusts, stocks and shares, ISAs)	
Joint or sole	

(continued)

Table 7-1 *(continued)*

Any savings scheme linked to your mortgage
Estimated maturity value and date
Current cash or surrender value
Household furniture and furnishings worth over £500 each
Type
Value if sold
Life or other insurance policies
Company where policy is held
Type of policy
Estimated maturity or death value
Surrender value (if any)
Stocks and shares
Name of holding
Joint or sole
Number of shares
Total value
Bank, building society, savings accounts, cash ISAs
Bank or company
a) Joint or sole
Current balance or value
Bank or company
b) Joint or sole
Current balance or value
Bank or company
c) Joint or sole
Current balance or value
Bank or company
d) Joint or sole
Current balance or value

National savings certificates and bonds including premium bonds	
Type of bond	
Joint or sole	
Current value	
Vehicles (cars, caravans, boats, and so on, worth more than £500 each)	
Joint or sole	
Value if sold	
Trusts and foreseeable inheritances	
Joint or sole	
Current value	
Valuables	
Joint or sole	
Value if sold	
Business interests	
Nature of interest/business	
Estimated value	
Money owed to your business	
Debtor	
Amount owed	

If your divorce is amicable and you and your spouse are committed to a fair settlement, you can create your list of assets together by assembling documents to prove that you own certain items and what they're worth. You're going to need the following documents throughout your divorce, because solicitors, mediators and the judge all need to see them:

✔ **Documents for your home**

- Two or three valuations for your house

- Title deeds or copy of land registry entry (see Chapter 3 for how to find out if you have these or how to apply for them if you don't)

- Mortgage deeds and recent mortgage statements

✔ **Documents for endowment policies or other insurance policies**

- Schedules

- Current valuations

- Up-to-date surrender or sale valuations

- ✔ **Documents for pensions policies**
    - • Policy booklet and schedule
    - • Statements, including cash equivalent transfer values (CETV, see Chapter 11)
- ✔ **Other documents you may need**
    - • Share certificates and recent share price listings
    - • Certificates relating to any collective investment funds
    - • Bank and building society statements and passbooks with current balances
    - • All vehicle log books and valuations
    - • Documents relating to any other investments, valuables or assets, and their valuations
    - • Bank deposit box details

Working together saves time and helps ensure that you don't overlook anything. In this case, two heads definitely *are* better than one. To make certain that your list is comprehensive, look through your home safe and bank safe deposit box for titles to property, deeds, securities, or other documentation relating to your ownership of valuables and property.

Listing what you owe

Your family's financial portrait is only half-finished until you list and value your household debts, which may include:

- ✔ Credit card debt
- ✔ Bank overdrafts and loans
- ✔ Hire purchase and other finance agreements
- ✔ Mortgage or secured loan commitments
- ✔ Tax arrears/HM Revenue debt
- ✔ Timeshare charge arrears
- ✔ Store card debts
- ✔ Catalogue debts
- ✔ Other personal loans, including student loans and business loans for which you or your spouse are personally liable

Without a list of your debts, you may forget about smaller debts, such as your store card, or anything that's being paid off slowly by direct debit from your bank account. When you've put together your complete financial picture, you're able to divide up your debts as well as your assets, making sure that neither of you is left with the lion's share of one or the other.

Gathering miscellaneous financial documents together

To collect together your assets and debts, you need to refer to a variety of other financial and legal documents in addition to bank and savings account statements. Those documents include:

- Copies of your tax returns for the past three years.

- Copies of all life insurance policies in which either of you is listed as a primary or contingency beneficiary or owner.

- Documentation about investments such as stocks, shares, ISAs, bonds and collective investments.

- Pension booklets, rules and statements.

- Copies of any financial statements you prepared separately or together when applying for a loan.

- A copy of your will and your spouse's will.

- Profit-and-loss statements and balance sheets for any business in which you, your spouse or both of you have an interest and copies of related partnership agreements or articles of incorporation.

- Copies of any pre-marital or post-marital agreements you've signed.

After you locate all the documents you need, keep them together in a safe place. If you use a mediator or a solicitor to help negotiate your divorce, he needs to see all this information and documentation. The more information you and your spouse willingly share with each other, your mediator and your solicitors, the less information your solicitor needs to secure through formal disclosure, and the more money you save. (We talk about disclosure in Chapter 5.) Make sure that you both have copies of all the documents.

In Scotland you must also identify when and with what funds (inherited, gifted or earned during the marriage) any assets were acquired. The solicitor is mainly interested in the assets and debts that existed on the day you and your spouse separated (the *relevant* date), not what you have when you go to see him. See Chapter 11 for more about the relevant date.

Creating income and expenditure worksheets

Assuming that you and your spouse negotiate child support, spousal support or both, on your own or with a mediator or solicitor, you need to know the actual take-home pay for both of you, and your investments, pensions, inheritance, child support from any previous marriages, bonuses, state benefits, tax credits and other sources of income. And you must know how you both spend that income. To determine how much money is coming into and going out of your household, have a look at Chapter 3, which gives you instructions and samples to follow.

If your spouse refuses to co-operate with you in the budget development process, you may have to take your best guess for certain types of income and expenses by using bank statements, cheque stubs and credit card receipts.

Planning for Your Life After Divorce

If you're likely to be separating before you begin divorce proceedings, you need to sort out some sort of plan for your future. See Chapter 6 for actions you must both take before one of you actually leaves.

An important aspect of planning for divorce is thinking about what life is going to be like after your marriage has ended and what you want out of your divorce settlement. You may want to consider the following:

- ✔ How much are you going to need to spend on your children's everyday expenses and out-of-school and recreational activities, including holidays and school trips. Remember that costs are paid by both parents in most of the arrangements you make for your children (see Chapters 10 and 13).

- ✔ How much are you going to need for living expenses after you divorce? (Think about developing a post-divorce budget that projects the income and expenses you anticipate.)

- ✔ What adjustments do you need to make in order to make ends meet and live a happy life on your own?

- ✔ Do you have adequate job skills if you plan to re-enter the job market after not working for several years?

- ✔ Where can you get those job skills? How long is getting them going to take and what will that education cost? (Remember to count educational expenses into your post-divorce budget, as well as any transport and child-care costs you may incur while developing your job skills.)

Thinking about these things when you're preoccupied by more immediate issues is tough, but having at least a general plan for your post-divorce life helps you better define your divorce priorities and determine what you really want financially from your divorce and what you're willing to give up.

Deciding on your goals and priorities

Write down your divorce goals and priorities in their order of importance. Then put the list away in a safe place. After a month or so, when you've had some time to think, take another look at your list. You'll probably find that you want to add, subtract, or re-order a few items.

When you're thinking about what you really want out of your divorce, try to be realistic. Don't ask for the moon, but then again, don't be a martyr. The expenditure list in Chapter 3 can help you keep your feet on the ground when you're thinking about what you want versus what you need.

Spend some time thinking about the kind of divorce you want and what you're willing to do to get that divorce, and articulate your desires to your solicitor. For example, ask yourself the following questions (and have a look at the chapters we reference for help in coming up with the answers):

- ✔ Are you willing to go all the way to a court hearing to get the top items on your list of divorce priorities, or is a negotiated settlement more important to you? (Chapters 14 and 16)

- ✔ What decisions are in your children's best interests, and how are you going to work with your spouse to achieve that end? (Chapter 10)

- ✔ How important to you is having a good relationship with your spouse after the divorce? How important is that to your children? (Chapter 10)

- ✔ Do you absolutely have to have the children living with you all the time, or are you willing to share their care with your spouse? (Chapter 10)

- ✔ Do you have to stay in the family home, or may you and the children be better off somewhere else? And how near do you and the children need to be to your work, schools, friends, family and ex-spouse? (Chapter 10)

- ✔ How big a house, realistically, do you need for you and the children for the next few years, and what can you afford? (Chapter 11)

- ✔ What are your minimum and maximum income needs, and what do you see as the optimum division of your time between your work, your children and your other commitments? (Chapters 11 and 19)

- ✔ How much of a priority for you is providing now for your longer-term security, such as when your children leave home or you reach retirement age? (Chapter 11)

- ✔ What difference does it make if you or your spouse re-marry or cohabit? (Chapter 21)

- ✔ How much time and money are you prepared to spend on your divorce? (See the next section 'How Much do You Have to Spend to End Your Marriage?' for how much your divorce is likely to cost.)

If you're clear about the kind of outcome that you want for your divorce, you're better able to choose a solicitor who can help you achieve it. (See Chapter 15 for tips on choosing the solicitor who's right for you.) You can also provide that solicitor with direction and feedback during the divorce process. If you use the first solicitor you hear about with little or no thought to your goals and priorities, terminating your marriage may end up being more stressful, lengthy and expensive than you ever imagined.

How Much Do You Have to Spend to End Your Marriage?

If you aren't careful, the thousands of pounds you spent on your wedding and honeymoon may be a mere pittance compared with the cost of your divorce. The cost of ending your marriage depends on a number of factors:

- **Whether your divorce is amicable and co-operative, or bitter and contentious:** The more you and your spouse can agree on, the less you have to spend on solicitors, barristers, legal fees and court costs. If your divorce is contentious, your solicitor may have to make a number of applications and court appearances. Your solicitor has to spend time to prepare each application and yet more time to argue each one out before a judge, and you have to pay for all that time.

- **What area you live in:** Legal fees cost more if you live in a city, because the overhead costs of most city firms of solicitors, especially in London, are higher and they cover the cost by charging you more.

- **What the reputation and experience is of the solicitor who represents you:** More experienced solicitors and barristers with 'winning' reputations can command bigger fees than those practitioners who haven't been practising as long or don't have established reputations as family law specialists. On the other hand, they may help you settle things much more quickly and efficiently. At the very least, make sure that your solicitor is a specialist family solicitor and preferably one who belongs to the Resolution (www.resolution.org.uk) and works to its code of practice and protocol.

- **How many of your divorce terms you and your spouse can work out together:** If you and your spouse can negotiate your finances together, instead of paying your solicitors to do all the work on your behalf, the result is almost always more economical.

- **Whether you and your spouse get into a battle about the children, which can be very expensive:** Co-operating over the plans for your children saves you the expense of your solicitors working out the fine details or the full costs of going to court.

- **What the amount is of assets and debts that you need to divide up, and their complexity:** Depending on the debts and assets involved, you may need to hire a valuer, financial adviser, forensic accountant, actuary or other professional to help with your divorce.

- **Whether you or your spouse are hiding any assets:** If you are, you may get involved in the potentially spiralling expense of formal disclosure proceedings.

- **Whether you and your spouse are willing to settle your divorce outside court or whether one or both of you is determined to have a court hearing:** If one of you is bent on a fight, it costs both of you.

✓ **What the legal strategies are of your solicitor and your spouse's solicitor:** You may choose a consensus-seeking family solicitor only to find that your spouse has chosen one who is adversarial or inexperienced in family law. Your solicitor may then have to change tack.

✓ **Whether you're eligible for any sort of public funding or legal aid:** The charging rates of solicitors and barristers doing publicly funded work are fixed annually by the government and are normally much lower than private charging rates.

Hoping for the best: The least it costs

If your divorce is extremely simple – you and your spouse have little or nothing to negotiate, you have no children or no children still at home, no marital property, few debts, neither of you is asking for spousal support, and you're willing to complete most if not all the paperwork yourself – you can get divorced for about £800, maybe even less. The court fees alone are – in 2008 – £300 for the divorce petition with an additional fee of £40 for the decree absolute.

Even if you own property or owe debts, your divorce may cost you no more than £2–3,000, if you and your spouse work out the terms of your divorce together after you have each had an initial consultation with your solicitors or the help of a professional mediator. Your solicitors review and formalise your final agreement. Public funding (which used to be called legal aid) reduces the cost even further. (Chapters 14 and 16 provide helpful information if you want to negotiate on your own or in mediation.)

Many solicitors offer an initial half-hour meeting for free or at a reduced rate.

Fearing the worst: The most it costs

Be prepared to spend a whole lot more money on your divorce if you and your spouse fight every step of the way, or if your divorce is complicated and active involvement of your solicitors from start to finish is essential. In this case, you may be looking at legal bills in five figures. At the end of a prolonged child residence battle, legal bills have been known to rise to £15,000. If you and your spouse go into battle over complex financial matters, those bills can *triple*.

The private hourly rate of an experienced family law solicitor can range from £120 to £400 or more, plus VAT, depending on where they practise and their level of experience. A mediation case can average a few hundred pounds. If you're publicly funded, different levels of funding apply to different stages of the legal process (see Chapter 15).

Pinpointing the cost with multiple estimates

To get a better idea of the likely cost of your divorce, you may get estimates from several family solicitors. When you're enquiring about or meeting potential solicitors (see Chapter 15), ask for fee estimates based on several divorce scenarios. These amounts help you to decide whether to hold out for a particular property settlement, child arrangement or specific amount of maintenance. By using the solicitors' estimates, you can do a very basic cost-benefit analysis comparing the value of what you may gain should you pursue a particular goal with how much it would cost you to get it. However, no solicitor can guarantee that you'll get the outcome you want, regardless of how much money you spend.

Do what you can to avoid a battle about your children. Not only is it extremely expensive, but also the battle may cause your children to suffer long-lasting emotional damage. If you're considering such a battle, analyse your motives, perhaps with the help of a counsellor (see Chapter 2 for help in finding a counsellor). After some serious reflection, you may decide that you're confusing your own needs with your children's – or that you are using the children as a way of getting back at your spouse. Refer to Chapter 8 for a thorough look at what your children's needs can include and to Chapter 10 to see what your alternatives are for child care.

Getting help from public funding (Legal aid)

If you're on a low income or have no income apart from your spouse's, you may be able to apply for financial help. We give you full details in Chapter 15 about what you need to qualify and how you can use public funding. The Legal Services Commission, www.communitylegaladvice.org.uk/ (or the Scottish Legal Aid Board if you live in Scotland, www.slab.org.uk), may be able to help with funding your legal and mediation costs.

Most forms of legal aid for family disputes are more like a loan than a gift. So, for example, if you're granted public funding to take your case to court, or for your solicitors to negotiate on your behalf, you have to pay back all your court and solicitor's costs out of any money or property that you receive as part of your settlement. This *legal aid charge* or *statutory charge* (also known as a *claw-back*) almost always applies regardless of whether your final settlement is by consent or fully contested. However, the one exception to this rule is that if you're eligible for public funding for mediation, you don't have to pay back any of the costs incurred by your mediator or solicitor so long as you reach an agreement in mediation and you and your solicitors go along with that agreement. This exception is an incentive for you to reach an agreement in mediation and to stick with it. But note that this exception isn't available in Northern Ireland.

Receiving state benefits and tax credits

The fact of the matter is that, after a divorce, the pot of money you were living on when married needs to be split between two households. You can try to cut back on your expenditure and you can try to increase your income, but you may not be able to avoid being hard up. If you have children, the drop in income and increase in expenditure affects them too.

The good news is that the government provides some safety nets to protect you financially. Public financial support includes *income support* and tax credits and benefits to help you provide for yourselves and your children, and to encourage you back into work where possible. Be aware of these benefits when you make arrangements for your family after divorce. All the professionals who have a contract with the Legal Services Commission have training in welfare benefits and tax credits because these benefits are such an important part of many divorced families' lives at one time or another.

Here we briefly summarise the main benefits and tax credits that you may be entitled to depending on your means and circumstances. For more information, pick up leaflet GL23 from your post office or download it from www.dwp.gov.uk, try www.hmrc.gov.uk/taxcredits, or make an appointment with your local Citizens Advice Bureau. See Chapter 13 for a detailed explanation of the benefits you may be eligible for if you have children.

- ✔ **Child Benefit:** A non-means-tested benefit, payable on a weekly or four-weekly basis to anyone responsible for a child living with them under the age of 16, or under 19 and in full-time education.

- ✔ **Child Tax Credit:** Paid to the main carer of a child under 16, or under 19 and in full-time education, the Child Tax Credit depends on your means. An amount is paid for each child in your household, plus extra for a disabled child or child under one year old.

- ✔ **Working Tax Credit:** You may be able to claim Working Tax Credit, depending on the number of hours that you work (you need to work at least 16 hours if you have a dependent child, or 30 hours if you don't). Working Tax Credit is more generous if you have children and you're their main carer, and you may be able to get help with child-care costs when you are at work. Maintenance or child support paid to you by your spouse or ex-spouse isn't taken into account as income.

- ✔ **Pension Credit**: Single people aged 60 or over living in the UK are entitled to a Pension Credit that guarantees an income of at least £124.05 a week (at present rates). If you're over 65 and single you may get up to £19.71 a week even if your income is up to £174 per week *and* you have savings or investments.

- ✔ **Income Support:** You can claim Income Support if you have less than £16,000 capital, work less than 16 hours per week, aren't in full-time education, and have income below a prescribed amount. Income support is a passport to several other benefits such as free prescriptions, housing benefit, council tax benefit and legal aid. You may also be able to borrow money from a social fund for certain essential household items.

Rules and levels of Income Support are liable to change, so check with HM Revenue and Customs to ensure that your information is up to date.

✔ **Jobseeker's Allowance:** To claim Jobseeker's Allowance you must be over 18, unemployed and available for work. You aren't treated as available for work if you have a dependent child living with you under the age of 16. Rates of payment depend on your National Insurance Contributions or are calculated in a similar way to Income Support.

✔ **Housing Benefit:** If you live in rented accommodation, are responsible for the rent, have less than £16,000 capital, and your income is below a prescribed level, you may be entitled to help towards your rent, up to a maximum of 100 per cent of the eligible rent for your area (which may be less than the rent that you're contracted to pay).

✔ **Council Tax Benefit:** If you're responsible for the council tax on your home, have less than £16,000 capital, and your income is below a prescribed level, you may be eligible for help towards your council tax, up to a maximum of 100 per cent. You can in any event claim a 25 per cent reduction if you're a single adult occupier.

✔ **Disability Benefits:** A range of benefits are available if you're temporarily or permanently disabled. Always get specialist advice from a Citizens Advice Bureau if you think you may be able to claim.

✔ **The New Deal:** Special deals are available to help single parents back into work, particularly if you've been on Income Support for more than six months. According to users, one of the most helpful features of the scheme is the personal adviser you're given to help you find work.

Anticipating a Hostile Divorce

If you suspect that your divorce is going to be a knock-down, dragged-out fight, or if you're certain it's not going to go smoothly, you may need to take some defensive measures.

Opening a bank account in your own name

If you share a savings account with your spouse and are concerned that he may abuse the account, you may want to withdraw some of the money in the account – maybe half, depending on your needs and the amount in the account – and deposit it in a new account in your own name. Make sure that you have a clear record of any such transactions.

After your spouse finds out that you've taken money out of your joint account and placed it in your separate account, expect some fireworks that may make your divorce negotiations more difficult. If you withdraw an unreasonable amount of money (and just what 'unreasonable' constitutes is something your solicitors may have to advise you on), you may end up increasing the costs of your property settlement.

Make sure that you have enough money in your current bank account to cover your monthly expenses. Bounced cheque charges and angry creditors are among the last things you need right now.

Closing or freezing your joint accounts

Cancel credit card accounts if your spouse is also a card-holder. If you can't close an account because of an outstanding debt that you can't pay, return your card to the credit card company and explain that you aren't going to be responsible for debts on the account beyond the current balance.

If you both have a joint account, ask your bank manager to freeze it so that you can draw on it only with joint signatures. Banks shouldn't be able to close a joint account without the consent of both of you. Make sure that you make arrangements for essential direct debits and standing orders first. Also, if you and your spouse have an overdraft limit with a bank or credit card, cancel or reduce these limits. Inform your spouse of what you've done and ask him to tear up his card or return it to you or the credit card company.

Finding a safe place for your important personal property

If you think that your spouse may try to damage, destroy or steal your personal property out of anger or revenge, find a safe place to hide your valuables. That can be a safe deposit box in your name, the home of a trusted friend or family member, or any other place your spouse can't access.

If your spouse steals or damages your personal property, you may be able to claim the value of that property from your spouse in any financial proceedings between you. Your solicitor can also use evidence of your spouse's destructive behaviour as leverage on the question of costs during your divorce negotiations or at the end of the final hearing.

Building your individual credit

Individual credit – credit in your own name – is essential to having a life on your own. Building a decent credit record takes time. If you don't have individual credit when you close your joint accounts, you may have to wait several years before you have access to credit on the best terms. (See Chapter 3 for more information on building your own credit record.) Check to make sure that any jointly held credit is recorded in your individual names rather than Mr and Mrs R. Smith. And ask your creditors to begin reporting information on these accounts in your name as well as your spouse's. Assuming that these accounts have positive payment histories, having them in your credit file may help you build your own credit history. Note that having a jointly held account is distinct from being an authorised user, which doesn't build your own credit record.

Protecting your mutual assets from being wasted by your spouse

If your spouse is angry about your divorce or wants revenge, he may try to use up your joint assets rather than allow you to get a portion of those assets in your divorce. If you're concerned that this may happen, consult a family law solicitor straight away about what steps you can take to safeguard your joint assets. Avoid maintaining large unprotected cash balances in your joint accounts. Your solicitor may be able to apply for an injunction and request an emergency hearing if the property in question is at risk from your spouse.

Identifying sources of ready funds

Protecting your legal rights when you're involved in a hostile divorce takes lots of money. If you seriously fear that your divorce is going to be hostile, start identifying the financial resources you have at your disposal at once, including your separate savings account, stocks, shares or bonds; borrowing against your insurance policy funds; getting a second mortgage on property you own in your own right; borrowing money from family members; and anything else along those lines. Keep a record of all transactions because you're going to be expected to account for them in any financial proceedings. Talk with an accountant or your financial adviser about the tax consequences and other implications of selling stocks or shares, borrowing against any insurance funds, or taking a second loan on any property you own.

Chapter 8

Helping Your Children Get Through Your Divorce

· ·

In This Chapter

▶ Putting your children's feelings first

▶ Deciding when the time is right to break the news

▶ Talking to all your children together or each child individually

▶ Preparing for your children's responses and questions

· ·

*P*utting your children first can seem like a tall order, especially if the break up of your marriage is full of conflict. After all, you have your own emotions to deal with, financial and legal matters to resolve, and worries about the future. Nevertheless, your children depend on you for the care and support they need to be happy and secure and to grow into well-adjusted adults.

In this chapter, we help you address your children's personal needs during your divorce and offer advice for minimising any emotional trauma they may experience. We also offer guidance on when and how to tell your children about the end of your marriage and alert you to some of the ways your children may respond to the news.

Remaining Sensitive to Your Children's Feelings

When you get divorced, you and your spouse aren't the only people affected by the change in your marital status. Your divorce means the end of family life as your children have known it up to now, something that has been their mainstay. They may feel anxious and be thrown off balance for a time – toddlers may revert to more childish behaviour, schoolchildren may lack concentration, older children may be more than usually moody or angry. These early reactions should pass unless the insecurity continues and is compounded by conflict.

Here are four ways in which you can best protect your children from the long-term damage of divorce and ensure the survival of their self-esteem:

- ✔ **Make sure that you don't get your children caught up in your adult arguments.**

- ✔ **Make sure that you don't subject your children to the insecurity of a succession of changes in their living arrangements.**

- ✔ **Make sure that your children don't lose either of you without very good reason.**

- ✔ **Make sure to keep your children in the picture about what's happening with your family.**

Be reassured, however, that not every child who experiences adversity is damaged by it. Your children can be resilient when they're given your help and support. They may experience a drop in household income. They may have to move out of their home and neighbourhood, attend a new school and make new friends. You may not have been able to keep them totally clear of a fraught or even hostile home environment. You may have to come to terms with the fact that your divorce is their first experience of you doing something for your own sake and apparently not theirs. However, your job is to do all that you can, co-operatively whenever possible, to prevent your children, resilient or vulnerable, from feeling anxious, unloved and insecure.

What your children may fear (but not tell you)

During and after their parents' divorce, young children in particular may become fearful that terrible things may happen to them or believe that they're in some way responsible for the break-up of their parents' marriage. Some of the more common fears and misconceptions children have about divorce include the following:

- ✔ The parent I no longer live with is going to disappear from my life.

- ✔ My parents' divorce is my fault.

- ✔ If I'm really good, my parents will get back together.

- ✔ I have to choose between my parents. I can't have a relationship with both of them after they're divorced.

- ✔ My parent's new partner will replace my other real parent.

- ✔ A new stepbrother or stepsister is going to replace me.

Understanding the thoughts that may be going through your children's minds can keep you alert to any signs that they're having trouble coping with your divorce.

When, What and How to Tell Your Children What's Happening

Both you and your spouse need to convey in words and deeds that you'll always be there for your children. They may fear that they're going to lose one of you in a divorce or that one or both of you will somehow abandon them and they're going to have to fend for themselves. Make sure that your reassurances are realistic and your promises are more than hot air. You want your children to trust you.

You can tell your children in several ways, and some are better than others. Consider the following options for making the conversation go smoothly:

✔ **Agree on what you're going to say.** If possible, you and your spouse should take the time together to decide what you're going to say about your divorce before you talk with your children. Getting your story straight beforehand means that you don't contradict one another or argue while breaking the news to your children.

✔ **Tell your children as a couple.** If at all possible, you and your spouse should tell your children about your divorce together, even if that means putting your animosity aside for a while. Telling them together conveys to them that although your marriage may be ending, you can co-operate as parents and that they still have a family – just a different kind of family – and you'll both remain actively involved in their lives.

✔ **Be fair to one another.** You must both agree that when you talk with your children – whether together or separately – neither of you blames the other for your break-up or encourages your children to side with one of you against the other. Both these scenarios are unfair to your children and can cause them a great deal of hurt. When you criticise their other parent, you're criticising someone they love. Your comments can also backfire on you – your children may side with the parent you criticised and not with you.

✔ **Be honest with your children about why you're getting divorced.** But keep their ages in mind and don't tell them things about your adult relationship that they neither understand nor need to know. Tell them as much as they need to know and no more. If you haven't been able to hide the discord in your marriage, you may want to acknowledge what your children already know by saying something like, 'We know that you've heard us fighting a lot and here's what's going to happen . . .'.

Don't hide the fact that life is going to be different for everyone in the family because of your divorce. Prepare your children for some of the changes to come. Then reassure them that your divorce hasn't changed and won't change your love for them, and that you'll continue to be involved in their lives. But don't promise them things you can't deliver.

✔ **Be very clear with your children that your divorce has absolutely nothing to do with them.** Young children may feel somehow responsible for the divorce and assume that if only they had behaved better you wouldn't be ending your marriage. A website especially for children, such as www.itsnotyourfault.org.uk, may help them (or you) understand better what's happening in your family.

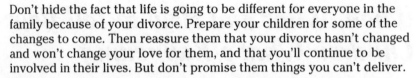

✔ **Don't let emotion get the better of you**. Try not to get emotional when you tell your children about your divorce. Watching a parent cry, shout or get very upset can be frightening for your children. Don't add to their anxiety with a highly charged account of what's been going on. You're likely to make them more concerned about your emotions than their own. As a consequence, your children may not let you know exactly what they're feeling.

Finding help with telling your children

If you need help deciding what to say to your children, talk things over with their health visitor (if you have a child under school age), their teacher (if they're at primary school and the relationship is a good one) or a school or children's counsellor (if they're of secondary school age). You can also ask your local Relate office (www.relate.org.uk) or Family Mediation Service (www.familymediationhelpline.co.uk) what service is available in your area, or use a mediator to help you work out together what you're going to say.

Helping your children cope with the news

If your children are having trouble coping with the news of your divorce, they may need a great deal more cuddling if they're young, and extra time and attention if they're a bit older. Adolescents may seem to take the news in their stride or protest vigorously, which can make giving them the support and understanding they need even harder – but you mustn't stop trying to reach out to them. Levelling with your teenage children as much as you can conveys respect for their growing maturity and helps them to grow – but not if you're tempted to confide in them to get them on your side!

Getting help from someone else

Sometimes helping your children isn't that simple. When your children need more than you, at the time, can give them, consider first involving a loved grandparent (UK research studies have shown many grandparents to be the people closest to children at such a time) or another trusted adult who's especially close to your children. (A grandparents' association is available: have a look at www.grandparents-association.org.uk.) Support groups for children whose parents have separated can be helpful to older children.

Tell your children's teachers, baby-sitters, other carers, the parents of their close friends, and any other adults they see regularly about your divorce plans. Informing these people helps them understand that any significant changes in your children's behaviour may be due to your divorce. Ask these adults to keep you informed of any changes they notice in your children.

In some areas, groups or short courses for divorcing parents are available where you can find out about children's reactions to divorce, effective parent–child communication, and resources that can help parents and their children. Find out from your local Relate or Family Mediation Service if support services operate in your area.

TIP

Resources to help you and your children

Many resources – books, leaflets and websites – are available to help you and your children cope with your divorce.

You may find *Help Your Children Cope with Your Divorce: A 'Relate' Guide* (Vermilion) helpful. For younger children, you may also find useful *Children Don't Divorce (Talking It Through)* by Rosemary Stones (Happy Cat Books), and for older children by the same author *It's Not Your Fault: What to Do When Your Parents Divorce* (Piccadilly Press). You can find further lists of books for children on several websites mentioned in this chapter or from a general divorce website such as www.divorceaid.co.uk/. And of course you can always use www.amazon.co.uk to check on availability.

These websites may help your older children:

- www.itsnotyourfault.org.uk
- www.coping-with-life.org.uk (a Rotary website)
- www.young-voice.org
- www.nyas.net
- www.thesite.org.uk

You may also find these websites useful:

- www.familyandparenting.org
- www.parentlineplus.org.uk
- www.parentscentre.gov.uk (the Government website)

For help over the phone, try the ParentlinePlus helpline (0808 800 2222).

Staying positive

Children's self-esteem is a precious thing and so is yours. Being too negative can destroy your self-esteem as well as your children's.

An American psychologist, John Gottman, invites couples into his studio for a weekend and measures the ratio between negative and positive statements in their conversation. Guess what? He has arrived at a startling glimpse of the obvious. If the ratio of positive to negative statements is five to one or more, he can predict that the relationship will survive. He claims 94 per cent success in his predictions over a period of about 20 years' study.

Imagine children hearing their parents say mostly negative things about each other or about them. Hearing negative things about their parents or themselves may be the key factor in losing their self-esteem. And the ratio of negative to positive is likely to get worse during a divorce.

So here are some things you can do to protect your own and your children's self esteem:

✔ At a contact handover, listen to yourselves talking together for about ten minutes and count the ratio of positive to negative statements you make.

✔ If you notice more negative than positive statements, reverse your own ratio next time. You may well find your ex-spouse becomes more positive too!

✔ Practise turning a criticism into a positive statement. For example, 'You're always late and I never know when you're coming! How do you think that makes Mary feel?' can become 'I appreciate your commitment to keeping in contact with Mary, and I find it really helpful when you arrive within 15 minutes of when we expect you.'

✔ Say what you think and feel rather than guess negatively what your spouse may be thinking and feeling – even if you feel you know her (and her thoughts) very well! However, stay as positive as you can. Rather than, 'You always look so bad-tempered when I arrive. Do you really hate me now?', try saying, 'I find it hard coming to collect Mary but I appreciate the fact that you let me come.'

✔ Be specific rather than generalise. Don't say, 'There you go! You always look on the black side'. Say instead, 'I feel that you're looking too much on the black side.'

Keeping your children out of the argument

Watch your own behaviour in the presence of your children. What you choose to do (or don't do, as the following list tells you) can either help reassure them that things are going to be okay or add to their anxiety about the future.

✔ Don't fight with your spouse when your children are around.

✔ Don't say negative things about your spouse to your children or to someone else within hearing distance of your children.

✔ Don't get highly emotional around your children about your divorce or your life after the divorce. You risk increasing their insecurity and fear about the future.

✔ Don't use your children as go-betweens between you and your spouse.

✔ Don't interfere in your children's relationship with your spouse by trying to manipulate them into thinking of you as the 'good parent' and your spouse as the 'bad parent'.

✔ Don't put pressure on your children to take sides.

✔ Avoid making big changes in your children's daily routines. As much as possible, keep everything in their lives just as it was. Children generally don't like change, and divorce is change enough.

✔ Don't spoil them because you're feeling guilty or because you want to get them on your side. And although you may feel tired, don't let discipline slip.

✔ Avoid making your children your confidantes. Keep your adult worries and concerns to yourself or share them only with other adults.

✔ Don't look to your children for comfort. It should work the other way around.

✔ Don't expect your child to become 'your little man' or 'your little woman' about the house. Your children are children not surrogate spouses. But don't let them off normal chores, either. If fewer hands are available to do things, share out the tasks. Involving them appropriately can help them to cope with change. We all cope with change better when we have something useful to do.

Deciding when to tell your children

You may tend to put off doing things that are unpleasant or you don't feel confident about (most people do). So, you may come up with countless reasons to put off telling your children about your divorce. However, make sure that you tell them before anyone else does. They need to hear the news from you, in your own words. And, in the same breath, you need to reassure them that you're always going to love them and take care of them.

The right time to talk with your children about the changes to come depends on their ages and on the circumstances of your divorce. For example, if your spouse announces that she has already filed for a divorce and is moving out next week, you need to tell your children about the split sooner and not later.

Informing your older children

Bear in mind that if you have older children (secondary school age and older) they usually need to be told sooner than very young children – assuming that you have some control over the timing of your conversations with them. Older children are more likely to find out about your divorce by overhearing a conversation or by coming across divorce-related papers, and partly because they're better at sensing that 'something is up'. They are also better at managing information over a period of time, digesting it, and coming up with explanations that they can live with – although they may sound more worldly-wise than they feel. When you're certain that the divorce is going ahead and have worked out at least some of the details, especially those affecting your children, talk with them as soon as possible.

Don't discuss your divorce plans with your older children until you've talked the plans over with your spouse. Making them confidantes and trying to seek their advice and opinions is unfair and inappropriate. If you need advice and counselling, go to an adult source. (See Chapter 9 for suggestions on finding a counsellor.)

Don't overlook the responses of your adult children. They're still going to be shaken by a divorce, even if you wait until they leave home or go to university. Like any children, they need to be told in a sensitive way. Your adult children may feel that the home they left is no longer there for them at a time when they haven't yet established themselves anywhere else. They may also seem to lose confidence in marriage (possibly explaining why many younger people choose to cohabit instead).

Talking to your younger children

If you have toddlers and primary school children, avoid telling them about your divorce plans too far ahead of the date when you and your spouse plan to begin living apart. Young children have a different sense of time from adults and older children; for them, a week can seem like a month and a month can seem like a year. If you tell your younger children too early, you risk intensifying the anxiety they have over knowing that their lives are going to change in ways they don't yet understand. Also, avoid using words like 'court' and 'law', because young children associate them with wrongdoing, perhaps without you realising it.

Regardless of their ages, whenever possible don't wait until just before you and your spouse begin living apart to break the news to your children. *Even worse is when one of you leaves without any explanation at all.* Instead, tell them far enough ahead of the day you plan to separate so that they have time to process your news, ask you questions, spend time with both of you in a relaxed manner, and enjoy your affection. All these things are essential preparation for the changes ahead.

Telling your children individually or all together

Should you tell your children about your divorce all at the same time, or have separate conversations with each of them? Only you can make that decision, but in this section we give you arguments in support of each approach.

Discussing your divorce as a group

If your children are close in age and maturity, telling them all together has important benefits:

> ✔ **You can help foster a 'we're all in this together' attitude among your children.** This feeling can be a comfort and a source of strength to them.

> ✔ **You can ensure that each of them knows exactly what her siblings know.** This may not seem important to you, but if you tell each of them separately, they may worry that they don't know what their siblings know or that you're going to treat them differently from everyone else in the family.

Talking to each child alone

If your children have significant disparities in their ages or levels of maturity, you may be better advised to have individual talks with them so that you can tailor an appropriate message.

Be sure to tell each child that you're having a similar conversation with her siblings. Unless your children are very young, they are probably going to talk with one another about what you've told them. Therefore, your message about why you're getting a divorce and what's going to change or stay the same in their lives must be consistent. If you tell each child something different, you only add to their anxiety and confusion.

Anticipating Your Children's Responses

You can't predict how your children are going to react to the news of your divorce. Their reaction depends on their ages and maturity levels, their personalities and their relationship with you, among other things. Interestingly enough, however, you may find that their emotions mirror yours and may include any or all the following:

> ✔ Disbelief

> ✔ Anger

> ✔ Fear

> ✔ Sadness

> ✔ Depression

> ✔ Rejection

To help keep an eye on how well your children are dealing with the news of your divorce, try to spend some extra time with them (but not in an interfering way). The time you spend together gives your children the opportunity to express their feelings and concerns about their daily lives in their own time.

Your children may well say things at odd moments of intimacy – young ones in the bath or at bedtime; older children in the car or even while washing up – if you're lucky and they ever communicate their feelings with you.

Listening to your children

Your children need to feel that they're being listened to while you're in the midst of your marriage break-up. You must find time to be in touch with their thoughts and feelings especially when they're finding it difficult to put these into words. Don't anxiously put words into your children's mouths but listen to how they're making sense of what's happening to them.

You may find it hard to hear what your children may say at times. For example, they may say 'Didn't daddy love me, then?' or 'If you hadn't been so cross all the time, mummy wouldn't have left'. You may be tempted to defend yourself by launching into explanations, but the important thing is that you hear and respond warmly to the anxiety behind their comments and that you aren't judgemental. Then your children are more likely to open up to you so that you can comfort and reassure them.

After your children find out about your divorce plans, they may begin to feel isolated and cut off from their friends. They may feel as though they're the only children whose parents ever got divorced and may be embarrassed about what's happening to them.

Although your children may appear to be coping, don't assume that they're not having trouble at school or at play, or aren't going to have trouble later on. Stay tuned in to their mood swings or any changes in their behaviour that may be a sign of emotional distress. See the section below on 'Recognising signs that your children are finding it hard to cope'.

If you separate before your divorce is final, your children must visit the parent who moves out as soon as possible to reassure themselves that she is all right and is still their parent. Young children have been known to worry that the parent no longer at home doesn't get enough to eat, for example.

However, if your children refuse to visit their other parent or seem reluctant to do so, don't force them. Contact needs always to be beneficial – not done for the sake of it. Under normal circumstances, your children must have the other parent's new address and phone number. In some rare instances, however, you may have strong reasons for keeping this information from them, for example if violence or abuse is involved, or you have reason to fear that it may be. (Refer to Chapter 2.)

If you or your spouse fought openly and often during your marriage, your separation may of course be a relief to your children as well as to you, and represent a positive, though strange, change in their lives.

The art of 'active' listening

If you've never before concentrated on listening attentively to your children, now is the time to start. Good, 'active' listening requires you to be attuned to the feelings behind your children's comments and questions, and then to let them know in a non-judgemental way that you heard what they were saying. Active listening doesn't mean preaching or lecturing, and doesn't necessarily involve analysis or problem solving. Its purpose is to encourage your children to open up to you and to tell you what they think about your divorce. Active listening promotes a feeling of love and trust between you and your children, something they need in order to deal with their parents' divorce.

Recognising signs that your children are finding it hard to cope

If you're divorcing, you need to be familiar with the more common signs of emotional distress in children and be on the lookout for these signs in your own children so that you're ready to step in as soon as possible. When children behave in the following ways, they're asking for help.

Toddlers and pre-school children may:

- ✔ Revert to more childish behaviour, such as bedwetting, thumb-sucking and crying.
- ✔ Have trouble sleeping in their own room or have nightmares.
- ✔ Develop behaviour problems at home or with other children.
- ✔ Become fearful of leaving you.

Primary school children may:

- ✔ Say they feel ill more than usual so that they can stay at home from school (headaches and stomach aches are particularly common).
- ✔ Choose one parent to be angry with and another to cling to for comfort.
- ✔ Begin spending more time alone in their rooms and less time playing with friends.
- ✔ Participate in fewer classroom activities.

Secondary school age children may:

- ✔ Withdraw from friends and family.
- ✔ Develop non-specific illnesses or nervous habits such as nail-biting.

✔ Spend more time alone in their rooms.

✔ Express anger towards the parent they think is responsible for the divorce.

✔ Try to behave like a surrogate spouse to the parent they feel has been wronged.

✔ Develop behaviour problems (such as getting into fights) at school, outside school or at home.

✔ Become more rebellious (for example, truanting, smoking, drinking, experimenting with drugs, or staying out late).

Although you may have no need to be alarmed if your children are under stress for a short period of time, if your child's obvious discomfort is prolonged or grows worse, you do have cause for concern. Alcohol and drug abuse, delinquency or criminal actions require immediate attention because these can put your child and others in danger. Read Chapter 2 for help on finding a counsellor or someone else who can help you and your child.

Handling your children's questions

After you tell your children about your divorce plans, give them an opportunity to ask questions. If they ask you something that you can't answer, say so by admitting that you don't know or it's too soon to tell. When appropriate, tell them that you promise to give them an answer by a certain date or as soon as you can. Be careful when explaining that you're divorcing because you and your spouse don't love each other any more – you don't want your children to think that you may therefore stop loving them. Reassure your children that you love them, and that you'll continue to do so.

During one of our mediation sessions, Sam, a 10-year-old boy, protested when his mother said she would tell him why she and his father were divorcing when he was older and would understand. He shouted: 'You tell me now even if I don't understand!' So she had to try.

Your children's initial questions probably relate to how your divorce is going to change their lives and what's going to stay the same. For example, depending on their ages, they may want to know:

✔ Where will they live?

✔ Will they still go to the same school?

✔ Will you and your spouse still live in the same town?

✔ Will they spend time with each of you?

✔ Will you continue to be involved with their favourite sporting activity?

✔ Can they continue their music or dance lessons?

  ✔ How will you share parenting responsibilities?

  ✔ Can they still go on school trips?

  ✔ Will there be enough money?

  ✔ Where will their dog or cat live?

Don't be surprised if your children don't ask you many questions at first. Discovering that you're getting a divorce is probably quite a shock, even if they already know that you and your spouse are having marital problems, and even if they have plenty of friends with divorced parents. Your children may need time to let the news sink in before they're ready to ask you questions.

Understanding how children vary with age

Your older children may come to you with questions after they've shared your news with friends, especially if their friends' parents are divorced and their friends tell them what the divorce experience was like for them.

Many resources are available for older children, and you may be better leaving some books or leaflets around instead of thrusting them eagerly on your reluctant adolescents. *Divorce is Not the End of the World* by Zoe Evan and Sue Ellen Stern (Tricycle Press) is suitable for 9–13 year olds.

Your younger children may have a hard time grasping the concept of divorce and find it hard to understand that you and your spouse will always continue to love them and care for them. If you have, for example, said that you no longer love each other, they may begin to think that love for them can also just stop. They may ask you the same questions over and over, which can really tax your patience. You need to understand that at the moment your children need constant reassurance.

You can help your younger children deal with your divorce by reading them age-appropriate books that deal with the subject. A very wise child psychiatrist says that one of the things that helps children cope with trauma is constructing a story about it or an explanation that they can then live with comfortably. You can gradually help your children to do this.

We recommend the following titles to help your younger children acknowledge and express their fears and worries about your divorce and the changes divorce brings:

  ✔ *Dinosaurs Divorce: A Guide for Changing Families* by Marc Brown and Laurence Krasny Brown (Little, Brown & Co.) for 3–7 year olds.

  ✔ *How Do I Feel About My Parent's Divorce* by Julia Cole (Franklin Watts Ltd) for 5–11 year olds.

'No one tells us anything'

Let your children know that you're willing and available to talk with them about your divorce and answer their questions whenever they want.

Four hundred and sixty-seven children from the west of England, aged between 5 and 16, were interviewed not so long ago for a research study. A quarter of them whose parents had separated said no one talked about the separation when it happened. Only 5 per cent said they were given full explanations and the chance to ask questions!

If your children seem reluctant to ask questions, take the initiative by talking with each of them individually about your divorce and asking them if they have questions about it. Obviously, if you've always enjoyed an honest, open relationship with your children they'll be more willing to discuss their fears and concerns than if you never before expressed an interest in finding out what they're thinking or having a meaningful conversation with them.

If you need help finding ways to communicate with your children, try any of the following titles. All the books we mention are usually available (sometimes second-hand) on www.amazon.co.uk:

- ✔ *But I Want to Stay With You* by Jill Burrett (Simon & Schuster Ltd), which is about communicating with your children.

- ✔ *Where's Daddy?* by Jill Curtis (Bloomsbury Publishing plc), which offers advice about how to tell children of all ages about a divorce.

Cafcass publishes some excellent leaflets for parents and children, for example: 'Putting your children first: a guide for separating parents' and 'My Family's Changing'. Take a look at www.cafcass.gov.uk for more info.

If your children have gone through a divorce before, don't assume that your second divorce is going to be easier for them. This divorce may trigger the very same emotions they experienced during your first divorce. Their lives are again disrupted by changes in their lifestyle and the discomfort of living with two adults who are preoccupied with the end of their marriage. You have to do the same things to help them through it.

Chapter 9

Taking Care of Your Emotional Self

. . . .

In This Chapter

▶ Preparing yourself for the emotional ups and downs

▶ Staying in control of your feelings

▶ Keeping in contact with family and friends

. . . .

*F*or better or worse, your marriage is an important part of your life and ending it isn't easy – whether you initiate the divorce, the decision is mutual, or your spouse is the one who chooses to finish things. As the reality of your divorce sinks in, clear and rational thinking may become difficult, if not impossible. Focusing on your day-to-day activities and getting a good night's sleep may become increasingly hard to do. You may find yourself distracted by questions such as: Will I have enough money to survive? Where will I live? How will the children be affected? Will I ever marry again? This chapter helps you understand the emotions you're likely to feel and provides you with suggestions for how to keep them under control.

Preparing for the Emotional Ups and Downs

Getting divorced can be an emotional roller coaster ride: one day you feel angry, sad, depressed and guilty, and the next you feel hopeful and confident. Your feelings may even change from morning to afternoon, or from hour to hour. They are likely to be most intense at first, and gradually ease up over time. You may also experience the same sorts of emotions when you separate.

Because divorce is a highly personal experience, predicting exactly how you're going to respond to it is impossible. Nevertheless, you'll probably experience at least a couple of the following emotions:

✔ Sadness or grief over the loss of your relationship

✔ Anger towards your spouse for past slights and oversights

✔ Embarrassment that your marriage is ending, especially if you've always tried to portray yours as the perfect marriage

✔ A sense of failure and disappointment that you were unable to make your marriage work

✔ Fear of the effect your divorce may have on your children and yourself (especially if you haven't been single for many years or you've never lived on your own)

✔ Guilt if you initiated the divorce

✔ A sense of rejection or abandonment if your spouse initiated the divorce, especially if he left you for someone else

✔ Depression

Even if you no longer want to be married to your spouse, you may still experience some sense of loss. The more you understand your feelings, the better able you are to put your emotional response in perspective, handle it in a positive way, and prevent your emotions from derailing your divorce.

Understanding the Stages of Grief

At first you may feel as though you're never going to get over the loss of your marriage, but in time you will. When you lose a loved one – whether it's your spouse or the marriage itself – you must progress through a series of stages in order to get over the loss and heal emotionally. The stages listed below apply to the loss of anything or anyone that's especially important in life, including the loss of a marriage:

✔ **Shock and denial:** Even if you knew that your marriage had problems and that your spouse was unhappy, the news that he wants a divorce can feel catastrophic. *Divorce?* That's something that happens to other people, not to you! If the decision to divorce is a mutual one, you may still find it difficult to comprehend that your marriage is actually ending. You may vacillate between thinking that it's all just a silly misunderstanding and that you and your spouse can work things out. You may find yourself questioning your judgement (were you too naïve?) and the assumptions you made about your marriage and your spouse (were you too trusting?). You may also feel anxious about all the changes about to take place in your life and unprepared to deal with them.

✔ **Anger:** Anger often follows shock (although not with everyone) and is a normal response, especially if your spouse initiates the divorce. As well as being angry with your spouse, you may be angry with yourself. Expressing your anger is a healthy way of relieving some of the pressure you feel. Keeping your anger bottled up can lead to depression. Punching a cushion or just shouting loudly can help you let off steam. Exercise is also a great way to burn off some of that anger; swimming, running or kickboxing can help to release some of the tension you're feeling.

When you can't seem to shake your anger, and especially if you become confrontational or violent, seek the help of a counsellor immediately. Confiding in someone who can help you put your feelings in perspective is imperative in this type of situation.

✔ **Depression:** You're bound to feel low during various points in your divorce. This response to a difficult life situation is perfectly normal. But if your depression doesn't go away or grows worse, if you begin drinking too much to numb your feelings, or if you're having thoughts of suicide, seek immediate help from your doctor or a counsellor. You may need help to get through the tough times and out of your depression. Refer to Chapter 2 for ways to find a good counsellor to help you.

✔ **Bargaining (avoiding reality):** At times during the healing process, you may respond to your divorce by trying to strike bargains with your spouse or yourself. In desperation, you may promise to do just about anything to keep your marriage together and to make the pain go away. _Avoid making such deals._ If your spouse accepts your offer and you stop your divorce proceedings, you're only postponing the inevitable. The promises you make may be impossible for you to keep, and you may find that you're more miserable than ever in your marriage.

✔ **Sorrow:** If you're feeling sad about what divorce is taking away from your life, try to tell yourself that no situation lasts forever. The future holds possibilities for your own new way of life and for your children, who are always moving forward anyway. You may find another partner, or a new career or job, or you may be able to pursue an interest that you weren't able to develop during your marriage – and you should be the wiser for what you've gone through.

✔ **Understanding and acceptance:** Eventually, you begin to accept your divorce. If you divorce after two years' separation, and you've made sensible arrangements during the period, you're more likely to be in a state of mind to negotiate with your spouse than if the divorce happens quickly while emotions are high. If you can't resolve your emotional conflict until after your divorce is over and have to wait until then before you experience peace of mind, don't worry – this is normal.

Understanding each of the stages you pass through when you're recovering from divorce doesn't make your pain go away, but it may help you to know that other people have felt the same way as you do. At times, you may feel that you're going crazy or that life is never going to be normal again. However, knowing what to expect and finding out that countless other people in your situation have gone on to find happiness in life can be very reassuring.

Because your judgement may be somewhat impaired during the early stages of the healing process, try to avoid making important decisions when you're still feeling unstable. If important decisions must be made, seek some objective input from a trusted friend or family member.

Keeping Your Emotions in Check

How you handle your emotions can mean the difference between creating a fulfilling life for yourself as a single person and remaining stuck in the past. It can also mean the difference between helping your children cope with the situation and jeopardising their happiness. You can end up bitter, angry and defeated, or you can emerge from your divorce a stronger and more self-confident person – the choice is up to you.

How your emotions can affect you

You need to recognise the possible negative effects of not dealing with the emotions you're feeling. Letting your emotions go unchecked can:

- Impede your ability to make sound decisions.

- Sap your energy at the time you need it most.

- Prevent you from recognising and acknowledging how you may have contributed to the demise of your marriage.

- Make you more apt to acquiesce when it comes to your divorce negotiations, especially if you feel wracked with guilt and remorse.

- Drive away your friends and family.

Ways of getting through the tough times

Here are some steps you can take to help yourself move through the emotional healing process as quickly as possible:

- **Reach out to close friends and family members, or join a support group.** Your friends and family are there to help, and talking to other people who are going through the same things you are can be a great source of comfort.

- **Keep a diary or journal.** The process of recording your thoughts and feelings can have a calming effect and help you gain a new perspective about your life.

- **Spend more time with your children.** Making your children an even more important part of your life than they already are helps reassure them that your divorce in no way diminishes your love for them and that you're going to continue to be a part of their lives, no matter what.

- **Exercise.** Physical activity helps release endorphins, which help lift your spirits naturally. You also become physically healthier.

✔ **Get re-acquainted with friends you may have lost touch with after your marriage began failing.** Catching up with friends you haven't seen for a while can help give you some perspective and remind you that things other than your divorce are happening elsewhere in the world.

✔ **Set up some counselling sessions for yourself.** Counselling can help you to put your marriage in perspective and assess what went wrong. Then you can think more clearly about what the future many hold. (See Chapter 2 for information on locating a counsellor.)

Women tend to be better than men at building emotional support systems and admitting when they need help. Men have a tendency to try to 'tough it out' by repressing their emotions instead of confronting what's bothering them. Whatever your sex, you need to acknowledge what you're feeling in some way, however you choose to do so.

Dealing with the Response of Your Family and Friends

No doubt most of you'll share the news that you're getting divorced soon after you've made your decision. You may even discuss the pros and cons of divorce with other people beforehand. Your family may offer you the greatest support after a marriage break-up, both practically and emotionally. If they're also grandparents they may be good at looking at the experience through the eyes of your children and offer them a safe port in the storm.

Although you should expect your family to support you through tough times, don't take their support or patience for granted. If they help you out, let them know that you appreciate their generosity and stay alert for ways that you can return their favours. Also, try to be sensitive to just how much you can lean on them – everyone has his limits – and avoid crossing that line.

Your decision to divorce shouldn't affect your close friendships; your true friends remain friendly no matter what your marital status may be. But be ready for those friends and family members who may view the divorced you a little differently from the married you.

Meeting with disapproval

Some people may suggest, in general terms, that you haven't tried hard enough at your marriage. However, they need to understand that had you been able to avoid divorce, you probably would have done so.

If you have children, you'll probably maintain a relationship with your ex-spouse and his family, and whether you have children or not, you may want to keep in touch with your ex-spouse's family. You and your spouse need to talk about this in order to adopt an agreed approach so that communication is still possible on all sides, especially when needed.

Keeping grandparents

Children and grandparents usually want to keep in touch with each other. Most parents want to share their children with their own parents from time to time. Why should children lose their grandparents just because your marriage is over? Their grandparents may be deeply affected if this should happen and it deprives your children of a part of their history and sense of security. You can also lose a valuable source of support.

The relationship between you, your ex-spouse, your children and their grandparents may need careful managing. If all the adults can conduct themselves with sensitivity and forbearance, your children stand to gain. If, however, a lot of tension is around, the risk exists that your ex-spouse's parents may give you a hard time or cast you as the villain of the piece; you may need to ignore this for the sake of their relationship with your children.

Coping if friends become more distant

Almost inevitably, some of the friends and acquaintances you and your spouse shared as a couple are going to feel uneasy about how to continue their relationships with both of you after your divorce becomes common knowledge. Others may seem more distant when you cross paths. This sort of behaviour can be very hurtful, especially if you're already feeling rejected.

Be open to the possibility that some friends may still be there for you, whereas others may feel the need to maintain links with both of you, and still others may recognise the importance of offering support and a listening ear to children and young people. If certain friends are important to you, consider making the first move – invite them over for coffee, ask them if they want to play a sport you used to share or go shopping, or invite their children to come and play with yours.

Sorting out tensions

No better way exists of sorting out these future relationships than talking about them with your spouse and agreeing to be generous if you can. You may be able to establish some ground rules about not inviting your mutual friends to take sides (something that may be harder with family). If talking over the issue is difficult and you choose to use mediation, it may be a topic to put on the agenda (see Chapter 16 for more on mediation).

If you can't agree at all, it may be best for you to initiate the topic with friends, family and neighbours; make plain that you want to continue your relationship as normally as possible while the break-up is taking place. Say that you appreciate that it may be awkward at times but that you value their friendship and hope that it will continue until everyone is in calmer waters.

Part III
Decisions, Decisions

'His form's certainly suffered since his divorce.'

In this part . . .

The decisions you need to make during your divorce are some of the most difficult of your entire life. You have to make arrangements for where your children will live and how you and your ex will take care of them, divide up your marital property (and debt), give consideration to whether either of you should pay maintenance to the other, and plan for your children's financial support. Because you may end up with less money to share between you, we also give you information about welfare benefits and tax credits that you may be eligible for. This part of the book provides guidance for making all those decisions, with one important caveat – you still need the guidance and advice of your own family solicitor about how to sort out many of these matters fairly and within the law.

Chapter 10

Deciding Who Cares for Your Children

. . . .

In This Chapter

▶ Avoiding a court hearing

▶ Understanding your parental responsibilities

▶ Working out where your children are going to live

▶ Maintaining contact with your children

▶ Using a parenting plan

▶ Satisfying a judge with your child care arrangements

▶ Keeping calm when you can't agree

. . . .

Grappling with decisions about the future care of your children can consume every ounce of your patience and resolve. If negotiating your arrangements seems about as likely as winning the lottery, we offer some encouraging statistics. Estimates show that over 80 per cent of all divorcing parents negotiate their own arrangements – by themselves, with the help of a mediator or with legal help – and the chances are you can too.

The law is clear in all decisions about children at the time of divorce: *your children's best interests must be paramount.* These decisions aren't questions of who wins or loses, but what's best for your children. Put aside any longings and fears for yourself as a parent while you think about your children's needs. Try to take a cool look together at what suits your children best.

Deciding for Yourselves

If you have children, you don't stop being parents just because your marriage has ended. If you and your spouse can decide one thing and one thing only in your divorce, decide how you're going to care for your children. Here we offer you just a few of the reasons why you – and not a judge – need to make these decisions. (More information on negotiating your own divorce terms outside a courtroom is provided in Chapters 14, 16 and 17.)

- ✔ **If you do go to court, you have no guarantee that you'll get the arrangement you want.** The judge may make no order or a different order from the one you were hoping for.

- ✔ **The courts are reluctant to make decisions about children unless it's absolutely necessary.** A judge or sheriff asked to make a decision about a child tries a number of alternatives to a court decision to settle the dispute between you. Have a look at the section 'Finding a Way Forward When You Can't Agree' later in this chapter for some of the options.

- ✔ **No matter how well intentioned they may be, because of their caseloads, most family court judges can devote only a very small amount of time to making these important decisions.** The judge usually thinks you know your children best and therefore encourages you to make the decisions.

- ✔ **In England, judges rely on the advice of a family court adviser (a *Cafcass officer*) and in Wales a family proceedings officer.** If a serious dispute with irreconcilable claims by each parent arises, the family court adviser may interview other people in your children's lives, such as teachers or grandparents, before reporting back to the judge. The procedures in Scotland are different – see later.

- ✔ **A serious court battle can become extremely costly, stressful and time-consuming, and have long-lasting effects.** One reason for the great amount of money and time involved is the testimony of any experts who are asked to give their opinions. Chapter 15 has more on legal aid.

- ✔ **Members of your extended family, friends, associates, people in your children's lives, and others may be brought into court.** Your children may have to be seen by the Cafcass officer or even by the judge. (In the Principal Registry of the Family Division, the biggest family court in London, and some other family courts, judges routinely see children who are over nine years old.)

Of the estimated 80 per cent of divorcing couples who come to a negotiated agreement about their children, many start off thinking they're going to wage a battle. But either they lack the financial resources to do so or deliberately avoid such a battle for fear of the emotional harm a court hearing would have on their children.

Understanding Parental Responsibility – Much More than Just 'Custody'

The law regarding children radically changed in 1989 when it shifted from talking about parental *rights* over children to talking about parental *responsibility* for children. (Refer to Chapter 4 for more about the legal aspects of parenting.) As a result, making decisions about your children requires you to think and act on two levels:

✔ How you and your ex are going to continue to be responsible for the big decisions for your children.

✔ How you're going to arrange for your children's day-to-day care.

Day-to-day arrangements are now referred to as *residence* and *contact* instead of 'custody' (or 'care and control') and 'access'. Not only have the words changed, but also the concepts behind them. The law encourages people not to treat children as possessions to be fought over, but as human beings and citizens in their own right. Overlooking your children's needs and desires is all too easy if you end up locked into a fight over possession of them.

Despite the change in legal terms, the media continues to refer to 'custody' and 'access' and most people still use those terms. They're no longer used in court and you're unlikely to hear them used during your divorce proceedings. Because you want to sound as if you know what you're talking about when you walk into your solicitor's office, we don't use them either.

The law expects you and your ex-spouse to continue to be responsible for your children after your divorce. Parental responsibility means that you share obligations for the big decisions concerning your children's home, education, discipline, financial support, medical care, choice of name and religion, and other important matters. Sharing this responsibility means that you have to be able to talk to each other after your divorce is over.

If in practice you decide to share decision-making authority about some things but not others, avoid conflict and misunderstanding after your divorce by clearly spelling out the areas of shared decision making. For example, you may agree that you'll both decide on your children's non-emergency medical or dental treatment only when the treatment involves invasive procedures, or about any psychiatric and psychological treatment, or that you'll share decision making when the time comes to consent to your children getting married or enlisting in the armed forces before they're 18.

Only rarely is parental responsibility ever removed by a court from a parent. At present other adults such as a step-parent or grandparent can only acquire parental responsibility if they have an adoption or residence order – that is, an order that the child live with them.

Deciding Where Your Children Are Going to Live

As well as being responsible for the big decisions about your children's lives, you also need to arrange for their day-to-day care. You're required by law to decide *residence*, or where your children are going to live, and *contact* – how they'll keep in touch with their non-resident parent. As with other decisions about their lives, your children's needs come first. Deciding arrangements is like a jigsaw – you must fit together a number of very different pieces in some sort of order. Some of the pieces to take into account are:

- ✔ Your children's needs and way of life
- ✔ Your and your ex-spouse's working lives and the amount of time you have to spend with your children
- ✔ Your soon-to-be-divided pot of money
- ✔ Your future separate housing

Consider who did what in your family before you and your spouse decided to separate and then see what has to change.

Staying primarily with one parent

Almost gone are the days when judges assumed that mothers were the only ones to look after small children. Many men take a much greater part now in the day-to-day care of their children, before and after divorce. In most cases after divorce or separation, however, children still spend more of their time with one parent than the other – usually their mother. About 10 per cent of fathers live with their children after divorce.

If you decide that living primarily in one place with one parent suits your children, you'll probably agree, as most parents do, that they must see their other parent as often as they need. No child wants to lose a loving parent. However, every family is different and you need to think through how things are going to work best in your situation.

Having your children live with you all or most of the time and being responsible for making the day-to-day decisions about their lives makes sense if your spouse can't be actively involved with them after your divorce. But be aware that having your children living with you all the time can be fraught with problems, especially if your spouse ends up with very limited contact but would have preferred to be a more involved parent after your divorce. Bear in mind some of the potential consequences of being a non-resident parent:

✔ When the children live with one parent, non-resident parents often feel excluded from their children's lives.

✔ About 40 per cent of non-resident parents slowly drift away from their children, especially if they remarry and start new families. When that happens, the divorced couple's children no longer have the benefit of a relationship with two birth parents and their extended families; and the non-resident parents often come to feel that they are no longer necessary to their children.

✔ Some non-resident parents begrudge paying child support if contact is more limited than they want.

Then again, the resident parent's situation isn't always a bed of roses. Consider the following:

✔ You may find, as most parents on their own can tell you, that shouldering all or most of the day-to-day responsibilities of raising children can be a tremendous burden – particularly if you're working full time or going to college. Juggling child care, work and college, not to mention housekeeping and keeping your garden tidy, all on your own, can leave you feeling completely drained at the end of each day.

✔ You may have little quality time to give your children, much less any time for yourself.

✔ Your children may spend more time in day care, after-school care or at home by themselves than when you were married and your spouse helped out. In such situations, some children end up doing more of the cooking and housework and playing parent to their younger siblings.

Whether you're a resident or non-resident parent, it's not an easy road. You can find advice and information on how to manage alone with your children from the One Parent Families/Gingerbread Helpline on 0800 018 5026 and they also have a good website: www.oneparentfamilies.org.uk.

You can also check on the website whether a branch of One Parent Families/ Gingerbread operates in your area. This self-help organisation gives support to parents on their own with children. (J.K. Rowling of Harry Potter fame is its President.)

If you're a resident of Scotland and are looking for some more local help, try the One Parent Families Scotland website at www.opfs.org.uk. The helpline is 0808 801 0323.

Non-resident parents often feel a sense of loss – of control, intimacy, routine and role. However, if you communicate with your ex-spouse, you're much more likely to maintain close relationships with your children.

Coping with being a non-resident mother

Although they're in the minority, some mothers don't seek to have the primary care of their children. Whatever the reason for not being the resident parent, many non-resident mothers say that they find the community around them less understanding in this situation than towards non-resident fathers. MATCH (Mothers living Apart from Their Children) has a good website (www.matchmothers.org) and you can write to its email address: enquiries@matchmothers.org.

Staying in contact as a non-resident father

A researcher wrote that divorce 'splinters fatherhood into many fragments' when fathers become non-resident parents. As a non-resident father, you have three options for handling your relationships with your children and your ex-spouse:

✔ Lose contact with both your children and your ex.

✔ See your children but have no contact with their mother.

✔ Keep in contact with your children and with your ex.

Contact the Parentline Plus Helpline on 0808 800 2222 or visit its website at www.parentlineplus.org.uk for more information. You can also contact Families Need Fathers on its website: www.fnf.org.uk.

Good Relationships Make Good Contact

Recent research by Liz Trinder and colleagues at the University of East Anglia looked at the way patterns of contact vary and why. In a detailed study of 60 families, they found that fortnightly contact was the most common, closely followed by weekly – these two forms of contact occurred in half of the families. In the remaining families, contact was more frequent in 13, less frequent in 11, but halted altogether in only 6 families.

But the really interesting finding is what made contact work or not work. The researchers say: 'There is no single factor that makes contact work or not work, but instead a wide range of factors at different levels', as follows:

✔ **Direct Factors:**

- Commitment to contact by resident and contact parents and children

- Clarity and agreement about parental roles

- A good relationship between parents and between parents and children

✔ **Challenges:**

- Nature of the separation
- New adult partners
- Financial support/child support
- Logistics: time, money, distance
- Parenting styles/quality
- Risk/safety issues

✔ **Other Factors:**

- Beliefs about contact
- Empathy and insight and ability to compromise
- Influence of other people - wider family, friends, legal advisers, mediators, counsellors

✔ **Time:**

- Children's ages and stages
- Time after separation.

The other really interesting thing is that they found a connection between the commitment to contact and the quality of the relationships between all those involved – both parents and children. Good relationships make good contact. Poorer relationships lead to a weakening of the commitment to contact, which in turn can lead to a further deterioration in contact.

Living in two households

Increasingly parents choose to share the day-to-day care of their children on a more equal basis. You may hear this called 'shared care' or 'shared residence'. Both terms are correct and we use them interchangeably. (See Chapter 4 for more on these terms.)

If you don't want your children to live with one parent and just visit the other, think creatively. Can you share out their care between you in a different way?

The benefits and pitfalls of sharing day-to-day care

The benefits of sharing care with your former spouse are obvious: your children get to maintain their relationships with both of you, and you both remain actively involved in your children's lives. Nevertheless, sharing care has some potentially serious drawbacks, including the following:

✔ **Shared residence is relatively expensive.** You and your former spouse both need to provide your children with a place to sleep and a place to store their clothes and other belongings when they are at each of your homes (unless you want them living out of suitcases and boxes). Plus, you each have to provide your children with separate sets of clothing, toys and other items that they use regularly.

✔ **Your children may prefer to live with one of you most of the time.** By the time your children reach adolescence, they may get frustrated with switching back and forth between homes. Living in one place gives your children ready access to all their belongings – and their friends always know where to find them.

✔ **You and your spouse must communicate and co-operate with one another much more than you do if the children are living with one of you most of the time.** You still have to put aside your differences and work together to agree certain rules and regulations for your children so that when they're with either parent, the same basic rules apply.

✔ **Shuffling back and forth between your home and your ex-spouse's home can be hard on some children.** This is especially true for very young children, because they may feel constantly unsettled. They often think of 'my mum's house' or 'my dad's house' but have trouble with the idea of 'my house'.

One for you, one for me – splitting up siblings

Rarely do siblings live in different homes. However, sometimes older children want so much to stay in their own homes and schools with their friends that they stay with whichever parent is living there or nearer, even if the parent moving out is going to be looking after the rest of the children. If you decide to separate your children from their siblings, this is likely to be for such special reasons. Halving the number of children between you in order to be fair to you both is not a good reason!

For most children, not living with both parents in the same house after a divorce is hard enough, but separating siblings from each other can feel cruel to them. Nevertheless, separating your children may just make sense in certain situations – for example, if a child needs special attention from one of you during a difficult time.

Although you can change the residence arrangement at any time if you agree to do so and the change is in your children's interests, a judge decides whether the change is merited if you and your ex don't see eye to eye. Most judges are reluctant to alter a residence arrangement unless the children's best interests are at risk.

Making shared care work

To make shared residence arrangements work, you and your spouse must do something that you may have had a hard time doing recently while married – get on with each other! To determine whether you and your spouse have what it takes to manage sharing your children's day-to-day lives while living separately, read the following rules:

✔ **Avoid post-divorce warfare.** Arguing over your children can be emotionally devastating for both you and them. When you do have disagreements about your children, talk things out. Don't shout them out, especially when your children are within earshot.

✔ **Don't use your children to try to get back at your former spouse.** Your marriage is over – it's time to move on. If you can't forgive and forget, you have no business sharing their care.

✔ **Respect one another's parenting abilities and styles.** You may not like the way that your ex-spouse parents your children but unless she endangers the children or unless you have good reason to believe that she is harming their emotional, scholastic or sexual development, how your ex-spouse acts as a parent is up to her. Plus, if you criticise your ex's parenting abilities, you can expect to hear some criticism of your own parenting.

✔ **Support one another's efforts to discover new parenting skills.** Even if you were both active, involved parents, each of you probably had primary responsibilities for certain things – one of you may have got the children dressed in the morning and prepared their lunches whereas the other helped with their school projects and got them ready for bed. Now you may have to discover new skills so that you can do all those things you used to share.

✔ **Agree on a schedule for when the children are going to live with each of you and stick to it.** Children depend on predictability. At the same time, don't be inflexible.

✔ **Mind your own business when your children are with their other parent.** Don't check up to find out what time your ex-spouse got the children to bed, what they ate for dinner, or to tell your ex what the children should wear to school the next day. Your ex-spouse is in charge of your children when they are at her home.

✔ **Support one another as parents.** Don't let your children play one of you off against the other in order to get what they want, and don't criticise your ex-spouse in front of your children.

Consulting your children

If your children are mature enough to know their own minds and especially if you and your ex-spouse are planning to share their care, you may need to consider their preferences. Your children may have already let you know what they think, directly or indirectly, but if they haven't and you want to know their feelings on the matter, talk it over with them. Decide beforehand whether to talk with them together with your ex-spouse or separately.

Residence decisions and their financial implications

Several generous state benefits and tax credits are available to supplement the income of families with children. See Chapter 7 for a summary of these benefits. However, the agencies that administer the benefits and credits do not share them equally between you even when you and your spouse are sharing the care of your children equally. HM Revenue and Customs, for example, pays the tax credits to the person who receives the Child Benefit, and that's usually the mother unless you agree otherwise.

CMEC (which is replacing the Child Support Agency over the two years from 2008 to 2010) treats the person who receives the Child Benefit as the parent with care, and requires the other parent to pay child support at the rate of 50 per cent of the full liability even though you may be sharing their care equally. If you have just one child, only one of you is able to claim the Child Benefit, but if you have more than one, you and your spouse may agree that you claim the Child Benefit for at least one child each. In that way you may each be able to claim the full range of benefits and credits and eliminate the need to pay each other child support. Most benefits and credits vary in amount according to the number of children you have living with you and your income, so you may need help working out what arrangement is best for you and how to maximise your income in this way. Your local Citizens Advice Bureau should be able to advise you. You can find its details in your local phone book or at www.citizensadvice.org.uk.

In Scotland, the Children (Scotland) Act 1995 expressly requires you – and the courts, if they have to make decisions about a child – to consult your children about your plans and take into account their views regarding decisions being made about them. If your children are old enough for the court to think they're capable of understanding and you've raised an action in court that directly affects them, they'll most likely receive a notice from the court about the action. This notice includes an invitation for your children to express any views to the sheriff on an 'F9' form. Their views are usually kept confidential by the sheriff, but they may be disclosed in court. A child over 12 is considered capable of conducting proceedings alone unless the facts show otherwise. Your child may therefore become a third party in court in a dispute between you and your spouse. In addition, any child – usually (but not necessarily) over the age of 12 – may instruct a solicitor to act on her behalf, and may apply to the Scottish Legal Aid Board for financial help to do this.

Despite good intentions, research has shown that many parents don't manage to talk to their children about their plans and many children regret this later on. You can put options to them, and you must pay close attention to their reactions and listen carefully to their views. Remember that some children – even older ones – avoid such situations and you may find it easier to talk while doing something together, such as cooking dinner or walking the dog. Make the occasion as easy as you can. When you do talk to your children about residence arrangements, keep the following things in mind:

- ✔ **Your children may automatically say 'you', when you ask them directly who they want to live with, because they don't want to upset you.** They may also feel that they're rejecting one parent by choosing the other. Make clear that it is your responsibility to weigh up all the factors and make a decision, but that you do want to hear what they have to say about their future.

- ✔ **Your children may base their ideas on unfounded assumptions.** For example, they may think that they'll be able to get away with more if they live with the parent they perceive as a lax disciplinarian or as more indulgent. They may believe that one of you has an emotional need to live with them and will put 'your' needs before their own.

  Also be sure that your children's preferences are not the product of revenge. For example, if you're leaving the marriage for someone else and your children know about it, they may want to stay with your ex-spouse out of loyalty to her and frustration with you.

- ✔ **Your children may tell your spouse the exact opposite of what they tell you, if you choose to talk to them separately.** Whether they're saying what they think you each want to hear or they're playing you off against each other, you and your ex-spouse may hear different things from the children. The best remedy for this problem is to keep the lines of communication open between you and your ex.

- ✔ **Your children trust you.** Avoid bribing your children into spending more time with you by making glorious promises about what their lives will be like if they do, and avoid making your children feel guilty by telling them how sad and lonely you'll be if they don't choose to be with you more often. When, not if, they realise that you manipulated them, they won't be able to trust you in the same way.

- ✔ **Your children love both you and your ex-spouse.** Don't criticise your ex in front of your children no matter what you feel. Your children don't need to hear what you think of their other parent. If you need to vent any anger or bitterness towards your ex, talk to anyone other than your children.

- ✔ **Your children very much want to please you, which means that you have to recognise if they're telling you what they think you want to hear, or whether they're saying what they really feel.** Try to avoid asking them outright who they want to live with until they're old enough and mature enough to assess honestly what they really want and feel comfortable communicating that information to you.

Have a look at Chapter 16 for how mediators can help you consult your children if you're having problems doing it on your own.

Keeping in Contact with Your Children

You and your ex-spouse may decide that sharing day-to-day care isn't the best option for your children and having them live with one of you most of the time is the way to go. If your children live mostly with one of you, you and your ex have to work out the arrangements for contact between the children and their non-resident parent. The legal term for a child's right to keep in touch with their non-resident parent is *contact*.

Contact usually means that children see their non-resident parent on a regular pre-arranged basis, perhaps weekly or fortnightly, by visiting or staying overnight, as well as on some bank holidays, birthdays and maybe during part of their school holidays. You may develop more flexible arrangements as the children become more independent, depending on how near to each other you live. If you and your spouse work out your own arrangements for your children, you can agree to anything you want so long as it is in the children's best interests. However, because a certain amount of planning is usually necessary, contact generally takes one of the following forms:

- **Staying contact:** Children stay overnight with their non-resident parent – usually in that parent's home on pre-arranged days and times and often at an agreed frequency, for example on alternate weekends.

- **Visiting contact:** The children meet their non-resident parent, often at that parent's or a relative's home, usually for an agreed period of time on a regular day and at a pre-arranged frequency, for example every Sunday.

- **Supervised contact:** The children meet their non-resident parent somewhere that is supervised by the other parent, or by an agreed or court-approved adult, for example a grandparent or a member of staff in a Contact Centre. (For more about Contact Centres, see the sidebar 'Using a contact centre' later in this chapter.) Supervised contact, when it takes place, is usually ordered by the court.

- **Indirect contact:** Children keep in touch with their non-resident parent by means of letters, presents, telephone calls, emails and so on, without physically meeting.

These options for contact carry with them decreasing degrees of closeness. You may opt for a mixture of them all or change between them at different times – for example, cooling contact a bit if a new partner comes on the scene or intensifying contact if your child misses her non-resident parent a lot or needs some special time. You must agree any arrangements beforehand with your ex-spouse if they're to work well for the children.

Arranging for your children to stay close to both of you is vital to their short- and long-term well-being. The only proviso under the law is that the contact must be *beneficial* to the child. (See the section 'Allowing indirect contact only' later in this chapter.) Indirect contact may be preferable if direct contact isn't beneficial, unless unusually strong reasons exist for a court to stop the relationship altogether – which is rare.

Contact can be hard to arrange if you end up living a long way away from your ex-spouse. Seeing your children at your ex-spouse's home may seem the only option but this works only if you have a good relationship with each other. Spending the time with your children in some other way may be better. (For the financial costs of contact, see Chapter 13.)

You don't have to fall into the conventional picture of a dad meeting his children at *McDonald's* for a quick Happy Meal. But then again, maybe you don't have anywhere else convenient to meet or you haven't used enough imagination! Or maybe your children love it! Where you see your children doesn't really matter, as long as you're spending your time together well.

Making your arrangements work for your children

Study after study shows that children do well when they have the affection and attention of both parents. They may, however, suffer long-lasting emotional, developmental and personal damage if their parents continue to act out their negative feelings toward one another after the divorce.

Positive male and female role models help your children develop into well-adjusted adults. Therefore, for their benefit, do what you can to help ensure that your children have an opportunity to maintain a strong relationship with both of you – even if you dislike or distrust each other.

The following list offers some suggestions for how to help maintain a positive relationship between your children and your ex:

✔ Agree on a visiting schedule that's as generous as possible. Also, let your older children have some control over when they spend time with their non-resident parent. Keep a record of the plan in both homes where it's easy to spot, perhaps on the fridge door.

- ✔ If you're the resident parent, encourage your children to phone their other parent, but let them have some say in when and how often they do so. They should be able to share their good news and their concerns, to get that parent's advice, or to get help with homework. Phoning shouldn't become a chore, duty or only for bad news.

- ✔ If you're the non-resident parent, try to agree a schedule for when to phone your children so that the calls are looked forward to and your ex-spouse doesn't feel that they're disruptive.

- ✔ Make sure that you both see school reports and share out homework assignments or projects whenever you can.

- ✔ Make sure that both of you attend parent-teacher events.

- ✔ When you take photos of your children, get extra copies made for your ex-spouse or send copies by email.

- ✔ If you're the resident parent, let your ex-spouse know the dates and times of your children's school plays and athletic events.

- ✔ Invite your ex-spouse to your children's birthday parties, and to share other important dates with you and your children.

Encouraging your children and your ex-spouse to maintain a good relationship can be tricky, especially when you don't have a good relationship with your ex. Here are some tips for avoiding points of tension:

- ✔ Don't try to shut your ex-spouse out of your children's lives by placing needless restrictions on their time together.

- ✔ Let your ex-spouse know of any big changes in your life – like a new partner moving in. Don't let your children tell her first if you can avoid it.

- ✔ Let your ex-spouse know well ahead of time when you plan to take your children away for the weekend or on holiday.

- ✔ Keep your ex-spouse informed of your children's medical problems.

- ✔ Consult your former spouse about the important decisions in your children's lives.

- ✔ Do not have arguments on the doorstep.

- ✔ Don't pass angry messages in written notes for your children to deliver. Your children may get curious and have a read, and if they don't, they still find it hard when their other parent opens the note!

- ✔ Take care when you phone your ex. If you want to sort something out with your ex-spouse and you think a row might take place, make the call after bedtime. Imagine what it's like for your children to listen to one half of the row.

✔ Don't argue at the school gate. Your children are sure to be mortified if you do so in front of their friends or teachers.

✔ Don't forbid your children to spend time with your ex's new partner. If you do, you force your ex-spouse to do things without your children, which can add to the stress they may already be feeling.

Remember that the worst experiences for children after divorce are losing contact with a loved parent and experiencing conflict between you – especially unresolved conflict and conflict involving them.

Tackling potential contact problems

Regrettably direct contact can sometimes become a sensitive issue for you, even with a court order. For example, as a non-resident parent, you may be tempted to deliberately return your children later than arranged, pick them up late, cancel plans to spend time with them, or withhold child support – just to get back at your ex. If you aren't the resident parent your ex-spouse may refuse to allow you to see the children or she may place unreasonable restrictions on contact. Often the only way to end this emotionally charged duel is when one of you takes the other to court.

Using a contact centre

Contact centres have been set up in many places to provide a safe place for children to meet their non-resident parent, when contact may otherwise be harmful or upsetting for the child. For example, it may be a good idea for you not to meet your ex-spouse at the time of contact, so you can arrive and leave the contact centre at different times. Being together with your children in a contact centre, which is friendly and has a whole range of toys and facilities for making drinks and even meals, can be a more positive experience for both you and your children than walking round the playground.

Most of these centres are run voluntarily. The contact centre staff, sometimes with the help of a Cafcass officer, work out with you how to make contact enjoyable for your children. They may also be able to provide for supervision if a court order requires it. Contact centres have a protocol for how they can best be used. In England and Wales, the National Association for Child Contact Centres (NACCC) makes clear that they offer safe contact and are available when no other solution is possible (contact them at www.naccc.org.uk or by phone on 0845 450 0280). In Scotland, contact centres are connected with Family Mediation Scotland; www.relationships-scotland.org.uk.

The judge sees contact as your child's right, not a right of either parent to have or bar. In most cases, the judge is very keen to make contact work if it's likely to be beneficial and safe for the children, and she may ask a Cafcass officer (family court adviser or family proceeding officer) to help determine if this is the case. The judge may order supervised contact if she feels that the well-being of your child warrants this. Supervised contact may take place at a *contact centre*. Note that going to court to try and make your non-resident ex-spouse see her children rarely serves any purpose.

Deciding if contact puts your children (or you) at risk

If your ex-spouse has threatened you or your children with violence or abuse, or you've experienced it, you must tell the judge, who investigates the risk before deciding whether or not to stop or continue contact. Cafcass should anyway have picked up this information from court forms before you even get to court. They make enquiries and inform the judge.

A judge can order that a contact centre is used if she thinks contact should still take place. Evidence suggests that contact can sometimes trigger episodes of violence that can be dangerous to you and frightening to your children. You must take threats seriously and report them to the Cafcass officer (if one is involved), your solicitor, or your local authority Children's Services Department Child Protection Team, which has a duty to investigate. See Chapter 2 for more on dealing with threats and abuse.

Some non-resident parents feel that their ex-spouses have denied contact unreasonably and even alienated their children from them. This situation is the time to be honest with yourself when you're the parent with care, in case your anger and hurt is governing your temptation to refuse to allow contact, instead of genuine fear for your own or your children's safety.

Allowing indirect contact only

When you have good reason to believe that your ex-spouse, the non-resident parent, may harm or endanger the children, contact *should* be restricted or even prohibited. Indirect contact can consist of letters and cards, or phone conversations, email and text messages, as long as these haven't been forbidden by the court. Indirect contact may be ordered in situations in which the non-resident parent has a history of the following:

- Mental, physical or sexual child abuse
- Child neglect
- Criminal activities
- Mental or emotional instability
- Alcohol or drug abuse
- Exhibiting explicit sexual behaviour in front of children

If allegations of abuse surface in a divorce, the court usually appoints a Cafcass officer to represent the children. This independent person conducts an investigation into the allegations and prepares a report to help the judge make the decision of whether to allow contact. When contact is restricted by the court, you may be ordered to have contact with your children at a contact centre. Sometimes indirect contact by letters and cards provides the link for the child and parent when other means are ruled out.

Some parents cruelly and maliciously use unwarranted accusations of child abuse or molestation by their spouses as a way to try to deny that parent contact with their children. If you're unfairly accused, get legal help from your solicitor or contact the Lucy Faithfull Foundation (0870 774 6354 or www. lucyfaithfull.org).

Stopping contact altogether

A big decision for a judge to make is whether contact should be stopped altogether. The important point to understand is that your children's right to contact with their non-resident parent is not for contact at all costs, but for *beneficial* contact. Research findings indicate that some mothers so much want their children not to lose contact with their fathers that they may agree to contact arrangements even though these are dangerous to themselves and the children. If you spot signs that your children are frightened of contact or they refuse to go, these signs must be taken seriously and dealt with. If you're concerned for your or your children's safety, contact your local refuge (see Chapter 2 for further information on dealing with abuse).

If you suspect your ex-spouse of child abuse

If you think that your ex-spouse is abusing your children, talk to a solicitor immediately. The solicitor can advise you of the appropriate steps to take, which may include any of the following:

✔ Contacting the police

✔ Starting criminal proceedings against your former spouse, and stopping all communication with her

✔ Asking the court to prohibit your ex-spouse from having any future contact with your child until your allegations are investigated

✔ Having your child examined by a doctor

✔ Taking photos of any unusual marks, bruises or cuts on your children that you believe are evidence of the abuse or molestation

✔ Asking the court to put pressure on your spouse to undergo evaluation and treatment for chemical dependency, alcohol abuse, psychiatric problems or anger management

✔ Reporting your allegations to your local authority's Children's Services Department Child Protection Team immediately

Burying the hatchet for your children's sake

When you and your spouse use contact as a vehicle for expressing your negative feelings for each other, you're inflicting emotional damage on your children. Children hate to see their parents fighting and, more important, tend to blame themselves for the discord. Those feelings can create many problems for your children, including a loss of self-esteem, emotional distress and even marital troubles of their own in the future.

Avoid this scenario at all costs! Your children deserve the opportunity to have both of you in their lives. Remember, a bad spouse doesn't necessarily equal a bad parent. Using your children to get back at your ex-spouse is a form of punishment for your children. You and your spouse must act like mature adults and put your children, not your hurt and angry feelings, first.

Going the Extra Mile with a 'Parenting Plan'

Like a growing number of divorcing parents, you may want to use a *parenting plan* in addition to agreements. A parenting plan is a detailed, written description of how both of you plan to be involved in the lives of your children after your divorce. In this way, your parenting plan can help you to avoid conflict and legal fights. (See Chapter 16 for how to use a parenting plan as part of mediation.)

Try using the excellent tools for developing a parenting plan provided by the Department for Children, Schools and Families. Have a look at the booklet *Parenting Plans* available at www.cafcass.gov.uk. Free copies of the parenting plan itself can be ordered from The Stationery Office on www.tsoshop.co.uk.

The parenting plan contains information on how to develop a plan and spaces to fill in to help you develop a plan of your own. You can use it as a guide and not complete it all or you can use it, as intended, as a way of spelling out how residence and contact are going to work in your situation. The parenting plan is a tool you can use with your children.

The family solicitors' organisation Resolution has produced a *My Time* chart. The A2-sized chart is aimed at children aged four to nine and is based around a two-week-to-view calendar. It comes with two different coloured dry-wipe pens so that children can see at a glance which parent they're seeing on a particular day. It includes space for writing reminders of things to tell or take to their other parent's house and special dates to remember. The *My Time* chart costs £9.50 (plus £3.95 p&p) and is available from www.encourage andpraise.com/.

Putting it all into the plan

Parenting plans spell out, in as much detail as you want, how each of you are going to be involved in your children's lives after your divorce. A good plan, such as the one recommended above, includes the following:

- **How you're going to communicate clearly with each other and your children:** How to talk about changes, how to make plans, remembering not to row or blame each other in front of your children, who explains what to your children, and listening to them.

- **What your living arrangements are going to be:** Who lives where, travel arrangements to and from your homes and who pays for what, who pays for and has the number of your children's mobile phones, setting rules for them (for instance, the rules on smoking, cycling helmets, times for bed, going out alone, and staying out late) and who baby-sits.

- **How your children are going to stay in contact with you both:** What happens when you need to postpone a visit, how to handle telephone calls, and how to keep in contact with other family members and anyone else.

- **What your children's religious or cultural upbringing is going to include:** What their religious education consists of, what arrangements to make for religious festivals, or speaking family languages other than English.

- **How to deal with plans for special days:** Including birthdays, weddings, funerals, anniversaries, Christmas, and so on.

- **Where your children are going to go to school and what to do about out of school activities:** How the school is to be informed, how both of you keep in touch with the school, how to make choices about schooling – examinations, course choices, school trips, and so on.

- **How to handle holidays:** How to agree them, travel arrangements for them, and plans for who will have the children for school in-service training days, and so on.

- **What to do about keeping your children healthy:** Who arranges dental and other check-ups, special health needs, and regular treatments, who cares for them when they're ill, and what to do in an emergency.

- **What to do about pets.**

- **How to review your plans from time to time.**

Improving your living arrangements with a parenting plan

A parenting plan can be useful to you for a number of reasons. A good plan does the following:

- Provides a visible arrangement that you all – parents and children – can see.

- Helps you and your ex-spouse to be more realistic about the amount of time and energy you need to care for your children on a day-to-day basis as single parents.

- Encourages you to get all your post-divorce parenting issues out on the table (acknowledging those issues and resolving them together, before your divorce is final, is best).

- Minimises the potential for post-divorce strife by helping you anticipate and resolve potential areas of conflict before they develop, and by spelling out on paper, before you're divorced, every detail that may make or break your agreement.

- Lets you establish mutually agreed procedures for resolving any post-divorce conflicts that develop relating to your children.

- Allows you and your ex-spouse to express your long-term goals for your children. For example, your parenting plan can state the following goals: 'It is our goal to support our children to the fullest extent possible in their school and extracurricular activities' or, if you're committed strongly to some issue, 'It is our goal to limit the amount of time our children spend watching TV and playing computer games, and to encourage outdoor activities, reading and conversation to the fullest extent possible'.

Making the plan flexible

If you and your spouse negotiate a parenting plan, avoid making your plan so rigid and inflexible that it can't bend and change to meet the developmental needs of your children. Remember that what your children need from each of you changes over time, depending on their personalities and their ages.

Your plan must also be flexible enough to respond to the changing circumstances in your own lives. That flexibility may include changing when or how often your children spend the night at your home and appropriately passing more of your decision-making responsibilities to them as they grow. These and other plan adjustments may be necessitated by changes in your professional lives, a serious illness or accident, changes in your living situation or finances, or changes in your children's needs.

Satisfying the Judge about Your Arrangements

Your divorce can't be granted until a family judge considers the arrangements for your children and decides that they are satisfactory. You or your solicitor specify the arrangements in a separate statement when you file your petition for divorce. You may base the arrangements on your Memorandum of Understanding (the concluding document; see Chapter 16 for more information on what this covers) developed in mediation, or on your parenting plan. If the judge is satisfied, she grants what's called a *Section 41 certificate* or *certificate of satisfaction*. You don't normally need to go to court for this, but if you can't agree or if the judge isn't satisfied with your suggested arrangements, a date is set for a court hearing.

In Scotland, if your children are under 16 when you decide to separate or divorce, you as parents can decide between you what arrangements are best for them, though you're required to take into account their views depending on their age and maturity. A child over 12 is presumed to be sufficiently mature, but younger children's views must also be considered. (Refer to the section 'Consulting your children' earlier in the chapter for more details.) If you can't agree on the arrangements and use a court, any arrangements the court makes for your children are governed by the principles of the Children (Scotland) Act 1995. This Act is based on similar principles to the Children Act 1989, which applies in England and Wales. Chapter 4 gives you more information about the Children Act 1989.

Finding a Way Forward When You Can't Agree

You and your spouse being at loggerheads over the arrangements for your children is understandable. After all, your decision making may be complicated by any number of things going on in your head:

- ✓ Fear that you may be squeezed out of your children's lives if you don't participate equally in all ways on decisions regarding them
- ✓ Guilt over how your divorce may affect your children
- ✓ Anger at your spouse
- ✓ Concern that if you don't see your children every day, your influence in their lives may diminish or they won't be well cared for

✔ Worry that over the coming years you're going to miss out on the special moments in your children's lives

✔ Fear that if a new man or woman comes into your spouse's life, that person will try to take your place when you're not around

If you and your spouse can't agree on the best way to care for your children, putting the issue in the hands of a judge is not your only alternative. You can try mediation to help you plan as parents together, even if you aren't on good terms. (In fact, if you apply in England and Wales for financial assistance from the Community Legal Service (legal aid) you're required to attend a meeting with a mediator to see if mediation is suitable before being granted financial aid for a solicitor or barrister to represent you in court.) Even if you take your case to court, you may still be referred to an out-of-court information meeting about mediation. (Chapter 16 explains how mediation works.) If you take up the option of mediation, research shows that you're very likely to agree arrangements for your children.

If your case goes to court, the judge will almost certainly ask a Cafcass officer to talk to you about your arrangements for your children and to report back immediately to the court on the meeting. The Cafcass officer tries to get you to resolve your dispute (called conciliation). Sometimes attendance at court can trigger a settlement. Your solicitor and barrister should also work together to find a solution while you're at court.

If you take your case to court in Scotland, the courts aren't allowed to make orders relating to your children unless absolutely necessary. Any sheriff who is asked to make a decision about a child can try a number of alternatives to a court decision to settle the dispute between you:

✔ **Refer you to a family mediation service for information about that service.** You're still free to decide whether or not you want to try mediation to help you to reach agreement with your spouse about your children. The sheriff can refer you to mediation at any stage in the proceedings.

✔ **Ask for a report on your family circumstances and those of any children from a person known as a reporter.** This report provides extra information to help the sheriff make a decision based on the welfare of your children. When the reporter interviews you, your ex-spouse and your children, a solution may become possible. The reporter can explain this in the report or can make recommendations to the sheriff about how the situation can be resolved.

✔ **Hold a child welfare hearing, which both you and your ex-spouse, as parents, must attend.** The sheriff takes an active role and may use this hearing to see what possible basis may exist for agreement between you and your ex. If your children have indicated a desire to express their views, they usually attend the hearing.

✔ **Must hold an options hearing before a case goes to proof – when evidence is led by both solicitors at a formal court hearing.** Like the child welfare hearing, the sheriff takes an active role and seeks any possible routes to agreement on the disputes between you and your ex-spouse as parents.

Preparing for a court hearing

Before you go to court, think twice (and maybe three or four times) about whether a court battle is *really* worth the expense and the stress it's going to create for you and your children. Maybe the time has come to settle out of court. However, for many reasons – both good and bad – some parents want to limit the time their former spouses can spend with their children after a divorce. Others want the sole right to make decisions about their children, or seek a residence order that's not consistent with the roles they've played in the lives of their children so far, perhaps to avoid paying child support.

If you're concerned that your spouse may try to limit your right to continue playing a meaningful role in your children's lives after you're divorced, or if you want to limit your spouse's involvement in your children's lives after your marriage has ended, you may be heading for a court battle. If that seems likely, you can take action now to improve your position:

✔ **Become aware of the general guidelines that judges use to make decisions about children.** The Children Act 1989 – or the Children (Scotland) Act 1995 – is the basis for decisions about children. You can find more about these Acts in Chapter 4.

✔ **Stay involved in all aspects of your children's lives.** This includes participating in parent-teacher events, taking your children to the doctor, dropping them off or picking them up from the childminder, nursery or school, being home at night to feed and bathe them and get them to bed, and helping them with their homework.

✔ **Be there for your children so that they view you as a 'go-to' parent.** They need someone they can count on for emotional, physical and psychological support and for general care giving.

Questions you can expect a judge to ask

If you take your dispute to court and it hasn't been resolved by other means, the judge, informed by the Cafcass officer, probably will consider most, if not all, the answers to the following questions before deciding on the arrangement that's in your children's best interests:

- ✔ Where are your children living now?

- ✔ What kind of relationship do your children have with each of you? To whom do they turn for help or support when they have problems?

- ✔ How did you and your spouse share parenting responsibilities during your marriage? Were you both actively involved in your children's lives – bathing, dressing and feeding them, helping them with their homework, playing with them, talking with them and helping them resolve their personal problems, attending parent-teacher meetings, taking them to their doctor's appointments, handling their emergencies, and so on?

- ✔ What arrangements do you and your ex-spouse want and can you co-operate with one another on behalf of your children after your divorce?

- ✔ Where will you each be living after your divorce and what kind of home life can you offer your children?

- ✔ Do any of your children have special educational or health-care needs? How do you and your spouse deal with them now?

- ✔ What hours do you work and does your work require you to travel? Do you think your work and travel schedule is going to change after your divorce?

- ✔ How stable are your finances?

- ✔ Do you suffer from any mental or physical problems?

Orders a judge can make

The judge is bound by the Children Act to avoid delay, and intervenes if she thinks that your children are likely to suffer from you or your solicitors dragging out the decision-making process. If you can't agree about where your children should live or how they're to see their non-resident parent, the judge can make the following orders (but remember that a judge doesn't make an order at all unless it's in your children's best interests):

- ✔ **Residence Order:** This order states with which of you your children should live.

- ✔ **Contact Order:** This order states how your children should keep in touch with the parent that they don't live with.

The judge can attach conditions to residence and contact orders if she thinks it's in your children's best interests. For example, if the judge thinks a risk of abuse or threat of violence exists, she may order supervised contact. You, your solicitor or a Cafcass officer then arranges contact at a contact centre or in the presence of some other trusted person, such as a grandparent.

If you have special concerns that you disagree upon or want to have the weight of a court order behind, a judge can make orders, in addition to those setting out residence and contact, which are in the children's best interests:

- ✔ **Specific Issue Order:** The judge can make an order to cover one specific issue. For example, the judge can order that your children should go to a specific school.

- ✔ **Prohibited Steps Order:** This order prohibits a specific thing, for instance, it may say that your children can't be taken out of the country.

- ✔ **Other orders:** The judge can make an order prohibiting any further applications for residence or contact if, for example, she considers that such applications may be thoroughly unmerited or harmful to your children. These orders are rare however.

The court doesn't like changing a child's surname unless you can show that a change is clearly going to benefit your child. Saying that you're going to remarry and you want your child to take your new surname is not sufficient.

Neither of you may get the children

Although this happens in only a very small number of cases, if both spouses have a history of child neglect or child abuse, the judge may decide that neither of the parents should have the care of the children. However, a judge doesn't consider making such a decision unless a third party – such as a social worker – raises the issue or the fact that neither spouse is fit to parent the children is undeniably obvious to the judge.

In cases such as this, the judge appoints a *children's guardian,* also known as a Cafcass officer, to represent the children in court and to help the court determine where the children should live. Often, a grandparent or another adult relative assumes temporary care of the children until a permanent living arrangement can be established.

The Local Authority Children's Services Department can enter a case if concerns exist about a child's welfare. In this case, as well as the Cafcass officer, children generally have their own solicitor representing them.

The National Youth Advocacy Service is an organisation that campaigns for children to be better represented in court. Visit their website at www.nyas. net; they also have a helpline: 0800 616 101.

If you have fears about your ex-spouse abducting your children, see Chapter 4 for guidance.

Children divorcing their parents

A child can make an application to the court herself, and receive legal aid, in certain circumstances, but the judge must first deem that the child is mature enough to do so. (The child is then called 'Gillick' competent, after a particular case brought by a Mrs Gillick.) In Scotland, a child over 12 is automatically considered competent to bring an action, and can do so under the age of 12 if of sufficient maturity and understanding.

Chapter 11

Dividing Up What You Own

In This Chapter

▶ Working out what you own

▶ Valuing and dividing up your property

▶ Deciding what to do with your home

▶ Dealing with your retirement benefits

▶ Sorting out your endowment and insurance policies

▶ Handling your debts

1 f your marriage has been relatively long and you've enjoyed a reasonably comfortable standard of living, you may be surprised when you realise just how much you've managed to collect over the years and how much everything is worth. Dividing up your property requires thought and deliberation, and possibly the advice and assistance of outside experts, because what you divvy up during your divorce has both short- and long-term financial implications for you both. The divorce court can make just one order for the division of capital and property. You get only one bite of the cherry, and so making sure that you don't miss out is a good idea.

This chapter focuses on how to handle the big stuff – your home, retirement benefits and financial investments – as well as some of the smaller items. We also give you suggestions for dealing with your debts. How you divide up your assets needs to be seen in the context of the whole picture of your financial settlement. (Chapter 12 looks at spousal support and Chapter 13 deals with child support, two other important parts of the settlement picture.) And remember that if you're in a civil partnership and want a dissolution of your partnership, this chapter applies to you as well.

Getting to Grips with Property Basics

During your marriage you may have bought a home, furniture, vehicles, computer equipment and maybe even fine art. You no doubt own other, less valuable items, too – kitchen equipment, bedding, a television, DVD player, books and bikes, for example. And, don't forget that pile of wedding gifts you've had stashed in the attic for years! Now that you're getting divorced, you need to do something with those things, too.

The less-valuable stuff you own can be divvied up rather informally. The process is usually a matter of making sure that your children have what they need, and then seeing that each of you gets your fair share of what you need to set up new households, plus taking at least some of the items that have special meaning to you. Chapter 14, which covers some of the divorce matters you can handle without the help of professionals, suggests some ways of accomplishing this division.

Distinguishing between tangible property and intangible property

In addition to the goods you own (such as vehicles and furniture), you must also take into account your *intangible property,* such as retirement benefits, stocks and bonds, when you're dividing up your property. (An intangible asset is an asset that has no intrinsic or marketable value in and of itself but instead represents or has evidence of value.) Your car, on the other hand, is *tangible property* that has value in and of itself (see the sidebar 'Placing a value on the vehicles you own' later in this chapter).

Identifying your marital property

Before you can divide up the value of your property, you and your spouse must first determine what property has to be included. The general rule in England and Wales is that you must take all property into account, regardless of whose name it's in or when it was acquired. Legally, you're each potentially entitled to a share of the value of any property that one or both of you own at the time of your divorce. That includes property acquired before your marriage, or after your separation if you've already separated, as well as all the property that you acquired during your marriage. If you haven't already done so, make a list and categorise your assets. (Chapter 7 gives you some advice on how best to do that.)

If you have a pre-marital agreement, this may include provisions for the division of your property on separation or divorce and you can keep to those provisions if you both want to do so. Pre-marital agreements are becoming more common in England and Wales. If either of you decide not to stick to the agreement, the court can enforce it only if the judge considers it fair to you both, taking into account all the circumstances; the judge always has the ultimate discretion. However, if you do have an agreement, the judge must take it into account as one of the many factors to consider. (See Chapter 21 for more information on pre-marital and post-marital agreements.)

You may agree on a division of all your major assets, only to end up with an argument over the dinner service or your family pet. Don't lose sight of the emotional and financial cost of arguing over such things, and be ready to compromise even if you've set your heart on something.

Understanding matrimonial property in Scotland

The position on property in Scotland is different from that in England and Wales. *Matrimonial property* is all the property belonging to you and/or your spouse, or acquired by either of you during your marriage and before the *relevant date* (see below for a definition of this term). Matrimonial property includes actual property – for instance, homes, caravans, holiday homes, time-share properties, endowment and insurance policies, pensions, bank and building society accounts, savings and investments, and so on – and also covers furniture, furnishings, jewellery, cars, boats and any other assets. A house or furniture bought before the marriage for use as a family home is also considered matrimonial property.

The relevant date

The date that matrimonial property is valued is called the *relevant date*. This date is the earlier of the following:

✔ The date when you and your spouse stopped living together.

✔ The date when the notice of intention to divorce – usually known as the summons or the *initial writ*, that is, the document that starts the divorce action – was served on you or your spouse.

Think of it this way: If the relevant date is 1 September and you win the lottery ten days later on 10 September, the winnings aren't considered matrimonial property – meaning you don't have to share them with your spouse. However, if you win the lottery ten days before the relevant date, on 21 August, the winnings are included as matrimonial property and are split between you and your spouse.

Exceptions to matrimonial property

Two types of assets that you can own before the relevant date aren't considered to be matrimonial property:

✔ Gifts to either of you from a third party

✔ Inheritances

So if one of your parents gave you a car, it isn't classed as matrimonial property. If your granny left you some money, it's not matrimonial property. But if you used the money you inherited to buy something for the family home, what you bought becomes matrimonial property. If you gave a gift to your spouse, it's matrimonial property.

Although only matrimonial property (or it's value) is normally divided equally between you, the court can divide it unequally in special circumstances – such as if you used inherited money to purchase a substantial item, or if you agree that something should be excluded from matrimonial property. The court also has the power to deal with items that aren't matrimonial property. Bear in mind that the court divides the net total of the property in money terms. In practice, a fair share of the total of the net assets may be more or less than half.

The net value of matrimonial property

The court looks at the net value of your matrimonial property. That means the matrimonial property (including pensions or life policies paid into during the marriage) at the relevant date, after you deduct all the legitimate debts incurred by you and your spouse during your marriage. These debts include mortgages, bank or personal loans, and outstanding transactions such as credit cards and household bills. Check with your solicitor about which debts are appropriate for consideration.

Valuing Your Assets

After you've made a list of all your property, including all property in your sole and your joint names, you need to assign a monetary value to each asset. Ordinarily, that figure is the item's *fair market value*, or what you may reasonably expect to sell the item for, assuming that you didn't *have* to sell it and that you have a willing buyer.

Although you can probably value many of your assets yourselves, you may need the help of outside experts, such as surveyors, estate agents, accountants and actuaries, to determine the worth of particularly valuable or complex assets, such as land or buildings, certain types of retirement benefits, fine antiques, a family business, and so on. You may find the services of an outside expert helpful if you and your spouse can't agree on how to value an important asset.

After you value your assets, you have to divide up their value, bearing in mind the guidelines a judge would use if such issues went to a full hearing in court, or by applying some other criteria that you and your spouse both agree to and that seems fair to you both.

When deciding which property to take from your marriage, keep in mind your personal goals for your life after divorce, and your post-divorce financial needs.

Placing a value on the vehicles you own

Determining the value of the vehicles you and your spouse own together is relatively easy and inexpensive. You can:

✔ Use one of the established car guides, such as *Glass* or *Parker*, which you can find in your local newsagent.

✔ Try www.parkers.co.uk or Google search 'used car prices'.

✔ Ask local car dealers what they would pay you for your vehicles. Because used car dealers tend to make low offers, you and your spouse may want to adjust the offers somewhat.

✔ Read the auto ads in the classifieds section of your local paper for vehicles comparable to yours, or try www.exchangeand mart.co.uk/iad/carinput.

Following the Legal Guidelines

If you involve solicitors in your property division negotiations, or if you look to a judge to decide who gets what, statutory guidelines take centre stage. The judge's personal preferences, and the persuasiveness of your solicitors, can also make a difference but the key words nowadays are 'equality' and 'fairness'. Judges in England and Wales are required to give priority to your children's needs and to consider all the circumstances including the following factors. The weight and value that the judge attributes to each factor varies from case to case and is up to the judge to decide.

✔ **How much money you and your spouse each earn now and can be expected to earn in the future.** Often, a judge awards a larger share of property to the spouse who has the lower earning potential. In evaluating your earning potential, the judge may consider your age, education level, previous work experience, physical and mental health, and other factors that may have a bearing on your ability to earn a living.

✔ **The value of any property or other financial resources that one or both of you may have.**

✔ **The financial needs, obligations and responsibilities that either of you have, or are likely to have, in the future.** That includes whether you have primary care of your children, and your respective housing needs and mortgage obligations.

✔ **Your standard of living during your marriage.** A judge usually tries to allocate income and assets between you and your spouse so that no great disparity exists between you and neither of you suffers a dramatic reversal in your lifestyle after you're divorced. In reality, however, your lifestyle may change (probably for the worse).

- ✔ **Your age and health, in particular whether either of you has any mental or physical disability.** Older spouses and spouses who are in poor health often receive a greater share of the property than younger or healthier spouses.

- ✔ **How long you were married.** The longer you were married, the more likely the court is to view you as equal partners.

- ✔ **Your individual contributions to your marriage and family generally.** The courts recognise that paying the family's bills is only one way that a spouse can contribute to the family. The courts now recognise that being a full-time parent, helping your spouse advance his career, or supporting your spouse through university and making other contributions to the marriage all have value, which although different should not be treated in a discriminatory way. Also, if one of you gave up a well-paid career to look after children, that can be taken into account. The key issues are equality and fairness.

- ✔ **The value to each of you of any benefit that either of you may lose because of the dissolution of your marriage.** The most obvious example of this kind of benefit is a pension. The law specifically requires a judge to consider your pension positions, and gives powers to the judge to *attach* or *share* death in service benefits, pension lump sum and pension income benefits between you. (See 'Dividing Up Your Retirement Benefits' later in this chapter.)

- ✔ **Your (and your spouse's) conduct.** A judge takes conduct into account only if disregarding it would be inequitable. In practice, conduct rarely makes any difference, however badly you feel your spouse has behaved towards you.

In Scotland, less emphasis is placed on factors such as what the future may hold. For instance, your marriage is considered an equal partnership and who does what doesn't affect the right to equal sharing of matrimonial property.

If you have a new partner, the judge only takes his means into account to the extent that those means affect your position, for example, when the new partner has a home that you can share or sufficient income to support you.

Money received from personal injury claims or past inheritances is taken into account (except in Scotland), but future inheritances aren't unless they're certain and likely to be received in the foreseeable future (usually within about five years).

If you've ever wondered what you'd do with that £1 million lottery prize on divorce, a Nobel Prize winner once agreed to give half of his million-dollar prize to his wife in their divorce. (By the way, he won the prize for economics!)

Working Out Your Money Matters When You Divorce in Scotland

When compared with divorce law in England and Wales, the law in Scotland has several major and important differences relating to your money and property arrangements. If you or your spouse applies for a divorce in Scotland, the key piece of legislation is the Family Law (Scotland) Act 1985 (refer to Chapter 4 for what this law entails).

The principles for valuing and dividing your property and assets (known as *matrimonial property,* described in 'Understanding matrimonial property in Scotland' earlier in this chapter), the provisions for *aliment,* also called *maintenance,* and the kinds of orders available to regulate these matters are all laid out in this Act. The Act also contains the provisions for *interim aliment* for a spouse after separation but pre-divorce, *periodical allowance* after divorce and aliment for a child. Financial support for new cases concerning children has been taken over by the Child Maintenance and Enforcement Commission (CMEC) running in tandem for the next few years with the Child Support Agency (CSA). See Chapter 13 for what CMEC and the CSA do.

Financial principles of Scottish family law

The Family Law (Scotland) Act has five main financial principles regarding divorce that you need to know:

- You must share fairly the net value of the matrimonial property.

- The court must balance your financial and non-financial contributions (or damage) to your spouse's wealth and vice versa. For example, if you work in your spouse's business for an artificially low wage or give up work and a pension to look after your children, the judge must take that into account.

- You must share fairly the burden of caring for your children aged under 16.

- If you've been substantially financially dependent on your spouse, he may have to support you for a period of not more than three years after the divorce to enable you to adjust to the loss of that support.

- If you're likely to suffer serious financial hardship as a result of your divorce (for example, when you're very ill) your spouse may have to provide for you to relieve this hardship over a reasonable period. However, this situation is the exception rather than the rule.

Financial orders in Scotland

The court in Scotland can make a number of financial orders. Here are the main ones:

- ✔ **Aliment:** The court can order a spouse to pay aliment, or child support, for a child of your marriage, but only if the Child Maintenance and Enforcement Commission, or CMEC (formerly the Child Support Agency, or CSA), can't make an assessment. For more about child support, CMEC and the CSA, read Chapter 13. Aliment may also be ordered for the interim period until your divorce has been finalised. In some circumstances you may get an award of aliment in addition to the child support assessment.

- ✔ **Capital sum:** A lump sum paid to you by your spouse. This order can't be awarded after your divorce decree.

- ✔ **Periodical allowance:** You may be ordered to pay a regular sum each week or month to your spouse after the divorce. Orders for periodical allowance are the exception rather than the rule and are made only if no other suitable remedy is available (such as a capital sum).

- ✔ **Transfer of property:** The court can order you to transfer ownership of a particular piece of property to your spouse or the other way round. Note that this order can't be awarded after your divorce decree.

The court can also make some incidental orders before or on divorce, including orders for the following:

- ✔ Valuation of property
- ✔ Sale of property
- ✔ Regulating occupation of your matrimonial home
- ✔ Regulating use of furnishings in your matrimonial home
- ✔ Setting a date from which interest is going to run on any capital sum awarded

The court can consider the following facts for you and your spouse when making these orders; they provide a fair degree of discretion (though not as much as in England and Wales):

- ✔ Health
- ✔ Age
- ✔ Earning capacity
- ✔ Child care costs
- ✔ Your needs and resources
- ✔ All the circumstances of your case

Getting Up-front Advice

If you and your spouse handle your own property division negotiations, especially when the total value of what you own together is substantial, consult a qualified independent financial adviser before you start dividing up your assets. Though you can do it on your own, we generally recommend outside help to make sure that you look thoroughly at the whole picture. (See Chapters 15, 16 and 17 about working with solicitors and mediators.)

With the help of computer models, financial services professionals can help you test various scenarios for dividing up what you own and what you owe together so that you can make strategically wise decisions. In essence, they can do a cost-benefit analysis of different property division schemes.

 Some financial advisers specialise in providing pre- and post-divorce money management advice. They can help analyse the best way to deal with not only the division of property but also child support and spousal maintenance. To find an independent financial adviser look at the Association of Independent Financial Advisers (AIFA) website at www.aifa.net/. For more information on financial advisers and to check their credentials go to the Financial Services Authority (FSA) website at www.fsa.gov.uk.

Deciding What to Do With Your Home

When everything around you is changing, you may be tempted to hold on to your home at all costs. You feel comfortable there – perhaps you spent time and energy decorating your home and doing the garden. If you have young children and you're going to be their primary carer after your divorce, you may want to stay in your own home to bolster their emotional security.

When it comes to your home, try to put your emotions to one side and approach the decision from a financial perspective. You may decide that keeping your home after you divorce isn't wise or financially realistic, or with some careful financial planning you may find a way to keep your house. The bottom line is this: Whatever you do about your home must be based on a financial decision that reflects the needs of your children and your ability to cover your costs. If you let your emotions rule, you may eventually end up losing your home because you can't afford to keep up with the mortgage payments, the bills or with essential repairs and maintenance.

Finding out what your home is worth

The least-expensive way (free in most cases) to determine the value of your home is to ask an estate agent for recent selling prices of comparable houses in your neighbourhood and how much you may get for your house. However, the agent's estimate represents an approximation of your home's value. In the end, your home is worth only what someone is prepared to pay for it.

A better method, albeit more expensive, is to engage a property surveyor to value your home. If you or your spouse apply to the court for a decision on your house and you can't agree on its value, you usually have to obtain a single independent professional valuation jointly.

Estate agent valuations tend to be imprecise. As a result, if you and your spouse both get your own valuations, the results can be quite different. *Don't* value your home based on its mortgage value. Mortgage valuations are often considerably less than your home's actual value and are mainly concerned with protecting the mortgagee's security.

If you do decide to get a valuation from an estate agent, try to obtain several valuations, say three, from different agents to make sure that you're on target.

Evaluating your options

Most divorcing couples resolve the problem of 'what to do about the house' in one of the following ways:

- ✔ Sell the house
- ✔ Keep the house
- ✔ Retain an interest in the house

Selling your home

When your home is the only asset of real value that you own, you may have to sell it so that you can both leave your marriage with some money in your pockets. You may also decide to sell because the house holds too many unhappy memories for both of you, it's too big for you to live in and maintain by yourself, or because you can't afford to keep it. A sale may be a good solution if the family home contains enough equity to rehouse you both.

If you do sell, remember that the selling price probably doesn't represent the actual amount of money you and your spouse can split between you. Most likely, you have a mortgage to pay off, selling costs and possibly other costs to deduct. If you use an estate agent to sell your home, you have to pay the agent a fee, usually a percentage of your home's gross sale price (that is, the estate agent's charges). After all is said and done, when those costs are subtracted from your home's anticipated sale price (leaving the *equity*), selling your house may not appear to be a very attractive option – but it still may nevertheless be the best one.

To understand the implications of selling your home, pick up a copy of *Buying and Selling a Home For Dummies* by Melanie Bien (2008).

Keeping your home

Taking the house as part of your property settlement is an option if you can afford to buy your spouse out or have enough other property so that your spouse can take another asset of comparable value. If your spouse agrees to transfer his interest in the marital home to you, the deeds have to be altered and any change of ownership registered at the Land Registry. (Refer to Chapter 3 for the process you need to go through to register ownership.) In turn, you probably have to secure your spouse's release from the mortgage, or give an *undertaking* – a promise to the court and your spouse – that you'll try your best to do so and will take full responsibility for the mortgage payments in the meantime.

Check out your mortgage capacity with an independent financial adviser or reputable lending institution and review the household budget you've projected for your life after divorce. You need to be sure that you can really afford to take over the monthly mortgage payments as well as the upkeep on your home. If you don't, you may have to sell your house eventually or even lose it if it's repossessed by your mortgage provider. If you haven't already developed a household budget for yourself, Chapter 3 tells you how to do so.

If your spouse keeps the home, takes over the mortgage, and then defaults on it, the mortgage holder can look to you for payment if your name is still on the mortgage deed, no matter what your divorce agreement says. This demonstrates why getting released from the mortgage is so important. Failing that, you need an *indemnity* from your spouse in the final settlement giving you the right to sue your former spouse for the money you may end up paying. However, you may have to go to court to enforce the indemnity and, even if you get a judgement against your spouse, you have no guarantee that you can actually recover what you're owed.

Retaining an interest in your home

You and your spouse may want to sell your house, but for practical reasons decide to delay the sale. For example, you may want your children to be able to live in the same home until they complete secondary school. If you have primary responsibility for your children, you can stay in the home with them, but your property settlement gives you both an interest in that property.

If you opt for this sort of arrangement, ensure that your agreement addresses the following questions:

- ✔ How much of an interest do each of you have in the home?
- ✔ At what point must your house be put up for sale?
- ✔ Who puts the house up for sale?

✔ How is the asking price determined?

✔ How are you going to pay all sale-related expenses?

✔ How do you want to divide up the net sale proceeds?

✔ If you still owe money on the mortgage, how is it paid each month?

✔ How do you want to pay the homeowner's insurance, rates and taxes?

✔ Who is responsible for the cost of minor repairs – and major ones, such as a new roof?

Specifying the regular upkeep your home requires in order to protect your investment in the property is a possible idea. You may also specify who's responsible for doing the maintenance and how often. Enforcing this provision, however, may be tough.

Advantages and disadvantages exist to retaining an interest in your home. On the one hand, it may be the only way that you can each keep an interest in the property and safeguard the needs of your children; on the other hand, one of you may have to wait quite a few years before realising your interest, and then there may not be enough to rehouse you both, plus neither of you will qualify for *social housing* (that's housing provided by the local housing authority or housing association).

Retaining an interest in your home can be done in one of two main ways: keeping it in your joint names with a *deed of trust,* or transferring it from one to the other subject to a *deed of charge* (called a *standard security* in Scotland). In the first case, you remain legal joint owners; in the second, only one of you is the legal owner. However, in each case the deed should spell out the answers to the questions above, such as the size of each share and when you're going to realise it. Either way, expressing your respective shares as a percentage of the value is usually better than as a fixed sum. This way you each benefit from any increase in the value of the property, or share the loss, proportionately.

When making decisions about your home, bear in mind that you and your spouse can agree certain things between you that the court doesn't have power to order, for example taking on a new mortgage or paying the existing one. Chapter 18 tells you more about the alternatives of settling between you or asking a judge to make the decision for you.

If your home is rented, your main option is to transfer the tenancy into one spouse's name. Usually the transfer is to the spouse responsible for the main care of the children. Make sure that you secure the transfer before your decree absolute of divorce if you're seeking a transfer into your name and the tenancy is in your spouse's sole name.

Hearing some good news about capital gains tax

The general rule is that disposal of your family home is exempt from capital gains tax (CGT) –. CGT is normally payable on any profit you make when you sell or transfer an asset such as shares or a second house. Husbands and wives can obtain CGT relief for only one house between them. If a property ceases to be your main residence before you sell it, you get a three-year period of grace for the CGT exemption.

After separation or divorce you can still claim exemption for your home if you sell it or transfer it to your spouse. If you stop living there, and transfer your home to your spouse as part of the financial settlement, you're still exempt from CGT as long as your spouse continues to use it as his main home. However, if you buy another property, you have to decide which property is going to be your *principal private residence* for tax purposes.

If, as part of your divorce settlement, you retain an interest in your property under a deed of trust on the basis that, for example, you realise your interest when your youngest child finishes school, you're technically liable for CGT. However, as long as you reach that settlement within three years of your separation, you don't have to pay any CGT. Be sure, therefore, not to delay settlement of your finances following separation.

If, as part of your divorce settlement, you retain an interest in your property under a deed of charge, you're liable for CGT when you receive your share. You can, however, claim your annual exemption (currently £9,600 each per annum) and maybe other forms of tax relief.

Always consult with your solicitor or accountant at the time of your separation for advice on your tax position, particularly if you own more than one property between you, or if you have other substantial assets. You can obtain a useful leaflet on CGT from HM Revenue and Customs – HS 281 Husband and Wife, Civil Partners, Divorce Dissolution and Separation.

Dividing Up Your Retirement Benefits

The retirement benefits you or your spouse may have earned during your marriage are treated as marital assets and are included among the assets you have to divide up. Such benefits may include:

- Occupational pension schemes, including public sector and private employment schemes

- Personal pension schemes

- State second pension (S2P)

- Retirement annuity contracts

- Stakeholder pension schemes

- Small self-administered schemes (SSAS)

- Self invested personal pension schemes (SIPPs)

- Additional voluntary contributions, known as AVCs

- Section 32 buy-out policies

You can claim the benefit of your ex-spouse's National Insurance Contributions to enhance your own basic state pension after your divorce without any loss to your ex-spouse. Write to the Department for Work and Pensions (DWP) within one month of your decree absolute, and send them a copy of your decree absolute as well as your own and your ex-spouse's National Insurance numbers. The court has no power to make orders relating to the basic state pension, although it does have powers in relation to S2P (see 'Knowing your pension options' later in this chapter).

In addition to getting state benefits from the government, you may earn your retirement benefits by working for an employer who makes a retirement scheme available to you as an optional benefit or provides it to you as an automatic perk of your job.

If you've worked for several employers during your career, you may have earned retirement benefits from each. Be sure that your list of assets reflects all those benefits.

Because of the variety and complexity of pension schemes, get advice from a pension actuary, an independent financial adviser or a solicitor – or all three – before you make any decisions about how you may adjust your pensions on your divorce. (Check out Chapter 3, which gives brief explanations of the different pensions that you may be dealing with.)

You can contact the following organisations for basic help on the different types of pensions:

- **Citizens Advice Bureau** (details in your local phone book) or visit their website at www.nacab.org.uk.

✔ **The Pensions Advisory Service (TPAS)** can give you information about any aspect of occupational, personal and stakeholder pensions. You can contact them by phone on 0845 601 2923 or visit their website at www.pensionsadvisoryservice.org.uk.

✔ **The Department for Work and Pensions** (DWP) has a specialist state pension department called The Pension Service. You can find your local pension office at www.the.pension.service.gov.uk or on 0845 606 0265.

Be aware that pensions accrued after marriage and before the relevant date (see the section 'Understanding matrimonial property in Scotland' earlier in this chapter) are always considered part of your matrimonial property in Scotland. You may be surprised by this fact, especially when you can't actually get hold of the money to divide between you! Where a pension has been earned or paid into partly before the marriage a simple formula of dividing it by the number of years before and after the marriage is used.

Finding out the value of your pension

To help you or the court decide how to deal with your pensions on divorce, you must find out their value. Assessing the value of your money purchase or personal pension scheme is fairly easy (see Chapter 3 for a definition of these types of plan). In most cases, the value is simply the amount of money invested in your plan at any given time.

To find out how much you've invested in your pension scheme, contact the pension administrator and ask for a note of the *Cash Equivalent Transfer Value* (CETV) or review your most recent summary statement. If you work in the private sector for an employer who offers an occupational pension, your employer is legally required to provide you with a summary annual report telling you the value of your pension. Similarly, the provider of your personal pension scheme should provide you with an annual statement.

If you have a final salary pension scheme, valuing it can be a rather more complicated process. (Have a look at Chapter 3 for a definition of this type of scheme.) To check the CETV produced by the pension scheme trustees, you may want to employ your own actuary to calculate the true value, particularly if the scheme is an armed forces or police pension scheme. The value of your final salary pension scheme can be affected by a number of different factors, such as whether any discretionary benefits are involved, your age and your health. Ask your solicitor or accountant for advice on whether you may need an actuarial valuation and to recommend a pension actuary if so.

Don't assume that getting the cash value of your pension scheme means that you can actually cash it in yet: you can't. The government restricts the percentage of the fund that you can take in cash, and the minimum age at which you can take it. (See 'Knowing your pension options' later in this chapter.)

Evaluating the options for dealing with your pension

When you divorce, you basically have three alternatives for dealing with your retirement benefits (they're described in the next section). When you're considering which alternative is best for you, take the whole financial picture into account, including the following:

- The value of the benefits of both your own and your spouse's pension (not only the CETV, but also what the pension income, pension lump sum and death benefits are likely to be)
- The value of your potential share of the benefits
- The value of your other family assets
- How much money you need now, and will need later
- How close you are to retirement age
- The likely costs of each option

If your participation in the pension predates your marriage or postdates your divorce, you may decide that your retirement benefits shouldn't all be taken into account in quite the same way. For example, if you've been married for ten years and a member of a pension scheme for 20 years, you can fairly argue that your spouse should have only a share in half your pension fund, not the full amount. But remember that you may have paid in more in recent years, and so the later years are more valuable. In the end, pensions are just another form of saving.

Check the actual benefits that your pension fund is likely to produce. The main benefits are:

- An income from your pension.
- A lump sum if you choose to take part of your pension in this form.
- Any benefits received by the beneficiary on the pension-holder's death.
- That you can draw benefits from your pension without retiring.

If you need help analysing your options in light of these factors, talk with a qualified financial adviser and/or family law specialist.

Knowing your pension options

You have several options when deciding what to do with your pension benefits. The most common options are as follows:

- ✔ Offsetting the benefits with other assets
- ✔ Attaching the pension benefits so you can both receive payment on the pension-holder's retirement
- ✔ Sharing the benefits on your divorce

Offsetting your pension benefits

Generally, whichever spouse has earned the retirement benefits retains all rights to them. The other spouse then usually takes an appropriate amount of other assets, such as a larger share of the house. This option is known as *offsetting* and is sometimes the cheapest way for you to deal with retirement benefits, especially when too few assets exist to go around. For this option to work for you and your spouse, you need to have enough other assets that you can use to offset the pension.

The value of your pension isn't directly comparable to the value of your other assets, such as your house, savings or car and you may need a specialist to help you come up with a fair division of them. Take these factors into account if you're planning to offset a pension against other assets:

- ✔ You can't cash in your pension until you're at least 50 years old (rising to 55 from 6 April 2010), and then the most that you can cash in is about 25 per cent of its value.
- ✔ You must take the rest of your pension fund as income – which is taxable.
- ✔ You may not live until retirement age and if you don't, you won't benefit personally from the value of the fund.
- ✔ You may find that the value of your pension fund, if it is a money purchase type scheme, goes up or down over time depending on the investment market.

Attaching pension benefits

This option provides each of you with a specified proportion of the various pension benefits when the spouse who's earning the pension benefits begins receiving them. The benefits can include the pension lump sum, the pension income or the death in service benefits. This option is available only if you have a court order for pension attachment on divorce and you have to get the approval of the pension administrators in advance. Several disadvantages apply to this option however:

- ✔ You can't earmark the state retirement pension or S2P.

- ✔ You remain dependent on your spouse, possibly decades after your divorce, because you need a spousal maintenance order if you want to share the pension income when your spouse retires.

- ✔ You have to wait until your spouse retires before you can draw your pension income or lump sum benefits.

- ✔ You lose the pension income if you remarry, although – as long as your order specifies so – you can keep the pension lump sum.

- ✔ Your pension benefits stop on the death of you or your spouse.

- ✔ You or your spouse can apply to the court to vary the order, and so you're at risk of losing the benefit.

- ✔ You may not be able to control your spouse's contributions to the pension, or to prevent him transferring the benefits to another pension fund.

Sharing your pension benefits

Sharing your benefits means that if your spouse has a pension fund, you share the value of that fund between you in specified proportions after your divorce. You still can't cash your share in, but you can invest your share in another pension fund of your choice (an *external transfer*) or keep it with the existing pension provider as your own distinct fund (an *internal transfer*), subject to the rules of the scheme(s) in question. You and your ex can share a pension only after you're divorced if you're granted a pension-sharing order and you get the pension administrator's approval in advance. Pension sharing isn't an option with the basic state retirement scheme, but it can be done with SERPs and S2P and most other kinds of pension.

Not all pension schemes allow you to make an external transfer; statutory schemes, for example, only allow an internal transfer. Conversely, not all schemes allow you to make an internal transfer. Where you have a choice, seek the advice of a qualified financial consultant.

The potential advantages of pension sharing over pension attachment are:

- ✔ You don't have to remain financially dependent on your spouse after your divorce. (So you don't need a spousal maintenance order as far as a pension is concerned.)

- ✔ You can decide when to draw the benefits (subject to your scheme's rules).

- ✔ You don't lose the pension if you remarry.

- ✔ You don't lose the pension if your spouse dies, and you can specify your own beneficiaries if you die before retirement.

- ✔ You know that your pension is safe because when the order has been made it can't be varied.

A large percentage of women in the UK don't have their own pensions or have much smaller pension funds than men, in part because women traditionally give up their careers to look after their children. If you're in this position, sharing in your husband's pension may mean the difference between living in poverty and living in comfort during your golden years.

Getting Down to Business: How to Deal with Your Joint Enterprise

If either of you owns a business or has a share in one, or if you and your spouse own a business together, its value is included in the assets to be divided between you. If you agreed to a different arrangement through a pre-marital agreement, a judge doesn't necessarily uphold such an agreement unless he considers that doing so is fair, given all the circumstances. (Chapter 21 explains how pre-marital agreements work.)

In Scotland, any business owned, or partly owned, by you and/or your spouse may be considered part of your matrimonial property (you can find the definition of this term in 'Understanding matrimonial property in Scotland', earlier in this chapter). The value of this asset is how much the business is worth on the relevant date. To determine this, you must obtain a valuation of the business at the relevant date. If you remain a partner after the relevant date, ordinary partnership law may also be involved.

If you and your spouse have both been actively involved in your business, you may find deciding what to do with it especially difficult. The idea that you may have to leave the business, shut it down or sell it can be tough to accept when your marriage is ending. On the other hand, making plans for a new career may be just what you need to get over the loss of your marriage.

Understanding your options, in a nutshell

To help you deal with the difficult decision of what to do with the business you and your spouse own, we offer you a number of options that have worked for other couples:

- ✔ **Keep the business in the hands of one spouse; the other receives assets equal in value to his interest in the business.** Usually, the spouse who takes the business is the one who has been most actively involved in it or whose skills and knowledge are most essential to its continued success. For financial reasons or if sufficient other marital property doesn't exist, the spouse who keeps the business may buy out the interest of the other spouse over time. You need to formalise the buyout in a written agreement. Also, to help secure your spouse's payments to you, placing a legal charge on his real property, on the assets of the business or on some other assets, if any exist, is a good idea.

- ✔ **Divide up the business with each of you taking a part of it.** This arrangement is practical only if you can logically divide up your business and if the division can be done without jeopardising the financial integrity of each part.

- ✔ **Sell the business and split the proceeds.** This may be your only option if all your assets are tied up in the business. However, if the continued success of the business depends on your combined skills and know-how, the business may not be worth much on the open market unless it has significant assets that would be of value to a new owner.

- ✔ **Wind up the business.** If neither of you is interested in continuing the business and you can't sell it as a going concern, winding it up is a reasonable alternative. However, to take advantage of this alternative your business's assets must have market value. *Marketable assets* can include machinery, equipment, land or buildings, or payments due to the business. Depending on the type and value of the assets you're selling, you may want to sell the assets yourself, employ a company liquidator to sell them for you (you have to pay a proportion of the proceeds) or have the assets auctioned off.

- ✔ **Keep operating your business together.** For obvious reasons, only a relatively small number of divorcing spouses who are also business partners choose this option. Most divorced spouses don't want to continue such an important and mutually dependent relationship. In fact, doing so may actually be harmful to the business.

If you worked in your spouse's business without compensation, your contribution to the business may be a factor in your financial settlement.

Assigning a value to your business

To implement any of the options just described you may have to assign a fair market value to your business. You need the following information if you want to make this determination yourself:

- ✔ Profit and loss statements for the past three years
- ✔ Balance sheets for the past three years
- ✔ Records of accounts receivable
- ✔ Records of accounts payable
- ✔ Tax returns and assessments for the past three years
- ✔ Bank statements for the past three years
- ✔ Contracts for future business
- ✔ Recent good-faith offers to buy the business, if any exist
- ✔ Purchase price(s) of businesses comparable to yours

When you're valuing your joint business, don't overlook its *goodwill value*. Goodwill consists of your business's reputation, name recognition, track record in pleasing its customers, role in the local community and other factors that make it a respected enterprise.

If you're going to leave the business you've shared with your spouse, be sure to take an active role in valuing it, or engage an independent forensic accountant or business valuation expert to value it for you. As much as you may trust your spouse, his best interest is to value the business for as little as possible – either your spouse has to pay you less if he buys you out over time, or you end up entitled to less of the other marital property.

If you can afford to do so, you and your spouse can each engage outside experts to value your business and then you can average their estimates or otherwise agree on a value. You can also arrange for a single valuation through a mutually agreed independent expert. Getting the help of an outside expert who's familiar with your particular type of business is advisable if your business is especially large, valuable or complex. However, be warned that the help of such experts doesn't come cheap.

Weigh up the risks of the business when you're considering it an asset as compared with any other assets that you're dividing between you, and don't forget to factor those risks into your settlement. Getting advice from your solicitor or accountant is advisable when you come to make decisions about businesses.

When you began your business, you and your co-owners may have decided how your share of the business would be valued if one of you decided to exit the business or sell it. Therefore, that agreement determines what your share of the business is worth, and the decision isn't one you and your spouse can make on your own.

Endowment and Other Insurance Policies

A common feature in the finances of married couples in England and Wales is endowment policies. You may have taken out an endowment policy as a savings scheme alongside an interest-only mortgage. Often this policy is considered a means of paying off the mortgage at the end of the term, maybe 20 or 25 years ahead, or on the death of you or your spouse if sooner. Premiums are paid on a regular basis, so that the cash value of the policy gradually increases, and the policy can become a significant asset. Increasingly, however, endowment policies aren't living up to their predicted targets because of the drop in the stock market in recent years, and you may now be advised to expect a shortfall between the terminal value of your policy and the mortgage that it intends to pay off.

If you and your spouse have such a policy, whether in your joint names or only in one name, you must decide what to do with it. The main options with these and any other policies that are acquiring a capital value are as follows:

- ✔ **Surrender or sell the policy.** The insurance company with whom you hold your policy has to provide you with details of the *surrender value* of your policy on request – that is, the amount the company pays you if you decide to cash your policy in. If you cash the policy in early, you don't have to pay any further premiums but you may lose the value of any bonuses. Not all policies are sellable on the open market, but if yours is, you may get slightly better value for money selling your policy rather than surrendering it. A financial adviser should be able to advise you on your options.

- ✔ **Treat the policy as paid up.** Paid up means that you don't have to pay any more premiums, but you're able to receive some benefit from the policy at maturity or on death. Part of the cash value of the policy may have to go towards maintaining the death coverage.

- ✔ **Transfer the policy from your joint names into your or your spouse's sole name.** Transferring the policy allows one of you to retain the policy as a form of investment, or as cover for the mortgage, without losing the terminal bonuses. Some policies are formally assigned to the mortgage lender, and so you may have to get the lender's consent if you want to transfer the policy to your spouse and you're retaining the mortgage.

You may also have to convert the mortgage from interest-only to repayment, so that you pay the capital and interest off together over time. Transferring an endowment policy can, however, be one way of providing your spouse with an immediate share of the family assets when you aren't able to sell the house until a later date and/or no other assets of any significance are available.

Dealing With Your Debts

If you owe more than you own, you're like countless other divorcing couples. In our credit-oriented society, your divorce may be more about dividing up your debts than about what to do with your assets. Although you can leave your marriage behind, you can't do the same with your debts. Divorced or not, the debts must be paid and you both must decide how to pay them.

Some of that debt may be *secured debt*, such as your mortgage or car loan. Secured debt is debt that you've collateralised with an asset. If you don't pay the debt, the creditor can take the asset that you put up as loan collateral. You probably also have *unsecured debt*, such as credit card debt, for example. For some of you, all your debt may be unsecured.

Unsecured debt has the potential to create a great deal of discord in a divorce because, unlike a secured debt, it's usually not associated with an asset of any significant value. In many divorces, if you agree to assume responsibility for a secured debt, you also get the asset that the debt is financing. But unsecured debts typically include the purchase of things such as restaurant meals, petrol for your car, clothing, holidays, groceries, and so on.

Tips for avoiding trouble

Here, we offer some suggestions for dealing with what is certainly an unpleasant task – figuring out what to do with your debts:

- **Pay off all your debt as part of your divorce.** This option is usually the best way to deal with debt, assuming that you and your spouse have enough ready cash or sufficient assets that you can liquidate easily. In this way you both begin your post-divorce lives unencumbered by financial obligations from your marriage. Paying off your debts also means that neither of you has to worry about how you may be affected if your ex-spouse doesn't pay the debts he agreed to pay. Remember, creditors can look to you for payment on any debts in your joint names, no matter what your divorce agreement may say.

- ✔ **Trade debt for assets.** If you can't wipe out all your debt, one of you may agree to take on more than your share of the debt in exchange for getting more of the assets – the financial equivalent of taking a spoonful of sugar to make the medicine go down – because you can afford to pay more of the debts than your spouse.

- ✔ **Take your fair share.** If you and your spouse own little, if anything, of real value, dividing up your debts may simply mean that each of you takes your fair share of the debt. For example, you may agree to pay off the balance on a credit card that was in both of your names but which you, not your spouse, used regularly.

- ✔ **Pay off your debts together after your divorce.** Avoid this arrangement – it requires too much co-operation and communication between you and your former spouse. However, if this is your best or only option, secure your spouse's obligation to pay his share of your unsecured debt (your credit card debt, for example) by placing a charge on one or more of your spouse's separate assets.

Where the law stands on your debts

When you decide the best way to deal with the money you owe, bear in mind that a judge considers the same property laws and guidelines that he applies to the division of your assets. (For an in-depth discussion of those laws and guidelines, turn to Chapter 5.) However, whenever third parties are involved the court's powers are very limited. A judge can't order either of you to pay or take responsibility for a debt to a third party. And you have to give secured creditors notice of any application you make that involves their security so that they can make representations to the court.

Chapter 12

Looking at Maintenance for You or Your Spouse

In This Chapter

▶ Understanding what maintenance means

▶ Examining the law's stand on maintenance

▶ Understanding the pros and cons of taking capital instead of maintenance

▶ Knowing when an increase or decrease in maintenance is justified

▶ Protecting yourself against the sudden loss of maintenance

▶ Considering the tax consequences of maintenance payments

*E*ven if you and your spouse concur that maintenance (also known as *spousal support* or *periodical payments*) should be included in your divorce settlement, you may have a tough time agreeing on the basic terms – how much maintenance is to be paid and for how long.

For example, if you're a husband who wants a divorce and your wife doesn't, she may bristle at the suggestion that she pay you maintenance, no matter how reasonable your request may be considering your ability to earn a living right away or at all. Or maybe as a wife, you're angry and hurt because your husband, who's a successful business owner, wants a divorce and you don't. You may retaliate by demanding maintenance, and a lot of it. You think that paying maintenance is the least that your spouse can do, given what he's doing to your life.

To deal with this issue as dispassionately as possible and make decisions that are fair to both of you, this chapter provides you with basic information about maintenance and the part it plays in divorce. Maintenance is just one part of the whole picture; you need to look at it alongside your decisions about your assets and child support (if you have children). Chapter 11 gives advice about dividing up your assets and Chapter 13 tells you about child support. The information in this chapter also applies to civil partners, but if you've never been married or had a civil partner you have no legal right to maintenance for yourself (although there's nothing to stop you agreeing that between you if you wish).

If you want to know what you can do to minimise the damage that a divorce can do to your money situation, see Chapter 3 for practical advice on managing your household finances and Chapter 7 for information on financial preparations for divorce.

What Is Maintenance and When Is It Paid?

Maintenance, *spousal support* or *periodical payments* are the payment of money by one spouse to the other after a couple are divorced. If you separate before your divorce is final, your spouse (or vice versa) may also have to pay *maintenance pending suit* or *interim periodical* payments, which simply means payments to tide you over until the final decree of divorce or final financial settlement.

The Family Law (Scotland) Act sets the provisions for the kinds of orders available to the courts for regulating these matters. This Act also includes the provisions for *aliment* for a spouse pre-divorce and *periodical allowance* after divorce. See Chapter 11 for a description of these provisions.

In generations past, unless a man paid his ex-wife maintenance, she had no way to pay her bills. Assuming that he could afford it, an ex-husband paid his ex-wife *maintenance* for her lifetime, usually by sending her a monthly cheque for a set amount of money. In reality, however, maintenance didn't last forever because the law required, and still does, that maintenance ceases if the ex-wife remarries. In almost all cases, it also ceases if the ex-husband dies (except in Scotland, where the deceased's executors have to apply to the court to terminate the allowance).

Over the last few decades, lifelong maintenance has become much rarer and judges have to consider in each case whether maintenance should be awarded or dismissed. Spousal maintenance continues to be a part of some divorce settlements – most often divorces involving wealthier couples or older couples who are ending lengthy marriages, or, as an added protection, where dependent children are involved.

In Scotland, spousal maintenance, or periodical allowance, following divorce is unusual.

Maintenance automatically ceases on the payee's remarriage, but it doesn't automatically cease on cohabitation. Today, therefore, many agreements and orders expressly provide that maintenance ceases when the ex-spouse has cohabited for a specified period of time, commonly six months.

Attitudes towards maintenance have changed as the roles of men and women in our culture have changed. Whereas maintenance used to be a standard part of most divorces, today only a small percentage of divorce orders or agreements provide for it. Furthermore, the law is gender-neutral when it comes to maintenance. In the eyes of the law, men and women are equally entitled to maintenance (in actual practice, however, far fewer men receive it).

If you do receive any maintenance, be aware that it may be for only a limited period of time. Such maintenance is intended to help you 'get on your feet' and usually lasts for a relatively short period of time, say three to five years. If you've been based at home looking after your children, you probably need time to retrain and then to earn enough to become self-sufficient. The amount and duration of maintenance payments depend on a number of factors:

✔ Your financial needs and resources.

✔ Your spouse's financial needs and resources.

✔ The value of the assets you receive in your divorce settlement.

✔ Your income and earning capacity both now and in the foreseeable future.

✔ Your education and your spouse's education level and qualifications.

✔ Your work experience and your spouse's experience.

✔ Your ages and the duration of your marriage.

✔ Your standard of living before the breakdown of your marriage.

✔ Your health and your spouse's health – both physical and emotional.

✔ The number and ages of children in your household and their physical and emotional health.

✔ The contributions that you or your spouse have made towards the family.

✔ Any other factors you want to consider if you're sorting out the terms of your divorce together, or other factors that a judge feels are relevant if that issue goes to a full hearing. Conduct is only relevant if *disregarding it is inequitable* (if serious abuse was involved, for example), and that is rare.

The approach to maintenance is premised on the assumption that most ex-spouses can, and eventually should, earn their own livings after a divorce. However, it also recognised that a woman (or a man, for that matter) may have put her own career on the back burner to raise the children or support the other spouse's career.

If your maintenance payments help your former spouse get the education needed to earn a good living, you may eventually be able to get a reduction in the amount, or a dismissal, of your spousal support payments.

In many situations, however, limiting the maintenance to a specific period of time isn't realistic. If you're middle-aged or older when you divorce and have never worked outside the home or have not done so in many years, this is particularly true. As a woman, you may have a very hard time finding good employment or even getting into the job market at all. In such cases, a maintenance agreement or order may be expressed to last during your and your ex-spouse's joint lives or until you remarry.

If you're a mother who views raising your children as a full-time job, you may face a dilemma. If you begin preparing yourself for the possibility of divorce by getting the education and training you need to be employable should your marriage end, you not only take time away from what you see as your primary job (child rearing) but you also get less maintenance when you do divorce. On the other hand, if you don't prepare yourself for the job market while you're still married, you receive more maintenance to begin with but aren't as prepared to support yourself when the maintenance ends (which it may eventually do).

Out of pride or a desire to be 100 per cent free of your spouse, don't summarily dismiss the idea of asking for maintenance. If you believe that you need time to become competitive in today's fast-changing and skill-oriented job market, your wisest course of action may be to swallow your pride and ask your spouse for financial help.

How the Courts View Maintenance

You may wonder whether maintenance is appropriate for your divorce, and the truth is, you don't have any hard and fast rules to go by. Maintenance-related decisions are made on a case-by-case basis, and no formula exists to help you decide the amount as with child maintenance (child support). As with all decisions about finances in divorce, if you don't agree on the question of maintenance between you, the judge has very wide discretion to decide on it for you, and that may include dismissing your claims altogether, or awarding more or less than you're hoping for.

A court rarely dismisses your own maintenance claims without your consent if you're the main carer of your children and the children are still dependent. However, a judge may award you only a *nominal* maintenance order such as 5p per annum. That nominal order, even though it has no immediate financial value, acts as a safety net because it allows you to apply to increase, or capitalise, the amount should you ever need to do so. (See 'Taking Capital Instead of Maintenance' later in this chapter.) However, when your maintenance claims have been *dismissed* they can't be reinstated, capitalised or varied, whether you consented to their dismissal or not. As maintenance orders are rare in Scotland, nominal maintenance orders don't exist.

If your maintenance is going to last only for a fixed period of time, the order may specify that you can't apply to extend that order. This is known as a *Section 28 bar*. If the order makes no such reference, you may be able to apply to extend the order if you think you have grounds, as long as you do so before the order expires.

When you agree to your maintenance claims being dismissed, or a judge orders it, this situation is sometimes referred to as an *income clean break*.

If your ex-spouse isn't living up to her maintenance obligation, you can try to enforce that obligation by asking the court to make any one of a number of orders. The most common orders include the following:

- **An attachment of earnings order,** which means that your spouse's employer has to deduct your maintenance regularly from your spouse's wages or salary and send it to you, with payment of the balance to your spouse. In Scotland, this order is known as an *arrestment of earnings*.

- **Registration of your maintenance order in the Magistrates Court,** in which case the court office takes over enforcement on your behalf.

- **A *garnishee* order for the arrears,** which means that you can take the money that's due to you from your spouse's bank or building society account. This order is known as an *arrestment of the account* in Scotland.

- **A judgement summons, or order for committal,** which means that your spouse is at risk of going to prison if she doesn't pay the arrears. This order is likely only if your spouse displays *wilful refusal.*

- **A charging order,** which means that you may be able to enforce the arrears through an order for sale of one of your spouse's assets.

Another alternative is to ask the judge to dismiss your maintenance order in return for a lump sum or asset similar in value to (or possibly slightly less than) the total amount of maintenance that you would have been due to receive. See 'Taking Capital Instead of Maintenance' later in this chapter.

Knowing the factors that a judge considers

Unless one of you makes a formal application to the court for maintenance, you and your spouse must decide on your own about maintenance, possibly with the help of your solicitors or mediators. To help guide you in your decision, the following is a list of factors a judge considers when ruling on maintenance. The greater the number of factors that apply to your marriage, the stronger your argument for maintenance.

- ✔ You've been married for a long time. You won't find a legal definition of 'long time' when it comes to marriage. However, if your marriage is less than seven years old, a judge is unlikely to treat it as a long-term marriage – even though it may feel like an eternity to you!

- ✔ Your spouse makes significantly more money than you do and can be expected to continue doing so, at least for the immediate future.

- ✔ Your age or health status make earning a good living nearly impossible.

- ✔ You've made significant contributions to your marriage or to your spouse's career. For example, you gave up your career to be a full-time parent, you continued to work throughout your marriage and let your career take a back seat to your spouse's so that you could help her advance professionally, or you helped build your spouse's business.

- ✔ Your educational background or employment history puts you at a disadvantage in the job marketplace.

- ✔ You're going to be your children's primary carer, making the pursuit of a career immediately after your divorce a difficult task.

- ✔ You have no other sources of regular income, such as income from trusts, property or investments.

- ✔ You're leaving your marriage with less capital than you may normally expect.

- ✔ You're going to have sole care of your children and one or more of them has special needs – perhaps due to serious physical or emotional disabilities or health problems – which preclude you from working or allow you to work on a part-time basis only.

In Scotland, orders for spousal maintenance following the divorce are the exception rather than the rule, and even if otherwise appropriate, they are unlikely to be made if the situation can be dealt with by a different sort of order such as payment of a capital sum or transfer of property.

Ideally, judges like to see the lifestyle you enjoyed when you were married continue after your divorce, but in reality, they know that most ex-spouses don't make enough money to support two households equally well, not even for a short period of time. However, a judge can try to make sure that the two of you don't end up with very different standards of living, particularly if your children are going to spend time with both of you.

Your conduct towards each other during and after your marriage rarely makes any difference to the order that a judge makes for maintenance because the judge regards your conduct as a matter between the two of you. The law says that conduct should be taken into account only if *ignoring it is inequitable in the judge's opinion.* For example, if your spouse injures you so badly that your earning capacity is adversely affected, a judge is more likely to award you maintenance as a result.

When it comes to income, divorce is still harder on women than men despite the large numbers of women who work outside the home. Most women, even those who receive maintenance, experience a drop in their standard of living after their marriage ends. However, some divorced men experience the same financial consequences. Both of you can benefit from individual advice on maintenance from your solicitors.

Taking Capital Instead of Maintenance

You can choose to receive your maintenance in the form of a lump sum or other capital asset instead of taking it as a series of payments over time. Known as *capitalising the maintenance*, this option can be particularly attractive if you have enough capital to do it and you don't trust your ex-spouse to live up to an agreement that provides for payments over time or if you're concerned that her financial situation may deteriorate after your divorce. It may also be a useful bargaining tool if you need a particular asset as part of your settlement, such as the house, but not enough other assets exist to meet your spouse's claims. Many spouses who are at risk of a maintenance order against them prefer the certainty of giving a bit more capital now in return for a dismissal of your maintenance claims.

Be sure that the lump sum or capital asset that your spouse offers you is adequate. Don't assume just because it sounds like a lot of money that you're getting a fair amount, especially if the asset doesn't produce an income flow or your spouse wants you to take the lump sum in lieu of other capital assets. Talk with a family law solicitor or possibly an independent financial adviser as well before you sign any paperwork.

Consider the consequences of capitalising your maintenance and what you can do to mitigate those consequences before you agree to accept a lump-sum payment. If you're dependent on Income Support for part of or all your income, the Department for Work and Pensions (DWP) treats the lump sum as if it's maintenance and deducts a corresponding amount from your Income Support each week until they regard the lump sum as paid up, so you may end up little better off. Also, if you've had the benefit of any legal aid or public funding to pay for your divorce expenses, the Legal Services Commission expects you to pay back your costs to them out of your lump sum as part of the *statutory charge*, whereas they don't expect you to do this out of your maintenance. (An exception to this rule may be made if you've reached an agreement through the use of mediation. See Chapter 7 for more on legal aid and how the statutory charge works.)

If you take a lump-sum payment and then put the full amount in your bank account, you may end up spending it all at once. The larger the sum, the more important it is that you have an investment plan that maximises the interest you can earn on the money and gives you ready access to at least a portion of it.

If you're giving your spouse a lump sum or other capital in lieu of regular maintenance, get the help of a family solicitor and possibly a financial adviser as well before you sign your agreement. If you think that your spouse is likely to remarry in the near future, you may be better off agreeing to maintenance now because the maintenance ceases in any event on your spouse's remarriage.

Seeking a Change in Maintenance

As long as your maintenance claims haven't been dismissed, the amount of maintenance you receive may be increased or decreased after your divorce is final, under certain circumstances:

- The amount can change if you and your former spouse both agree to the change.
- The amount can also change if the court orders it.

Some couples agree to include in their divorce settlement provision for an automatic review of, or change in, the amount of maintenance every year or so, perhaps in line with inflation. If you and your spouse agree to something on those lines, your maintenance shouldn't lose value through inflation. The two of you can implement such an agreement; you don't have to refer to the court. If you're paying maintenance and are struggling financially, try to negotiate a reduction or make an application to the court, rather than just ignoring the problem and hoping it will go away.

If you don't have any provision for an automatic change in the amount of maintenance payments, you and your ex-spouse can still agree a change, but then you're advised to formalise the agreement by applying to the court for a change to the terms of your original court order. You can do this by consent and by post, but you usually have to pay a court fee.

Always try to negotiate a solution rather than rush straight to court but if you and your spouse can't agree on a change in the rate of maintenance, one or other of you may make an application to the court. You need to support your application with a statement or *affidavit* (an affidavit is a statement that you sign on oath in front of an officer of the court or any solicitor other than your own) setting out the reasons why you believe that a change is justified and what you think is a fair amount. If you think that your spouse is going to object to the application, weigh the costs of making such an application against the benefit of the change in maintenance that is likely to be ordered *before* you make your application. A family solicitor can advise you on your prospects, but the judge has the ultimate discretion to decide.

Preparing for Life without Maintenance

Unless you have a *secured periodical payments order*, your maintenance payments stop when your spouse dies. Secured periodical payments orders are very rare these days and occur only when the paying spouse has substantial spare capital assets or property against which such an order or maintenance can be secured. In the absence of a secured periodical payments order, you have no legal right to be paid maintenance by your ex-spouse's estate. Obviously, if those payments are an important source of income for you, the death of your ex-spouse may be financially devastating for you.

If you live in Scotland and have the benefit of a periodical allowance, your payments don't automatically cease on your spouse's death, but the executors of your spouse's estate must make an application to the court to terminate the payments. Sometimes the court orders payment at a reduced rate or sets a time limit on the allowance, rather than terminating it.

Although death can come unexpectedly to people of any age, this issue may be of particular concern to you if you're ending your marriage to a spouse who's elderly or in poor health. This issue can be addressed by your spouse purchasing a life insurance policy and naming you as beneficiary or by you taking out a maintenance protection policy. A good independent financial adviser or your solicitor should be able to tell you about your options.

Another important point is that a spouse or ex-spouse with the benefit of a maintenance order has the right to make a claim against the paying spouse's estate under the Inheritance (Provision for Family and Dependents) Act 1975, if the paying spouse didn't make reasonable financial provision on her death. (This Act doesn't apply in Scotland, although if you're still married, you may have other rights.) The court looks at what the deceased spouse's financial position was on death and what other responsibilities she had in deciding what reasonable financial provision needs to be. If a spouse's maintenance claims have been dismissed by the court, whether by consent or not, an order is almost always in place preventing that spouse from claiming against the estate as well.

Maintenance and Tax

Tax relief on maintenance payments that you *make* to your spouse was abolished back in April 2000, unless one of you is over 65, and even then the relief that you can claim is limited and modest in amount. Maintenance payments that you *receive* aren't taxable, nor do they have any effect on any child support payments that your spouse is liable to pay.

Don't make your maintenance payments in cash without getting a written receipt. If you do, you don't have a record of your payments and if any question arises concerning how much you may have paid your former spouse, or exactly when you made a particular maintenance payment, you lack the documentation you need.

Chapter 13

Providing Financially for Your Children

In This Chapter

▶ Determining who pays child support

▶ Working out the appropriate amount of child support

▶ Negotiating your own child support agreement

▶ Accounting for child support extras

▶ Ensuring you receive the child support that you're due

As a parent, you have a moral and legal responsibility to support your dependent children so that they have a roof over their heads, clothes to wear, enough food to eat, and an education – the basics, in other words. Divorce doesn't change this obligation whether your children live with you or with your ex. If you have dependent children, deciding how to share the cost of raising them is a key issue in your divorce.

This chapter explains which parent usually pays child support to the other and how the Child Maintenance and Enforcement Commission (CMEC) or the Child Support Agency (CSA) determines a minimum level of support. We help prepare you to negotiate your child support agreement and explain when the court may become involved. We also cover the expenses beyond the basics that you need to include in your divorce agreement – or that a judge may order you to pay.

Whether you're divorcing, separating, dissolving a civil partnership, or separating after living together makes little difference to your obligations under this heading. You may end up using different legislation if you go to court but the principles are just the same and the CSA/CMEC treats everyone in the same way.

Supporting Your Children

Child support is an amount of money one parent pays to the other, after the couple are separated, to help cover the cost of bringing up their dependent children.

From 1993, the Child Support Agency (CSA) was the statutory agency primarily responsible for determining the amount of child support due in each case. In November 2008 that responsibility passed to the Child Maintenance and Enforcement Commission (CMEC) but the changeover process is likely to take until at least 2014. (This chapter refers throughout to CSA/CMEC – either or both might apply to your situation depending on when you're reading this.) In 1993 the CSA took over much of the power to decide child support issues that used to belong to the courts. Although both of you reaching agreement on child support is still possible (and better), neither you nor your ex can prevent the other from applying to the CSA/CMEC for a calculation of liability – except where an order for child maintenance was made prior to March 2003 or you have a written maintenance agreement from before April 1993.

CMEC's role is to promote the importance of child maintenance and to raise awareness among parents of the importance of taking responsibility for maintenance and making appropriate arrangements. CMEC also has a duty to provide information and guidance services, with a view to encouraging parents to enter into their own maintenance arrangements (take a look at www.cmoptions.org for more info).

You don't have to wait for divorce proceedings to apply to the CSA/CMEC for a calculation of the amount; you just have to be living apart from your spouse. Either of you can apply to the CSA/CMEC when you've separated and no fee applies.

Check out the CSA/CMEC website at www.csa.gov.uk or phone the helpline 0845 713 3133 for details on the formula that the CSA/CMEC uses to calculate support. The CSA/CMEC bases its calculations of liability on the following principles:

- The number of qualifying children to which the child maintenance applies
- The non-resident parent's net income and circumstances
- The number of children living with the non-resident parent (the CSA/CMEC calls these children 'relevant other children')

You can use the CSA/CMEC formula as a starting point for your own agreements. In fact CMEC has its own website (www.cmoptions.org) designed specifically to help you come to your own arrangement.

Caring for your children all the time

Ordinarily, when one parent has primary care of the children (the *parent with care*), the other parent (the *non-resident parent*) is obliged to pay child support. If your ex-spouse was a step-parent and not the biological or adoptive parent of the child, the CSA/CMEC has no jurisdiction to require him to pay child support; however, see the section later in this chapter 'Applying to the court: Special circumstances a judge may consider'. (The parent with primary care is usually regarded as meeting his child support obligation by raising the children. In fact, he typically spends as much as three times the amount of money as the non-resident parent on their children's necessities!)

The amount of child support due is based on the non-resident parent's net income and doesn't take account of the following:

✔ Income of the parent with care

✔ Income of the current partner of either parent

✔ Housing costs of either parent

✔ Travel to work costs of either parent

Sharing your children's care

If you and your ex-spouse share the care of your children, one parent, usually the parent who receives the Child Benefit (see the section later in this chapter on 'Claiming Child Benefit'), is designated the parent with care. The other parent is liable to pay child support at a reduced rate. The CSA/CMEC bases this rate on the proportion of nights spent with each parent. Supporting your children when you share care can take two forms:

✔ **Splitting care equally:** If you share the care of your children on a 50:50 basis and are designated the parent with care, you'll probably still receive child support from your spouse. For example, if the CSA/CMEC calculates a monthly child support amount of £350 to be paid by your spouse but your children spend half of their time living with each of you, your spouse is only required to pay you £175 of support per month and is allowed to deduct a further £7 a week for each child.

✔ **Sharing care in other ways:** If you and your ex-spouse share the care of the children in different proportions, the CSA/CMEC allows a reduction in their non-resident parent's child support payments in proportion to the average number of nights the children spend with him. For example, if you're the non-resident parent and the children spend an average of one night per week with you, your liability, say £350, is reduced by one-seventh to £300; if they spend an average of two nights per week with you, your liability is reduced by two-sevenths to £250. The average number of nights is worked out over a period of one year.

Working Out What You Pay or Receive

The amount of maintenance or child support is based on the non-resident parent's net income only. For most people 'net' means your earnings after any tax, National Insurance and pension contributions are taken off. If you're self-employed, it means your gross profit after tax, National Insurance and pension contributions. For non-resident parents whose income is £200 or more per week, the rates are:

✔ 15 per cent of your net income if you have one child

✔ 20 per cent of your net income if you have two children

✔ 25 per cent of your net income if you have three or more children

If you have an income of less than £200 per week you pay a reduced rate of maintenance. Non-resident parents with a net income of £100 or less, and those on certain benefits such as Income Support or Jobseeker's Allowance, pay a flat rate of £5 per week (unless the child stays overnight for an average of at least 52 nights each year in which case no child support payment is required). A few people – such as full-time students and prisoners – don't have to pay anything. A non-resident parent pays less if any other children (including stepchildren) live in his household.

Your child support payments are also reduced if your children stay with you for at least 52 nights per year – refer to the section 'Sharing your children's care' earlier in this chapter for details.

The CSA/CMEC limits the amount of net income it can consider for child support to £2,000 a week.

By 2010, the CMEC is likely to have brought in the following changes:

✔ Child maintenance will be calculated on the gross income of the non-resident parent.

✔ Percentage rates will be set at 12 per cent for one child, 16 per cent for two children and 19 per cent for three or more children.

✔ Income limit will increase from £2,000 a week to £3,000 a week.

✔ Current flat rate will increase from £5 a week to £7 a week.

If you pay maintenance to your spouse voluntarily and you think the CSA/CMEC may become involved, try to agree with your spouse in advance how much of these payments represent child support, because that amount can be credited to you by the CSA/CMEC while the calculation is being carried out.

The formula for calculating child support payments can be varied only in very limited circumstances, including:

✔ You can receive an allowance for special expenses, such as contact costs, prior debts, boarding school fees, and payment of the mortgage for your spouse. These special expenses can't be less than £10 to £15 per week if they're to be taken into account for the non-resident parent.

✔ You believe, as the parent with care, that the calculation is unduly favourable to your ex-spouse because, for example, he has assets worth over £65,000 or his declared income and lifestyle are inconsistent.

If you're a non-resident parent and you don't co-operate with the CSA/CMEC, it can make assumptions about your income and impose an interim maintenance decision. The CSA/CMEC also has wide powers, including disqualifying you from driving, to enforce child support payments.

Getting state benefits and tax credits

Before October 2008, if you were on Income Support or income-based Jobseeker's Allowance, the CSA/CMEC considered you to have made an application for child support unless you were able to claim 'good cause' for opting out. This assumption has now been abolished. Parents with care can now choose to leave the CSA/CMEC and make their own arrangements for child maintenance with the other parent of their child(ren).

Before October 2008, when the CSA/CMEC made an assessment of your spouse's liability, you were allowed to keep only the first £10 per week that he paid. The rest was taken by the Department of Work and Pensions (DWP) to help pay for your Income Support or Jobseeker's Allowance. After October 2008, if you stay with the CSA/CMEC, any child maintenance collected on your behalf is paid directly to you and you can keep up to £20 a week of any child maintenance paid before it affects the amount of benefit you receive. Also, all child maintenance payments are ignored from that date when calculating Housing Benefit and Council Tax Benefit.

However, child support payments that you *receive* as the parent with care are ignored completely in calculating your entitlement to Working Tax Credit. If you *pay* child support to your ex-spouse, any Working Tax Credit you receive may be considered part of your income, depending on your net income compared with that of your ex-spouse. Flip to Chapter 7 for more about state benefits.

For more information on CSA/CMEC have a look at the HM Revenue and Customs website (www.hmrc.gov.uk/taxcredits/) or the CSA/CMEC website at www.csa.gov.uk. You can also try the CSA/CMEC information line on 0845 713 3133, or write to the CSA/CMEC National Helpline, PO Box 55, Brierly Hill, DY5 1YL.

If you live in Scotland, you can contact One Parent Families Scotland (www.opfs.org.uk) for more information. For help in Northern Ireland, visit the Child Maintenance and Enforcement Division's website at www.dsdni.gov.uk/index/CSA/CMEC.htm.

Claiming Child Benefit

Child Benefit is payable regardless of your income to anyone responsible for, and living with, a child under the age of 16, or under 19 and in full-time education. Currently, in 2008, it amounts to £18.80 a week for the eldest child and £12.55 for any other child. Some lone parents may be entitled to a little more. (Check the rates on www.direct.gov.uk each year because they are subject to change.) Therefore, if your children live mainly with you, you're entitled to claim the Child Benefit for them. If you and your ex-spouse share the care of your children equally, the Child Benefit is normally paid to the woman unless you agree otherwise. Alternatively, you may claim the Child Benefit for one child, and your ex-spouse may claim it for another child. Contact HM Revenue and Customs (www.hmrc.gov.uk) or the Department for Work and Pensions (www.dwp.gov.uk) for more information.

Receiving Child Tax Credit

Like Child Benefit, Child Tax Credit (CTC) is also paid to the main carer of children under 16, or under 19 and in full-time education. You can qualify for the Child Tax Credit whether you're employed or not, but it's dependent on your means – your income must be less than £58,000 per annum. An amount is paid for each child in the household and extra money is available if you have a child with special needs, or a child under one year old. So, as with Child Benefit, whether this extra source of income is available to you or not depends partly on whether or not you're considered the children's main carer. If you share the care of the children equally between you, the Child Tax Credit is normally paid to the woman unless you agree otherwise.

Qualifying for Working Tax Credit

If you're working, you may be entitled to claim Working Tax Credit (WTC), depending on the number of hours that you work and your income. Working Tax Credit is more generous if you have children and are their main carer, and in addition you may get some help with their child-care costs. Single parents are also able to keep all their maintenance payments and still claim Working Tax Credit. For more information, read Tax Credits: A Guide for Lone Parents available free from One Parent Families/Gingerbread (www.oneparentfamilies.org.uk).

Applying to the court: Special circumstances a judge may consider

The court's powers to determine child support payments (also known as *child maintenance* or *periodical payments for the child*) have been greatly limited since the Child Support Act 1991 came into effect in April 1993 and the power to determine most child support payments went to the CSA. The main circumstances in which a court can make an order for such payments are limited to the following:

✔ You both, as parents, agree on an amount of child support and ask the court to make an order by agreement.

✔ You, as the parent with care, ask the court to make an order to top up the child support calculated by the CSA/CMEC where your ex-spouse has a net income of over £2,000 per month (increasing to £3,000 per month by 2010).

✔ Your child has special needs.

✔ You want an order for payment of school fees.

✔ You aren't the natural parent of the child but have treated the child as a child of the family.

✔ Your child is still in full-time education but over the age of 19, although if he is over 18, the child has to make the application himself.

If you have a court order for child maintenance predating 3 March 2003, or a written maintenance agreement dated prior to April 1993, the CSA/CMEC can't get involved with calculating the payments (unless the parent with care is on Income Support – in this case the CSA/CMEC is automatically involved). If you want to change the level of, or enforce, child support, you have to go back to court to do it. If your court order postdates 3 March 2003, the CSA/CMEC can become involved if either of you applies to it not less than one year after the order for child support was made. The CSA/CMEC then takes over responsibility for calculating and enforcing the payments.

Bear in mind that when deciding whether to have a court order for support or to go through the CSA/CMEC, one or both of you are responsible for the costs of making an application to the court to vary or enforce the order, whereas the CSA/CMEC doesn't charge for doing this on your behalf.

If a judge is involved in determining the level of child support, he has to put the needs of the children first and consider a whole range of factors including the income, needs and resources of each of you and the children, as well as any mental or physical disability of the children, and the manner in which your children were being, or expect to be, educated.

If you, as the non-resident parent, are thinking of transferring the house to your ex in return for not claiming child support – don't. You can't hold your ex to that agreement or prevent him from applying to the CSA/CMEC for a calculation of your child support liability, and the CSA/CMEC makes no allowance for the transfer of the house.

Agreeing on Extra Expenses

A number of other expenses are associated with the upbringing and support of children that you may or may not agree to pay. Among these possible expenses are:

- ✔ Life insurance, where your children are the beneficiaries
- ✔ Private health care
- ✔ Disability insurance

Purchasing life insurance for the benefit of your children

If you die while your children are still dependent on your financial support, life insurance proceeds help provide for their care. You may want to provide your ex-spouse with proof every year that your life insurance policy continues to be in force. If you and your ex-spouse share the cost of bringing up your children, you must both purchase life insurance policies.

You must appoint a trustee – an adult who would manage the policy proceeds on behalf of your children should you die before they're of age. Your ex-spouse is a logical choice, assuming that he can be trusted to manage the money responsibly. However, the trustee can be another financially responsible adult.

Providing private medical cover

Usually, if you have private medical cover, the parent with employer-sponsored medical insurance maintains the children on his policy. Private health insurance may not cover all medical expenses – dental or orthodontic expenses and glasses, for example, may be excluded. Nor does private health insurance pay 100 per cent of covered medical expenses. Therefore, you and your ex-spouse have to decide how those costs are to be shared. If you're the parent with primary care, unless these costs are specifically dealt with during your divorce negotiations, you may end up having to cover them. You may include private health care as part of your child support agreement. However, if you do so, check the details of your spouse's health plan before coming to a final agreement about child support.

Some private health plans cover all medical expenses if you pay a little more each month than the standard premium, or provide a lower level of medical expense reimbursement if you use doctors 'outside the plan' – something that may be important to you if your children are currently being treated by doctors who aren't on the list of preferred providers issued under your insurance plan. You and your ex-spouse must decide how to deal with these and other possible issues related to the scope and cost of your private medical cover.

Purchasing disability insurance

Disability insurance and/or critical illness cover provide a working parent with a percentage of his income if he becomes unable to work due to illness or injury. Carrying disability insurance is more common when the parent paying child support is self-employed.

Disability insurance is especially important if a parent's business is a sole proprietorship, a partnership or a small limited company. In such businesses, the active involvement of the business owner is critical to the business's financial success. If the owner becomes incapacitated due to illness or an accident, he will have little or no income and would probably be unable to meet his child support obligation after a period of time.

Even if your children are very young, don't overlook the issue of how you'llfund their college education – you can't start saving too soon for this major expense.

Providing 'extras' for your children

Gifts, trips, clothes and anything else that you give a child because you *want* to (and not because you *have* to) do *not* necessarily count as child support when you have a court order or CSA/CMEC assessment for the support. Therefore, you can usually assume that if you're paying child support, you *can't* deduct the value of those gifts from the total amount of support you're obliged to pay. To be certain, however, check with your solicitor if you can't agree with your spouse.

If you initiated your divorce and feel guilty about its likely effect on your children, don't try to ease your guilt by agreeing to pay more support than you can afford. If you have a hard time coming up with the payments after your divorce, you can find yourself in legal trouble if your former spouse takes you to court to enforce the terms of your child support agreement.

Calculating your share of child support 'extras'

Under the CSA/CMEC, child support is essentially a regular amount that is presumed to provide adequate support for a child. But that amount may not cover the 'extras' you want your children to have – private education, music or other lessons, holiday courses, sports gear or extra tutoring, for example. If a judge is deciding child support in your divorce and you want certain extras to be included in the court order, you must ask the judge to consider those special expenditures in the child support amount or through an order for payment of school fees.

Even if you agree to share responsibility for paying the basic day-to-day costs of your children's care, you still have to decide which extras to fund and how to split the cost of any big extras you both feel your children need. A good idea is to calculate first how you're going to split the cost of special activities and other extras for your children. One easy way to calculate the split is for each of you to pay a

percentage of the cost of the extras based on your individual incomes relative to your total combined income.

For example, assume that the total annual cost of the extras you want to fund is £5,000, and that you earn £40,000 a year and your spouse earns £45,000 a year, for a total combined annual income of £85,000. In this case, your income represents 47 per cent of the total, and your spouse's income represents 53 per cent of the total. If you apply these percentages to the £5,000 total cost of the extras, in order to pay for them you contribute £2,350 a year, and your spouse's share is £2,650. Realistically speaking, given the cost of maintaining two households, you may not have enough money left over to give your children all the extras they're used to or you want to provide, or paying for them may require some cutbacks in your post-divorce budgets.

Negotiating Your Own Child Support Agreement

Like almost everything else to do with divorce that you can accomplish without the help of a court, negotiating your own child support agreement has its advantages, for example:

✔ The negotiation process encourages both of you to assume equal responsibility for deciding how you'll take care of the financial needs of your children.

Mothers often end up being their children's financial advocates in divorce court cases. Sometimes – whether true or not – it can appear to their spouses that mothers are really arguing on their own behalf, not for their children.

✔ Negotiating together reinforces the fact that although your marital relationship is changing, you have a relationship as parents and you're both legally responsible for your children's welfare.

✔ Working things out together also helps increase the likelihood that when you're divorced, the parent who's obliged to pay child support actually does so.

CMEC (www.cmoptions.org) provides information and guidance services to raise awareness among parents of the importance of taking responsibility for maintenance, encouraging parents to enter into effective maintenance arrangements. The message from CMEC is that it should only get involved when parents can't come to agreement themselves or when one parent tries to evade his or her responsibilities.

Your child support agreement must clearly spell out how child support is to be paid, how often it is to be paid, the amount of each payment, and the date by which it must be paid. Preparing a child support agreement that meets the approval of a court requires legal help. Judges look for a tightly drafted agreement that leaves little open to question.

Increases in the *inflation rate* ultimately decrease the value of the child support you receive. A practical way of dealing with this potential problem is to build into your agreement increases in the amount of child support your ex-spouse must pay that are in line with inflation. Or, if you have a court order for child support without any such built-in increase, you can ask a judge to order an increase. If the CSA/CMEC works out your child support, they automatically review it every two years.

Understanding child support and contact

Don't underestimate the importance of working out a parenting plan and using a negotiated agreement that helps ensure that your ex-spouse pays child support as agreed. (Refer to Chapter 10 for more on parenting plans.) According to the CSA/CMEC, a marked relationship exists between the amount of child contact and the payment of child support. Just consider the following facts:

✔ 93 per cent of non-resident parents who see their child at least once every two weeks pay something.

✔ Only 69 per cent of non-resident parents who see their children less often than once every two weeks pay child support.

Changing the agreement as your lives change

Another advantage to negotiating your own child support agreement is that you and your spouse can craft one that readily allows you to anticipate and accommodate changes in your lives and in the lives of your children over the years. For example, you can spell out how you plan to deal with future possible expenses related to your children – such as orthodontics, sports, extracurricular school activities, clubs, an opportunity to study abroad and student fees. (American research suggests that children from divorced families often suffer financially when they get beyond 18 and enter higher education.) You can also deal with salary increases or decreases either of you may experience. Working all this out saves you time and money later on.

The courts aren't bound to honour provisions you include in a pre-nuptial agreement concerning the care or support of your children. The judge has the ultimate discretion as to the question of care or residence, and the authority of the CSA/CMEC almost always prevails in questions of child support.

Making Sure the Child Support Gets Paid

You have no way of knowing what the future may bring, and the truth is that being single again sometimes changes the priorities of a previously devoted parent. As a result, that parent may begin to take his child support obligations less seriously. Or, if you and your former spouse fall out, your ex may decide to withhold child support as a way to get back at you. Other developments that can affect your former spouse's commitment to your child support agreement include a failing business, a new marriage, another child, excessive debt, and substance abuse problems.

Getting a court order

If you negotiate your own child support agreement, the best idea is to submit the agreement to the court for approval so that you have a consent order within the divorce. This precaution is an important one even if you believe that your spouse is totally trustworthy and you're certain that he will live up to your agreement.

Without a court order for child support, you don't have the full force of the law behind you if your former spouse stops making regular child support payments, begins paying less than he is supposed to, or fails to make any payments at all. Chapter 20 has additional information on what you can do if you begin to have trouble in getting your child support.

Using automatic deductions from wages

If your spouse fails to make the regular payments due to you through the CSA/CMEC or under a court order, you can arrange for the payments to be deducted from your spouse's salary and paid to the CSA/CMEC by his employer. This arrangement is known as an *attachment of earnings order* if it's done through the court, or a *deduction from earnings order* if done through the CSA/CMEC. The errant parent's employer is served with a court order for the deduction and if that employer fails to comply with the court order, the *employer* is in breach of the order and subject to penalties. The deduction from earnings option doesn't help you collect the payments due if your former spouse is self-employed.

If your former spouse has a stable work history, the deduction from earnings option is an excellent way to ensure that you get the child support you need. But it isn't as effective if your ex-spouse often changes jobs – you have to ensure that each new employer is served with a new attachment of earnings court order or CSA/CMEC deduction from earnings direction – and it's particularly difficult to enforce if you don't know about the job changes.

To help deal with these potential problems, and if your spouse is willing, your consent order can state that your ex-spouse has to let you know whenever he changes jobs. Also, the court order for attachment of earnings requires your former spouse's employers to inform you and the court of any change in his employment status. Despite these safeguards, you may still not receive notification of any changes in your former spouse's job situation or the notification may not come on a timely basis.

Initially, your spouse may resist the idea of having child support payments automatically deducted from his wages (the automatic deductions may seem like an invasion of privacy or your ex-spouse may think the automatic deductions make him appear dishonest or unreliable). Automatic deductions are mainly used when the payer has defaulted on payments. However, it does make paying child support somewhat hassle free and your ex may end up appreciating the automatic deduction. Plus, he may find that managing his money is easier when the child support is already taken care of and the rest of the pay cheque can be spent as needed.

Knowing when child support obligations cease

Ordinarily, a parent's child support obligation through the CSA/CMEC ends when a child reaches 16 years of age, or when he is 19 if the child is still in full-time secondary education. However, that obligation can continue through the court while your child is a full-time college student or attending a full-time vocational course. But, degree or no degree, your responsibility to provide child support usually ends when the child reaches his early twenties.

If you pay child support under a court order and your child moves in with you on a full-time, permanent basis, ask the court for an order cancelling your child support obligation. If you don't, your legal obligation to pay child support to your former spouse continues. If you pay child support under a CSA/CMEC decision, ask the CSA/CMEC for a *supercession* – a completely new decision, backdated to the date of your application.

Understanding Child Support and Tax

As far as adjustments to taxable income go, if you pay child support, you *can't* claim your payments as a tax deduction. If you receive child support, you don't have to declare it as income and you don't pay tax on it.

The CSA/CMEC and HM Revenue and Customs usually assume that the parent who receives the Child Benefit is the parent entitled to receive child support and the Child Tax Credit. (See the section 'Receiving Child Tax Credit' earlier in this chapter.) Even if you're sharing the care of your children on a 50:50 basis, the Benefits Agency and HM Revenue and Customs can't split the Child Benefit or Child Tax Credit between you. If, however, you have more than one child, you can agree that one parent claims for one child and the other parent claims for another. That way each of you can have the benefit of the Child Benefit, Child Tax Credit and child support for at least one child. You may each be entitled to claim Working Tax Credit as well. See Chapter 7 and the section 'Getting state benefits and tax credits' earlier in this chapter for more on the generous tax credits that are available to families with children or to families on low incomes.

Part IV
Working Out the Terms of Your Divorce Agreement

'Are you sure this is a genuine mediator?'

In this part . . .

If you and your spouse hope to negotiate your divorce co-operatively and, where possible, together, this part of the book is helpful. It provides a framework for negotiating, tells you how your negotiating can be supported by both mediation and your family solicitor, and when you need to get legal help. If you have children, this part helps you focus on their needs as well as on your own futures.

We also explain the important role that mediation can play in helping you and your spouse avoid the expense and emotional trauma of a divorce trial. We offer tips on finding the best family solicitor for your situation, maybe one who offers collaborative law, and we tell you how to build and fund a mutually co-operative partnership with your solicitor as your divorce proceeds.

If, in the end, you fail to negotiate a co-operative divorce settlement with your spouse, the last chapter in this part gives you a taste of the divorce court process. At that point, the big decisions are left up to the judge.

Chapter 14

Doing Some of the Negotiating Yourself

In This Chapter

▶ Being on your best behaviour

▶ Planning a negotiating strategy

▶ Picking a time and place for your negotiating sessions

▶ Determining the kind of information and outside help you need

▶ Negotiating children arrangements, child support and spousal support

▶ Devising a property settlement

*N*egotiating your own divorce agreement (or at least some of it) can definitely save you money on solicitors' fees and court costs. But it does require that you work in a co-operative way with your soon-to-be ex-spouse, which can be a challenge. You both have to be very sure that you're on good enough terms to attempt it. No mediator is in the room with you to keep your meetings civilised and productive, and no solicitor to do the negotiating for you.

Although we don't tell you *what* to decide (that's up to you), we do try to prepare you to make good decisions by suggesting how to plan and organise your negotiation sessions and offering some basic negotiating advice. In this chapter, we also provide a primer on the basic issues that you may have to resolve before you and your spouse can make your divorce legal.

First, a Word of Caution

When you read this chapter, keep in mind that the plan of action we describe is an ideal scenario to attempt. Realistically, you may not have the desire or inclination to do everything we recommend, which is fine and understandable. Just accomplish what you can – you still save yourself time and money.

Negotiating on your own is not for every couple and can be downright danger-ous for some. When you negotiate on your own, you're less protected than in mediation, or when your solicitors negotiate on your behalf, or in court. You may end up with a number of problems: a divorce agreement that gives you less than you're legally entitled to, a parenting plan that's emotionally harmful to your children, or an agreement that's completely unenforceable.

What you say to your spouse during your negotiations can be used against you if you end up in court, unless you and your spouse have a written agree-ment guaranteeing that whatever you say during your one-to-one negotiations remains confidential and unless you head your correspondence 'Without Prejudice'. If you don't have such a written agreement, what you say to your spouse may come back to haunt you. For example, if you use mediation you must sign an Agreement to Mediate, which deals with safeguarding the confi-dentiality of your discussions and its limits and exceptions. (Mediation is cov-ered more fully in Chapter 16.)

Remaining on Your Best Behaviour

Successful negotiation takes hard work on your part, a commitment to the negotiation process, and a willingness to act like mature adults. That's a tall order for many happily married couples, let alone those who are splitting up. You and your spouse have to sit down together, one-to-one, talk honestly, work out how to solve your problems in a rational manner, and be willing to give as well as take. Treat one another fairly and politely during your negotia-tions. If you don't, your negotiations are likely to become more than a little painful and a harsh reminder of why you're getting divorced in the first place.

Negotiating your own divorce means that both of you must:

- Let reason, not emotions, rule.
- Listen without interrupting one another. Waiting to have your say can be tough to do, especially if you don't like what you're hearing.
- Resist forming a response to what your spouse is saying while she's still talking. Stay cool. If something your spouse says or does during a nego-tiating session upsets you, bite your tongue. Try not to respond in the heat of the moment.
- Allow your spouse to express her opinions and respect what she says. Ridiculing your spouse's choice of words is one way to put that person on the defensive and shut down two-way communications entirely.
- Be open to compromise. Neither of you are going to get everything you want from your divorce, so be ready to make some trade-offs.
- Avoid using intimidation and threats to get what you want. Tactics like that are sure to backfire on you.
- Be honest and polite.

When you and your spouse are negotiating, stay seated. If you stand or walk around and talk to your spouse at the same time, you're less apt to hear what your spouse is saying and more apt to get over-emotional.

Starting Off on the Right Foot: The Preliminaries

You and your spouse are sure to want to get your negotiations over with as quickly as possible. But taking the time to plan how you negotiate can mean the difference between progress and frustration. Before you begin your formal negotiations, you and your spouse should ideally have decided the following:

- When and where to negotiate.
- What issue(s) you plan to address at each negotiation session.

  Unless your divorce is very simple – with little to divide up, no dependent children and no spousal maintenance – you need more than one session to negotiate it. For example, you may have to wait from time to time for information you require from different agencies, businesses, banks, and so on.

- How you're going to structure your negotiation sessions.
- What information and documentation you need and what kind of record-keeping system you're going to use to record your progress.

A deadlock is always possible no matter how hard you try to come to a meeting of minds, and so you must also decide ahead of time what to do if your decision making reaches an impasse; perhaps mediation or using solicitors to do your negotiating. You must also decide ahead of time where you're going to get information or clarification from when a matter of law or finance arises that you don't understand.

If you and your spouse negotiated a pre-marital agreement prior to your marriage, you may well have less to negotiate. (For an explanation of how these agreements work, turn to Chapter 21.)

Planning a Method of Negotiation

No single, right way exists for you to negotiate. A method that works for another couple may not be appropriate for you. However, prior to starting your negotiations, you and your spouse should come to at least a general agreement about how you're going to structure your negotiation sessions to make them as efficient and effective as possible. The following steps outline one plan of action that may work for your situation:

1. **Share your goals and priorities with one another, and discuss any special concerns you may have, *prior* to tackling a major new issue in your divorce – such as your parenting plan, child support, spousal maintenance or the division of your property.**

   Try to speak in terms of your or your children's realistic needs. Then identify where you agree or disagree and where your shared interests lie.

2. **Develop a list of possible options for settling the issue, keeping in mind your individual goals and priorities and your areas of agreement and disagreement.**

   When you're identifying your options, be creative and try not to censor or prejudge any ideas. A seemingly silly idea may inspire a new, more practical one that works for both of you. You may each want to develop your own list of options and then share both lists with one another.

3. **Eliminate all the ideas on your list that you both dislike or both agree are unrealistic.**

4. **Use the options that still remain to develop written proposals for resolving whatever issue you're negotiating.**

   You can each develop your own proposal for the issue, present it to one another, and respond with counterproposals, or you can write a proposal together. After you settle on a decision, put it in writing. Each time you concur on a specific issue, you're that much closer to a final divorce agreement. However, a decision on one point may impact on another, so don't close any doors until you've got the complete picture.

The negotiating process you use doesn't have to be as formal as the one just described. Find a method that you both feel comfortable with and that facilitates a fair resolution of each issue in your divorce.

Choosing the Right Setting

When deciding on a place for your negotiation sessions, pick a quiet, comfortable (but not too comfortable) location that's relatively free of distractions. That probably rules out negotiating in front of the television or any time at home when your children are up and about. Wait until they've gone to sleep or, better still, do your negotiating away from home in a neutral location – in a corner of your local library or in a park, for example.

When you negotiate in a public place, you're more likely to be on your best behaviour, which means that you're less likely to yell at each other, burst into tears or stomp away in a huff.

Chill out before you storm off

Keeping your cool can be tough to do no matter how hard you try. Old hurts and insecurities may resurface during your negotiations, especially if your spouse exhibits an uncanny knack for pushing your emotional buttons and deliberately or unwittingly hurting your feelings. Rather than letting your emotions get the better of you or threatening to derail the negotiations, try these options:

✔ Take a short 'time out'. Walk around the block, get a snack, listen to calming music or read a magazine. Then resume your negotiating.

✔ If you need more than a quick break, tell your spouse you can't continue negotiating and rearrange your negotiation for another time.

✔ Acknowledge that you need third-party help.

Don't rush your negotiations. Take all the time that you need – you're making important decisions that affect your life and the lives of your children for years to come.

Scheduling the Time

Negotiating your divorce agreement probably takes at least a couple of sessions, depending on what you have to resolve and how quickly you and your spouse can come to a consensus on things. Therefore, fix your sessions ahead of time and make them a priority in your life. They need to be every bit as important as business meetings, doctors' appointments, parent-teacher meetings and your children's birthdays.

Set a time to begin and end each session. Generally speaking, your sessions shouldn't run for more than two hours. Longer sessions may well become unproductive.

Don't back out of a scheduled session without a very good reason. (Incidentally, wanting to play golf, having dinner with friends or 'just not feeling like it' aren't good reasons.) However, unexpected events do come up, and so if one of you has a legitimate reason for rescheduling, try to provide the other with at least a few days' notice.

Deciding on the Order of Business

Develop written agendas for your negotiating sessions and determine ahead of time who prepares them. You can take turns writing the agendas, or one of you can agree to prepare them all. Whatever you decide, make sure that both of you have a copy of the agenda well in advance of the next negotiating session. Plan to take up the major issues in your divorce in the following order:

- ✔ **A parenting plan and child support:** If you have children, their well-being must be your number-one responsibility in your divorce. See Chapter 10 for tips on developing a parenting plan.

- ✔ **Maintenance:** You need to decide whether a case exists for one of you to pay maintenance to the other. Maintenance is covered more fully in Chapter 12.

- ✔ **Division of your property:** Remember to include any pensions and outstanding debts you may have.

Using written agendas may sound like needless work, but in fact preparing them ahead of time means that you:

- ✔ Know what sort of 'homework' you must do before your next session.

- ✔ Get down to business at the start of each session instead of trying to decide what you're going to discuss.

- ✔ Stay on track during a negotiating session, because you have a written reminder of what you're supposed to be talking about.

Making your negotiations as painless as possible

Obviously, negotiating the end of your marriage isn't going to be much fun. Here are some suggestions that may make things easier:

- ✔ Start your negotiations off with some easy stuff – something both of you can probably agree on. Early success is a confidence builder and helps create momentum for continued progress.

- ✔ Remember your goals: sound and co-operative arrangements for your children, a less-expensive divorce, an agreement that satisfies you both, and a mutual commitment to making your agreement work after your divorce is official.

- ✔ Avoid overreaching or posturing to gain control.

- ✔ Acknowledge when your spouse makes a concession that benefits you. (Go on, swallow your pride and do it!) In this way you help encourage your spouse to make yet more concessions and compromises. But don't forget that in order to keep the concessions and compromises coming, you must make some of your own.

- ✔ Be sure that your spouse doesn't mistake your willingness to concede a few points as a desire to get back together, unless that's definitely what you want.

- ✔ Try not to make important decisions 'in the heat of the moment' or when you're feeling especially depressed or guilty about your divorce. Although this may be difficult, you're more likely to make decisions that you regret later.

When you can't resolve an issue the first time round, agree to return to it later or get outside help. An issue that initially seems irresolvable may be easier to address the next time you tackle it, especially after you and your spouse have a few successful resolutions under your belts.

Educate yourself about your divorce-related legal rights and responsibilities before you begin negotiating. You can do that by each booking an appointment with a solicitor, reading divorce-related literature (such as this book), or consulting a website such as www.divorceaid.co.uk.

Acquiring (and Paying for) Expert Advice

You and your spouse must determine what sort of information you need in order to make intelligent decisions and which of you is responsible for getting that information. First, make a list of what you need, and then take turns to choose a research topic. Next, you may need to engage some of the following professionals:

- ✔ A qualified accountant to help you understand the possible tax implications of your financial decisions and how to plan for them

- ✔ An estate agent or professional valuer to help you value your home, other property, collectibles, fine art, and so on

- ✔ A financial adviser to help you determine what to do with the assets or pensions you may receive in your property settlement

If you're going to share the cost of outside experts, decide early how to pay for them. Any of the following options may be feasible:

- ✔ Liquidate an asset. For example, you may be able to sell one of your cars or some stocks or bonds, or dip into your savings.

- ✔ One of you pays all the expenses involved in hiring professional help in exchange for getting an equivalently larger share of your property or taking on less of your shared debt.

- ✔ One of you pays all the expenses. The other spouse then reimburses that spouse.

- ✔ You split the expenses 50:50, 60:40, 75:25 – whatever you agree is fair.

- ✔ One of you pays the full cost of hiring one expert and the other pays for hiring another expert. However, for this arrangement to be fair, the cost of hiring each expert needs to be relative to your individual salaries.

Write it all down and save it

During your negotiations, keep an accurate record of what you agree on and what areas of disagreement remain.

Without a written record of your discussions, you don't know where each of you stands in the negotiating process, and writing your final divorce agreement is difficult if not impossible.

Decide which of you is in charge of record keeping. If one of you agrees to be responsible, make sure that your records are always readily available to the other spouse.

So that you have no doubt about the fairness of an outside expert's advice, choose experts who have no personal or business relationship with either one of you. Meet the expert together (not separately) and make sure that the expert understands that she is working for *both* of you.

Bringing in a Solicitor to Help You

If you're like most people, one of the key reasons you may want to negotiate your own divorce is so that you can keep your legal costs down. However, excluding solicitors entirely from your divorce is almost bound to be penny-wise and pound-foolish. Solicitors have a valuable role to play at some point in most divorces, including yours. (For more on how to choose your solicitors wisely, read Chapter 15.)

You must each employ your own solicitor. The profession's rules mean that no solicitor is allowed to accept both of you as clients. The Law Society in the UK prohibits solicitors from working with both spouses in a divorce.

Getting some basic information

Each of you should meet your solicitor prior to starting negotiations. Use this interview to acquire an overview of the divorce law and guidelines, gain an understanding of what must be included in your divorce agreement, and determine the issues and proposals you may want to consider making during your negotiations. Unless you read law books just for fun or have been divorced a number of times, you're unlikely to know about these subjects.

Be sure to get advice about any special concerns you may have related to the decisions ahead of you, and find out about potential legal pitfalls or problems. After talking with your solicitor about the issues in your divorce, you may decide that your divorce is much too complicated for you to negotiate yourselves.

You may also want to use your solicitor to help with specific tasks during the negotiating process – for example, to review financial documents, provide you with feedback about a proposal your spouse has made, or review the counter-offer you're considering. You can also talk to your solicitors about the role a mediator can play.

If money is an issue, be upfront about it. For example, you may want to tell your solicitor you can afford to purchase only an hour or two of her time. Your solicitors are under a professional duty to tell you what their time costs.

Asking your solicitors to review and draft your final agreement

Whether you and your spouse are able to resolve all the issues in your divorce, or you work out just some of them, before you sign anything, ask your solicitors to review what you've drafted. Having your solicitor review your draft agreement assures you that nothing important has been overlooked and that you haven't created potential future problems between you and your spouse. Solicitors are more prepared to do this nowadays as long as you give them full information. In addition, you and your spouse must decide which of your solicitors drafts the final agreement. You can make that decision by tossing a coin, or you may agree that the spouse who has public funding (see Chapter 15 for more details) or the one with greater financial assets engages the solicitor to prepare the final agreement, or you may agree to share the costs in some way. If your solicitor drafts the final agreement, your spouse's solicitor should review it and vice versa.

The solicitor you employ can tell you whether the agreement you and your spouse negotiate by yourselves is equitable (fair) to both of you under the law. The agreement may sound like a great deal to you, but after reviewing it, your solicitor may tell you that you're entitled to more. Although you may decide that you're happy with what's in the draft agreement, at least you know what you're giving up after meeting your solicitor. Your solicitor can also make sure that your draft agreement doesn't overlook certain issues that may create problems (with taxes, for instance) down the road and that it's legally enforceable.

Your solicitor is trained to protect your interests and may therefore have to pose a worst-case scenario and provide legal advice to prevent or mitigate such a situation. So, if your solicitor says something that alarms you or makes you question whether you should negotiate your divorce on your own, don't panic. Your solicitor is legally bound to inform you of all possible outcomes. Such a scenario that you find alarming may have little chance of actually occurring, but you must consider it seriously so that down the line you don't regret not listening properly.

Creating a Parenting Plan that Works for Everyone

If you're like most divorcing parents, both of you want to be actively involved in your children's lives after your marriage has ended. Plenty of research shows that children do best when they have two parents actively involved in their lives.

Therefore, your negotiations about your children's future care are likely to focus on deciding how both of you can continue to spend time with your children, how you can continue sharing parenting responsibilities with one another after you no longer live together, and how you can both assure your children of your continued love. (For more on parenting plans and children's arrangements, see Chapter 10.)

The plan you finally decide on may not be as good as having two parents under the same roof but can be the next best thing. And, if your marriage was tense and full of strife, parenting under two roofs may end up being better than parenting under one. The website www.cafcass.gov.uk-publications can help you ensure that you don't overlook anything while developing your plan.

Working Out Child Support

If you and your spouse share dependent children, your child support arrangement may be the most important item you negotiate. The Child Maintenance and Enforcement Commission (CMEC)/Child Support Agency (CSA) formula (covered in Chapter 13) is a useful minimum guide.

Determining a reasonable standard of living

When working out child support arrangements, you must first come to an agreement about the standard of living you want for your children after your divorce. Although you may both agree that you want the very best for your children, if you're like most couples and money was tight during your marriage, even less of it is likely to be available after you're divorced. Therefore, to provide your children with the extras that you want them to have, you and your spouse may have to agree to cut some items out of your own post-divorce budgets.

Another possibility, sad as it may be, is that after your marriage ends, you find it hard to maintain your children's current lifestyle: you may not be able to provide them with all the extras that you hoped they'd have. Deciding what to cut is probably a tough decision to make.

When you're developing budgets for the cost of raising your children, be sure to include the cost of their share of household expenses, including the rent or mortgage, utilities, food, clothing, travel, school lunches, child care, sporting activities, music lessons, and so on. Look at the expenditure sheet we include in Chapter 3. Also, don't forget to consider how you and your spouse are going to pay for other expenses, such as dentistry, university or further education, any special health care, extra tuition and even weddings. You and your spouse can decide how you plan to fund your children's education when you draft your agreement, or, if they're very young, you can include a clause providing that you'll return to that issue as each child turns a certain age (entering secondary education perhaps), when you should have a clearer idea of her aptitudes and abilities and the relevant educational or employment implications.

Getting a court order, even if you agree

Even if your divorce is amicable and you both agree to share the cost of supporting your children, you may want to ask for a consent order for your child support plan from the court to ensure that the agreement is upheld. If your spouse doesn't live up to the agreement, the full force of the law can help you collect what you're due. Securing a consent order can be an important just-in-case step; without one, your options for getting the agreement enforced are more limited. Although you can get a court order for child support after your divorce, the process takes time, and while you're waiting, you and your children may suffer financially. (Chapter 13 talks more about the options for child support and enforcing child support agreements.)

In Scotland, formal written agreements (provided that they have the necessary legal content and have been registered) are enforced by the courts in the same way as court orders and therefore your agreement is probably sufficient there. In addition, the Scottish court can't make an order for child support if the CMEC/CSA has jurisdiction even if you and your spouse are in agreement – except where *additional* payments are justified, perhaps for a disabled child.

If the spouse who's paying child support can afford to pay more than just the minimum according to the CMEC/CSA formula, your negotiations must also address how much that additional payment amount is to be.

Don't forget to spell out in your agreement exactly how the child support is to be paid – personal cheques, direct debit or other arrangement. Before you sign a child support agreement, ask your solicitor to review it so you can be sure that what you and your spouse agree to is legally enforceable and fair to both of you.

Having a court order for child maintenance, if it's made after March 2003, doesn't prevent either one of you from making an application to the CMEC/CSA when the order has been in effect for a year. If one of you does apply, the CMEC/CSA takes over the calculation and enforcement of child support.

Discussing Spousal Maintenance

If you feel that you need some financial support after your marriage has ended and can present solid reasons why your spouse should pay for it, your divorce negotiations need to include discussions about maintenance. (Turn to Chapter 12 for more in-depth information on the subject of maintenance.) Be aware that maintenance can be a difficult issue to negotiate, so don't give up if you can't come to an agreement right away.

If you're the spouse who needs or wants maintenance, in order to make your case, compare your post-divorce financial needs and resources with your spouse's. Note the contributions you made to your marriage or to your spouse's career. Steer clear of phrases such as 'I must have', 'I require' and 'I deserve'. Don't behave resentfully about the sacrifices you may have made in the interest of your spouse or marriage. At the time you made those choices, you probably did so because you believed they were for the best.

If possible, frame your thinking in terms of how you may both benefit from any maintenance she may pay out. For example, perhaps you need maintenance now so that you can develop good job skills to earn a better living in the future. Depending on your circumstances, it may be that when you have a good job, not only will your spouse be able to stop paying you anything for yourself, but you may also be able to begin contributing more to the support of your children. In other words, your spouse may trade a short-term sacrifice for a long-term gain.

When you're preparing your projected post-divorce budget and estimating your monthly income without maintenance, do *not* include in your income figure any child support you're going to receive. Child support is for your children, not for you.

Dividing Up Your Property and Debts

If you don't have young children to support, and you and your spouse both earn good money, the only decisions you have to make may relate to the division of your property and debts. Before you can get down to deciding who gets what, developing a comprehensive inventory of your assets and debts (including your pensions) and assigning accurate values and amounts to each item is *critical*. (See Chapter 7 for information on creating a list of your assets.)

If you and your spouse own and operate a business together, or if one of you runs a limited company, don't try to negotiate what to do about the business without the help of solicitors. The financial issues are too complicated to work out on your own – they're vexing even for solicitors!

If you're divorcing after just a short marriage, you and your spouse may be able to accomplish that division in a single negotiating session. Usually, the longer your marriage, the more you own and owe together, and the more time you need to reach a property settlement agreement.

Splitting it down the middle – or not

Many divorcing couples begin by thinking that they'll split up their property and their debts 50:50 for practicality's sake. Depending on the circumstances of your marriage, your assets and your debts, this method may or may not be fair. (Flip to Chapter 11 for more information on ways to divide property.)

Here are some of the factors suggesting that you need to consider a non-equal split:

✔ One of you has contributed significantly more to your family than the other. Being the main carer of your children and home is usually seen as equal to going out and earning a salary.

✔ One of you has a greater need than the other for more than half of the assets or less than half of the debts. For example, one of you has the main care of the children or makes much less money than the other or one of you has never worked outside the home and has little earning capacity.

✔ One of you is significantly older or younger than the other or has health issues that are going to affect your ability to pay half of the debt or replace the assets you'd otherwise give up.

As a point of reference or a reality check, take a look at the section on following legal guidelines in Chapter 11. You can also find out from your solicitor what criteria a family law judge would have to use if deciding how your property and debts should be divided. You can get this information if you meet your solicitor before you start your negotiations, or you can get it from a solicitor later, after your negotiations have begun.

Regardless of what percentage split you use to divide up the value of your property and debts – 50:50, 60:40, 80:20, for example – both of you need to be 100 per cent clear about the rationale for that percentage split and feel comfortable with it, and preferably state your reasons for agreeing on that percentage in your agreement.

First divide the big assets, and then the miscellaneous ones. Before dividing up your assets and debts, make lists of your expected incomes and your projected needs.

You've probably seen media reports about 'Big Money Cases' where very rich people argue in the High Courts – even the House of Lords – about how their million pound assets should be shared. Those cases bear very little resemblance to the normal divorce – those bitter arguments arise over what they call 'necessaries' but we would call 'luxuries' (for example, £4,000 a year for dog food) with huge amounts to spare. Paul McCartney and Heather Mills were not arguing about their 'needs'. The case was also unusual, apart from the enormous wealth involved, because the marriage was short.

Dividing up the big stuff

The first stage focuses on the division of your significant assets – your home, other real property, bank accounts, pensions, investments, vehicles, and so on – and the debts that may go with them. Don't overlook the tax consequences of your decisions during this stage. Be open to selling assets if doing so helps to create a win-win situation. (You're most likely to need the help of outside professionals during this phase.)

When you divide up assets that secure a mortgage or loan – your home, vehicles, and so forth – look at both the debt associated with the asset and the asset itself. Value that asset according to the amount of equity you have in it (that is, what's left from the market value of your house or vehicle minus what you owe on the mortgage or loan) and don't forget the costs of sale.

Sharing out smaller items

Use the second phase to share your miscellaneous property, such as your stereo system, furniture, CDs, computer equipment, kitchenware, linens, the lawnmower, power tools, and so on. You may not be able to assign specific values to these items – approximate values may do. During this stage you can also divide up credit card debts and other miscellaneous unsecured joint debts.

Don't overlook your family pets when dividing up your property. If you have children, you may want to let the pets live with whichever parent is going to have the children most of the time after your divorce is final. Having their pets around increases your children's sense of stability and security after your marriage has ended.

You can trade off debts for assets or vice versa. For example, you can agree to pay off more of your debt in exchange for getting a larger share of your assets; or you can agree to take less property so that you don't have to pay off as much of your debt.

If realistic or cost-effective – wipe out as much of your joint debt as you can by selling assets. Minimising your post-divorce financial ties is almost always a good idea. You may also want to sell joint assets to provide both of you with the cash you may need to start your lives as single people. Be careful, however, that in your quest for cash you don't sell items for less than their actual value. (Take a look at Chapter 11 as well for more info.)

Working Out What to Do With the House

Your home is probably the most valuable asset you own together. What you do with your home after a split can be tough on you emotionally as well as financially. Nevertheless, what happens to your house is a bottom-line issue that should be based, at the end of the day, on financial considerations. See Chapter 11. To help you make a sound decision, ask yourself the following questions and talk over the answers to those questions with your spouse:

- How much does comparable housing cost?
- What emotional ties do each of you have to your home and to your neighbourhood?
- How much can you sell your house for?
- What are the costs of buying and selling?

✔ Is it important for your children to continue living in the same neigh-bourhood or school district?

✔ Are other houses in the same neighbourhood or school district available that you and your children can move into?

✔ If you want to keep your home, can you afford to do so, taking into account your mortgage payment, insurance costs, taxes, upkeep and maintenance?

✔ What does your spouse get in return if you keep the house?

Remembering Your Taxes

Don't overlook income and capital gain taxes when negotiating your divorce agreement (see Chapter 11). Ask your accountant, if you have one, or your solicitor to advise you on any possible tax liability. For general information on taxes, you can look at the current *Tax Handbook* from Which Essential Guides. Other tax-related issues you may need to consider include:

✔ How you're going to share any tax refund you may have coming.

✔ How you're going to share responsibility for any taxes you may owe.

✔ How you're going to share liability for any interest, penalties and arrears you may owe if you're audited sometime in the future.

Getting to a Solution

After you and your spouse think that you're close to an agreement on all the issues in your divorce, draft an agreement that reflects your decisions so far. Even if a few issues remain unresolved, start drafting anyway, noting what stands between you and your final agreement. When you see how close you are to a final agreement, you may be encouraged to get down to business and tie up those loose ends with the help of your solicitors. Head to Chapter 15 for how to find a good solicitor to help finalise your agreement.

Chapter 15

Choosing a Family Solicitor

In This Chapter

▶ Knowing when you need a solicitor

▶ Evaluating and engaging the best solicitor for you

▶ Changing solicitors

▶ Seeking affordable legal help and public funding

*R*egardless of your opinion about lawyers (solicitors and barristers) – that they're wise and informed legal advisers or a necessary evil – you almost can't escape having to use one when you're getting a divorce. If yours is a complicated and contentious divorce, the help of a solicitor is absolutely essential. If your breakup is more straightforward and amicable, a solicitor's input and assistance is advisable, even when you and your spouse handle most of the divorce negotiations yourself.

After reading this chapter, you'll feel a little less intimidated by solicitors and much more confident about employing one. We show you what to look for in a solicitor, how much they charge, and how to begin your search for a solicitor you can trust and afford. We also equip you with a set of questions to ask solicitors and an awareness of other issues to consider when choosing a solicitor. Remember that you have no direct access to barristers – you always have to instruct a solicitor first. For more information on what barristers do, take a look at Chapter 4.

When to Engage a Solicitor

Assuming that you're a law-abiding citizen and have never been sued or had to sue, you may well have never employed a solicitor before. Therefore, you may find the prospect of engaging and working with a solicitor downright intimidating, especially if you've always looked to your spouse to make the important decisions in your household.

Most divorces aren't simple and therefore the active involvement of a solicitor is critical. In any of the following situations, seriously think about employing the services of a family solicitor:

- You and your spouse have dependent children.

- You've been based in the home during your marriage and don't have the job skills and contacts you need to begin earning a good living right away; or you're an older person who has never worked.

- Your property is substantial or complicated; you have capital gains taxes and other tax issues to consider; you've made very different contributions to your marriage; or other similar factors.

- You, your spouse, or both of you own your own business, or you and your spouse are business partners.

- You and your spouse share a lot of debt.

- You're reluctant to speak up when you disagree with your spouse and tend to back down when he disagrees with you.

- You don't trust your spouse to be honest, open and fair.

- You and your spouse are so estranged that civil discourse and compromise are no longer part of your discussions.

- Your spouse has become physically or emotionally abusive.

- Your spouse has engaged a solicitor.

Keep in mind that professional ethics don't allow solicitors to represent both you and your spouse at the same time, even when you believe that you're going to be in complete agreement over all major issues. Ethically, the solicitor can't give both of you independent legal advice if any conflict or potential conflict arises, however minor.

What to Look for in a Solicitor

A solicitor may be involved in your divorce from start to finish or work with you on a very limited basis. (Generally, if you and your spouse both feel confident about your ability to work out your own divorce agreement, you can limit your use of a solicitor to initial advice and information, final evaluation and feedback, and the drafting of your final order or agreement.)

Engaging a family solicitor is more than just a matter of looking in *Yellow Pages*, making a Google search, or simply employing the solicitor's firm which helped you negotiate your office lease or draw up your will. Your solicitor needs to:

✔ Be experienced in family law.

✔ Talk to you in plain English, not legalese, and pay attention to what you have to say.

✔ Be someone you trust and feel comfortable with, because you may have to reveal highly personal information about yourself and your marriage.

✔ Make clear that, if you have young children, during your divorce you must put your children's needs first and that he won't pursue unreasonable demands for child support or help you pursue vindictive child residence and contact arrangements.

✔ Answer the phone promptly and professionally.

✔ Be affordable.

Appropriate skills and experience

An old adage states that 'there are horses for courses'. This saying is as true for a solicitor as for any other professional. In other words, when you select a family law solicitor, you want one with the legal skills and knowledge needed to get the job done for you:

✔ If you need help negotiating your divorce agreement, the ideal solicitor is a problem solver, works well with people, is adept at compromise and is comfortable in court. Although you and your spouse may have no intention of going to court, a solicitor's advocacy, experience and history of success in court can have some bearing on his ability to negotiate a settlement with your spouse's solicitor.

✔ If you know from the start that you're heading for a contested hearing, you may want a solicitor who has considerable courtroom experience: not all solicitors do. Alternatively, your solicitor needs to have a good working relationship with the local family law barristers. See Chapter 4 for more about the different roles of solicitors and barristers.

✔ Try to choose a solicitor familiar with the family law judges in your area. Knowing the court style of the judge who's likely to hear your case and how the judge has decided previous cases similar to yours helps your solicitor adapt his legal strategy and style to that particular judge.

Don't base your decision on which solicitor has the nicest office. A fancy office in an expensive building says nothing about the adequacy of a solicitor's legal skills. At the same time, don't assume just because you pay a lot of money to a solicitor that his legal representation is appropriate to your needs or of high quality. Also, don't let a solicitor's physical appearance influence your choice.

If your financial situation is complex, the solicitor you engage should either have a solid understanding of the issues and laws that pertain to your divorce or work closely with a barrister or financial experts who have that knowledge, such as an independent financial adviser, accountant or valuer. Remember, negotiating your divorce agreement is as much about financial matters as about ending your marriage.

Personal style

If you're relying on a solicitor to do more than simply review your divorce paperwork, you must be prepared to share details about your personal life, marriage and finances. Therefore, you must feel comfortable with the person representing you. In addition, your solicitor should share and support your basic philosophy or attitude towards your divorce. For example, if you want to keep things as calm, co-operative and non-adversarial as possible, avoid solicitors who like to 'go for the jugular'.

Affordability

Most family law solicitors bill for their services on an *hourly basis*. A few may agree to take a *flat fee* based on the total amount of time and work they think your divorce requires and if your legal needs are very specific and very limited – for example, you may just need some paperwork filled out and filed.

Estimating upfront just how much time is necessary to finalise your divorce is difficult, because no solicitor knows exactly how any divorce is going to work out. Depending on where you live, on average the services of a family solicitor when you're a private (and not a publicly funded) client cost you anywhere from £120 an hour to more than £400 an hour in some top-notch London firms – *plus* expenses (also called *disbursements*) and VAT.

Most solicitors want an upfront payment 'on account of costs' of anything between £500 and £1,000. This amount is to cover the initial work they have to do – and of course to make sure that they get paid.

Among other things, a solicitor's private hourly (as opposed to publicly funded) rate depends on where you live in the UK and whether your community is rural or urban. If you live in London you can expect to pay the most. See the section later in this chapter 'What if You Can't Afford Your Solicitor's Fees?' for more about finding a solicitor who does legally aided, or publicly funded, work.

Knowing What You Can (and Should) Expect from Your Solicitor

In some ways, your solicitor is like a general practitioner, in the middle of a network of services that have grown up to help you and your family during your divorce. At the same time, he must have the legal skills and a compatible approach to get you safely through your crisis.

A good family solicitor listens to your story with several things in mind. One of the first things should be to clarify how ready you are to begin divorce proceedings. If you're uncertain about whether your marriage is over, or if your partner is seeking the divorce, and you're in shock about the situation, a good solicitor tells you how to contact a counsellor. If your solicitor discovers from your story that you're being abused, he takes action (see Chapter 2) and may tell you how to contact a refuge.

Your solicitor should consider whether you and your family are likely to benefit from mediation. This depends on your approach to how you want to conduct your divorce and also on how you convey your spouse's likely approach. You may think that only co-operative couples (see Chapter 5) can use mediation, but mediation can work even if you and your spouse aren't at the point of co-operating because you've stopped talking to each other. Your solicitor may think this over and suggest mediation to you if it seems a good idea in your situation (see Chapter 16 for more information on how mediation works).

If you're eligible for legal aid, you're obliged to consider mediation and meet a mediator. You and the mediator decide if mediation is suitable or not – for example, because domestic abuse has occurred. In most circumstances your solicitor can't be paid by the Community Legal Service to represent you until you check mediation out.

Your solicitor can – and should – also find out whether you're eligible for any state benefits or tax credits and tell you how and where to claim them. See Chapters 10 and 13 for more information on getting state benefits.

Finding the Right Solicitor

Locating the right solicitor takes time. To start your search, you can develop a list of potential solicitors by:

✔ Asking friends and family members who have gone through a divorce and were happy with their solicitors.

✔ Asking solicitors you've worked with in the past. Before requesting the name of a family solicitor, explain the nature of your divorce and the kind of legal help you think you need.

✔ Consulting the Law Society's *Directory of Solicitors and Barristers*. Published regularly, it lists solicitors and barristers by county and city and gives details of their qualifications including the year that they were admitted as a solicitor. Your public library should have a copy. You can also go online to www.lawsociety.org.uk-find a solicitor.

✔ Contacting the family law solicitors' professional association Resolution (01689 820272, www.resolution.org.uk), which can provide you with a list of solicitors in your area who specialise in divorce and family law. See the sidebar 'Locating a specialist' later in this chapter.

✔ Looking under 'Solicitors' in the phone book or *Yellow Pages*.

✔ Asking your mediator, counsellor or social worker.

✔ Searching the Internet. Many divorce solicitors have websites and one of them may be located in or near your community. Some divorce-related websites also have links to divorce solicitor sites. You can also try the Community Legal Service website at www.clsdirect.gov.uk – legal aid solicitors do private work, too.

✔ Asking the other members of your divorce support group for names, if you belong to one.

Locating a Specialist

Some Resolution members are accredited specialists who are proven experts in different areas of family law – such as divorce finances, domestic abuse or international cases. They've gone through rigorous tests designed to show knowledge, practical application of the law, and best practice. The Resolution website at www.resolution.org.uk lists these specialists

The Law Society also has specialist accredited panels, one for children matters only and others for family law and for family mediation. The Law Society's 'Find a Solicitor' page of the website www.lawsociety.org.uk allows you to narrow your search to accredited solicitors. When the list of firms comes up, the site shows which have specialist solicitors and who they are.

Avoiding Certain Solicitors

If you anticipate an especially rancorous divorce, you want a solicitor who acts as your legal ally and your advocate, not one who's merely interested in collecting fees. Steer clear, therefore, of solicitors who brag about themselves a great deal, act distractedly when you speak, trivialise your questions by not answering them or telling you 'not to worry about that', or who ignore your questions entirely.

Avoid solicitors who talk down to you, don't ask you any questions, or allow themselves to be constantly interrupted by phone calls or conversations with people who come into their office while you're meeting. And make sure that your solicitor doesn't leave other clients' files where you can see or read information confidential to them.

If any of the solicitors on your list ask you few, if any, questions about your marriage, your finances or your divorce goals, cross that solicitor's name off your list.

Meeting Potential Solicitors

After you narrow your list of solicitors down to a small number, a good idea is to telephone their offices to check the individual's availability and any other essential criteria (such as whether they offer legal aid if you think you may need it). By this time you should have just one or two with whom you want to arrange a meeting to ask how they would treat your case. Don't engage a solicitor just because someone you know and respect gives him a glowing review. Make up your own mind after an in-person meeting.

During your first meeting, don't be afraid to ask questions. Find out about the solicitor's experience and talk about possible approaches to your divorce case. Make sure that you and the solicitor you decide to work with are in agreement regarding the type of divorce you want to pursue and that he concurs with your divorce goals and priorities (unless the solicitor can give you good reasons for revising them).

Requesting a free consultation

Many solicitors give you a free 30-minute to one-hour initial consultation, but you may have to ask for it. Solicitors who don't offer you free consultations may charge you a nominal sum – £5 to £50 – for an initial meeting or may charge their normal hourly rate. However, the amount of money solicitors charge for an initial meeting with you has no bearing on their skills in divorce law.

Questioning the solicitor, and responses you need to hear

Bring a notebook with you to your meetings so that you can record the important points and how each solicitor replies to your questions. Don't be shy about taking notes. Also, as soon as possible after each meeting has ended, write down your impressions of the solicitor you've just met.

To get you started on developing a list of questions, the following are some of the most important ones to ask. (These questions are most appropriate if you're engaging a solicitor to help with your divorce negotiations or because you need to be represented in court.)

- **How long have you been practising divorce law, roughly how many cases have you handled, and how many hearings have you been involved in?**

  Look for a solicitor who has been a family lawyer for at least three years. If you anticipate that your divorce may end up in court, make sure that the solicitor has some advocacy experience, and preferably has successfully represented other clients at contested hearings.

- **Do you take other kinds of cases as well? If so, what percentage of your practice is represented by family cases?**

  Not less than 50 per cent of the solicitor's caseload should be family cases.

- **Have you ever had a case like mine? How did you handle it?**

  Avoid a solicitor who has never dealt with the particular issues in your divorce case, such as your spouse being a foreign national or if you were married abroad. Solicitors can't give you specific details about another case, but they can tell you enough for you to determine whether they have sufficient experience to deal with a case such as yours.

- **Who actually handles my case – you, another person in your firm, or both of you?**

  Don't assume that you're receiving inferior legal care if a skilled paralegal under the supervision of a solicitor or a legal executive works on your case. Both can do a good job of handling certain aspects of a divorce for considerably less money than if your solicitor deals personally with you.

- **What do you think about mediation?**

  If you and your spouse reach a stalemate on some aspect of your divorce and you want to give mediation a try, select a solicitor who believes in mediation and has used it successfully in divorces such as yours.

- **How do you charge, and how do you expect to be paid?**

Find out the solicitor's hourly rate, whether he does any publicly funded work (or *legal aid*), and get an estimate of how much your divorce is going to cost. If you're worried about how to pay for the legal help you need, be upfront about your concerns. See the later section 'What if You Can't Afford Your Solicitor's Fees?' for more about public funding.

✔ **Do you provide me with an estimate of your expenses and an explanation of what those expenses may include?**

You may have to pay the cost of long-distance calls, facsimiles, copying, delivery fees, outside expert fees, court fees, and so on.Solicitors call these *disbursements*. If you object to paying certain expenses, ask for an explanation in advance of why you should be billed for them. If the expenses aren't essential to your case, let the solicitor know that you're unwilling to pay for them. Solicitors should not incur any substantial disbursements without your prior authorisation.

✔ **How often am I billed for your expenses, and do I get an itemised bill?**

You should expect to receive itemised bills. Asking for them monthly is the best idea, even if little work has been done, because it helps you to budget and keep up to date with your costs.

✔ **If I have questions about my case, can I call you? How quickly can I expect to have my calls returned?**

Expecting your calls to be returned within 24 hours is reasonable, unless you make clear that you're calling with an emergency. Then your call should be returned within an hour or two, possibly by another family solicitor in the team, if yours is unavailable.

✔ **What's your approach going to be, based on what you know about my divorce?**

The solicitor should be able to provide you with a preliminary assessment of the strengths and the weaknesses of your case (and your spouse's case) and a clear explanation of how he intends to maximise your strengths and minimise your weaknesses in order to get you the best divorce possible. Steer clear of solicitors who emphasise 'playing hardball' rather than negotiating and trying mediation. Hardball tactics cost money.

✔ **If you can't negotiate a settlement and any issue in my divorce goes to a full hearing, will you or someone else from your firm represent me in court or will you recommend a barrister?**

If you think that an issue in your divorce may be fully contested, you may want a solicitor who has advocacy experience and who can handle your divorce from start to finish. Alternatively, the solicitor may use a barrister, or *counsel,* for your representation in court. Barristers are not necessarily more expensive than solicitors, and they usually have more experience presenting cases in court. However, some extra time and cost are involved in your solicitor instructing the barrister on your behalf, and you may well need a personal meeting with the barrister before your hearing, for which you're expected to pay.

✔ **What can I do to minimise my legal expenses?**

Some solicitors are more amenable than others to letting you conduct certain aspects of your case yourself – picking up documents, copying, conducting simple research and doing other tasks a layperson can handle.

✔ **What do you expect from me?**

Any reputable solicitor expects a client to provide full disclosure of all relevant facts, provide information on a timely basis, return phone calls promptly, be honest, pay bills on time, and respect the solicitor's advice regarding what to do or not do in terms of the case. However, ultimately you're the one who makes the decisions and the solicitor must follow your instructions as long as he is acting within the law and the ethics of the profession.

✔ **Are you trained as a collaborative lawyer?**

If you want your case to be dealt with in a co-operative way, using this alternative form of dispute resolution, your spouse's solicitor must also be a collaborative lawyer. For further information on collaborative law see Chapter 5.

Producing the documents you need

When you meet prospective solicitors, try to bring along some key documents and a summary of information regarding your family's finances, including the following:

✔ Your marriage certificate.

✔ A list of your assets and debts.

✔ Copies of your and your spouse's current will.

✔ Details and evidence of your income, both gross and net (that is, before and after deductions for tax, National Insurance, and so on).

✔ Copies of deeds to property and details of any mortgages.

✔ A copy of any pre-marital or separation agreement that you may have signed.

✔ Any correspondence that you've received from your spouse or your spouse's solicitor about the divorce or from the Child Maintenance and Enforcement Commission, or CMEC (formerly the Child Support Agency, or CSA).

Chapter 7 provides a comprehensive list of the types of financial and other information you should have already prepared and assembled in preparation for your divorce. When you engage a solicitor, you may have to provide additional background information and documentation.

Finding out what a solicitor wants to know about you

Your initial meeting is a two-way exchange – you aren't the only one asking questions. The solicitor needs to get some information from you before he can answer your questions. Solicitors must also ensure that they don't have a conflict of interest if they represent you. A conflict exists, for example, if their law firm represents your spouse's business.

The following list gives you an idea of the types of questions you can expect a solicitor to ask you:

- How long have you been married and where were you married? Why are you getting a divorce?

- Are you and your spouse still living together? If not, with whom are your children living (if you have children) and who's in the family home?

- Have any previous proceedings taken place or have you used solicitors before in relation to your marriage or separation?

- Do you and your spouse have a pre-marital, post-marital or separation agreement?

- What major assets do you and your spouse own, and what do you estimate each of those assets is worth?

- What are your family debts?

- What kind of employment-related benefits, if any, do you and your spouse have?

- Are you and your spouse retired or do either of you have plans to retire soon?

- What are your goals for your divorce in terms of spousal support, property settlement, child residence and contact, and child support?

- Do you have any dependent children from your marriage?

- What kind of relationship do you have with your children and what role do you play in their day-to-day lives as a parent?

- Has a social worker or child protection officer had any dealings with you or your children?

- What do you think would be the best arrangements for your children?

- Has there been any violence or abuse in your relationship?

- Are any third parties involved?

- Do I need to know anything else about you, your spouse or your marriage?

Be prepared to provide honest answers to questions that may make you feel uncomfortable, such as: 'Do you have any present intention to cohabit or remarry?' and 'Is your spouse aware of your affair?'.

Getting the Terms and Conditions of Business in Writing

After you decide on a solicitor, ask for a contract, written agreement or letter and terms of business before you pay any money over and above the cost of your initial interview. According to the Law Society's client care code, the document should detail all the specifics you and the solicitor agreed to during any of your meetings, including financial arrangements and an estimate of the costs, certain services the solicitor will or will not provide, payment arrangements, and so forth.

Don't hesitate to take a day or two to re-read the contract or agreement thoroughly before signing it. Ask the solicitor about anything you don't understand and keep asking until all your questions have been answered to your satisfaction. If you and the solicitor agree to add or delete anything, make certain that those changes are reflected in the document before you sign it. Keep a copy of the final signed contract or agreement for your files.

Changing Your Solicitor if You're a Private Client

The solicitor who helps you with your divorce is working for you. So, if you're unhappy with something your solicitor does or doesn't do, communicate that dissatisfaction to him, but be reasonable about it. If you do have cause to complain and aren't satisfied with the outcome of your complaint, you can write to the Legal Complaints Service (LCS) at Victoria Court, 8 Dormer Place, Leamington Spa, Warwickshire CU32 5AE; helpline 0845 608 6565. You can also contact the LCS at www.legalcomplaints.org.uk.

If you're sure that your solicitor isn't doing a good job of representing you, and you're a privately paying client, you can dismiss him. (If you're publicly funded, see the next section.) However, you do have to pay for any work the solicitor has performed up to that point and for any and all expenses the solicitor has incurred on your behalf. Your solicitor is entitled to hold onto your file of papers until he receives payment.

Before you dismiss your solicitor, consider getting a second opinion from another solicitor. You may find that your solicitor is doing the very best job possible under the circumstances and you may not be any happier with someone else.

Changing Your Solicitor if You're Publicly Funded

If you're publicly funded and for any reason you decide that you want to change solicitors, you can't do so without the co-operation of the Legal Services Commission (LSC). If you want to change solicitors because, for example, you're moving to a different area, you need to approach your newly chosen solicitor to help you apply to the LSC to amend your certificate. If you want to change because you're dissatisfied with your solicitor, the LSC may expect you to go through the solicitor's firm's complaints procedures before considering whether to allow you to change.

Discovering What to Do if You Can't Afford Your Solicitor's Fees

You may not be able to afford to pay the fees of even a relatively inexperienced solicitor. If you check your finances and come up short, some form of public funding or some other legal resources may be available to help you with your divorce.

Qualifying for public funding: legal aid

You may be able to receive help with the funding of certain sorts of cases under a scheme operated by the government of England and Wales. The scheme is known as the Community Legal Service (CLS) and is run by the Legal Services Commission (previously the Legal Aid Board). The Legal Services Commission (LSC) has strict criteria for the granting of any sort of public funding, and it only pays firms and agencies that hold LSC contracts to do this work.

For more information about public funding and legal aid, look on the Community Legal Service website at www.communitylegaladvice.org.uk. This site has family information leaflets that can be downloaded, contains a directory facility for finding an LSC-contracted provider/solicitor, and also has a legal aid financial eligibility calculator. You can download a leaflet on public funding called *A Step-by-Step Guide to Legal Aid, help with paying for civil cases.* This describes the legal aid system, what it covers and what you may have to pay. You can phone on 0845 345 4345 and a family telephone helpline is expected to be rolled out nationally. The LSC website www.legalservices. gov.uk has useful information about legal aid generally.

If you live in Scotland and are on a low income or have no income apart from your spouse's, you may be able to apply to the Scottish Legal Aid Board, also known as SLAB (www.slab.org.uk), for financial help. This financial aid goes towards advice and correspondence your solicitor provides on your behalf. It doesn't cover the cost of raising a divorce action. For this you must have a certificate for full legal aid. To be assessed for legal aid, you need to fill in detailed forms about your finances and await the decision from SLAB about your eligibility.

Northern Ireland also has its own legal aid system run by the Northern Ireland Legal Services Commission. Look at www.nilsc.org.uk or call on 0289 040 8990 for further information.

The statutory charge

You need to regard most forms of public funding for family proceedings as a loan rather than a gift. That is because you have to repay any costs that your solicitor reasonably incurs on your behalf out of any money or property that you recover or preserve in the proceedings (apart from maintenance). Your solicitor isn't allowed to release the money or property owed to you until you repay your costs to the LSC or you have an agreement to postpone repayment, as described in the following paragraphs. This amount is known as the *statutory charge* or *legal aid charge.*

Limits apply to the amount of work that solicitors can do for publicly funded clients and to the rates that they can charge. Although these limits vary for different sorts of work, a publicly funded bill is generally a great deal lower than private charges. If you're publicly funded (or *legally aided*) and your spouse isn't, your total bill for the divorce is likely to be significantly lower than his, even if the work that your solicitors do is very similar.

If you do have the benefit of public funding, you may have to pay little if anything upfront to the LSC while your case is in progress. However, don't lose sight of the fact that ultimately you're responsible for your costs. You and your solicitor always need to weigh up the costs of any particular action against the benefits that you're hoping to achieve. And because you're ultimately responsible for the final bill, you're entitled to expect your solicitor to give you regular estimates and updates of your costs just as you would if you were privately paying.

Mediation and the statutory charge

You'll be pleased to know that one of the current perks of using family mediation is that you don't need to make any financial contributions and the statutory charge doesn't apply (check out the next section, 'Qualifying for public funding: the Family Help scheme'). If you manage to reach an agreement on all key issues in your divorce through mediation and your solicitor puts your mediation agreement into legal form and helps you implement it, you don't have to repay the costs incurred by your mediator or your solicitor, which can represent a major saving to you and your spouse. The family 'pot' to be divided between you doesn't suffer any significant deduction for costs.

The system for public funding (legal aid) of family mediation is different in Scotland and Northern Ireland from the position in England and Wales. If you receive legal aid for advice and assistance in Scotland, your solicitor can apply to the Scottish Legal Aid Board for your share of the fees for mediation to be covered. This situation applies only where the mediator or the family mediation service charges mediation fees.

Northern Ireland has its own Legal Services Commission that provides more limited assistance with the costs of Family Mediation than in the rest of the UK. Do discuss this with your solicitor or the Family Mediation Service provider, so that you're very clear about how much you may be asked to pay.

Qualifying for public funding: the Family Help scheme

Different levels of service are available for publicly funded (legally aided) work within the area of family law with differing criteria for eligibility and scope, and with different levels of remuneration for solicitors, in some cases by way of standard fees rather than hourly rates based on actual time spent. All applications for public funding (legal aid) are assessed on their merits, and you may also be assessed on your means. Receipt of Income Support, Income-Based Jobseeker's Allowance, or Guarantee State Pension Credit, however, are passports to eligibility. To help you understand this area, we set out below a guide to the levels of service that you're most likely to come across in England and Wales during your divorce. But if you find it bewildering, phone 0845 3454 345 or take a look at www.communitylegaladvice. org.uk or www.legalservices.gov.uk.

Family Help is a service of several levels that covers family disputes, and includes help in resolving those disputes through negotiation or other means. Family Help doesn't include the provision of mediation services by the solicitor, but does allow the solicitor to give you help and advice in support of family mediation. The solicitor normally starts by arranging a meeting for you with a mediator (have a look at the 'Publicly funded family mediation' section later in this chapter and at Chapter 16 for more info). Family Help also doesn't cover preparation of your case or representation by a solicitor or barrister at a contested final hearing in court. For that you need to go to the *Legal Representation* level, which costs more because of the statutory charge.

Family Help (Lower) – Level 1 advice

Level 1 is the basic level of legal advice available, and covers you for preliminary advice and assistance on most aspects of divorce and child matters. Assuming that you're financially eligible, Level 1 covers the solicitor's initial meeting with you and any work immediately flowing from that, which can be a letter of advice, a telephone call or a referral to another organisation. It also covers general advice about your dispute and methods of resolution, such as mediation.

The fee received by the solicitor at this level is a single fee, which is usually a standard amount, and at this level no statutory charge applies unless the dispute proceeds to other levels (see the later sections 'Family Help (Higher) – Level 3 advice' and 'Legal Representation') and your home or other assets are in dispute.

Level 1 allows your solicitor to assist you in undefended divorce proceedings (the vast majority of cases) but not to start court proceedings or attend court with you (other than help in obtaining a court order which confirms a financial agreement – called a *consent order*). If the divorce is very straightforward, he may suggest that you deal with the procedure yourself. In almost all cases you don't need to attend court anyway, but if you do need to attend personally, your solicitor tells you what arrangements can be made to represent you (again, take a look at the 'Family Help (Higher) – Level 3 advice' and 'Legal Representation' sections later in this chapter).

The income and capital limits for eligibility are reviewed each year but up to April 2009, if your gross income is £2,530 or less per calendar month, and your disposable capital £8,000 or less, you may be eligible for Family Help. Assets that are the subject of dispute between you and your spouse can't be taken into account for these purposes. If you're financially eligible for Level 1 help you don't have to pay any contribution towards your costs, but see the earlier section 'Qualifying for public funding (legal aid)' regarding the statutory charge. At Level 1, the solicitor assesses your eligibility and can provide advice straight away.

Family Help (Lower) – Level 2 advice

Level 2 of the Family Help scheme allows your solicitor to assist you where a significant dispute exists relating to children and/or finance, which requires work beyond the initial interview and follow-up:

✔ In children cases, Level 2 goes up to, but doesn't usually include, the issue of court proceedings.

✔ In finance cases, Level 2 goes up to, but doesn't include, the issue of court proceedings, except where proceedings are issued for the purpose of obtaining a consent order (a court order that confirms a financial agreement).

When a person is participating in family mediation or has successfully reached an agreement or settlement as a result of family mediation and is in need of legal assistance, this may be provided under Family Help (Lower, Levels 1 and 2). Even when you're assisted under the Levels 1 and 2 of Family Help, this isn't an automatic passport to exemption from payment of court fees (in 2008, £340 for a divorce). To claim exemption you're given forms to complete and sign and you have to send the court up-to-date proof of your finances.

For Level 2, the solicitor must check your financial eligibility, but he is able to provide advice straight away. This level of service entitles you to a limited amount of advice and assistance with the negotiations or disclosure process.

You automatically qualify for all levels of legal aid if you're on Income Support, Income-Based Jobseekers' Allowance, or Guarantee State Pension Credit.

Where the case completes at the Family Help (Lower) level, the statutory charge doesn't apply unless the costs in the case are exceptional and are claimed at an hourly rate. In these cases the statutory charge applies to costs and disbursements (expenses paid on your behalf) above the exceptional case threshold; that is, actual costs incurred above three times the standard fee. Where a case doesn't conclude at Family Help (Lower) but proceeds to Family Help (Higher), the charge is attached to all costs including those incurred at Family Help (Lower).

Family Help (Higher) – Level 3 advice

If you and your spouse aren't able to resolve any key issues in your divorce without going to court, you may want to apply for a Legal Funding Certificate to help with your legal costs and expenses – known as Level 3 advice.

The LSC takes responsibility for assessing your means, and they may ask you to pay a monthly contribution (on a sliding scale according to your means) for the lifetime of your case, and/or a one-off contribution from your capital, by making a written 'offer' to you. You need to accept the offer and pay any capital contribution (your disposable capital in excess of £3,000 assessed in accordance with the relevant rules) and the first monthly contribution from income before a certificate is issued and the solicitor can start work for you (although, see below regarding urgent work). Any contribution that you make is credited to you when the costs are calculated at the end of your case and set against any liability you have under the statutory charge (refer to the earlier 'The statutory charge' and the later 'Solicitors' time/costs and the statutory charge' sections).

Family Help (Higher) authorises help in relation to a family dispute, including assistance in resolving that dispute through negotiation or otherwise. This Help includes starting court proceedings and representation by your barrister or solicitor in proceedings when you and your spouse have not agreed about the finances. Family Help (Higher) doesn't cover you for preparation for or representation at a contested final hearing or appeal. For that, take a look at the later 'Legal Representation' section.

Family Help (Higher) requires an application to the LSC for a certificate before help can be provided, but the solicitor may be able to grant limited cover immediately in an urgent case such as one involving domestic violence (see the 'Solicitors' time/costs and the statutory charge' section later in this chapter).

Financial eligibility and merits criteria apply to the provision of Family Help (Higher).

Legal Representation

Legal Representation covers representation by your solicitor or a barrister in 'family proceedings'. The LSC divides 'family proceedings' into a range of different case types, such as finances or cases about children, and applies different criteria to each. These criteria reflect the nature and priority of the subject area and, in many cases, the need to ensure that Legal Representation is indeed the most appropriate form of service. Solicitors can grant emergency representation in urgent cases. Otherwise decisions on funding are made by the LSC's regional offices.

In most circumstances, the client must attend an assessment meeting with a mediator – to consider the suitability of mediation in the particular case – before an application can be made for Family Help (Higher) or for Legal Representation in family proceedings. However, some cases are excluded from this requirement and various exemptions also apply – for example where the matter is urgent (see the 'Emergency certificates' section later in this chapter) or the other party is unwilling to attend an assessment meeting or consider mediation.

Solicitors' time/costs and the statutory charge

The amount of time spent on your case depends at what level your solicitor is assisting you. He always has to consider how far the work is reasonable and necessary, and whether a client of moderate means would pay for it. Your solicitor also tells you if your case is exceptional – for which an unusual amount of extra work needs doing at Family Help (Lower, Level 2) and which might involve the statutory charge. But usually a point comes where the work requires further funding through Family Help (Higher, Level 3).

If the only work done is under Level 1 and/or 2 and you don't have an 'exceptional case', you don't have to pay any costs (that is, the statutory charge). However, the statutory charge does apply in the following circumstances:

- ✔ If extra work is done as an exceptional case under Level 2 and the case stops there, the statutory charge is payable on the value of that extra work, but your home is exempt.

- ✔ If extra work is done as an exceptional case under Level 2 *and* you get or keep money or property because of work done under Family Help (Higher) and/or Legal Representation, *all* the Level 1 and/or 2 costs must be repaid to the LSC. For example:

  - Advice with divorce proceedings under Level 1 connected with a Level 3 Legal Funding Certificate covering financial disputes with your spouse in that divorce attracts the full statutory charge.

  - Advice about domestic violence concerning your ex-spouse under Level 1 connected with a Level 3 Legal Funding Certificate covering financial disputes with that ex-spouse attracts the full statutory charge.

  - Advice about children and/or financial issues concerning your ex-partner under Levels 1 and/or 2 connected with a Level 3 Legal Funding Certificate covering financial disputes with that ex-partner attracts the full statutory charge.

Publicly funded family mediation

Public funding can be given to you for mediation whether you're referred by a solicitor or you contact the mediation service before, during or after seeing a solicitor. Some mediations, especially about children, can be completed without solicitors being involved at all and you can still be publicly funded for the costs of the mediation.

If you qualify for public funding, not only do you get completely free mediation but also a legal aid solicitor can give you legal advice to support mediation, which means that you don't have to pay any contribution towards your costs for the whole process. Nor are any of your costs the subject of the statutory charge if you go ahead with an agreement reached in mediation, and so you need not repay these charges at a later date. (See the earlier section, 'Mediation and the statutory charge'.) The income and capital limits for eligibility are the same as for other forms of legal aid (see the earlier section 'Qualifying for public funding: the Family Help scheme'). The mediator assesses your means and can tell you at your initial appointment if you're eligible, providing you take evidence of your means.

You don't have to undergo a means test if your children are the subject of proceedings by the local authority for a care or supervision order, or if your children have been abducted abroad. You're granted public funding for representation in those proceedings without any means assessment or contribution from you. Free legal advice is also available to parents where a local authority gives written notice of its intention to commence proceedings for a care or supervision order.

Emergency certificates

If your case is urgent (your spouse has seriously threatened or abused you, for example), your solicitor may be able to grant an emergency certificate without waiting for a full response from the LSC. You still need to fill out the application forms and your solicitor needs to be satisfied of the merits and urgency of your application, and of your financial eligibility. You have to promise to repay the LSC if you don't co-operate in the LSC assessment of your finances; if it turns out, after all, that you're not eligible; or if you refuse an offer of public funding requiring payment of a contribution. Your solicitor is then also entitled to recover additional costs from you at private client rates.

Discharge or revocation of your certificate

If your solicitor can no longer justify you continuing to receive public funding, he has a duty to notify the LSC. This may be because your case has successfully finished, the merits of your case have changed, you're behaving unreasonably, or because your means have changed so that you're no longer financially eligible. Your certificate may then be discharged.

Your solicitor also has to notify the LSC if he thinks that you're being dishonest about your circumstances. In that case, the LSC may revoke your certificate, which means that you're treated as never having been eligible for legal aid and you become personally liable for all your costs from the outset. This measure is harsh but is used only where justified. The LSC has to give prior notice of most discharges and all revocations.

Finding alternative ways to pay

You may have other means at your disposal to pay for legal help even if you don't have sufficient cash or aren't entitled to legal aid:

- ✔ **Payment plan:** You may be able to find a solicitor who allows you to pay for his services over time, depending on your future earning potential. Also, some solicitors take credit card payments.

✔ **Charge on your property:** If you own property or other significant assets that you're fairly certain of keeping as part of your settlement, a solicitor may be willing to take a charge on that property or make an agreement that you pay your costs out of it at the end of your case. If a charge applies and you sell the property, your solicitor is in line to receive all or some of what you owe him from the sale proceeds. If you have such an agreement with your solicitor, get the terms of agreement in writing and check it out with another independent solicitor before you sign.

✔ **Loan:** You may be able to get a bank loan. Some banks on the Internet offer such loans. But take care – costs can increase rapidly and unexpectedly and loans can be expensive.

✔ **Matrimonial fee funding schemes:** A variety of schemes are now available through which a finance company may give you credit and then pay regular amounts to your solicitor to fund your case. Ask your solicitor for details.

Considering a DIY Divorce

You may be tempted to handle your divorce yourself. Although nothing is intrinsically complicated about the divorce procedure, like other things such as plumbing in a washing machine or building a flat pack wardrobe, the first experience is the worst and you can spend a lot of time finding out just how everything is done and reading the instructions.

Nevertheless you can get a lot of information and download forms from the Courts Service website www.hmcourts-service.gov.uk/infoabout/divorce/index.htm. This website takes you through the procedures step by step and is very clear. You can also find (but not in Northern Ireland) several DIY divorce websites that provide forms (for a fee) and help you fill them in (also for a fee).

However, unless your marriage is short and you have no children or complicated finances, getting the help of a solicitor and/or mediator is the safest way. You have a lot to think about and take into consideration during a divorce and unless you're both in total agreement about everything (which is unusual) you may well find the whole business too stressful.

Chapter 16

Using a Mediator to Help You Work Things Out Together

In This Chapter

▶ Defining mediation

▶ Grasping how the mediation process works

▶ Appreciating the benefits of mediation

▶ Understanding the role of your solicitor in mediation

▶ Wrapping up the mediation process

*W*hen you and your spouse are working out the terms of your divorce, no matter how hard you both may try, you're likely to encounter issues that you can't resolve on your own. If that happens, you don't have to tear your hair out in frustration or throw in the towel and prepare for a court hearing. Rather than let sticky issues derail co-operation over your divorce, you and your spouse may still be able to work out a negotiated settlement by using mediation.

This chapter explains what mediation is and how it works, and describes the characteristics of a good divorce mediator. It also sets out the role of your solicitor when you use mediation (because opting for mediation doesn't eliminate your need for a solicitor).

What is Mediation?

Mediation is a voluntary confidential dispute-resolution method that relies on the open exchange of information, ideas and options to help you and your spouse resolve your differences without going to court. Although mediation can help resolve a wide variety of matters, it has proven to be an especially cost-effective tool for divorcing couples. Over 70 per cent of couples using mediation reach an agreement – two-thirds of those come to an agreement on all their divorce issues during mediation.

Mediation can help both you and your spouse to come out winners and avoid a court hearing in which typically one of you wins and the other loses. It also enables you, if you have children, to work together in your children's best interests.

When do you start mediation?

The starting point for family mediation is when you've already separated or divorced, or you plan to do so. After you reach this point, mediation can take place at any time – before you begin to take court action, when you encounter something you can't agree upon, or when you get as far as court and the judge suggests you consider mediation instead of having the court make a decision for you. Courts vary a great deal in their approach to mediation, but generally a judge is more likely to suggest mediation for children matters than for financial matters.

Most mediators give you each an opportunity to find out about mediation and the mediator before you commit yourselves to the process. This is called a *pre-mediation interview* or *intake appointment.* If one of you wants to apply to the Legal Services Commission (LCS) for public funding (or legal aid) for your case, you're first asked to meet a mediator to see if mediation is suitable for you. In most cases, you have to consider this option before financial assistance can be granted for a solicitor to represent you in court. (See Chapter 15, and the section 'Getting Help With the Cost of Mediation' later in this chapter for more about public funding.)

About readiness for mediation

If you're feeling a great deal of anger or other strong emotions about your divorce, you may need to go for counselling before you can sit down constructively with your spouse to make use of mediation successfully. (See Chapter 2 for a list of counselling organisations and their contact details.)

About the safety of mediation

If your marriage involved a history of violence or you fear that going together to mediation sessions may trigger violence, mediation may not be right for you. You can talk about this issue on your own with a mediator first if you still want to find out about mediation. Mediators are required by their professional Code of Practice and membership of their professional body to ensure that their practice of mediation is safe. If you opt for mediation, the mediator discusses with you how to make it safe, but see the sidebar 'Sometimes, mediation isn't such a good idea.'

What do mediators do?

If you decide to go ahead with mediation, the mediation sessions normally involve a three-way meeting with you, your spouse and your mediator. At your first session, the mediator establishes the ground rules for your negotiations, clarifies the issue(s) that you want to resolve and sets an agenda for your discussions. Your next step is to work through the agenda one item after another. Depending on the complexity of the issues you need to resolve, and how well you and your spouse are able to work together, you may be able to resolve matters in a single mediation session, or it may take three or more sessions before you reach an agreement.

A mediator doesn't take sides, interject opinions or provide legal advice. Even if she is a family lawyer, giving legal advice to you or your spouse is unethical. In addition, a mediator isn't a counsellor. If one of you is too upset to work during sessions, the mediator may suggest that she mediate with you in separate rooms, or recommend counselling alongside mediation. A mediator can't make decisions for you or order you or your spouse to do anything you don't want to do. Instead, the mediator sets out to create an environment in which you and your spouse feel comfortable and are able to express your opinions calmly, talk over your differences and work out your problems together.

You may want to use a mediator only to help you talk through the arrangements you make for your children, with or without the help of a parenting plan (see Chapter 10). You may work everything else out with your solicitors. Or you may want only to sort out finances through mediation. Increasingly, couples are using mediation to sort out everything, called 'All Issues Mediation.'

Who are mediators?

Family mediators come from a family law background or a background in another profession that equips them to work with other people's relationships or decisions. For example, your mediator may also be a counsellor, a social worker or a teacher. Whatever their professional background, mediators have to undergo additional training to prepare them to mediate between divorcing or separating couples.

Family mediators must meet a set of agreed standards, be deemed competent and undergo continuing education. They aren't, for example, allowed to do work in England and Wales that's paid for by the Legal Services Commission unless they've been assessed as competent by the College of Mediators, or one of the mediators' professional bodies or the Law Society.

Sometimes, mediation isn't such a good idea

Mediation may not be good for you if:

✔ You're intimidated or threatened by your spouse.

✔ You haven't really decided yet whether your marriage is over or begun to clarify your own divorce priorities and goals, and so you don't know what to negotiate for.

✔ You can't get the information you need to negotiate on an equal footing with your

spouse – you suspect that your spouse is hiding assets, for example; a good solicitor doesn't let you go into mediation unprepared.

Although mediators can help you and your spouse to communicate again if you're no longer able to do so, you both need to *be prepared* to do so if mediation is to be effective. If you aren't, mediation is not such a good idea.

Working with a qualified mediator helps you ensure that whatever you and your spouse agree to complies with the law. However the outcome of mediation isn't legally binding. You decide whether to make your decisions in mediation legally binding, through a solicitor or by other means. You're always given the opportunity to receive individual legal advice before you finalise your decisions, and doing so is important.

Because your mediator understands the law and legal processes, she is able to defuse potentially explosive situations during your mediation sessions. For example, if your spouse threatens to storm out because you ask her exactly how much she earns, a mediator can remind your spouse that your solicitor requires that information and can get it anyway through a formal *disclosure* process if it isn't provided voluntarily in mediation. (Chapter 5 gives you the lowdown on disclosure.)

Any reputable family mediator tells you upfront that each of you also needs a solicitor. This is because a mediator works with you both impartially and therefore can't at the same time advise you individually about the proposals you reach in mediation. Because you're employing a mediator, however, you need to make much less use of your solicitor than if she was doing all the work for you.

If you need any help or advice with legal issues you can consult your solicitor at any time during the mediation. (See 'Asking for Mediation Help from Your Solicitor,' later in this chapter.)

Reaping the Benefits of Mediation

It takes two to tango, to sing a duet, and to make mediation work. So, if your spouse isn't serious about making mediation work, you're probably wasting your time as well as the mediator's. However, if your spouse is uncertain about whether or not to mediate, ask her to consider these important mediation benefits:

- You're helped to focus on the needs of your children.

- You can save money. Working out the sticky issues in your divorce using mediation can be much cheaper than going to court to resolve those issues. For example, some court cases have cost anything up to £30,000, although the average court case in which one key issue needs to be decided costs probably between £4,000 and £6,000.

Depending on where you live and whether your mediator works in the private or not-for-profit sector, a mediator in England and Wales can charge anywhere from £60, up to £300 an hour for some private mediators in London, with the average being about £80 per hour for each of you. Some mediators charge per session, one of which usually lasts about one and a half hours. When you realise that you're likely to attend three to five sessions on average, if you mediate all issues, you can see that compared to going to court, mediation is well worth the money. Also, you're likely to attend fewer sessions if you mediate only the arrangements for your children. And if you receive public funding, you pay nothing.

Family Mediation Scotland (FMS) services operate in the not-for-profit sector and have charitable status. A nominal charge applies for the service, which may be waived in circumstances of hardship. However, fees do apply if you use FMS to work out your property and financial matters. You need to ask them for a note of the fees. If you're on legal aid or have legal advice and assistance, your fees may be covered if the Scottish Legal Aid Board (www.slab.org.uk) approves the application for expenditure on mediation. Scottish solicitor mediators who work in the private sector charge fees at the commercial rate for mediation, and so you need to ask them about their fees (www.calmscotland.org.uk). If you're on legal aid, these fees can be reclaimed, too. See the later sidebar 'Family mediation in Scotland' for details of these organisations.

Similarly, Family Mediation Northern Ireland operates in the not-for-profit sector and has charitable status. However, the service is only free to you in certain circumstances, for example, when paid for by a social services trust or when you qualify for legal aid and your solicitor has obtained authority from Northern Ireland Legal Services Commission to pay for mediation.

- You may find a mediation session considerably less formal, less intimidating and less stressful than a court.

✔ You may resolve things faster. Depending on the caseload in your area's family court, your final hearing can take months – even a year or more – to arrive. On the other hand, after you decide to mediate, your first session can probably be fixed within the month – although just how long you and your spouse take to work things out is in your hands.

✔ You and your spouse can brainstorm about divorce agreement options. As a result, you may come up with fresh options for the care of your children, for the division of your assets, for maintenance for one of you, if you think it's needed, and for child support, which you may never have thought of otherwise.

✔ You're in control. You make the tough decisions in mediation, not a judge, and no one forces you to do anything.

✔ You preserve all your options. If mediation doesn't work, you can still go back to your solicitor to negotiate on your behalf, using all the information you may already have collected, or you can go to court.

✔ You preserve your privacy. When you use mediation, only you, your spouse and the mediator hear what you say.

✔ You and your spouse are more likely to be happy with your agreement and to honour it in the future, because you work it out together instead of a judge deciding.

Finding Family Mediators

Before using a mediator, you can ask your solicitor questions about the ones she recommends, or you can contact one or two directly and ask them questions such as:

✔ How much do the mediators charge for their services? Do they charge by the hour or do they charge by the session? Do they offer publicly funded mediation?

✔ What are their professional backgrounds?

✔ Is their professional body a member of the Family Mediation Council (National Family Mediation, the Family Mediators Association, Resolution, the Alternative Dispute Resolution Group and the College of Mediators – see www.familymediationcouncil.org.uk) or are they members of the Family Mediation Panel of the Law Societies in England and Wales or approved by the Law Society in Scotland?

✔ Can they mediate all the issues you need to resolve or just some of them? Some mediators handle the full gamut of divorce-related issues, but others don't mediate financial matters or children issues. You may want to use mediation only for one or two sticking-point issues.

✔ Does your solicitor have good reports of their use by previous clients?

You can find a qualified mediator in your area by contacting the Government's Family Mediation Helpline on 0845 602 6627 (www.family mediationhelpline.co.uk).

In Northern Ireland, try Family Mediation NI on 028 9024 3265 (www.family mediationni.org.uk) or the Mediators' Institute of Ireland on 00 353 1 284 7121 (www.themii.ie).

Find out whether the mediators in your locality do publicly funded work and what they charge. You may want to ask whether they mediate alone or in pairs for all or some of the sessions and how many sessions are involved.

Family mediation in Scotland

Two organisations are approved to provide family mediation in Scotland:

✔ **Local family mediation services affiliated to Family Mediation Scotland (www. relationships-scotland.org. uk).** Family Mediation Scotland has joined forces with Couple Counselling Scotland to become Relationship Scotland. Its mediation work is directed at families with dependent children and can include children over 16 and in full-time education or further education.

✔ **Solicitor mediators accredited by the Law Society of Scotland (www.lawscot. org.uk).** The Law Society of Scotland is the governing body for Scottish solicitors who act as mediators, and the Society offers mediation on all issues – property, finance and your children. They also mediate with you if you have no dependent children. Solicitor mediators are usually members of CALM (Comprehensive Accredited Solicitor Mediators; www.calmscotland. org.uk).

These organisations meet standards set by the Lord President of the Court of Session (Scotland's highest civil court). They have to regulate their mediators and ensure that the mediators abide by a standard code of practice.

Mediators working for these organisations are protected by Scottish law from giving evidence in court. This protection means that no matter what you say in mediation, it can't be used as evidence if you go to court. Certain exceptions do apply, though – for instance, where a criminal offence has been committed or a child's safety is at risk, or if each of you agrees that the mediator should give evidence.

All Family Mediation Scotland's services offer individual, separate and confidential appointments when you contact the service. At these appointments you each hear the same information about what mediation can offer you and what other services are provided. You're also asked about your family situation and your mediator should check with you that mediation will be safe, especially if your relationship has included any violence or abuse. If mediation is a risk, you have several other options for getting help:

✔ **Contact centres:** Most family mediation services in Scotland provide contact centres. Children can spend time here with a parent they don't live with, if parents find that making these arrangements is difficult. You can find more information on contact centres at www.familymediation scotland.org.uk, or have a look at Chapter 10.

(continued)

(continued)

✔ **Support groups:** Many of the family media- tion services offer support groups for adults and also for children going through sepa- ration or divorce. Some services also have children's workers who offer individual ses- sions to children experiencing short-term difficulty. (See Chapter 2 for a list of support groups.)

✔ **Time to Talk:** This specialist service is mainly for children whose parents can't meet in mediation, but who want to find out their children's views on matters to do with the separation or divorce. Sometimes this service is used as an alternative to the court seeking the children's views. Refer to Chapter 10 for other ways to find out what your children are thinking.

Ask your mediator what she can offer you, your spouse and your children, because new services are being developed all the time. For example, all family mediation services offer mediation that includes (where appropriate) your children, grandparents and members of step-families. However, not all family mediation services offer mediation on property and finan- cial issues. If they don't offer it themselves, they can put you in touch with a solicitor or mediator in your area or a neighbouring family mediation service.

Taking Your First Mediation Step

When you decide on mediation, and a mediator, your first contact is usually in person, to discuss in confidence whether mediation is truly suitable for you and the issues you want to resolve.

Your mediator should also talk to your spouse to make sure that you both choose and intend to use mediation and that you both understand what it involves.

The mediator can give you an idea of how many meetings you're likely to need – depending on the number and complexity of the issues you want to resolve – and the likely cost to each of you. (See 'Getting Help with the Cost of Mediation' later in this chapter about applying for public funding for mediation.)

You're strongly encouraged to get a solicitor to advise each of you at the end of mediation and possibly along the way.

If you discuss how much your mediation is going to cost and decide to move forward with it, you're asked to sign an agreement to mediate when you begin to work with your mediator.

An agreement to mediate

An agreement to mediate looks something like the following, and may include some of the following statements, depending on your mediator's usual practice:

By signing this agreement we express our sincere intention to:

✔ Be fair to each other

✔ Leave fault and blame out of the negotiations

✔ Be co-operative

✔ Consider the needs of our children, our individual needs and the needs of the family as a whole

✔ Work for the least emotional and financial upheaval

✔ Make full and frank disclosure of our finances

✔ Not transfer, change or conceal any assets in advance of reaching an agreement

✔ Make no charges on any account unless agreed by both of us

✔ Only talk to the mediator during sessions, not at other times

✔ Agree that all communications (except the disclosure of finances that are open for use by solicitors and the court) are made on the basis that they are confidential (unless they pose a real risk of harm to anyone or are evidence that one of you has benefited from the proceeds of a crime) and not to be referred to in any court evidence or affidavits

✔ Acknowledge that the Memorandum of Understanding (the concluding document) is not legally binding unless and until we choose to make it so, through our solicitors or by other means

✔ Recognise that the mediator can't give legal or other advice, and that it is our individual responsibility to obtain any such advice as appropriate

Understanding How Mediation Works

Mediation works for you by building up mutual understanding, co-operation and problem solving; it's *not* about winning or losing. During your mediation session, the mediator acts as coach, consensus builder, facilitator and, if necessary, referee, and provides or helps you to accomplish the following:

✔ Clarify exactly what you need to work out

✔ Organise your discussions by determining what you discuss first and how you approach each issue

✔ Keep your discussions moving forward

✔ Provide legal or other information as necessary (but not legal advice)

Identifying the issues and making an agenda

You're likely to enter mediation with separate agendas and may need to work with the mediator to agree on a common agenda. For example, you may think that you stand to lose everything – your spouse, children, home and way of life – and if you didn't initiate the divorce, it's all undeserved! Or, if you initiated the divorce, you may see yourself as managing better without your spouse, staying in the house with your children, and being generous about contact between your ex-spouse and your children. The mediator doesn't let you argue this out straight away, but instead encourages you to agree on an agenda of the things that need to be tackled, such as:

- How to separate
- What the arrangements will be for your children
- What to say to your children, when and how
- Who will live where
- How you'll share out money and property
- When all these arrangements will be put in place

Exploring the issues in detail

Unless you choose to use mediation only for settling arrangements for your children, you need to collect and share all the details of your finances just as you would if you were negotiating yourselves (Chapter 14) or through your solicitors (Chapter 15). You need to collect the information on the forms that are given to you by the mediator. These forms are similar to the forms you would use in England and Wales if you were asking a judge to decide things for you, commonly known as the *Form E*. Using this form means that the information is applicable and usable (or *portable*) for you in either context. (See Chapter 3 for an example of a worksheet for assembling this information.) You need to go through these forms together in your mediation sessions, and then the mediator can display the agreed facts from these forms for you both to see clearly.

When you talk together about how to look after your children when you're apart, the mediator helps you to look at your children's future through their eyes. Hopefully, looking at things from your children's perspectives helps you begin the transition of your relationship from partners to co-parents.

Calculating your individual incomes

You each must fill in an income sheet on which you list the following:

- ✔ Your monthly salary or wages from your main and any other employment.

- ✔ The deductions, such as National Insurance, income tax, pension contributions and any work-related subscriptions.

- ✔ Any state benefits such as Child Benefit, Working Tax Credit, Child Tax Credit, disability benefits, rent or council tax rebates.

- ✔ Any other sources of income, such as from property, trusts, shares, dividends, fees, casual payments or maintenance from a previous spouse, deducting your likely tax liabilities.

You then need to work out your separate total net monthly incomes. (See a sample in Chapter 3.)

Working out your expenditures

You must list separately what you currently spend and estimate what you need to spend in the future, to work out how much money you each need after your divorce. (Chapter 3 provides a guide to help you estimate your needs.)

You need to list separately expenditures for your children. Your children's expenses are likely to include:

- ✔ Child care.

- ✔ Education – travel, school meals, school trips, uniform and sports gear, any extra tuition (for example, music or sports) and support for further or higher education.

- ✔ Recreation.

- ✔ Clothes, including out-of-school clothes and equipment, nappies and so on.

Recording your assets

You must list all your assets, as follows (for help in establishing a full list of your assets and their values, see Chapter 7 for a worksheet):

- ✔ **Properties:** The value of your home, any other properties and any mortgages attached to them, and brief details of the purchase date and price (for assistance, see Chapter 7).

- ✔ **Bank accounts:** The name and address, account number and type, and balance at a given date.

- ✔ **Building society and savings accounts:** Same as the preceding.

- **Investments:** Name, type, size of holding, value and date.

- **Life insurances:** Company, policy number, date of maturity and value, surrender value.

- **Pension plans:** Company, type, date of maturity, lump sum, annual pension, cash equivalent transfer value, and widow or widower benefits, if any.

- **Cars and other vehicles:** Manufacturer, model, year and second-hand value

- **Valuables:** such as jewellery or antiques.

- **Other assets:** including money owed to you or any certain inheritances expected in the next few years.

Listing your debts and liabilities

Make a list of how much you owe and to whom, stating beside each item whether you're jointly or solely liable (for help creating this list, see Chapter 7):

- Bank overdrafts and loans
- Other loans
- Hire purchase and finance agreements
- Credit and store cards

Verifying the details

You need to verify that you really have the assets and liabilities that you say you have. To do so, collect and bring in detailed proof or *verification* of all your income, assets, pensions and debts (see Chapter 7). Following are some examples of the kind of proof you need to provide:

- **Income:** Payslips, benefit books, business accounts, and so on.

- **Assets:** The valuation of your house and a copy of the mortgage statement for your property or properties, including more than one estate agent's estimate of its value and a record of your mortgage payments to date. From these documents, you can work out what your house is currently worth to you (that is, the capital balance or *equity*).

- **Bank accounts:** Bank statements and building society pass books.

- **Policies:** Schedules and valuation statements.

- **Pension plans:** Pension statements.

- **Any other documentary evidence:** For example, credit card statements.

As you bring in your separate and joint financial information, the mediator displays it on a flip chart or a computer so that you both can see it all put together. This way you can see where you stand and whether a surplus (unlikely) or a shortfall (likely) exists between what you have and what you need.

Negotiating your future budgets

When you both see your income, expenditure, assets and liabilities clearly listed, you can get a measure of your future needs and resources. When a deficit exists between what you have and what you need, you have to do something to reduce that deficit – increase your income, cash in some assets, pay off some debts or reduce your future expenditure. To work out how best to accomplish this reduction, you need to decide on a few things:

- **Your goals and priorities:** You're encouraged to work towards agreeing on your goals and priorities as a basis for negotiating how you divide your assets and liabilities and your future expenses for yourself and your children.

- **Your options:** After you and your spouse establish some common goals, you can start thinking about the various options for meeting them. For example, if one of your common goals is that you each have accommodation large enough to house your children, you can then look at how you can achieve that, such as one of you staying in the family home and the other buying or renting elsewhere, or selling the home and each of you buying another smaller property.

  The goals and options that you discuss in mediation are not just confidential to you and the mediator; they are *privileged.* This term means that neither you nor your spouse – nor your mediator – may quote your discussions in court or in any court statements. The purpose of this restriction is to create an environment where you and your spouse can freely discuss any options you want without worrying that you may prejudice yourselves in any future court proceedings. In Scotland this privilege is protected by law (see the earlier sidebar 'Family mediation in Scotland' for details).

- **A parenting plan:** You must decide, on the basis of what's desirable and feasible for your children, whether you share the care of them equally or whether one of you is the resident parent. If you decide on the latter, you need to decide how the other person can succeed in, and sustain the cost of, staying close to the children. For more information on creating a parenting plan, see Chapter 10.

- **Child support:** You also need to work out how you share the cost of supporting your children. You can do this in the context of all your future income and expenditure or by reference to the formula adopted by the

Child Maintenance and Enforcement Commission/Child Support Agency. Asking for an estimate of this amount from the CMEC/CSA is always wise. See Chapter 13 for more about child support.

✔ **What to do with your home and pensions:** Some of the more common options for keeping or selling your home and for dividing your pensions are set out in Chapter 3 and Chapter 11. When you have the 'big picture' displayed before you, you're able to see more clearly what options are going to work out best for you.

Consulting your children during mediation

One great advantage of mediation is that you and your spouse can talk together about the future of your children. If you find this a painful thing to discuss, as it often is (see Chapter 10), a mediator can help you manage your emotions so that you can continue to value and talk to each other as parents, rather than just as divorcing spouses.

As you begin to shape your plans, moving where necessary away from competing for your children to co-operating for them, the mediator may suggest that you consult your children about the plans you're about to make. You can try talking to your children about the divorce in general (as we suggest in Chapter 10), but you can also involve them in your planning so that you can get their perspective, depending on their age and ability to deal with it.

If you're working on a parenting plan in mediation, you can show it to the children before settling it, if they're old enough to understand it. You can ask them to express their priorities on whether they'd prefer to move between two homes, or mostly live with one of you, and if so, how they want to keep close to their other parent. Children are often quite clear about some of these issues. You can't let them make your decisions for you – you're responsible for how you parent them – but you can consult them.

If you find consulting your children difficult for any reason, the mediator may suggest that she consult them separately and bring back their comments to you both in your next session. Not all mediators do this, but those who do have been trained to talk to children sensitively and carefully. The mediator should discuss meeting with your children very thoroughly with you beforehand and issues of confidentiality must be sorted out. The mediator only meets your children if you all agree that this approach is likely to help you make decisions for their benefit.

Your children may find it a relief to see a mediator, because they can then talk fairly freely and feel that they're contributing to the arrangements being made for them, especially if it has been hard for either or both of you to listen to them. However, the mediator is always careful to ensure that she doesn't become a counsellor for your children. If that's what your children need, the mediator suggests how counselling can be arranged.

TRUE DIVORCE STORIES

Sometimes the children *do* know best

Richard and Jenny, aged 11 and 8, were invited by their parents and a mediator to have their own meeting with the mediator – without their parents – to discuss their parents' plans for sharing their care. Their parents were talking about having Richard and Jenny change households several times during the week, whereby one parent would meet them from school on certain days and the other on other days. The parents had been rowing a lot and this meant they wouldn't have to meet each other face to face.

When the mediator described the proposed plan to Richard and Jenny, they said without hesitation, 'There will be too much rushing about.' Taking account of their separate after-school activities, Richard and Jenny suggested a series of simple adjustments, which seemed to resolve the issues for their parents and for themselves.

They asked the mediator, when she discussed with them how she was going to feed this information back to their parents, to emphasise that they loved both their parents and to ask the parents not to row in front of them. When the mediator met again with the parents to discuss their children's ideas and feelings with them, they were visibly moved and were proud that their children had been more practical than they had been.

Including other family members in a mediation session

During your mediation sessions you or your mediator may feel that other adults may usefully be included in the discussion, perhaps for a special meeting. A new adult partner may be living with your children or be present at their contact visits, or one or both of you may have remarried and your children have acquired step-parents and perhaps step-brothers and step-sisters. Life, having become complicated, may also have become stressful for you all and produced disputes or misunderstandings. Your children's grandparents, who may be able to offer help or may be getting excluded, can be involved in mediation. Battle lines may even have been drawn up unhelpfully between your families of origin (see Chapter 9).

If you're in such circumstances, no reason may exist why you shouldn't use mediation, which is a method of sorting out disputes and misunderstandings in all kinds of situations, not only those associated with the actual process of divorce. You can discuss this option with your mediator and see whether a viable idea is to include a particular person or people who may need to be heard and to listen to what you're planning. As with your children, mediation with other people in your life is done with great care, with the purpose and the ground rules clarified to everyone in advance of the meeting.

Four sisters were living with their father and his new partner. Their mother had also re-partnered. Tensions had been building up between the two households over the girls' visits to their mother. One night, two of the girls were so worked up about the phone rows going on that they ran away – fortunately to their grandparents. In the next mediation session, the parents blamed each other for causing the girls to run away, though it was clear that the problem involved more than just the two of them. They decided with the mediator that their new partners should be invited to attend a one-off meeting with them and the mediator. During the meeting, the two women began shouting at one another, each saying that the other was trying to take away the children. The mediator pointed out that they were both saying the same thing. After they realised that they shared identical fears, their relationship improved dramatically. The tension between the two households dissolved and the girls were able to spend time with both families – without so many rows.

The Memorandum of Understanding

As you negotiate your way through the big decisions together, step by step with the help of your mediator, she should be writing down what you propose. At the end of your sessions, your proposals are set out in written form, usually called an Outcome Statement or Memorandum of Understanding. This name is meant to draw attention to the fact that it is not legally binding unless and until you both agree to make it so through your solicitors or by other means. You may have worked together on a parenting plan such as the one described in Chapter 10; if so, the nuts and bolts of this plan are integrated into your final proposals. You need to take this to your solicitors or your mediator can send it, with your agreement. Your solicitors can then advise you individually regarding your agreement.

Including your financial details in an Open Statement

The details of your income, assets, pensions and liabilities, with a list of the verifying documents, are set out in an Open Statement separate from your proposals in the Memorandum of Understanding. The information is usually in schedule form, which is easy for you and your solicitors to follow.

Even if you and your spouse fail to reach agreement on any of the issues between you, you're still able to use the Open Statement as the basis of your court form if necessary. You shouldn't have to duplicate any of the hard work that was involved in collecting that information for the mediation.

Making your Memorandum of Understanding legally binding

After you've had a chance to discuss the Open Statement and Memorandum of Understanding with your separate solicitors and financial advisers, you're given a chance to make it legally binding if you so desire. If you're both happy with your work, your solicitors prepare your agreement for the court in the form of a draft Consent Order (or a Separation Deed if you aren't yet going to divorce). Your solicitors send the draft order to the court along with a short summary of your means, called a Statement of Information. If the judge accepts that your proposals are fair for the children and for you, and that you've both agreed freely to the proposals after fully disclosing your finances to each other and receiving legal advice, the order is *sealed* by the court and made final, and is legally binding upon you both. Neither of you has to attend court for this process – everything can be done by post.

Asking for Mediation Help from Your Solicitor

While you're attending mediation sessions, you can consult your solicitor about the proposals you're working on at any time. If you decide to use mediation, your solicitor shouldn't simply hand you on to a mediator and wait for you and your spouse to resolve all your outstanding divorce issues. At a minimum, your solicitor can prepare you for mediation by helping you to:

- ✔ Develop a list of the specific issues you want to resolve.

- ✔ Work out your goals and priorities.

- ✔ Assess your options.

- ✔ Review any information your spouse may share with you prior to mediation so that you understand it all and know the right questions to ask about it.

- ✔ Develop a mediation plan or strategy.

- ✔ Assess whether you may need any other sort of professional help, such as from an independent financial adviser, forensic accountant or pension actuary.

Depending on your ability to negotiate with your spouse during a mediation session and the complexity of the issues you want to resolve, your solicitor may also help you in other important ways:

- ✔ By serving as a sounding board on occasions.
- ✔ By confirming or questioning any information the mediator or your spouse may give you.
- ✔ By reviewing with you any written agreement that the mediator drafts.

Your solicitor can't discuss your situation with your spouse's solicitor or with the mediator without your consent, because you and your spouse are the people doing the negotiation.

Getting Help with the Cost of Mediation

The government actively encourages the use of family mediation in England, Scotland and Wales, and, as part of that policy, has made public funds available to support people of low to moderate means with the cost of mediation. If you think that you may be eligible for public funding, you need to make sure that you see a mediator who's approved by the Legal Services Commission. (See the 'Who are mediators?' section earlier in this chapter.)

The mediator assesses your financial eligibility for mediation during your first introductory session, so you need to take details of your means to that session, along with recent evidence of your salary or state benefits or other income. If you're eligible, and mediation is otherwise suitable, the whole process including the preparation of the Open Statement and Memorandum of Understanding is free. Your spouse is assessed separately for her eligibility.

After the mediator confirms your eligibility, you become entitled to some free advice from your solicitor, both during the course of mediation and at the end. Your solicitor gives you publicly funded 'Family Help (Lower)' to cover this expense and also the cost of putting your mediated Memorandum of Understanding into legal form and implementing it (see Chapter 15 for more on public funding).

Family Mediation Scotland (FMS) services are free unless you use them to work out your property and financial matters. See 'Reaping the Benefits of Mediation' earlier in this chapter for more information.

If for any reason, mediation isn't suitable for you and your spouse, the mediator gives you or your solicitor a form CLS APP7 confirming that mediation can't proceed. This confirmation enables you to apply for public funding to take your case to court instead, if that's appropriate.

Bear in mind that most forms of legal aid for family disputes are more like a loan than a gift. So, for example, if you're granted public funding by the Legal Services Commission to take your case to court, or for your solicitors to negotiate on your behalf, you have to pay back all your court and your solicitor's costs out of any money or property that you receive as part of your settlement. This is known as the *Legal Aid Charge* or *Statutory Charge* and almost certainly applies to you regardless of whether your final settlement is by consent or fully contested (see the section on public funding in Chapter 15 for more info about this charge).

By contrast, if you're eligible for public funding for mediation, you don't have to pay back any of the costs incurred by your mediator or solicitor so long as you reach an agreement in mediation and you and your solicitors finally approve that agreement. This arrangement is an incentive to you to reach an agreement in mediation and stick with it.

Going to Your Solicitors if You Can't Agree in Mediation

If you don't agree on all or some of the issues in mediation, you can pass on to your solicitors the work you do in mediation to try to reach agreement with your spouse's solicitor. Therefore, the time and effort you've put into mediation isn't wasted (see Chapter 17).

If your solicitors also fail to find an agreement, either you or your spouse can take your case to court. See Chapter 18 for an idea of what to expect if your case goes to court.

Before entering mediation, you're asked to agree that what you say to each other in sessions is *confidential* to you and your mediator, and that neither you nor the mediator can reveal the content of your discussions to anyone else without each other's consent. This confidentiality gives you freedom to speak without being quoted, which your mediator also respects. The only times that confidentiality can be broken are when a real risk of harm exists to a child or another adult that needs to be reported, or evidence exists to suggest that one of you has benefited or is benefiting from the proceeds of a crime (for example, through tax evasion or benefit fraud). You're told about these exceptions at the beginning of mediation.

Privilege means that the court can't enquire into the content of your mediation discussions and you can't quote each other without each other's consent. If your case goes to a hearing, neither your solicitors nor the court can enquire into or use conversations that took place in mediation. The Open Financial Statement is the only thing that can be taken from mediation and used in court. This grants you the freedom to explore goals and options in mediation together without fear of prejudice. Here again, the exception to this rule is if a real risk to someone's safety exists.

Chapter 17

Helping Your Solicitor Get the Best Results Possible

In This Chapter

▶ Knowing what to expect from your solicitor

▶ Knowing what your solicitor expects from you

▶ Seeking emergency orders

▶ Providing your solicitor with all the necessary information

▶ Hammering out a final divorce agreement

▶ Finalising the agreement

*W*hen you engage a solicitor to represent you in your divorce, you and your solicitor become partners – you give and get, and your solicitor gives and gets – and the progress and outcome of your divorce, not to mention its cost, depend in part on how well your partnership works.

To help make your solicitor-client relationship productive and efficient, this chapter explains what you and your solicitor can expect from one another and the type of information your solicitor needs in order to represent you in the most effective (and economical) way possible.

Because the divorce process becomes more formal when you engage a solicitor, this chapter also explains how round-table conferences and draft proposals work. Finally, this chapter provides some information on the preparation of the final divorce agreement.

What to Expect from Your Solicitor

You and your solicitor need to understand from the outset what you need and expect from each other. At the very least, you should expect that your solicitor does the following:

✔ **Provides a written contract or agreement that states the terms and conditions of your solicitor-client relationship and an estimate of the costs.** (Don't work with any solicitor who refuses to provide one.)

✔ **Lives up to the terms of your written agreement or contract, or lets you know ahead of time when something you agreed to needs to be changed.** (You did make sure to get something in writing from your solicitor, didn't you?)

✔ **Lays out a plan for, and general approach to, your divorce and explains it to you, after becoming familiar with the facts of your case.** The plan doesn't need to be elaborate, but at a minimum it should give you a general sense of how your solicitor intends to proceed with your divorce to achieve an agreement that works for you. Your solicitor should also give you a rough timetable for the completion of your divorce.

✔ **Provides clear explanations of all your options as your divorce progresses, answers your questions honestly, and shows respect for your preferences and decisions.**

✔ **Pulls out the stops to reach a negotiated settlement.**

✔ **Gives you straightforward answers to your questions.** Be prepared, however, to hear things you may not like – that your divorce expectations are unreasonable, that you should give up certain assets or pay money to your spouse, or that your spouse is unwilling to concede on an issue that's really important to you.

✔ **Tells you when your divorce priorities and goals are not legally or financially feasible.**

✔ **Returns your phone calls within a reasonable period of time (24 hours is acceptable) unless you're very clear that you need a quicker response.**

✔ **Consults with you before putting an offer on the bargaining table or taking other important actions related to your divorce.**

✔ **Gives you copies of all correspondence and documents sent out of his office that relate to your case.**

✔ **Keeps your personal and financial information confidential.**

✔ **Stores any important documents you produce in a safe place and provides you with copies on request.** Your solicitor should return them to you promptly after your divorce is over or, if you ask for them, sooner.

✔ **Acts as your interim adviser, as well as your solicitor, by recommending certain services, other professionals, courses, seminars and support groups that you may want to consider using to help you deal with the non-legal aspects of your divorce.** Good family law solicitors want to help with their clients' emotional or mental healing while handling the legal aspects of their divorces.

> ✔ **Explains to you the option of using a mediator as well as a solicitor and makes a referral if you want one.**
>
> ✔ **Follows the Law Society Family Law Protocol.** You can download a copy from www.lawsociety.org.uk/documents/downloads/dynamic/familylawprotocol.pdf.

When your negotiations are under way, you can't rule out the possibility that your spouse's solicitor may do things that change the tenor or direction of your divorce. When that happens, your solicitor's approach may well change and the cost of your divorce increase as a consequence. These changes can also mean that your divorce takes longer.

Expect some disappointment and frustration along the way as the terms of your divorce are being negotiated. But don't take your feelings out on your solicitor, assuming that he is working hard on your case. Your solicitor can't always produce instant solutions.

What Your Solicitor Expects from You

To help get you the best divorce possible, your solicitor expects you to provide information, direction, and feedback when needed. Respond to your solicitor's requests as quickly and completely as you can. Staying actively involved in your divorce and being responsive to your solicitor's requests is the best way to help ensure that the legal help doesn't cost you a fortune and that your final divorce settlement reflects at least some of your goals and priorities.

Your solicitor may tell you things that you should and shouldn't do while you're getting divorced. These instructions are intended to help protect your legal interests or your safety. Don't disregard them! If you do, you may undermine your solicitor's efforts and put your interests or your children's interests in jeopardy. The following sections of this chapter describe what your solicitor expects of you as a client.

Speaking your mind and not being afraid to ask questions

Trusting your solicitor's judgement doesn't mean that you can't ask questions, request an explanation when he says something that you don't understand, or speak up when you aren't sure that you agree with his recommendations.

When your solicitor provides you with advice and options, carefully weigh up what he says. Talk it through with your solicitor but, in the end, follow your intuition – only you know what really satisfies you and how far you're willing to go to get there. Remember, you make the decisions; your solicitor only recommends the decisions that you can make.

Paying your bills on time

If you have trouble paying your legal bills, don't let them pile up. Instead, as soon as you feel financially pinched, find out if your solicitor is willing to work out a payment plan or some other financial arrangement with you. Don't just disappear or become unavailable to talk to your solicitor because of your money problem. You may hurt your case if you do. If you're publicly funded and you have to pay a contribution towards your costs (see Chapter 15 on public funding), make sure that you pay it promptly, and let your solicitor and the Legal Services Commission know if you get into difficulty.

If you don't pay your legal bills, your solicitor may well stop working on your case and make an application to the court to withdraw so that he can legally stop representing you. If the court approves the application (which it usually does if you don't pay your bills), you have to engage a new solicitor, and your divorce takes longer. You're still contractually bound to pay your solicitor's outstanding fees, as well as the costs of your new solicitor. Your solicitor is entitled to refuse to send your file of papers to your new solicitor until you pay any outstanding costs.

Keeping your solicitor up to date with any changes in your life

Your solicitor needs to know about any changes in your personal situation or in your spouse's life that may affect your divorce or your safety. For example, inform your solicitor if your spouse begins threatening you with a battle over the children, if your spouse's business is experiencing financial problems, if you develop a serious new relationship, or if your spouse becomes abusive.

Be especially on the ball if you or your spouse receive warning letters about debt. Debt can ultimately lead to bankruptcy proceedings, which, if not dealt with, have major and serious implications in divorce.

Avoiding using your solicitor as a therapist

Your solicitor is your legal adviser, not your therapist. Taking up his time with tirades about your spouse, worries about your future, or laments about what may have been is a quick way to run up your legal bills. When you're having difficulty dealing with your divorce or just need a shoulder to cry on, talk to a trusted friend or relative, or a counsellor. Refer to Chapter 2 for a list of counselling organisations, and Chapter 9 has some good information about caring for yourself.

First Things First: Seeking Urgent or Interim Orders

If your divorce is contentious, one of the first things your solicitor may do is file an application asking the court to grant an *interim* or *emergency order* or an *injunction* (or *interdict* in Scotland). Such orders can help you make sure that certain things happen or don't happen while you're working out the terms of your divorce. For instance, your solicitor may request an order for:

✔ Spousal support.

✔ Child residence or contact.

✔ Control of assets if you're worried that your spouse may waste or hide family assets.

✔ The right for you to remain in your home.

✔ An injunction against improper behaviour of many types (including physical abuse) on the part of your spouse.

If you have to apply for an order excluding your spouse from the home or to prevent abuse, you may be able to get an order at the same time that your spouse pay the rent or mortgage until the longer-term property issues are decided.

In Scotland, the Family Law (Scotland) Act 1985 provides guidelines for *interim aliment* (maintenance). Aliment can be for a spouse or for a child, but only if the provisions of the Child Support legislationdon't apply. (See Chapter 13 for more information on the Child Support legislation.)

When you need action now: *Ex parte* orders

When the need for action is immediate, your solicitor may be able make an *ex parte* application (now known as a without notice application) to the court. *Ex parte* refers to a legal action ordered on behalf of one party without the other party being notified about it or having an opportunity to participate in the action. You and your solicitor need to spell out in your application and any statement in support why the order should be granted on an *ex parte* basis. Examples are that your safety would be at risk or that your spouse may destroy or dispose of property or valuables if he finds out about the application before an order is made.

With an *ex parte* order, your spouse doesn't find out about the court's decision, and a full hearing doesn't take place, until after the court has made an initial decision on your application and granted its order. Therefore, an *ex parte* order is normally of very short duration. Both parties in the action are usually ordered to attend a hearing to determine whether the terms of the *ex parte* order should be extended or varied.

If you request an *ex parte* order and one is granted, you may be held responsible for any damage that your spouse suffers because no court hearing was held, so think through the implications with your solicitor before you make the application.

If you're concerned that your spouse may disappear with your children, your solicitor can also ask the court to prohibit your spouse from doing so or ask the court to order supervised contact if evidence exists that he may attempt to abduct your children (see Chapter 10).

After your solicitor files the appropriate paperwork with the court, the solicitor or the court arranges for a court hearing to deal with the application. At this hearing, your spouse (or your spouse's solicitor, assuming that one has been engaged) has an opportunity to argue why your application should *not* be granted. Remember that many people aren't using a solicitor at all these days, mostly because they think they're too expensive. If your opposite number chooses not to, he is perfectly entitled to represent himself.

Providing Your Solicitor with Essential Information

You need to provide your solicitor with basic information about your family, marriage, finances, reasons for divorcing, and so on during your initial meeting. But after your client-solicitor relationship is formalised, your solicitor needs to know a lot more about you.

Your solicitor collects much of the information we mention here through one-to-one interviews with you, and by asking you to fill out forms and provide as much back-up documentation as you can – payslips, credit card statements, title deeds to property, insurance policies, lease agreements, bills, loan applications, business profit-and-loss statements and balance sheets, records of investments, household budgets, and other documents (refer to Chapter 3 for a list of everything you should need).

Don't decide for yourself whether your solicitor needs the requested information. Clarify with him, if you need to, why the information is necessary. Do your best to provide everything your solicitor asks for; don't hold anything back just because you think the information is unimportant or irrelevant. Failing to share that information may derail your solicitor's negotiating strategy or complicate your divorce in other ways. For example, if you withhold information from your solicitor that your spouse's solicitor knows about, your spouse's solicitor may damage your case by introducing that information into evidence during a hearing.

If you read Chapter 7 of this book and follow its advice, you're a couple of steps ahead of the game. But if you delay pulling together essential information because the whole process sounds oh-so-tedious and time-consuming – which it is – you can't avoid assembling the necessary paperwork after you engage a divorce solicitor. Remember, the more information your solicitor gets from you or through the co-operation of your spouse, the less you need any formal disclosure or court proceedings and the less your divorce costs. (Chapter 5 covers the disclosure process in detail.)

The following sections of this chapter provide a rundown of some of the things your solicitor needs to know.

Personal information

To help develop a constructive approach for ending your marriage and to determine what you may be entitled to in your divorce, your solicitor needs information on your personal history, your marriage and your dependent children. Therefore, among other things, your solicitor questions you about:

- ✔ Why you're getting a divorce.
- ✔ The history of your marriage.
- ✔ Biographical information about you and your spouse.
- ✔ Your individual health histories, including whether either of you has a history of serious medical or emotional problems.
- ✔ Your children – their ages; where they're living, if you and your spouse are separated; whether they have special needs (educational, physical, emotional); whether they're attending state or private schools; and so on.

Writing it all down: The story of your marriage

It may be helpful if you prepare a written narrative describing your marriage: how you and your spouse shared child-care responsibilities, what you think led to your divorce, what you want from your divorce and for your life after divorce, and what you believe your spouse wants.

A succinct narrative can be a good way for your solicitor to get at the facts and issues related to your divorce that may not be apparent from a review of the financial, legal and personal data forms you fill out or from your client-solicitor interviews. Furthermore, putting everything down on paper can be both cathartic and healing, and may help you put your marriage and divorce in proper perspective.

Legal and financial information

Your solicitor also spends time reviewing the ins and outs of your finances and any legal agreements into which you and your spouse may have entered. Among the things your solicitor needs to know are the following:

- ✔ Whether you have a separation agreement. If so, your solicitor needs to read it. (See Chapter 6 for more on separation agreements.)

- ✔ Whether you and your spouse own property, including homes, buildings or land. Be prepared to provide your solicitor with copies of the title deeds and any mortgage documents relating to the property if you owe money on it.

- ✔ Whether you signed any pre-marital or post-marital agreements. (For full information on pre-marital and post-marital agreements, take a look at Chapter 21.)

- ✔ Whether you or your spouse have done any inheritance planning, such as writing a will, buying life insurance, or setting up a trust.

- ✔ Whether you or your spouse own shares in a limited company or have a business partnership together or separately, or if you have other shared business interests.

- ✔ An accounting of your assets and debts and where you got the money to pay for any of the property you may own (that is, your home and any other homes, buildings or land).

- ✔ How much each of you earns annually from all income sources – including salaries, bonuses and other employment-related income, dividends, trust income, pensions, annuities, royalties, state benefits, tax credits, and so on.

✔ Whether either of you made special contributions to the other spouse's career or business or to the family generally (for example, you helped finance the business or worked in the business; your spouse supported you through college or university; or you used your separate or inherited funds to purchase assets or to pay for your family's living expenses).

✔ Whether either of you has wasted family assets by gambling, engaging in extramarital affairs or through addiction to drugs, alcohol or even the Internet.

✔ Your current household budget and your projected post-divorce budget.

✔ Evidence of your spouse's fault, if you plan to petition for divorce against your spouse based on his adultery, behaviour or desertion, or evidence of the length of your separation if you want to divorce on that basis (see Chapter 5).

Other important information

Finally, your solicitor asks you questions about what you expect from your divorce and what you're willing to do or not do to get what you want. Your solicitor needs this information in order to meet your needs but also because he has to be certain that you have realistic expectations about the possible or likely outcome of your divorce. Given this, you can expect your solicitor to ask you about:

✔ Your divorce goals and priorities.

✔ Why you feel that the children's arrangements you want are reasonable and why your spouse's desired children's arrangements aren't reasonable, if you and your spouse don't agree on these aspects.

✔ Under what, if any, circumstances you're willing to go to a full court hearing to get what you want.

Hammering Out the Details of Your Settlement

Your solicitor works out the details of your proposed divorce settlement and presents them to you for your approval and then to your spouse's solicitor in detailed written or oral form. Your spouse's solicitor should do the same thing. These oral or written presentations can be little more than trial runs to get your or your spouse's reaction to certain provisions, or they can represent something closer to a final and complete divorce agreement.

After everyone feels that they're very close to a final agreement, one solicitor prepares a written draft *consent order* (or a draft *separation agreement* if you're delaying your divorce until you've been separated for two or five years – see chapter 5 for more info). Depending on the complexity of your divorce and how willing you and your spouse are to do some compromising, a single draft order or agreement may be all that's necessary before you and your spouse have something you can both approve.

Expect to review all drafts, whether they're prepared by your solicitor or your spouse's solicitor, and then be ready to provide your solicitor with feedback. Don't agree to any proposal if it makes you feel uncomfortable. You and your spouse aren't obliged to accept any draft agreement you don't like. You can accept or reject the draft agreements, or you can use them as the basis for additional negotiations.

When your solicitor fully briefs you about key points and legal issues, he may suggest that you and your spouse work out the terms of your final agreement on your own instead of working through your solicitors (assuming that you and your spouse are communicating with each other). After that, your solicitor can draft a written divorce agreement or order. Your solicitor may also suggest mediation if a stumbling block arises, for example about the arrangements for your children, which you may be able to overcome by directly negotiating with each other with the help of a third party.

Evaluating the Proposal

You have to evaluate whatever agreement your spouse may propose, or that either solicitor may draft, and decide whether you like the agreement, don't like it, or like it enough to use it as the basis for your final negotiations in your divorce settlement. When you do your evaluating, ask yourself the following questions:

- ✔ Is the agreement fair to me?
- ✔ Can I afford the agreement?
- ✔ Is the agreement in my children's best interests?
- ✔ What was I looking for in an agreement that this one doesn't have? Are items missing that are worth the cost and the time involved in continued negotiations?
- ✔ Is my reason for not settling yet that important items are missing from this agreement, or is it that my emotions are getting the way?
- ✔ What may I have to give up if I really push for any of the missing items? Is it worth it to me? What are the risks of not settling now?
- ✔ Is my spouse likely to make any additional concessions?

✔ Will I be any better off if I refuse to settle and take this case to a full hearing? What is the worst that can happen? (Your solicitor should be able to give you a strong sense of the best and the worst judgements that are likely, given the statutory guidelines and the past decisions of the judges who may hear your case.)

✔ What kind of financial and emotional toll is not settling likely to take on my children and I? Is not settling in order to gain what I want really worth it?

You and your solicitor need to discuss the pros and cons of the proposed agreement. Share your thoughts and concerns with your solicitor and ask for an opinion about the agreement. Your solicitor may tell you that the agreement is about as good as you're going to get, that you can probably get a few more concessions if you keep negotiating, or that the agreement is not in your best interests. In the end, however, how you respond to whatever offer is on the table is your decision.

Making a Deal: The Final Settlement

After you and your spouse come to a final agreement about the terms of all the key issues in your divorce, your solicitor or your spouse's solicitor drafts a version in the form of a consent order detailing everything you agree to, including many standard provisions and precedents – language that you find in many consent orders. Either your solicitor does the drafting, and submits it to your spouse's solicitor for review and changes, or vice versa. Children orders are drafted separately from financial orders. If issues over the divorce itself remain, your solicitor deals with those separately as well.

Don't get impatient with all the back-and-forth negotiations. Getting everything just right is important because after you and your spouse sign the agreement it becomes a legally binding contract or order, which means that both of you are legally obliged to live up to what it says, like it or not.

A draft consent order that includes terms for your capital, property or pensions can't be submitted to the court for approval until after your decree nisi is granted. Also, the terms themselves can't take effect until your decree absolute is granted. Your solicitor, however, may be able to advise you on legal ways around these restrictions if some urgency is involved in your case.

After you and your solicitors agree on the terms of your draft consent order, usually one of your solicitors sends a copy of the draft order (and any court fee) by post to the court. If the order is a draft financial one, your solicitor must send a simple agreed summary of your respective finances and intentions known as a *Statement of Information* or *Rule 2.61 Statement*. A judge then examines the paperwork in your absence and, if he approves it, the court seals the draft order, or else lets your solicitor know of any queries.

If you do have to attend a hearing, your solicitor usually goes with you or may be able to go in your place. So long as the draft consent order is within the powers of the court and appears to be fair, the hearing should be more of a formality than anything else and be over quickly.

Changing the Agreement Later

After a financial order dealing with your property or capital is sealed by the court, changing it is almost impossible, even if you and your spouse agree. Only in the most exceptional circumstances does a judge review such an order after it's made. Only orders concerning your children, or child or spousal maintenance, can be reviewed, and then you and your spouse have to agree those changes or you need to justify why the changes should be made.

Applying for the Final Decree

If you're the petitioner, your or your solicitor's responsibility is to apply for the final decree of divorce – the *decree absolute* – when a final order has been made on your property and finances. Unless your finances are very straight-forward, your solicitor usually advises you to wait before applying for the decree absolute until the final financial order has been made. In most cases, a court officer can grant your decree absolute without reference to a judge, and sends a copy of the final decree to both solicitors.

If more than a year has elapsed between the decree nisi and the application for decree absolute, you have to explain the reason for the delay to the court. You or your spouse can also apply for the decree absolute – on payment of a fee – even if you're not the petitioner, if at least three months has elapsed since the decree nisi and no good reason exists for the petitioner's delay in applying.

Make sure that you keep a copy of your final court order and your divorce decrees in a safe place. They're important documents and you may need them for future reference, or have to supply them if you're applying for a passport or want to remarry. If you do lose them, you can apply to the court for another sealed copy, but you need to supply the court with your court reference number and a fee. You can find the court reference number in the top right-hand corner of all court documents. The number is exclusive to you and your ex-spouse.

Using the Collaborative Law Process

The collaborative family law process is a relatively new way of dealing with family disputes. Solicitors have to undergo special training to act collaboratively. Each person appoints his or her own solicitor but instead of conducting negotiations between you and your spouse by letter or phone you meet together to work things out face to face.

Each of you has your solicitor by your side throughout the entire process and therefore you benefit from legal advice as you go. The aim of collaborative law is to resolve family disputes without going to court.

How does the collaborative process work?

After you both meet your respective solicitors, discuss the different options and processes available, and decide that the collaborative process is for you, what happens next?

You both meet individually with your separate solicitors to talk about what to expect in the collaborative meetings, which are usually referred to as *four-way meetings* because they're meetings between the four of you – you and your spouse and your respective solicitors. You and your solicitor discuss what you both need to do in order to prepare for the first four-way meeting.

Your solicitor and your spouse's solicitor speak to each other face to face or over the phone in order to plan for your first meeting.

The first four-way meeting

At the first four-way meeting, the solicitors make sure that you both understand that you're making a commitment to work out an agreement without going to court, and all four of you sign an agreement to this effect.

You and your spouse are invited to share your own objectives in choosing the collaborative process and you all plan the agenda for the next meeting. This agenda depends on your own individual circumstances but may typically include a discussion about how the children are responding to the separation.

If time permits, you may also go on to discuss how financial information is to be shared and agree on who brings what financial information to the next meeting.

Subsequent four-way meetings

Subsequent meetings deal with your and your spouse's particular priorities and concerns. The aim of these meetings is to enable you to reach agreement on how the finances are to be shared or what arrangements need to be made for any children. You may, for instance, look at involving other professionals such as specialists in pensions and financial planning, or people trained to assist children in understanding and coping with the changes that your divorce or separation brings to their lives.

The final meeting

In the final meeting documents detailing the agreements you reach are signed and your solicitors talk you through anything else that needs to be done in order to implement those agreements. Sometimes a firm timetable for implementation isn't possible – for instance, if the family house needs to be sold.

How long does the collaborative process take?

One of the benefits of the collaborative process is that it's not driven by a timetable imposed by the court. Therefore, to a large extent the process can be built around your family's individual timetable and priorities.

How expensive is the collaborative process?

Collaborative solicitors generally charge by the hour as do all family solicitors. Rates vary from locale to locale and according to the experience of the solicitor. No one can predict exactly what you'll need to pay for this kind of representation because every case is different. However, although the cost of your own fees can't be predicted accurately, a general rule is that collaborative law representation costs from one tenth to one twentieth of the cost of being represented conventionally by a family solicitor who takes issues in your case to court.

You can find a Resolution collaborative solicitor at www.resolution.org.uk or on 01689 820272.

Chapter 18

Putting the Decisions in the Hands of a Judge

In This Chapter

▶ Analysing your options if your spouse makes you an offer of settlement

▶ Reviewing what happens at a pre-trial hearing

▶ Preparing for a fully contested hearing

▶ Understanding the role of the judge and the trial process

▶ Weighing the pros and cons of an appeal

*W*e're going to give it to you straight: If your divorce is heading for a contested hearing (sometimes referred to as a trial), the experience is not going to be pleasant. The cost of your divorce skyrockets; you probably have to pay for it out of your family property (which means you and your ex each take less property from your marriage); your stress level soars; and you still have no guarantee that you're going to like the judge's decision. If you think a contested hearing sounds like a kind of hell on earth, you're getting the idea. Contested hearings are serious business. If you're heading for such a hearing, fasten your seat belt, because you're in for a bumpy ride.

To help prepare you for some major turbulence in your life, we discuss out-of-court settlements and evaluating any offers that your spouse sends your way. We explain what happens prior to a court hearing, and offer you general advice about proper in-court behaviour. We also provide an overview of the procedure at court hearings and conclude with information on appeals, in case the outcome isn't as you hoped.

A major overhaul of the procedures in family courts in England and Wales has been going on over the last few years. If you're reading this chapter after 2010, check with your solicitor as to whether the new rules are in force or not. (Skip ahead to the 'Preparing for the New Family Procedure Rules' section later in the chapter to read about some of the language changes you can expect to see after 2010.)

Making Certain You Want to Go to Court

Before you move full speed ahead with a formal application for a court hearing on any major issue within your divorce, think long and hard about its financial and emotional costs. Putting any issue within your divorce in the hands of a judge is a gamble: the judge may not view matters quite the way you do, and you may not get the divorce order you hoped for. Never assume that you have such a strong case that the judge is automatically going to decide in your favour. Be prepared to be disappointed.

Before committing to a full court hearing, ask yourself the following questions:

- Does the risk of losing or having a disappointing outcome outweigh any benefits you may receive from going to court?

- Would you be better off compromising with your spouse to ensure that you get at least some of the things that are really important to you, rather than rolling the dice and hoping that you come up with a lucky number?

- Do you have the time for a lengthy court hearing? Remember that getting divorced takes longer when you go to court. Preparing for the hearing takes a great deal of time and you may also have to wait for a hearing date – as long as *six months* or more depending on how many other cases are ahead of yours. If you want a speedy divorce, going to court isn't the way to get it.

- Do you want to put your children through the emotional stress of a fully contested court hearing? Although they may not fully understand what's going on, they're likely to sense that you're under an unusual amount of pressure, which may scare them.

Despite all the negatives associated with a court hearing, sometimes it's your best or only option. For example, you may need to go to court because:

- Your spouse refuses to negotiate, or negotiations haven't worked.

- Your spouse is hiding information essential to a fair settlement.

- Your spouse insists on an arrangement for your children that you don't think is in their best interests, but refuses to discuss it in mediation.

- You need more maintenance than your spouse agrees to.

- You think your spouse may be wasting or hiding assets.

- Your spouse has an alcohol or drug problem or abused you or your children.

Settling Out of Court

Most issues within divorce never get to a full hearing, although they may get as far as the steps of the court. Therefore, while your solicitor and your spouse's solicitor prepare for your court hearing (maybe with the assistance of a barrister) they may also try to negotiate an out-of-court settlement.

Receiving the offer

After you and your spouse give the go-ahead to your respective solicitors, one of them may send the other a written offer, the other may counter it, reject it or (if you're lucky) accept it. (By the way, your solicitor can't accept or reject an offer without your consent.)

Eventually, all the terms of your agreement may be worked out. This back-and-forth process is a more formal version of what you and your spouse may have done if you had tried to negotiate your own divorce by yourselves or during a mediation session. (To find out more about doing it yourself, look at Chapter 14 and for how mediation works, head to Chapter 16.)

You may get an offer during this back-and-forth process that you believe is relatively reasonable and fair. The offer may not be everything you hoped for, but it may be close. Although your solicitor should provide you with her opinions about the offer, the final decision about how to respond is yours.

If you get an offer from your spouse, read it very carefully. The offer may not be close to what you're legally entitled to, what your spouse can really provide, or what you think you need.

Deciding on the offer

Following are some questions that you should ask yourself to help you decide what to do when you get an offer:

- ✔ How close is the offer to what you're asking for, and is the offer fair?

- ✔ Does the offer reflect most, if not all, of your divorce priorities?

- ✔ Are you likely to benefit if you reject this offer, given what you know now about your legal rights and responsibilities, the value of the property you own, and how your children are being affected by the divorce?

- ✔ How much have you spent on your case and can you afford to spend any more?

✔ Are you willing to take the offer just to stop the agony of going through a protracted and expensive legal process?

✔ Are you likely to do better if you go all the way to a final hearing than if you accept what your spouse offers?

To help you decide what to do, your solicitor may be able to offer information regarding how the judges who may hear your case have decided cases similar to yours.

✔ What are the advantages and the disadvantages of settling now?

You may think that threatening to take your case to court is likely to pressure your spouse to give in on certain points that are important to you. Before you try this tactic, you should think about which scenario is more likely: you hold your ground and your spouse agrees to a compromise, or your spouse holds her ground and calls your bluff.

Settling Issues through a Pre-trial Hearing

A *pre-trial hearing* or *pre-trial review* offers you and your spouse a formal opportunity to resolve your differences and come to an agreement when you have enough information to make a decision. The judge participating in the hearing may actively push for a settlement when she knows the facts of your case. Judges have been known to instruct divorcing spouses and their solicitors (or barristers if the solicitors have instructed them) to talk over their case first. If you and your spouse can't reach a settlement, the judge may note her displeasure and give reasons for why you should have come to an agreement.

Your lawyers use pre-trial hearings to settle issues relating to the arrangements for your children following receipt of the Cafcass report, and financial issues following full disclosure between you. (See Chapter 5 for basic information about these procedures.) Your lawyers may also try to resolve other immediate issues, such as who pays what bills while your divorce is proceeding and so forth.

The pre-trial hearing is an opportunity for both lawyers, the judge, and maybe even you and your spouse, to discuss your case and accomplish the following:

✔ Clarify the specific issues to be resolved at your final hearing.

✔ Address all uncertainties that must be resolved before the final hearing.

✔ Develop a timetable for interim and final hearings.

✔ Determine who's going to be called as witnesses.

✔ Decide the arrangements for preparing the necessary bundle of documents for use at the final hearing (see the later section 'Preparing the court bundle').

Procedures are different in Scotland and Northern Ireland. Check with a solicitor there before you make any decisions.

If your case involves your children, the court may list a pre-trial review hearing a week or two after the Cafcass officer files her report, and a week or two before the final hearing date (see Chapter 5 for a description of a Cafcass officer's role). This period gives you and your solicitors the opportunity to discuss any recommendations that the Cafcass officer made and to see if you're able to resolve the outstanding issues.

In financial cases, the *Financial Dispute Resolution* hearing (FDR) is the main opportunity to explore the possibilities for settlement with the judge's help. This hearing is usually listed a few weeks after the first court appointment and a few weeks before the final hearing. Sometimes it is combined with the first appointment to save time and money. See Chapter 5 for more on the court procedure for children and financial cases.

The court doesn't usually let you postpone a court appointment without the judge's prior permission. You must have good reason if you ask for a postponement; otherwise you may have to pay your spouse's wasted costs.

The monetary costs of a court hearing

Going to court can be a serious expense. The exact cost of a court hearing depends on a number of factors: what part of the country you live in (divorcing in a major metropolitan area, for example, usually costs more than divorcing in a provincial town); the specific issues the judge is deciding on; your lawyer's legal strategy; and the legal strategy of your spouse's lawyer. Your costs are likely to be higher if your or your spouse's lawyer has a particularly confrontational strategy.

You can expect your legal bills alone to run into the four- or five-figure range – maybe as much as four times the cost of a negotiated divorce.

At a minimum, you should be prepared to incur the following expenses:

✔ Lawyers' fees – not just your solicitors' fees but barristers' fees as well

✔ Court fees

✔ Expert fees

✔ Cost of preparing evidence, bundles of documents and witnesses for the hearing

✔ Miscellaneous legal expenses – copying, long-distance charges, postage, delivery fees, and so on

This list covers just the monetary costs of a court hearing. It can't begin to calculate the cost to your family's health and happiness if you're embroiled in an ugly divorce court battle.

Your lawyer may use the pre-trial hearing to see how a judge is likely to decide the issues in your case. If she gets the feeling that things may not go your way at a final hearing, your lawyer may urge you to settle out of court.

If you don't agree to a negotiated settlement at a pre-trial hearing, you and your spouse can agree to one later, even after the final hearing begins.

Preparing for the Final Hearing

Getting ready for a final hearing is time-consuming work, which is why hearings are so expensive. Your solicitor reviews and gathers information relating to your case, develops and refines her legal approach, co-ordinates the production of evidence and a bundle for the court, prepares witnesses to give evidence, and makes other preparations. Often your solicitor, with your consent, engages a barrister or *counsel* to help with the preparation and presentation of your case. Chapter 4 describes the main roles and differences between solicitors and barristers: both these branches of the legal profession can be called lawyers as well.

Setting the stage

Preparing for a final hearing is somewhat like staging a play, with you and your spouse as the reluctant 'stars'. The witnesses who give evidence in court are your supporting, or not-so-supporting, players depending on whether they give evidence for or against you.

To help stage your final hearing, your solicitor outlines a strategy. This serves as an overview of everything your solicitor does to get you a favourable out-of-court settlement as quickly as possible, assuming that is a realistic goal, or to win your case if it goes all the way to a final hearing. Your solicitor's strategy may be an aggressive or non-aggressive one:

- ✔ An *aggressive strategy* involves bombarding the other side with allegations of abuse, indifference, child neglect, wasting assets, infidelity, dishonesty, delay or general instability. To a lesser extent, an aggressive strategy can involve pressuring the other side with interim applications, questionnaires, requests for disclosure and requests to produce documents, among other things.

- ✔ A *non-aggressive strategy* relies more on informal disclosure to get at the facts of your case and co-operation between your solicitors to work out the terms of the issues in your divorce.

Both tactics are designed to encourage an early out-of-court settlement. These tactics, however, can make your spouse all the more determined to go to court. An aggressive strategy is almost guaranteed to make you and your spouse enemies forever, but this may be your only option.

The strategy that your solicitor chooses depends on several factors, including:

✔ Your own desires and resources

✔ Your solicitor's opinion on what's best for the case

✔ Your spouse's solicitor's likely strategy

✔ Your solicitor's style and the style of your spouse's lawyer (some are scrappy street fighters and others are wily tacticians)

If you contest the validity of a pre-marital or separation agreement, a judge may have to rule on that issue – whether holding you to that agreement or not is fair – before she can decide how to divide up your property and debts or decide whether one of you has to pay the other spousal support. (See Chapter 21 for more on pre-marital agreements.) To save time and money, your solicitor must try to get this issue resolved as quickly as possible because the judge's decision determines exactly what issues your final hearing addresses and influences how much disclosure you may need to do.

Understanding the disclosure process

In all divorce and family court proceedings in the UK, a duty of *full and frank disclosure* exists of all relevant information and documentation between the parties. In children matters in particular, this duty can even extend to information that is adverse to your own case, if it affects the welfare of your children. The judge doesn't permit you, your lawyers or your witnesses to introduce at your final hearing important evidence that you haven't previously disclosed to your spouse. If one of you does produce new evidence that's essential for a fair hearing, you and the judge decide whether an adjournment (or postponement) of the final hearing is necessary, and if so, who should pay the costs of the adjournment.

One of the ways that your solicitor gathers information is by using the standard *disclosure* process, which involves the use of legal tools such as requests to produce documents, and questionnaires. (Your spouse's solicitor does the same thing.) This disclosure is in addition to any that both solicitors may have already done – formally or informally – if you've been trying to work out a negotiated agreement on any issue in your divorce with your spouse. Chapter 5 tells you more about the disclosure process.

The current rules for procedure in financial cases – the *ancillary relief procedure rules* – are designed to make the process of disclosure less overwhelming and costly for you and require both parties to exchange all essential information and documentation in advance of the final hearing.

Disclosure costs can skyrocket in a litigated divorce. Ask your solicitor what she can do to keep those costs down.

Producing evidence

Your solicitor may use various kinds of evidence to bolster her arguments or to undermine your spouse's position. Your solicitor also works out how to address evidence your spouse's solicitor may introduce that's damaging to your case. Among other things, evidence can include:

- Financial records
- Police reports
- Valuations
- Doctors' records
- Photos, letters, diaries and videotapes and audio tapes
- Psychological or medical reports
- Witness statements

Calling witnesses

Your solicitor and your spouse's solicitor may call witnesses to give evidence at your final hearing. Your friends, family members and business associates may be called as witnesses. *Expert witnesses* who have special training, education or knowledge, such as psychologists, business valuation specialists, doctors, valuers and estate agents, social workers and others with professional expertise, may also be called.

If you use expert witnesses they need to be paid for their time. Depending on the kind of witness and her reputation, an expert witness can charge you at least a hundred pounds an hour. If these witnesses are asked to do certain things in preparation for your final hearing – review documents or write a report, for example, they bill you for the time taken to do that work as well as for their time in court.

The family and civil proceedings rules expressly require expert witnesses to be *jointly* instructed by you and your spouse whenever possible. The expert's first duty is to the court, and not to either of you. You're jointly responsible for the expert's fees. If one of you wants to instruct your own independent expert, you have to justify your reasons to the judge, and, if you can do so, the judge normally allows one expert each for the particular subject in issue. You're responsible for your own expert's fees (although, if you win the case, the judge may order your spouse to pay part of or all your costs including those of your expert, although this is rare).

If you're worried that one of your witnesses may not turn up to court voluntarily, or your witness needs a summons or court order to attend, you may apply to the court office for a witness summons, or to a judge for a court order, requiring your witness to attend on the date and time specified. You have to provide your witness's out-of-pocket expenses for attending court upfront at the time of serving your witness with the summons.

If you do have a witness who you think may be reluctant to attend court on your behalf, think very carefully before summonsing her. A reluctant witness may end up giving evidence that's not helpful to you, or may collapse under cross-examination. In addition, your solicitor or barrister isn't allowed to ask your witness any leading questions (questions that may suggest the answer), unlike your spouse's lawyer who *can* ask your witness leading questions.

Ordinarily, witnesses are used to help establish certain facts. For example, if you and your spouse are fighting over the residence of your children, witnesses may be called to help establish which of you is their primary carer – the parent who spends most time with them, takes them to the doctor, attends parent-teacher meetings, takes them to and from school and nursery, feeds them, clothes them, and so on. Or a surveyor may be called to help decide the value of your home. Most witnesses, including you and your spouse, are expected to file and exchange beforehand a written statement or report detailing the evidence on which they're relying. Witnesses must be available to give oral evidence (and be cross-examined) at your final hearing.

Professionals who have been involved with your children, such as their teacher or doctor, rarely agree to give evidence as witnesses on your behalf because they don't want to take sides. Any evidence they give should be primarily in order to help the judge decide what's best for your children, not what's best for you or your spouse. As a result, they normally meet the Cafcass officer instead, who includes any relevant information from the witnesses in her report. Let the Cafcass officer know before the report is prepared if you think she should speak to anyone in particular.

During the course of the preparations for your final hearing, your solicitor meets any witnesses on your behalf to get a sense of what they're going to say and to draft a statement of their evidence. She may advise them about the most important points that they should try to make and the best way to get those points across. However, your solicitor does *not* tell witnesses what to say.

Preparing the court bundle

Before any major hearing, particularly the final one, the judge expects your solicitors to agree on all the documents that are needed for the hearing. The documents include all the applications, orders, statements, reports and other miscellaneous documents relevant to your case. Your solicitor has to take responsibility for collating all the documents for your application into one fully indexed and paginated *bundle*. The bundle also includes a chronology of all the main events relating to the issue in question (agreed if possible by your lawyers in advance), a copy of any questionnaires and responses, and a summary from each of your solicitors of the main facts, issues and arguments in your case. Your solicitor must file the bundle with the court by a date fixed by the judge so that she can read the papers before the final hearing. Your solicitor should consult you about the contents of the bundle, but she has to abide by the court's requirements.

Rehearsing for your big day (or days)

Prior to the start of your final hearing, your solicitor, and possibly your barrister as well if you have one, should spend time with you, preparing you for what's to come. For example, your solicitor or barrister may:

- ✔ Talk you through the trial process – the procedure for the final hearing.

- ✔ Review her strategy with you.

- ✔ Explain the points that you should make when you give evidence, even suggesting words or phrases that help clarify your thoughts or add weight to your statements.

- ✔ Anticipate questions that your spouse's barrister or solicitor may ask and help you come up with answers for the more sensitive or difficult ones.

- ✔ Build your confidence by role-playing or grilling you as your spouse's lawyer would if she were trying to unnerve you or make you angry.

- ✔ Advise you about how to look and act in the courtroom.

Tell your solicitor about any concerns you have about the hearing. She can probably help alleviate your worries. For more information about giving evidence, see Chapter 5.

Dressing the part

Appearances count and your appearance can detract from the real issues in your divorce and even undermine your solicitor's legal strategy. Be sure that you and your solicitor talk about how to dress for your final hearing.

Your solicitor is likely to suggest that you wear something simple and understated (for example, if you're the wife, no bright colours, plaids or prints, steer clear of flashy jewellery, ensure that your hair is clean and neat with no wild hairstyles, and avoid excessive make-up and too-short skirts). Even if understatement is not your style, make it yours for the final hearing – if you're the husband, now is the time to wear a shirt and tie. Judges often prefer simplicity to extravagance, and you don't want any unnecessary distraction from the key issues of your case.

Acting the part

You may seethe with anger, quake with fear or feel totally defeated when you're in the courtroom, especially when you're on the witness stand, but try to keep your cool. Also, be polite to everyone – including your spouse's lawyer and, yes, even your spouse.

Your lawyer may tell you not to worry if you cry when you're on the witness stand. You won't be the first witness to do so, but don't be tempted to turn the tears on just for effect.

Listen attentively to the courtroom proceedings. Take notes and when you hear someone say something that you know isn't the truth, let your solicitor know. The best way to do that is by passing your solicitor a note, rather than whispering in her ear. Whispering may make your solicitor miss important evidence, and someone on your spouse's side may overhear your comments.

When you're called to give your evidence, keep a few things in mind:

- **Answer the questions you're asked in as few words as possible.** Giving long, involved answers may say too much and hurt your case. If the lawyer wants to know more, let her ask you another question.

- **Pause before you answer a question so that you give yourself time to think about what to say and so that your lawyer has time to object to the question you're asked.** If your lawyer objects and the judge sustains the objection, the judge tells you not to answer the question. Otherwise, you have to answer any question you're asked.

✔ **Take some time to compose yourself if you're unnerved by a question or not sure how to respond to it.** Give yourself time to think by pouring yourself some water and having a sip or by asking the lawyer to repeat the question. A jug of water and a glass should be sitting on the witness stand. If not, ask the judge for a glass of water. You may find counting to ten before you answer helps.

✔ **Sit up straight; don't slouch.** Keep your hands folded in front of you on your lap. Avoid wild gesticulations.

✔ **Don't be rude, sarcastic or argumentative with your spouse's lawyer, even if her questions are offensive or upsetting to you.** Offending or upsetting you may be part of the lawyer's strategy.

✔ **Address your answers to the judge slowly and clearly.** The judge records your responses and, in the end, the judge decides the case.

✔ **Don't send dirty looks or expressions of exasperation in the direction of your spouse or your spouse's lawyer when you get off the stand.** Maintain your dignity no matter what.

Understanding the Judge's Role

The judge who hears your case is responsible for ensuring that you get a fair hearing and that the barristers or solicitors follow the appropriate court procedures, and she will have read yours and your spouse's important documents in advance. The judge also rules on any objections the lawyers may make. If your and your spouse's lawyers get into a disagreement with one another or if someone in the courtroom gets unruly, the judge steps in.

During the hearing, the judge listens to the evidence and the lawyers' submissions and reviews any documents, statements and reports that are entered into evidence. The judge may also ask questions of the witnesses and almost certainly takes notes, although a court transcriber or machine is also recording every word that's said.

Many family court judges used to be family lawyers. Most judges have reputations for the kind of courtroom they run and for the way they tend to decide certain issues. For example, the judge in your case may run the courtroom with an iron hand or give your lawyers a great deal of leeway. She may have a reputation for favouring mothers over fathers in child residence battles, or be less inclined than other judges to order spousal maintenance.

If your solicitor knows which judge is going to hear your case and has been practising in that judge's jurisdiction for some time, she should take the judge's style and reputation into account when preparing for your hearing. If your solicitor isn't familiar with the judge, she should talk to a solicitor who is.

In some courts, you may not know which judge is due to hear your case until the day of your final hearing. Therefore, your solicitor may have to 'fly blind' as far as preparing for the final hearing with a particular judge in mind.

Having Your Day in Court

You and your spouse finally get your day in court weeks, maybe months, after your application is filed (assuming that you still haven't been able to settle the issues out of court). The solicitors should provide a brief summary of the case and issues in writing, along with a draft of the order sought. These summaries are exchanged between the solicitors and a copy given to the judge no later than the day of the hearing.

In the courtroom, you and your spouse sit with your respective barristers or solicitors at tables or benches directly in front of the judge. If you haven't seen or spoken with your spouse in a while, the sight of her in the courtroom may be unnerving and upsetting; on the other hand, you may feel just plain glad that you're finally getting things resolved.

Most family proceedings are heard in *chambers*, meaning that only you, your lawyers and the judge are allowed in court. Witnesses are allowed into court only when giving their own evidence. Occasionally, an expert witness such as a child psychologist may be invited to stay for the whole proceedings.

Court hearings follow a very predictable sequence of events. To help you make sense of what's happening in your hearing, here's a brief rundown of what you can expect:

1. **Opening speeches**

   The lawyer for the spouse who has made the application outlines the agreed facts of the case to the judge and summarises the issues between you and your spouse and the witnesses to be called. These summaries set the stage for the evidence and arguments to come.

2. **The applicant's case**

   The lawyer for the spouse who made the application (the *applicant*) goes first. The applicant's lawyer presents evidence as to why that spouse should get what was asked for in the application – for example, residence of the children or a transfer of the house and maintenance. To help prove the case, witnesses are called to the stand and questioned on oath, first by the applicant's lawyer (*examination*) and then by the other spouse's (the *respondent's*) lawyer (*cross-examination*).

The applicant's lawyer may then ask more questions of some of her witnesses who gave evidence earlier (*re-examination*). Re-examination is more likely to be used if the respondent's lawyer damages the applicant's case during cross-examination. It is used when something she said needs to be clarified or explained in a way that's more favourable to the applicant.

Sometimes, if an expert witness has been jointly instructed, or if a Cafcass officer has been involved, she is called before any of the other witnesses and both lawyers and the judge have a chance to question her. The judge then usually releases the expert or Cafcass officer to avoid any unnecessary costs and time.

3. The respondent's case

The lawyer for the respondent presents her case following the same procedures used by the applicant's lawyer, except that she doesn't have the opportunity to summarise the respondent's case orally first. The respondent's lawyer starts by calling the respondent to give evidence and then any other witnesses on her behalf. The applicant's lawyer cross-examines each of the respondent's witnesses in turn, and then the respondent's lawyer re-examines them if she needs to.

4. Closing arguments

During closing arguments, both lawyers get one last chance to make their cases. The respondent's lawyer goes first. If only a few issues need to be resolved, final arguments may exceptionally be waived.

5. The judgement or order

Depending on the complexity of the case, the judge may give her decision right away or take time to deliberate and return with a decision later. In most cases, the decision is given straight away. The judge also hears arguments and makes a decision on who pays for the costs of these proceedings. Usually, you're each responsible for your own costs, but sometimes, if one of you has clearly lost or has conducted the proceedings unreasonably, that party is ordered to pay all or part of the other's costs.

No matter how long you think you may be sitting in front of the judge, never bring food, drinks or reading materials into a courtroom. And make sure that your mobile phone is switched off.

Finally, the Judgement

When the judge gives the decision, she may ask one or both of your lawyers to write a written draft of the order made. Your lawyers may go straight off and do this together, or one lawyer may draft the order and send it to the other for review and approval. When both lawyers agree, or if the given time limit expires without an objection, the order is submitted to the court for the judge's final approval.

After the judge approves your court order, you can expect the following to happen:

✔ The provisions of the order usually replace any interim or pre-trial court orders unless otherwise specified.

✔ A court officer seals the court order and sends it to your solicitors. Your solicitor gives you a copy of the sealed order.

✔ The solicitor for the petitioner applies for the decree absolute – the final decree of divorce – if she has not already done so. The granting of the decree absolute is usually a formality and dealt with by a court officer on the day of receipt.

Yes, your divorce is officially over and for better or worse, you're single again. You and your now ex-spouse must comply with all the provisions of the court order, including transferring and returning property, paying money, adhering to a specific contact schedule, and other such terms. Chapter 19 gives you a helping hand here.

You probably remember Paul McCartney and Heather Mills's divorce in 2008. A better example of how *not* to divorce is hard to imagine. Of course, not many of us would attract such media interest but then not many of us would pour a jug of water over our ex-husband's lawyer in the courtroom. Luckily the judge was not present at that moment otherwise Heather Mills may well have been in contempt of court. It was, anyway, a bad hair day for Paul McCartney's solicitor.

Appealing the Decision

You can appeal the judge's decision if you're unhappy with it, but an appeal takes yet more time and money. In addition, you have to file your appeal within a certain period of time, usually 14 days for financial matters and 7 days for children matters. How long you have to file an appeal depends on the nature of the order, who made it, and in which court it was made. If you're considering an appeal, ask your solicitor about the time limits for filing.

You can't appeal a judge's decision just because you want to, and in some cases, you may need the permission of the judge to do so. You must have a legal basis for the appeal. Generally, an appeal is entertained only when some clear procedural irregularity is evident, or you can show that the original judge took into account matters that were irrelevant, ignored matters that were relevant, or otherwise arrived at a conclusion that was plainly wrong.

Wrapping things up

You and your solicitor should review the details of the judge's decision and any aspects of your divorce that you've negotiated with your now ex-spouse so that you understand your legal responsibilities to one another and are clear about any other steps you need to take as a result. You may need to:

✔ Transfer property, sort out charges on property, make deeds of trust and see to other ownership documents.

✔ Exchange cash and other valuables. You may want to make this exchange through your solicitor or in front of a neutral third party so that neither of you can accuse the other of dishonesty.

✔ Amend your insurance policies as necessary or purchase new ones.

✔ Make changes to your will and to other inheritance planning documents.

✔ Notify or pay off your creditors. For more on the practicalities of life after divorce look at Chapter 19.

Time and money aren't the only factors to consider when you're deciding whether to appeal. You should also consider these facts:

✔ Your appeal may not be heard for months, and when it is, you face another court hearing and yet more costs.

✔ While you're waiting to discover the outcome of your appeal, you, your spouse and your children are living in a sort of limbo. You may have to delay the application for the final divorce decree yet further. The result: you're still not divorced.

✔ Everyone in your family may be emotionally worn out already by the first hearing.

✔ You may have to find a new solicitor, especially if your current solicitor thinks that filing an appeal is risky or pointless given the facts of your case.

✔ The judge's decision may not be thrown out, and even if it is, you have no guarantee that the outcome of your next hearing will be more to your liking. In fact, you may end up with a judgement you like even less!

Preparing for the New Family Procedure Rules

Just when you'd got used to the legal jargon, new rules called Family Procedure Rules are due to come in after 2010 in England and Wales. As well as changing divorce procedure, the rules also change some of the terminology. A few of the suggested changes are shown in Table 18-1.

Table 18-1	Terminology Changes Coming into Effect in 2010
Current Term	*Proposed New Term*
Decree Nisi	Conditional Order
Decree of Divorce	Divorce Order
Decree of Nullity	Nullity Order
Decree of Judicial Separation	Judicial Separation Order
Decree Absolute	Final Order
Ancillary Relief	Financial Order
Cause	Case or Proceedings
Maintenance pending suit	Maintenance pending outcome of proceedings
Petition	Application
Petitioner	Applicant

Part V
After Your Divorce Is Finalised

'This is what happens when both sets of grandparents are divorced too.'

In this part . . .

This part of the book helps you prepare for the post-divorce experience. We give you advice on handling your personal finances, seeking a well-paying new job, and getting the education you need to pursue that new career. We also alert you to some of the more common (and serious) problems newly divorced people face, give you advice on how to deal with those problems, and point you towards other resources that can help. Finally, for more peace of mind the next time you marry, we offer information on pre-marital and the rarer post-marital agreements.

Chapter 19

Handling the Practical Matters of Life after Your Divorce

In This Chapter

▶ Attending to post-divorce legal and financial matters

▶ Rethinking or writing your will

▶ Managing your money after you're divorced

▶ Locating the job you need

▶ Making life okay for you and your children

*N*ow that you're divorced, what do you do first? Depending on the details of your final court order, you may have plenty to deal with in the way of paperwork and payments. You need to begin managing your own money, perhaps find a job outside the home, and build a new social life for yourself or pick up your old one where you left off. Whether your children are living with both of you or one of you, you must work out together how you're going to care for your children now that you're on your own.

This chapter provides the information and advice you need to tie up the loose ends of your divorce and face the challenges ahead. It highlights inheritance planning issues to consider, offers information that can help you reach your educational and career goals, and suggests things you should do to manage your money wisely, no matter how much (or how little) income you have. This chapter also offers you some valuable advice about post-divorce parenting and developing new friendships.

Tying Up the Loose Ends of Your Final Court Order

Read the details of your final court order carefully, and do exactly what the order says. If you fail to carry out your legal obligations (and that's exactly what they are), the battles that may have plagued the end of your marriage are likely to continue. If your ex-spouse decides to take you to court, you may find yourself in legal trouble all over again.

Ask your solicitor which of the loose ends relating to your divorce court orders you need to deal with yourself and which he can take care of. Your solicitor should clearly advise in writing who needs to do what. Use that letter as a checklist to make sure that you don't overlook any of your legal responsibilities.

Transferring real property

If your former spouse is to become the sole owner of real property (houses, other buildings, or land) you own together, you must transfer your interest in the property by both signing a formal deed of transfer. Your solicitor sends a copy of the deed of transfer to the Land Registry where the property is registered. If your property is jointly rented, you need to sign an authority to your landlord to transfer the tenancy into your ex-spouse's sole name. (See Chapter 3 for more about the Land Registry.)

If the transferred property has an outstanding mortgage or charge attached to it, you're still legally liable for it, unless and until your spouse pays the mortgage off, or the lenders join in the deed of transfer and formally release you from the mortgage. This situation is the case even if your final order says that your former spouse is to take responsibility for the mortgage. In such an order, your ex-spouse usually promises to do whatever is possible to secure your release from the mortgage and to pay you back (or *indemnify* you) if he defaults on the mortgage payments. That promise is binding as far as you and your ex-spouse are concerned but not so far as the lenders are concerned. The lenders can still sue you for the debt if it's not paid. (See Chapter 11 for a discussion of the legal actions you can take to protect yourself if your ex-spouse defaults on the loan associated with the transferred property.)

If your final order obliges your ex-spouse to pay you a lump sum of money, you should secure that debt with an asset if you can – just as a bank or other commercial lender may do. In this way, you increase the likelihood of seeing that money. For example, if your ex gets the house and, in return, is going to pay you £30,000 within the next five years, you can secure that debt by placing a *charge* on the house and registering it with the Land Registry. If your ex-spouse doesn't pay up, he can't sell, borrow against or transfer the asset without paying you first.

If you place a charge on the house, and your ex-spouse defaults on payment to you, you can foreclose and sell the house. Enforcing the charge through sale is a good option if you have enough equity in the house to then pay off the mortgage, pay the costs of sale, and keep the money you're due.

Transferring other property

If you transfer stocks, bonds, policies, shares or other funds to your former spouse, you may have to pay capital gains tax if their value has appreciated since they were first purchased. Timing may be crucial here. You need to check this out with your solicitor or accountant.

If you need to transfer ownership of a vehicle, you register the transfer at the DVLA, Swansea, SA99 1BL. You can make customer enquiries by telephone on 0870 240 0010 or by email at vehicles.dvla@gtnet.gov.uk. Their website address is www.dvla.gov.uk.

Paying off debts

At all costs, try to avoid a divorce agreement that requires your ex-spouse to pay off your debt. If he fails to honour that agreement, your credit rating is damaged, despite what your agreement says. This is a real concern if your ex-spouse is angry about your divorce and you think he may try to get revenge by not paying your debts. Chapter 11 gives you more tips for avoiding trouble.

If your former spouse does take over some of your debts, however, notify your creditors in writing and ask them to transfer those debts into your ex-spouse's name in order to relieve you of responsibility for them. Although the creditors are not legally obliged to comply with your request and although they can still collect the debt from you if your former spouse does not pay, your letters help underscore who's supposed to be satisfying those debts. And, as a friendly reminder of what you expect, send your ex-spouse a copy of those letters.

If you want to be sure that your ex-spouse is paying off the debts that used to be yours, see if you can get him to provide you with proof of each payment – a copy of the monthly statement is sufficient. You may also want to ask the creditor to notify you straight away if your ex-spouse defaults.

Collecting state benefits and tax credits

Now that you're finally separated or divorced, your status changes and you may become eligible for certain state benefits or tax credits. See Chapter 7 for a summary of the main benefits and credits that may be available to you: they can make a big difference to your financial position. Make an appointment with your local Citizens Advice Bureau (CAB) to make sure that you're claiming all the benefits to which you're entitled, or for help in completing the forms. You can find their details in your local telephone directory. The sooner you apply, the sooner your application is dealt with. Most benefits and credits are backdated to the date of your application, not to the date that you first become eligible.

You can claim a 25 per cent reduction in your council tax if you're a single person living on your own, with or without children. You can also claim if your offspring are students.

Protecting your pension rights

If you have the benefit of a pension sharing or pension attachment order (see Chapter 11), you need to take a number of important steps to make sure that the order is put into effect. Your solicitor may deal with these for you, or advise you on the steps that you can take yourself. If you have to wait for your share of the benefits until your spouse draws his or dies (under a pension attachment order), keeping the pension administrators informed of any change of address is crucial; otherwise, you may lose the benefit.

If you want to obtain the benefit of any additional contributions that your ex-spouse has made to the state pension scheme (without any loss to your ex-spouse), you must send a copy of your decree absolute to the Pension Service (www.thepensionservice.gov.uk) within one month of the grant of the decree.

In Scotland, a pension sharing order or agreement must be sent to the Pension Service within two months of your decree of divorce – this is particularly important to remember if you have a 'Do It Yourself' divorce.

Changing your final order

If you're unhappy with something in your final order, comply with it anyway; most of the order stands whatever you think, particularly the property and capital provisions. However, if you believe that the terms of your maintenance or pension attachment order should be modified due to changes in the circumstances of your life or your ex-spouse's life, you can apply to the court for a variation. Similarly, if the arrangements for your children that you agreed to or that were ordered are no longer meeting their needs, you can apply to the court to vary the order. But talk to your solicitor first to get an idea of your prospects of success.

Rethinking Your Estate Planning

If you had a will when you were married, you need to revisit that legal document now that you're divorced. Any provisions in that will appointing your ex-spouse as an executor or beneficiary automatically lapse on the granting of your decree absolute. (An *executor* is the adult responsible for making sure that the provisions of your will are carried out after you die. You appoint your executor in your will. A *beneficiary* is a person you name who benefits from part of or all your estate.)

If you don't have a will, now's the time to write one

Getting divorced is a good excuse for you to write a will if you don't have one already or even if you do. You may be able to get public funding for your solicitor to draft your will for you if you're financially eligible and if you're appointing a guardian for your minor children. A will isn't just for millionaires. You need one if you care about who inherits your property after you die and who looks after your children if you and your ex die. Without a will, the *rules of intestacy* determine who inherits everything you own. In England and Wales, the rules of intestacy require that your estate passes to the following people, in the order given, but subject to certain financial restrictions:

1. Your spouse if you have one, but if not, to

2. Your children and grandchildren if you have any, but if not, to

3. Your parents, equally if both alive, but if none, to

4. Your full brothers and sisters or their issue, but if none, to

5. Your half brothers and sisters or their issue, equally if more than one.

If you don't have any of the above, your property then goes to grandparents, full aunts and uncles, half aunts and uncles, and then the Crown, the Duchy of Lancaster, or the Duke of Cornwall.

Your will can also serve the following functions:

- ✔ Provide for your children if you die while they're still financially dependent on you.

- ✔ Appoint the adult to manage the assets you leave to your children in your will. That person is called a *trustee.* If you don't name a trustee in your will, the court may appoint your ex-spouse to play that role.

- ✔ Appoint the adult to be legally responsible for your children if you and your ex-spouse both die while your children are still *minors* (which means they're under 18 years old). This appointee is called a *guardian*, or *testamentary guardian.* Your children's guardian automatically acquires parental responsibility for them on the death of you and your ex-spouse (see Chapter 4).

Ordinarily, your ex-spouse becomes responsible for bringing your children up if you die whilst they're under 18. If that's not what you want, state your preference in your will and provide your executor with a separate written statement of your reasons. However, despite your stated preference, a judge may award residence to your ex-spouse unless he doesn't want it or is an unfit parent, or other strong reasons exist for a non-parent to bring up your children.

Estate planning tools to help you

In the event of your death, you can make sure that your children are financially provided for in other ways besides including them in your will. To find out which estate planning tools are most appropriate for you, talk with a wills specialist, or a trust or probate solicitor. Inheritance tax implications may also apply.

Trusts

A *trust* holds and manages assets for one or more beneficiaries. It can be *revocable* (one you can change later on) or *irrevocable* (a trust you can't change). You must appoint a trust corporation or not less than two *trustees* to oversee and manage the assets held in trust for the benefit of young children or where real property is involved. To help you determine whether a trust is appropriate, consider the following:

- ✔ Children under the age of 18 (or 16 in Scotland) can't inherit money or property in their own right.

- ✔ Trusts can provide tax benefits and reduce the number of assets in your estate that must go through probate, depending on the type you set up.

✔ Trusts are most appropriate when you're leaving your children a substantial amount of property, because they're expensive to set up and maintain.

✔ Trusts are complicated legal entities. To establish one, you need the help of a trust specialist or probate solicitor.

Other estate planning options

Another option is to name your children as the *beneficiaries* of your life insurance policy or nominate them for any benefits that your employer offers. Again, you have to name an adult to manage the benefits for your children should you die. Your solicitor, financial adviser or work personnel department can provide helpful advice. If you're paying private school fees for your children, you may also want to take out a school fees policy to cover the fees in the event of your death.

Assessing Your Financial Situation

What you asked for during your divorce process and what you actually ended up with are probably somewhat different. For example, you may have received fewer assets, been saddled with more debt, and received less child support and maintenance than you had hoped for. On the other hand, if you're the one making those child and spousal support payments, those payments may be higher than you expected. Either way, money is likely to be tight now. Developing a budget helps you determine just how much you can afford to spend and where you need to be cutting back. Chapter 3 can help you come up with a budget for your family.

If you're obliged to pay spousal or child support, managing your money is particularly important because the law expects you to make those payments on time and in full. If you don't, and your former spouse takes you to court to enforce arrears, arguing that you 'just ran out of money' doesn't cut any ice with the judge. Going back to court costs you more time, money and stress, and you may well be ordered to pay your spouse's costs. Ultimately, you can find yourself spending time in prison.

As a general rule, your mortgage payments (principal and interest) should not consume more than 30 to 35 per cent of your gross or pre-tax income. Taking your mortgage and any other debt into account, you need to ensure that your budget can cope with at least a 1 per cent rise in interest rates, and preferably 2 per cent.

For help in putting your budget on track or to increase your financial skills, get in touch with your local community education college to see if it runs courses on personal finance. Also, if you owe more than you think you can pay given your monthly income, a debt counsellor may be able to help you negotiate lower monthly payments to your creditors. Good sources of debt advice include:

- ✔ **Citizens Advice Bureau (CAB):** www.adviceguide.org.uk
- ✔ **National Debtline:** www.nationaldebtline.co.uk or 0808 808 4000
- ✔ **Consumer Credit Counselling Service:** www.cccs.co.uk or 0800 138 1111
- ✔ **Payplan:** www.payplan.com or 0800 389 3431

Using the services of a financial adviser

Unless you're an experienced financial manager, planning and implementing an appropriate investment strategy takes the help of a qualified financial planner or adviser. When you're looking for one, as a general rule steer clear of professionals who are tied to a particular company and sell specific financial products. Instead, engage an independent financial adviser.

Working with an independent financial planner who makes money by charging you a percentage of the total value of the assets he manages or invests for you, or employing a financial planner who charges you by the hour for advice and assistance, may be better alternatives. Financial planners who charge you by the hour are most likely to consider *all* your investment alternatives – policies, stocks and shares, bonds, property, and so on. Ask the financial adviser about the different options for payment of his charges.

The Institute of Financial Planning has a search facility that helps you find a qualified financial planner in your area. You can phone them on 0117 945 2470, or try www.financial planning.org.uk. The sector is regulated by the Financial Services Authority and anyone giving advice must have a Financial Planning Certificate (FPC).

You can identify an adviser's status without asking directly: the letters after his name show whether the person is a member of one of the financial associations that promote professionalism within the industry and provide an indication of his expertise. For example, if he is a member of the Personal Finance Society (www.thepfs.org) or the Chartered Insurance Institution (www.cii.co.uk), the following designations apply:

- ✔ **CFP:** has passed the entry-level examinations Certificate in Financial Planning.
- ✔ **DipPFS:** has completed the diploma qualifications.
- ✔ **APFS:** has obtained sufficient passes of advanced diploma examinations and has a minimum of three years' experience.
- ✔ **Chartered Financial Planner:** has accrued at least 290 exam credits, 120 of which must be at the advanced level, has at least 5 years industry experience, and has completed 3 years continuing professional development (CPD).
- ✔ **FPFS:** has accrued at least 350 exam credits, at least 5 years industry experience, and has a minimum of 3 years CPD.

Finding a Job or Landing a Better One

When you take a hard look at your budget and assess all your options, you may decide that if you're going to be financially solvent, you need to work outside the home (if you don't already) or find a better-paying job.

If you're unsure about what kind of new career you may be suited for, meet a career counsellor. He can help you assess your skills and interests and discuss the types of jobs for which you may be suited. Younger people can look at www.connexions-direct.com. Other possible sources include your local further education college and your local Jobcentre Plus office. Look online at www.jobcentreplus.gov.uk or in *Yellow Pages* for your nearest Jobcentre Plus.

Acquiring the education you need

If you already have a job but need to make more money, finding more lucrative work may simply be a matter of updating your CV and beginning a job search (especially if you have good job skills and strong qualifications). But, if you're re-entering the work world and your skills are outdated or very limited, or if you want to change careers, you may well need job training or continuing education to achieve your employment goals.

Financing a college degree

Depending on your job skills and education level, achieving your career goals may require getting a degree from a three- or four-year college or university course, completing a further education college course, or attending a trade or technical college (see the next section 'Choosing a vocational course or college'). But you may find financing the cost of higher education hard to do when money is tight, especially if you need to put money away for your children's education.

If you need help funding your education or training, the student loan, grant or work-study initiatives may be able to help you. Extra help may be available to you if you have children or are a single parent. You may need to complete an access course to get into university if you don't have appropriate GCSEs. For more information look at www.direct.gov.uk under extra financial help for adult students.

If your goal is to get a well-paying job after graduating from college, select your course of study carefully. Some college qualifications lead to a bigger and more immediate financial payoff than others.

Choosing a vocational course or college

You can find both good and bad vocational courses and providers. Attending one of the good ones can be a great way to gain very specific job skills. The bad ones take your money and give you little in return.

Before you enrol in a privately run vocational college, find out if your local community education college offers you the same education at a cheaper cost.

The following tips can help you shop wisely for a vocational college course:

- ✔ Visit the college. Check out its classrooms, computers and other classroom resources. Do the surroundings look well cared for and is the equipment state of the art?

- ✔ Find out if the college is accredited and by whom.

- ✔ Ask to sit in on some of the classes.

- ✔ Get information about the curricula, staff, costs and refund policy.

- ✔ Talk to students who have completed the course you hope to enrol in. Get their opinion of how well the course prepared them for a career. If they're willing to share the information, find out what salaries they earn.

- ✔ Find out about the kind of career counselling and job-finding assistance the college offers its students and ask about the college's placement rate.

Searching for the right job

You have many avenues open to you when you begin looking for a job. The right method for finding that perfect job depends on your particular job skills, work experience and the kind of job you want. You may want to consider the following job search methods:

- ✔ Read the classified ads in your local paper, or check out its website.

- ✔ Go to job fairs. They're a great way to find out the potential employers in your market and what skills they're looking for.

- ✔ Talk with some of the larger employment or personnel agencies in your area. Some are general and some specialise in a specific industry.

- ✔ Work with an executive recruiter if you're fairly well qualified already (better known as a *head hunter*).

- ✔ Visit your local Jobcentre Plus or look at `www.direct.gov.uk` to find out about job vacancies in the public and private sector.

- ✔ Tell your friends and professional associates that you're looking for a new job.

✔ Use the Internet. Searching for key words such as 'job openings', 'employment' or 'careers' yields a wide variety of job openings all over the country. Narrow your search by specifying the area you want to work in or indicating the type of job you want, or go directly to the organisation you want to work for and click on its 'employment' link.

Some career-oriented websites offer more than just job listings. You can post your CV at these sites, conduct your own job search, arrange for a personal search agent to email you information about listings that match your job criteria, and get advice from career counsellors:

- www.jobsite.co.uk
- www.proteus-net.co.uk

Dealing with Personal and Family Issues

After your divorce is over, you enter a new phase in your life. You may feel happier than you've felt in a long time, free of the tension and strife that plagued your marriage. Life after divorce can represent a time of personal growth, rediscovery and new opportunities for you.

On the other hand, you may find being single again an intimidating and lonely experience – particularly if divorce was not your idea and you're unprepared for life on your own or if you have sole care of your children. Even if you sought this last arrangement, having full-time responsibility for your children seven days a week, night and day, can be overwhelming, not to mention exhausting. Maybe you're planning to enter a new relationship, perhaps with someone who isn't used to living with other people's children (that is, your children), or who may have children with whom you – and your children – come to live. Or maybe your ex-spouse is entering a new relationship, and your children have to adjust to that. In other words, your future, and your children's, can be much more complicated than your past.

If you need parenting support, try parentlineplus.org.uk or one parentfamilies.org.uk, or look for *Co-parenting Survival Guide* by Zimmerman and Thayer or *Parenting after Divorce* by Stahl, both available on www.amazon.co.uk.

Being easy on yourself

To help you adjust to all the changes in your life, avoid piling unreasonable expectations on yourself. Just do what you must to tie up the loose ends of your divorce; otherwise, take a breather and regroup mentally and physically. Although you may have big plans for what to do with the rest of your life, give yourself a chance to recover from what you've been through.

In other words, being a little lazy – letting your house get messier than it usually is, eating fast-food dinners once in while, skipping a few workouts at the gym – is okay. Pressuring yourself to make important decisions right away, before you can think them through with a clear head, may cause you to make mistakes that you regret later on.

On the other hand, maintaining those habits can make you feel good about yourself and about life in general. If you get too lazy, you may slip into a state you can't crawl out of, which definitely interferes with your ability to get on with your life.

Taking time to reflect on what happened

Try to put your recent experiences into perspective. Take time to understand why your marriage didn't work out and how you may have contributed to your marital problems. Otherwise, you may end up making the same mistakes twice. Keeping a diary is a good way to do this and counselling can be a big help, too (see Chapter 2 for advice on how to find a counsellor).

Accept the fact that your life is no longer the way it used to be and never will be again; which doesn't mean that your new life is a disappointment – just different. Identify some benefits to being single again. For example, you have more privacy and time to yourself, and you can sleep better because you're no longer stressed out by your divorce.

Finding a support group

Consider joining a divorce support group. The members can help bolster your confidence through the inevitable down times as you rebuild your life and can provide you with advice and feedback when you encounter problems you're not sure how to handle. Contact the Divorce Recovery Workshop at www.drw.org.uk for support after your divorce. One Parent Families/Gingerbread can put you in touch with a local group of parents on their own: go to www.oneparentfamilies.org.uk or call the helpline on 0800 018 5026. And don't forget that if you start feeling depressed, you don't have to be suicidal to ring the Samaritans on 08457 909090 – even in the middle of the night.

Becoming handy around the house

You may have to take on new household chores – cooking, food shopping, balancing the accounts, home repairs, mowing the lawn – chores your ex-spouse used to do. If you need to get up to speed quickly on unfamiliar household tasks, relatives and friends may be willing to give you a quick lesson (don't be ashamed to ask them for the help you need). Reading how-to books or taking classes are also good ways to acquire new skills. Soon you'll feel proud of what you can accomplish on your own and gain confidence in your ability to discover even more.

Focusing more attention on your children

If you have children, much of your energy is probably focused on helping them adjust to life after your divorce. If you and your spouse were separated while getting divorced, your children most likely began making the adjustment then. Now that your divorce is final, they may have to deal with a new set of changes and need more of your attention as a result.

Your divorce may actually provide an opportunity for you to improve your relationship with your children. Now that you're no longer distracted by the troubles of your marriage or the process of your divorce, you can refocus some of your energy on your children.

Finding activities you and your children enjoy

Being with your children, as a non-resident parent, may be awkward for everyone at first. Seeing you living in a new place and not having you in their everyday lives may feel weird to your children. To help everyone adjust to the new situation, avoid making every get-together a special event. Simple activities such as a trip to the supermarket, a bike ride, doing homework together or watching a DVD – the kinds of things you used to do together – take some of the pressure off and help reassure your children that not everything in their lives has changed.

If you're a non-resident parent, don't be upset if your children don't appear overjoyed to see you when you pick them up. Their initial nonchalance may be their way of protecting themselves emotionally, or it may reflect their confidence that you'll always be in their lives and the divorce hasn't changed your love and concern for them. Don't make assumptions about the ways your children are responding to the changes occurring in their lives. Instead, try to understand the true reasons for their behaviour.

Working at rebuilding a sense of family

As you recover from your divorce, rebuilding a sense of family with your children is important for you all. Whether you're a resident parent, a non-resident parent, or you share residence with your spouse, your children need to feel that they're still part of a real family, which is essential to their sense of self-worth. To help maintain a sense of family, hold on to as many of your family rituals as you're comfortable with. Go with your children to special school festivals or arrange for holidays with your extended family.

Think about establishing new family traditions (going on an annual family holiday or taking up a new hobby with your children, for example) to make your children feel as if some benefits to their new life do exist and to help them enjoy spending time with you as a family.

Special family time doesn't have to cost a lot of money. It can be as simple as a walk after dinner, weekend bike rides, playing Monopoly or decorating the Christmas tree. Your children benefit from spending time together as a group and growing up in a household where open communication, humour, clear values and rules, nurturing and respect for one another exist.

Making New Friends

When you get divorced, you almost inevitably lose touch with some of your friends. They may well be people you knew through your ex-spouse, or people who related to you solely as one half of a couple. Some of your friends may feel the need to choose sides in your divorce. Others may drop out of both of your lives.

But your most important and significant friendships will remain intact. Even so, making new friends can be fun and can bring new energy and hope to your life. Volunteer for a cause you care about; sign up for a class; join a singles group (a group for divorced people is a particularly good idea), a book reading group or a health club; or try some other new activity.

Make a point of rediscovering your local community and all that it offers you and your children. Find out how to do something you've always wanted to do but never got around to doing, or take up a hobby you put aside when you were married. Chapter 23 is full of ideas for helping you adjust to and make the most of your new life. The point is this: *Get out of the house and add some variety to your life!*

Chapter 20

Solving the Toughest Post-divorce Problems

In This Chapter

▶ Your ex-spouse doesn't let you spend time with your children

▶ You don't get your maintenance or child support payments

▶ Your ex-spouse leaves the country

▶ Your ex disappears with your children

▶ You want to change your divorce settlement

▶ Your ex-spouse declares bankruptcy

*U*nfortunately, divorce may not bring to an end the problems that destroyed your marriage. Some divorced couples persist in arguing and going out of their way to make each other miserable instead of getting on with their lives. Consumed by anger and a desire for revenge, they fight over the outcome of the divorce, withhold child support or spousal maintenance, purposely delay making support payments, or interfere in each other's child residence or contact arrangements.

This chapter can't solve everyone's post-divorce problems, but it does provide you with specific information about some of the most common (and serious) problems divorced couples face and what you can do about them – if necessary.

Your Ex-spouse Interferes with Your Child Contact Arrangements

If you're a non-resident parent and your ex-spouse makes seeing or contacting your children difficult, or even impossible, she may be in breach of a court order, and is almost certainly putting the wellbeing of your children at risk. Contact is the right of the children, rather than the right of either parent. If your ex is denying you contact with your children, get in touch with your solicitor for advice on the next steps to take.

On the other hand, no law requires a non-resident parent to have contact with their child. You can use your ex-spouse's repeated failure to stick with any order or agreement for contact as justification for why the court should modify your current arrangement. You may even be able to go to court and ask the judge to restrict your ex-spouse's contact if, in the end, you think that is what's best for your children.

Avoiding retaliation by withholding payments

If your spouse interferes with your child contact arrangements in any way, you may be tempted to withhold payment for child support. *Don't do it!* Not only are you in breach of your obligations – just like your ex-spouse – but you may also jeopardise your children's wellbeing. Two wrongs in this case definitely *don't* make a right.

A far better course of action is to continue paying your child support and try to work things out with your ex. Mediation is your best bet if you want to resolve your disputes outside of court (see Chapter 16 for more on the subject of mediation), but mediation doesn't work unless you're both willing to give it a try. If your ex-spouse is unwilling, going back to court or to the Child Support Agency/Child Maintenance and Enforcement Commission (CSA/CMEC) may be your only options. Talk to your solicitor to find out exactly what steps you should take next. You can also contact Families Need Fathers (www.fnf.org. uk) or the One Parent Families/Gingerbread (www.oneparentfamilies. org.uk) for information and support for non-resident parents.

Making an application to the court

If you've already tried out-of-court resolutions without a result (see Chapter 10 for more on this), consider making an application to the court – for a fresh contact order or for a variation of a previous order. An application to *enforce* a court order is a last resort; the main remedies for breach of a court order (or *contempt of court*) are a fine or imprisonment, and they may not succeed in getting you what you really want: contact with your children. Unless your ex can prove that she has good reason to keep you from seeing your children – you've abused them, sexually molested them, you have a drug problem, and so on – your ex-spouse is likely to be ordered to allow you to resume seeing your child, albeit at a pace that suits the children.

From 2009, courts have new enforcement powers and can order 'contact activities'. They can make people involved in a contact case attend 'contact activities', such as a parenting programme or an information session about mediation, The courts can ask a Cafcass or a Welsh Family Proceedings Officer to monitor contact orders and/or compliance with a 'contact activity' and report to the court if necessary. Where a contact order is breached without reasonable excuse the courts can make the person in breach of the order do unpaid work. Courts may also award financial compensation from one person to another, for example, when the cost of a holiday has been lost.

Child Support Payments Don't Arrive

The sad reality is that tens of thousands of divorced parents with agreements, court orders, or Child Support Agency/Child Maintenance and Enforcement Commission (CSA/CMEC) assessments for child support never receive their child support, or receive it only on a sporadic basis. As a result, many of these parents struggle to provide for their children, some may lose their homes, and still others fall into poverty. If your ex-spouse falls behind with her child support payments, the overdue payments become known as *arrears*. Chapter 13 tells you about the arrangements that you and your spouse may make for child support during your divorce.

If you're having trouble tracing your ex-spouse, you may be able to get the Department of Work and Pensions to disclose her whereabouts to the court. If your ex is the sort of person who can pay but won't, you can scream, cry and tear your hair out, or you can use legal means to force your ex-spouse to pay up. The main legal means available to you are slightly different, depending on whether you have an agreement, a court order or a CSA/CMEC assessment for your child support.

Enforcing a child support agreement

A child support agreement made between you and your spouse is a form of contract, and contracts are normally enforceable by the courts according to contract law. However, if your agreement has been made in the context of family proceedings, the court is likely to enforce the agreement in one of the same ways that they would if you had a court order for child support, as described in the next section.

If your agreement has been in force for more than a year, you or your ex-spouse can apply instead to the CSA/CMEC for a fresh calculation of the child support liability. The CSA/CMEC then takes over all the administration and enforcement of the child support payments. The CSA/CMEC doesn't deal with any arrears that have accrued *before* your application to the CSA/CMEC.

Fulfilling an order for child support

A court order for child maintenance is also sometimes called an order for child support payments, or an order for *periodical payments for or to the child.* Agreements as to child maintenance can be included in a consent order. If you have an order for child support that predates 3 March 2003, you have to apply to the court if you want to enforce that order. If your court order for child maintenance has been in effect since that day and for more than one year, either of you may apply to the CSA/CMEC as described in the preceding section.

The court's powers are as follows:

- **Attachment of earnings order:** If your ex-spouse is in regular employment, one of the most cost-effective ways of ensuring that you get your child support payments (and any arrears) is by applying for an attachment of earnings order. If you're successful, your ex-spouse's employer is obliged to deduct the child support payments directly from your ex-spouse's wages or salary and pay them to you. The court has to specify a limit of earnings below which the employer can't deduct the child support payments, in order to ensure that your ex-spouse still gets the minimum necessary to survive.

- **Execution against goods:** The court can authorise a bailiff to enter your ex-spouse's home (or other premises belonging to her) and seize goods to the value of any child support arrears that have accrued. The bailiff can then sell the goods and pay the proceeds to you.

- **Charging order:** If the arrears are substantial, you may be able to secure a charge against your ex-spouse's property up to the amount due to you, plus interest. Ultimately, you may be able to get an order for sale of the property and take your child support arrears from the proceeds.

- **Garnishee Order:** If you know that your ex-spouse has a bank or building society account, or that your ex-spouse's solicitor is holding money for her, you may be able to obtain a Garnishee Order that the contents of the account be frozen until the child support arrears have been paid to you from it.

- **Bankruptcy:** If your ex-spouse has been made bankrupt, you may still be able to collect the child support payments due, although you may have to compete with other creditors for a share of your ex-spouse's income. You can still apply for the arrears when the bankruptcy order has expired (normally after one year) by one of the other means referred to in this section, but whether your ex will have the means to pay is another matter.

- ✔ **Judgement summons or committal:** Under this method of enforcement, your ex-spouse can be committed to prison if evidence of wilful refusal to pay exists. Beware, though, of killing the goose that lays the golden egg!

- ✔ **Registration of the order in the Magistrates Court:** If your child maintenance order has been made in the County Court, which is likely, you can apply to register the order in the Magistrates Court, and then the Clerk of the Magistrates Court takes over enforcement of the order for you.

An application to enforce arrears of child support payments may prompt an application by your ex-spouse for a reduction in the current payments. If she can show that the current payments are genuinely unaffordable, an order may be made to reduce the payments and possibly waive some of the arrears. In addition the court doesn't normally enforce arrears that are more than 12 months old.

Enforcing a CSA assessment

Many applications for child support are dealt with by the Child Support Agency/Child Maintenance and Enforcement Commission, rather than by the court. If your ex-spouse regularly fails to pay support based on a CSA/CMEC calculation, the CSA/CMEC has the powers described in the following three sections to enforce payment.

Payment by bankers' standing order or direct debit

The CSA/CMEC can order your ex-spouse to make payments by a bankers' standing order or direct debit, and direct her to open a bank account for this purpose if she doesn't already have one. The frequency of payments usually matches your ex-spouse's salary or wage payments.

Deduction from earnings direction

Your ex-spouse can agree to a deduction from earnings voluntarily or, if arrears exist, the CSA/CMEC can require your ex-spouse's employer to deduct the child support payments at source and pay them directly to the CSA/CMEC. The deduction from earnings direction has two main parts: a normal deduction rate to cover the current child support payments and any arrears, and a protected earnings portion that states the minimum amount of take-home pay your ex-spouse is left with after making the deduction – 60 per cent of her net earnings for that employment. Any shortfall can be carried forward to the next pay period. CMEC, which is taking over from the CSA during the period 2008–2011, is going to introduce deduction from earnings orders as a first method of collecting maintenance payments, in order to allow it to take the maintenance directly from the wages of the non-resident parent before arrears begin.

A liability order

If neither of the above methods of enforcement are appropriate, the CSA/CMEC can apply to the Magistrates Court for a liability order. The order can include interest, penalty payments and fees, as well as child support payments. The court must make an order if it is satisfied that the payments are due and unpaid. It can't question the basis of the child support calculation. CMEC plans to introduce an administrative process to replace the court-based liability order process.

Until then, when a liability order has been made, the CSA/CMEC can try to recover the debt by various means:

- ✔ **Distress action**, using bailiffs to seize and sell goods and household items.

- ✔ **Third party debt order**, requiring a bank or building society to release funds to the amount of the liability order.

- ✔ **Charging order on property or assets**, so that when the property or assets are sold, the monies due are paid to the Secretary of State.

- ✔ **Registering the liability order in the Register of County Court Judgements**, which affects your ex-spouse's credit rating and possibly her membership of a professional body.

- ✔ **Committal to prison**, for a maximum of six weeks.

- ✔ **Removal of driving licence**, or disqualification from obtaining one for up to two years.

Ultimately, the court decides which means of enforcement is most appropriate. The court is unlikely to disqualify your ex-spouse from driving if she needs to drive to earn a living. But if your ex-spouse is committed to prison or disqualified from driving, and at the end of the prison sentence or disqualification still hasn't paid the arrears, the CSA/CMEC can make a further application to the court.

The CMEC's new powers don't come into force until about 2011, and it will eventually have even more enforcement weapons, such as freezing assets and confiscating passports.

Your Ex-spouse Leaves the Country

Unfortunately, some parents are so intent on not paying their child support that they move out of the country, often without leaving a forwarding address. When that happens, enforcing a child support court order and collecting that support can be particularly difficult.

Means to enforce maintenance orders abroad do exist, but they can be expensive and time-consuming, and don't apply to every country in the world. Ask your solicitor for some preliminary advice before you launch into any enforcement proceedings abroad.

Scotland has a different legal system, and so taking the children out of England into Scotland, or vice versa, may raise many of the same problems, such as having to return the children to the country they were taken from so the courts can decide where they should live.

Your Ex-spouse Disappears with Your Children

If you have residence of your children and your ex-spouse kidnaps them or refuses to return your children to you, she is committing both a criminal and a civil offence. *Leave no stone unturned if your ex-spouse takes off with your children.* The longer you wait to act, the harder finding them is going to be. You should:

- ✔ **Call your local police station immediately.**

- ✔ **Contact your solicitor straight away.**

- ✔ **Hire your own private investigator.** *Private enquiry agents* who track down missing persons using national computerised databases can be very effective at turning up missing people through National Insurance numbers, driving licence numbers, and plenty of asking around.

If you suspect that your spouse may be thinking of taking off with your children, you must also alert your children's childminder, nursery or school about your concerns. However, unless a court order applies forbidding your ex-spouse to remove the children from your care, the school, childminder or nursery don't have the power to prevent your ex-spouse from doing so. The best they may be able to do is to call you and stall your ex-spouse until you arrive.

If you think that your ex-spouse may be planning to leave the country with your children, and you have a residence order, contact the Passport Office and ask that your children not be granted passports if your ex-spouse applies for them. If your ex-spouse manages to get out of the country with your children, contact the government's International Child Abduction and Contact Unit on 0207 911 7127. They can put you in touch with a solicitor who's authorised to take abduction proceedings on your behalf. *Do not delay.*

The organisation Reunite can be helpful if your children are ever taken out of the country without your permission. Phone them on 0116 255 6234 or contact them by email (reunite@dircon.co.uk) or through the website (www. reunite.org).

Your Ex-spouse Owes You Maintenance

Many ex-spouses who are legally obliged to pay spousal maintenance fail to make the payments or don't make them consistently, often because they resent having to pay the money or because their new spouse pressures them not to pay. Other ex-spouses don't pay because they develop serious money troubles after their divorce and instead of asking the court to let them pay less, they simply stop paying or pay only when they can afford.

When your spouse owes you maintenance the best idea is to contact your solicitor, who can lay out your options and help you carry out a plan of action. Refer to the earlier section 'Fulfilling an order for child support' for a list of some of your options.

The best time to ask your solicitor about potential problems with your spouse's payment of maintenance is when the terms of your divorce financial settlement are being written.

Your Ex-spouse Fails or Refuses to Sign Property Over to You

If you have an order that your ex-spouse is to sign the house or other valuable property over to you, and she fails or refuses to do so, your solicitor can apply to the court for an order allowing a district judge or a partner in your solicitor's firm to sign the deed of transfer in your ex-spouse's place. You have to give your ex notice of the application, and serve a copy of the original order on her, endorsed with a penal notice – which states that if your ex-spouse doesn't comply with the order, she is guilty of contempt of court and may be committed to prison. If your ex-spouse still doesn't respond and you have to proceed with your application for the judge or solicitor to execute the deeds, you can get an order that your ex-spouse pays the costs of your application.

You Want to Change Some Terms of Your Divorce Settlement

Over time, situations change and the agreement or judgement that seemed fine at the time it was written may no longer be what you need or want now. Or maybe you've never been happy with the outcome of your divorce – you've done your best to abide by your order or agreement but have decided that now is the time to do something about it.

If you and your ex-spouse see eye to eye on the changes, modifying your agreement or the judge's order may be relatively hassle-free, assuming that the judge shares your perspective and assuming that the changes don't harm your dependent children in any way. However, if one of you wants things changed and the other doesn't (which is more likely), you may be in for a replay of your divorce battles.

Demonstrating a change in your circumstances

Ordinarily, if you ask the court to vary the terms of an order made within your divorce proceedings, you must justify your request by demonstrating that a definite change in your circumstances exists. A judge is unlikely to regard your simply 'not liking' the terms of your court order as sufficient justification for a change.

To vary the terms of your child residence and contact arrangement, you must be able to demonstrate that the proposed change is in the children's best interests. On the whole, the court doesn't like to change things unless a legitimate need exists for the change due to significant changes in your life, in your ex-spouse's life or in the lives of your children. Those changes may include the following:

- You're moving a long distance away.

- Your children aren't being properly supervised when they're with their other parent. This may be due to a substance abuse problem, because her work hours have changed and the children are left alone for long stretches of time, because your ex is busy partying into the wee hours of the morning, or other similar situations.

- Your child becomes seriously ill and the present arrangements are unsuitable.

- ✔ You or your ex becomes seriously ill, is arrested for a violent crime, or is accused of child molestation or child abuse.

- ✔ You and your teenage children are in constant conflict, and you can no longer control them.

- ✔ Your ex-spouse's new partner or spouse is improperly relating to or influencing your children.

- ✔ You believe that your ex-spouse is abusing or sexually molesting your children.

- ✔ The arrangements are simply not working out.

Whatever the reason(s) you give to justify your request for a variation, the judge makes her decision according to what's in the best interests of your children.

After you're divorced, you or your ex may also want to make changes in your child maintenance court order. Usually, the parent who receives the support wants more money, and the parent paying the support wants to pay less. What a surprise! The parent who's requesting the variation must provide the court with proof that changes in her life, changes in the life of the other parent, or changes in the lives of the children merit the variation. Remember, though, that if your court order was made after 3 March 2003, and it has been in effect for more than one year, nothing is stopping either of you from applying to the CSA/CMEC instead for a calculation of liability. If you have more children with another partner after you get divorced, a judge may view that as a valid reason for lowering the amount of child support you're obliged to pay to your ex-spouse. The CSA/CMEC formula also treats your net income as reduced by a certain percentage for each new child that you have. See Chapter 13 for more information on child support.

Courts aren't permitted to agree to a variation of a couple's *capital settlement* or *property settlement* when it has been made into an order, except in the most exceptional circumstances.

Securing a court order if you change the agreement yourselves

If you and your ex-spouse informally decide to change your child residence and contact arrangement, you don't need to tell the court unless you're changing the terms of a court order. If you do want to deviate from the terms of an existing court order, you're advised to get a new order that reflects all your changes. Otherwise, if you and your spouse have a later disagreement over the arrangements, you may have more difficulty persuading the court that the original order should be changed.

Put your new agreement in writing and, to be certain that it is enforceable, get a solicitor's help in wording it. Make sure that you both get copies of the new agreement.

If you're paying court-ordered child support and you and your ex agree informally that you can begin paying less child support than what was ordered, that you can suspend your payments for a while, or that you don't have to pay any child support at all, the court may view your new informal agreement as non-binding, even if you put it in writing. In that case, the court order for child support remains in effect.

Even if your requested changes are mutual, a judge may not consider them to be in the best interests of your children. Therefore, if you and your ex-spouse reduce, cease or suspend your child support payments, the court may consider the non-paying person to be in breach of the order and that parent can end up in legal hot water. If you want to vary your current court order, do so by applying for a new one.

Your Ex-spouse Files a Bankruptcy Petition

Given that consumer debt is an ever-increasing feature of modern life and the finances of many people take a turn for the worse after divorce, the possibility exists that your ex-spouse, or her creditors, may file a bankruptcy petition. Your ex-spouse can file her own bankruptcy petition if she owes any one creditor more than £750 and can't afford to pay.

If you believe that your ex-spouse may be thinking about filing a bankruptcy petition, and if she is currently paying you maintenance, child support, or both, or a consent order exists transferring money or property to you from your ex-spouse within the last three to five years, get in touch with your divorce solicitor or a bankruptcy solicitor immediately!

Support obligations – theory and practice

Here's the theory: Although going bankrupt wipes out many of your ex-spouse's debts, including some of the debts she may have agreed to pay according to your divorce agreement or court order, the bankruptcy does *not* affect her obligation to pay you maintenance or child support.

However, in practice, the trustee in bankruptcy, who takes over all your ex-spouse's financial affairs, can apply for an order from the court to help discharge some of the debts, and that may mean that your own order for maintenance or child support is reduced during the period of bankruptcy. Although you can apply to enforce any arrears when the bankruptcy order has been discharged, the courts don't normally enforce arrears that are more than 12 months old.

Capital and property orders

If an order is made within the divorce proceedings for your ex-spouse to pay you a lump sum, and your ex subsequently files a bankruptcy petition, you can claim in bankruptcy for matrimonial lump sums. Transfers of property cannot be made in bankruptcy, and so in most cases you have to express the order sought as a lump sum rather than a transfer of property.

If you've already received the lump sum payment, the trustee in bankruptcy can apply to the court to 'set aside' the order and reverse the payment, if she can show that fraud or collusion existed between you and your spouse. But as a matter of public policy the courts decided in 2008 that it can't be right that court orders made in divorce ancillary relief proceedings (including transferring the family home to the ex-spouse) can be set aside almost as of right by the trustees.

If your ex-spouse has applied for the bankruptcy petition, and you think that the petition may be an attempt to frustrate an order made in your favour, you can try to prove that your ex-spouse isn't really bankrupt at all. Alternatively, if you think that your ex is genuinely in financial difficulty, you may be able to persuade her to enter into an *individual voluntary arrangement* or *IVA* with her creditors. This process is cheaper than bankruptcy, doesn't carry the same stigma, and may be agreed by the creditors so long as your ex-spouse keeps up with promises of payment.

Good practice for your divorce solicitor is to include a declaration that your spouse is solvent in the final divorce settlement. Although this declaration may not prevent a trustee in bankruptcy later questioning the true nature of the order, it may help.

Chapter 21

Thinking Ahead:
Pre-marital Agreements

In This Chapter

▶ Bringing up the subject of pre-marital agreements with your spouse-to-be

▶ Sorting out what to put in your pre-marital agreement

▶ Making your agreement legally acceptable

▶ Negotiating a post-marital agreement

Sooner or later, you're likely to meet someone new, fall in love and maybe even think about tying the knot again. If you've been divorced before, you know that marriage can be something of a gamble, and when it ends it can drain your emotions and your bank account. So you may wonder if you can do anything to make splitting up a little bit easier, just in case things don't work out the way you hope the next time around.

A *pre-marital* (sometimes called a *pre-nuptial* or *pre-nup*) agreement may help you achieve some peace of mind because it lets you and your future spouse work out some of the details of your divorce *before* you get married. Although it may seem somewhat cynical (let alone unromantic) to discuss such an arrangement with your spouse-to-be, drafting a pre-marital agreement (PMA) may make good sense given today's divorce rate. (Of course, we hope you don't need to use it.)

This chapter tells you all about what a pre-marital agreement can and can't do, what gives the best chance of making such an agreement legally influential, and the role that solicitors play in the drafting process. (We also offer you some advice for raising the subject with your intended.)

Accepting that PMAs Aren't Just for the Wealthy Anymore

The legal status of pre-marital agreements in England and Wales has been the subject of recent court cases and political debate. Currently, PMAs aren't enforceable and can't exclude the jurisdiction of the court, – the judge decides how much weight, if any, is given to a pre-marital agreement in each case. However, judges are increasingly prepared to take a pre-marital agreement into account as one of the factors they have to consider, particularly with shorter marriages, if doing so is fair to you and your spouse.

In Scotland, PMAs are generally valid and binding if they're entered into without coercion or intimidation, consent has been freely given by both parties, and the terms were fair at the time they were entered into. Anyone in Scotland of sound mind and over the age of *legal capacity* – that is, 16 years old – can enter into a legally binding agreement, including a pre-marital agreement.

Celebrity pre-marital agreements

According to a 2008 article in *Family Law*, the leading journal on family law in the UK, the first famous pre-marital agreement was probably that of the American actor Lee Marvin, but he was preceded by some two centuries by Wolfgang and Constance Mozart in 1782 ('a written assurance of my honourable intentions towards the girl'). More recently John DeLorean of sports car fame, presented a PMA to his beloved (a model half his age) – and to her lawyer who advised her against signing – just hours before the ceremony. Other American stars said to have entered into PMAs include Donald Trump (twice) and Woody Allen and his step-daughter, Yi Previn. (He reportedly refused to marry her unless she agreed to get nothing if they split.) Others who ended up divorced after signing a PMA include Don Johnson and Melanie Griffith, Boris Becker and Barbara Feltus, Sharon Stone and Phil Bronstein (if they split within two years he would get only £300,000 of her roughly £60 million fortune), Liz Taylor and Larry Fortensky

(£1 million only), Steven Spielberg and Amy Irving, and Joan Collins and Peter Holm.

Among the still-marrieds, Michael Douglas and Catherine Zeta Jones signed a PMA in 2000 (although at that time he was the superstar and she was the also ran – some may say the positions are a bit reversed now in 2008). A PMA signed by American magician David Copperfield and supermodel Claudia Schiffer was rumoured to say that she agreed to never reveal Copperfield's 'tricks of the trade' if they divorced, but they denied this.

On the home front, some of our 'celebs' still appear to be taking the 'it's unromantic' line. Following the example set by the Beckhams, Colleen Rooney is said to have refused to consider a PMA in 2008 on that very basis. Other reasons can also prevail, though. When asked in 2008 why he hadn't got a PMA, the (divorcing) John Cleese replied, 'I was naive.'

Traditionally, PMAs have been associated with very rich people, especially when a wealthy person is marrying someone with a lot less wealth or earning power. In recent years, however, throughout England and Wales people of more average means have begun using PMAs, such as the following:

- ✔ People who have already gone through a difficult and expensive divorce and want to make any future split less divisive and distressing – and cheaper.

- ✔ Spouses-to-be who own their own businesses and want to protect their enterprise from the potential repercussions of divorce.

- ✔ Older people heading into marriages with a substantial amount of property, stocks, shares and other valuable assets.

- ✔ Couples, especially older ones, who want to write their own inheritance rules so they can ensure that their children from a previous marriage, and not their future spouse's children, inherit certain assets when they die. (By law, when a spouse dies, the remaining spouse has a legal right to claim a share of the deceased's estate, no matter what the will says.)

- ✔ Couples who want to negotiate the rules of their marriage – how they'll share in the housework, what religion their children will be raised in, and other issues relating to the management of their marriage and family life. (However, the courts don't usually enforce such lifestyle provisions if the couple have any disagreement over them. They're more of a memorandum than a contract.)

You may feel that you're tempting fate, but working out the details of your divorce before you get married by negotiating a pre-marital agreement can be one way to minimise the potential negative financial and emotional repercussions of divorce. Doing most of the end-of-your-marriage negotiating at the start of your relationship – when everything is still rosy – can make your divorce negotiations more straightforward, less emotional and cheaper, and can help protect important assets in the aftermath of any divorce. It can even improve the quality of your relationship because you feel more secure and certain about your future.

Broaching the Subject With Your Spouse (Delicately)

So, you like the idea of a pre-marital agreement, but you're wondering how to broach the subject with your intended. You realise that your soon-to-be spouse may not consider negotiating a pre-marital agreement to be the most auspicious way to begin a marriage. We can't guarantee you a risk-free way to raise the subject, but we can give you some general ground rules for opening the discussion:

- ✔ **Be honest without being hurtful about your reasons for wanting a pre-marital agreement.** If you've had a bad previous experience, cite this as the reason for your request rather than doubt about the honesty or commitment of your future partner. If you sound as though you're being evasive or are lying, or if you appear to be acting out of greed, you may have a tough time getting to the negotiation stage and may even derail your marriage before it begins.

✓ **Consider using a session with a counsellor to explore the pros and cons together if you're nervous about bringing up the idea of a pre-marital agreement or you try and the discussion becomes heated.** A good counsellor does his best to ensure equal participation in the discussion and works to prevent either of you putting unfair pressure on the other. (See Chapter 2 for advice on how to find a local counsellor.)

✓ **Be absolutely clear with yourself as well as with your future spouse that your desire for a pre-marital agreement says nothing about any doubts about your love for and commitment to him.**

✓ **Explain how your spouse can also benefit from the pre-marital agreement.** Fully consider this aspect beforehand so you have your reasons ready.

✓ **Avoid becoming defensive or angry if your spouse becomes upset.**

✓ **Consider arranging a session or two with a trained mediator if you and your future spouse try to draft your own pre-marital agreement and reach a stalemate.** (Mediation is discussed in detail in Chapter 16.) If mediation helps you resolve your differences and you end up with an agreement, give your draft agreement to a solicitor so you can be sure that it has the best chance of being enforceable. You and your intended should each engage your own independent solicitor to review the agreement from your perspective.

Deciding What Goes in Your Agreement

The provisions you include in your agreement should reflect your individual interests and financial concerns. You may have some thoughts already about what to include, and your solicitors can also make suggestions. Think about how long you want the agreement to last, and consider the following questions (the answers you come up with may give you some fresh ideas):

✓ How will you be compensated if you're making a sacrifice, for example by agreeing to give up your career to help build up your spouse's career or business, or to raise your children?

✓ Will one of you pay the other maintenance if your marriage ends? If so, how much will the payments be and how long will they last?

✓ Who will pay the legal fees if you get divorced?

✓ What will be the nature of your joint ownership if you purchase property together? (See Chapter 3 for the different options.)

✔ Who will get the house and any other significant property if you get divorced?

✔ How will you deal with inheritance issues?

✔ How will you share expenses during your marriage?

✔ What will you do about your debts if you get divorced?

✔ How will you be compensated if you intend to support your spouse while he goes through university, medical school or another training course, and the marriage ends?

✔ Will your spouse have any interest in your business if you get divorced?

✔ How will you be compensated if your spouse-to-be has bad credit and, therefore, during at least the early years of your marriage all credit has to be in your name? (You're responsible to your creditors for that debt, even if your spouse agrees to pay off some of it if you get a divorce.)

If you and your spouse-to-be are buying a property together, and one of you is putting in a much greater contribution than the other, your main concern may be to protect that greater interest. In that case, the solicitor dealing with the purchase for you can word the purchase deed in such a way that it reflects your respective contributions. In addition you can draw up a deed of trust spelling out your respective contributions, and your intentions regarding your joint ownership and responsibilities. If you have such a deed, you may not have to go to the trouble and expense of a pre-marital agreement. (However, as always with divorce and PMAs, the divorce court has the ultimate power to adjust your respective interests in any property.)

Negotiating the terms of your pre-marital agreement may have an unexpected effect. Depending on what you discover about your future spouse by going through the process, you may decide to call off your marriage instead of signing on the bottom line.

After you've prepared your pre-marital agreement, read it periodically to make sure that it continues to reflect your interests and needs. If things have changed, you and your spouse can agree to amend the agreement or to cancel it. The amending or cancelling process has legal implications, so talk with a solicitor if you're thinking about taking such action.

Making Your Pre-marital Agreement Fit for Court

The laws of England and Wales guide judges in making decisions about how to divide up a divorcing couple's joint property and debts. Bear these laws in mind if you're thinking about having a pre-marital agreement. Chapter 4 summarises the main factors that a judge has to take into account during divorce proceedings if he is asked to decide on a division of your property.

If you and your future spouse write a pre-marital agreement, you can include whatever terms you want (with the provisos we state here) as long as they're acceptable to both of you. But to have any chance of your pre-marital agreement being taken into account on divorce, you need to ensure that the following guidelines are observed. Although you have no guarantee that the court is going to enforce your agreement even if you do follow these guidelines, you can be pretty sure that the court won't enforce it if you don't.

- ✔ **Your agreement must be in writing, and the terms of the agreement must be clear.**

- ✔ **You must both sign your agreement because you want to, not because you're being threatened or coerced, or because of other external pressures.** Pregnancy may be regarded as such a pressure unless the implications of the pregnancy are recognised between you. Neither of you should exploit a dominant position.

- ✔ **Your agreement should be negotiated and finalised well before the date of your marriage.** This lessens the likelihood that either of you feels pressured to agree to your partner's requests in order to avoid jeopardising your impending marriage. The more distance you can put between the date of your marriage and signing the agreement, the better.

- ✔ **You must both be involved in negotiating the agreement, although you can use solicitors to negotiate for you.** The court is more likely to enforce an agreement if you both have proper independent legal advice.

- ✔ **You must be 100 per cent forthcoming with one another about your incomes, assets and liabilities.** Both of you must be aware of what the other is giving up or getting before you sign the agreement. The more information you share with one another, the better. If you don't have full disclosure, the court will want to know who made that choice, and why.

- ✔ **You must both fully understand what you're agreeing to.**

- ✔ **You should expressly consider whether the agreement will still apply, or differ in any way, if you have children.**

- ✔ **Your agreement shouldn't be likely to create any injustice to either of you.**

If you or your spouse can prove that one or more of the characteristics just listed were missing from your pre-marital agreement negotiations, the court is more likely to change or reverse certain provisions in the agreement or, after holding a hearing, disregard your pre-marital agreement entirely.

Reciting in your agreement the reasons why you want to make such an agreement (for example, to avoid litigation in the event of divorce), while recognising that you can't exclude the jurisdiction of the court, may help you win the support of the court.

You may be able to include provisions for spousal support in your pre-marital agreement. However, family courts aren't necessarily bound by those or by provisions relating to the care and support of any children you have during your marriage, because those provisions may not be in your children's best interests. Remember too to include a clause that you'll review the agreement periodically, especially if you have children.

Getting Legal Help with Your Agreement

Each of you should have your own solicitor to help you during the pre-marital agreement negotiation process. Engaging your own solicitor is always a good idea whenever you negotiate the details of an important legal document that has implications for your financial wellbeing. A solicitor can help you ensure that the agreement is fair to you, explain how the agreement can affect you if your marriage ends in divorce and can make certain that the agreement has the best chance of being taken into account by a judge.

The solicitor you use should be a family law practitioner, preferably with specific experience in the area of pre-marital planning. Depending on the circumstances, you may also need the assistance of a solicitor with special expertise outside the area of family law or the help of other professionals. For example, if you own a business, you may want a business law specialist or a business valuation expert involved in your pre-marital planning. Or, if you want to set up a trust as part of your planning, the assistance of an estate planning solicitor is advisable.

You and your spouse should discuss your pre-marital goals and concerns and what each of you thinks is fair before you meet your solicitors. Then you can determine if writing a pre-marital agreement is even possible. You need to identify and categorise the issues you agree on, the issues that need legal clarification, and what you want your solicitors to help negotiate. Using a solicitor to help you work out the terms of your pre-marital agreement can cost anywhere between £750 and £20,000 for something very complicated. The final cost depends on where you live, the complexity of the issues you address in the agreement, and the value of the assets involved. For a typical couple in their 40s or 50s entering a second marriage with a small pension that needs to be protected, a PMA may cost in the region of £5,000 to £7,500 in London. If you consider the cost of a litigated divorce, spending money now on a pre-marital agreement may save you some money in the long run.

Drafting a Post-marital Agreement

Just as its name implies, a *post-marital agreement* is one that you and your spouse draft after you're married. Although this type of agreement is even more rare than a pre-marital agreement, it can be useful on occasion.

Understanding how to use a post-marital agreement

You can use a post-marital agreement in much the same way that you can use a pre-marital agreement. For instance:

- ✔ You can spell out in a post-marital agreement what happens – if you get divorced or die while still married – to any business you start after your marriage.

- ✔ You can use the post-marital agreement to try to ensure that all your estate goes to your children when you die, instead of a portion of it automatically going to your spouse.

- ✔ You can use a post-marital agreement to work out most of the details of your divorce but, as with PMAs, you can't exclude the jurisdiction of the court.

Doing your best to make your post-marital agreement stand up in court

Post-marital agreements are very rare in England and Wales, and the guidelines regarding what makes a post-marital agreement most likely to be taken into account by a court tend to be even less well defined than those applying to PMAs. Basically, neither type of agreement is automatically legally enforceable. Generally, however, the guidelines mirror one another. So, when you negotiate your post-marital agreement, abide by the same rules that apply to PMAs, including full disclosure, no coercion and honesty.

Because a post-marital agreement is relatively rare, using separate solicitors is essential to ensure that your agreement stands up in court if one of you contests its terms further down the road. Also, if you want your post-marital agreement to be considered by the court, you're better off negotiating it while your marriage is still on solid ground, not after your relationship begins to fall apart. Otherwise, if you split up and one of you later contests the terms of the agreement, the court may view the post-marital agreement as little more than an effort by one of you to take advantage of the other. Also, if you petition for divorce too soon after you finalise your post-marital agreement (and what constitutes 'too soon' is up to a judge to decide), the agreement may not hold up in court if your soon-to-be-ex challenges it.

Part VI
The Part of Tens

"'My goodness, Snow White,' said her friendly, kind, generous, loving & <u>extremely</u> beautiful stepmother, 'I wouldn't eat that apple if I were you.'"

In this part . . .

The Part of Tens contains quick and handy bits of advice and information, packaged ten to a chapter, including:

- ✔ Steps you can take to help make your children's lives as happy and stable as possible.

- ✔ Suggestions for how to put your divorce behind you, get on with your life, and jump back into the social swim.

- ✔ Tips on how to make your next marriage or serious relationship a happy and lasting one, because you never know when you're going to meet someone new.

Chapter 22

Ten Ways to Help Make Everything Okay for Your Children

In This Chapter

▶ Being there for your children when they need you

▶ Supporting your ex-spouse's parenting efforts

▶ Refusing to burden your children with your worries

▶ Being sensitive to the issue of dating

*O*ver half of the couples divorcing in 2006 had at least one child aged under 16 (that's 125,030 children); 20 per cent of these children were under 5 and 63 per cent were under 11. So to say that nearly every child these days knows someone her own age whose parents are divorced or divorcing isn't stretching the truth. Even so, few children expect divorce to happen in *their* family, and so when it does, the effects can be devastating.

At first, your children may feel as if their lives have been turned upside down, with everything that they know and love being taken away from them. Your divorce is your children's divorce, too. As a parent, you have the responsibility of helping your children cope with the profound changes that are happening in their lives. This chapter provides suggestions for how you can bring some stability to an otherwise uncertain situation.

Showing Your Children that You Still Love Them

Tell your children that you love them and make sure that your actions prove it. Spend time with them, show them affection and be ready and willing to listen when they want to talk and share their feelings with you.

Encouraging Your Children to Respect and Love their Other Parent

Give your children permission to love their other parent. Don't paint such a negative picture of your ex that your children feel guilty about their love for their mum or dad. Instead, support your ex-spouse's parenting efforts and speak in positive terms about each other. Tell your children funny or affectionate stories about your family, about how you and their other parent met, or about your former spouse's relatives. Such conversations show that you're comfortable talking about your ex-spouse and give your children a sense of pride in their family history and roots, something all children need.

Keeping Your Burdens from Your Children

Treat your children like children, not like grown-ups. Although they may have to assume more responsibilities in the home after your divorce – maybe even getting a job – never forget that they aren't yet adults. Be careful not to burden them with your problems and avoid sharing all your worries with them. If you're going through a rough time, your children probably sense it and may feel scared about what may happen to them as well. If you're feeling stressed – perhaps you're concerned about how to pay the bills – let your children know what's going on but don't go into lurid details. Assure them that no matter what, everything is going to be all right. Chapter 8 suggests some books that may help your children, and don't forget about your local library – it's a great free resource.

Trying to Agree with Your Ex-spouse on the Ground Rules for Parenting

If you and your former spouse are sharing the day-to-day care of your children equally, try to agree on the big issues such as curfews, discipline, schoolwork and homework. Living by one set of rules in one home and by a totally different set of rules in the other can be tough on your children – and in turn tough on you and your ex-spouse (refer to Chapters 4 and 10 for tips on how to make this easier). On the other hand, if your former spouse doesn't parent your children as you do, don't complain about it to your children or argue about it unless her parenting style is, in your view, clearly doing emotional or physical harm to your children.

Making Your Children Feel at Home in Your New Place

If you've moved out of your old home and now have a new one, make sure that your children have a special place there that's all their own. If your finances allow, let them decorate that space. At the very least, make your new home as comfortable as possible for your children so that they enjoy visiting or living with you.

Your children feel better if you and your ex agree to maintain a supply of their clothes, toiletries and toys – within reason – at each of your homes. This arrangement avoids your children having to pack and unpack a full suitcase each time they travel from one parent's place to the other.

Avoiding Manipulation

Don't argue with your ex-spouse in front of your children, use your children as go-betweens when you're fighting with your ex, or try to prevent your ex or her family from seeing them. If your ex-spouse starts dating, don't attempt to sabotage that relationship or make your children think that you're going to disapprove if they like your ex's new girlfriend or boyfriend. Children can't have too many caring, supportive adults in their lives, and if you behave resentfully because your former spouse has a new love relationship, you're inadvertently giving your children a lesson in jealous behaviour.

Keeping Your Promises

Being true to your word helps to make your children's lives as predictable as possible. For example, if you say you're going to pick them up at a certain time, be there; if you tell them you're going to do something together, do it. If you have to change your plans, give your children as much notice as possible and, if your ex is agreeable to it, re-arrange the planned activity.

If you live too far away from your children to see them regularly, the next best thing is to write to or phone them as often as possible.

Many non-resident parents dread seeing their children because saying goodbye and returning their children to the other parent at the end of each visit is so painful. If you feel this way, try to take comfort in the fact that over time saying goodbye becomes easier. Don't let these feelings prevent you from seeing your children. Feeling that they can depend on spending time with you on a regular basis is important.

Waiting to Date

Avoid bringing home new partners straight after your divorce is final and certainly avoid introducing your children to multiple dating partners straight afterwards. When you first begin dating, your children may resent you spending time with new people so soon or feel threatened by the presence of these strangers. For a while, you may want to arrange times with someone you're dating for when your children are staying with your ex-spouse, if you think that may make your children more comfortable. (For more re-partnering advice, turn to Chapter 23.)

If you begin dating someone regularly, your children may become emotionally attached to that person, treating her as a regular and special adult in their lives. Be aware that if your relationship ends, your children may have a tough time accepting the fact that it's over (especially if your ex-spouse is no longer an active participant in your children's lives).

Creating Stable and Predictable Lives for Your Children

Maintain as many routines, rules, and traditions from your past family life as you can. Children thrive on predictability. After your divorce, you can try creating stability for your children by serving their meals at the same time, letting them keep their pets if possible, being available to help them with their homework, and maintaining the same standards of discipline as before. And be sure not to interfere in your children's relationships with the parents, brothers, sisters and other relatives of your ex-spouse. Your children have already experienced a significant loss – don't compound it by attempting to scuttle new friendships that your children may need and value.

Avoiding Becoming a 'Super Parent'

If you feel guilty about the effect your divorce may be having on your children, or if you're angry because they live with your ex-spouse, don't try to compensate for your feelings by becoming a 'Saturday treats' mum or dad who lavishes them with gifts and money, or becoming a smothering and over-protective parent. As difficult as it may be, try to maintain the same relationship with your children that you had before the divorce. They need predictability and stability at this moment, not excessive gestures. The best way to provide them with what they need is through your simple love and affection.

Chapter 23

Ten Tips for Putting Your Divorce Behind You and Moving On

• •

In This Chapter

▶ Finding moral support

▶ Seeking counselling if necessary

▶ Meeting new people

▶ Getting your finances under control

▶ Putting some fun back into your life

• •

*I*f you feel like crawling into a hole and hiding until your divorce is over, it's no wonder. But life definitely does go on and things will get better (sooner, rather than later, we hope). You may even fall in love again and your next marriage may be a perfect match. To boost your spirits a bit, we offer ten tips for moving forward with your life and planning for happier times.

Finding an (Adult) Shoulder to Lean On

Find someone with whom you can talk openly and honestly about your situation. Who it is doesn't matter – as long as that person is a good listener. Pick someone you trust who has given you good advice in the past.

Express your thoughts in the safest way you can. In other words, don't rant and rave to your former spouse or to your children. Get rid of those negative feelings so that you can get on with your life. (See Chapter 9 for help in understanding the emotions you may be feeling.)

Above all, avoid loading all your worries onto your children. They have their own insecurities, and you need to put up a strong front for them (see Chapter 10).

Starting to Keep a Diary

Starting a diary or journal is an excellent way to get a handle on your emotions. A diary is an effective way of expressing your thoughts and keeping track of how they change from week to week; you may even find that you become less reliant on friends and family to help you get your head together again.

Write as though you're talking to your best friend or to yourself. Draw pictures to illustrate your thoughts. Every week, read what you wrote the previous week. You may be surprised at the depth (or the triviality) of your emotions, or you may discover that – in just a week – your feelings about things have changed quite a bit.

Seeking Help If You Need It

If you're crying all the time, harbouring a lot of anger towards your ex-spouse, feeling depressed or having a tough time getting on with your life, you need more than a shoulder to lean on – you need professional counselling. An accredited counsellor or therapist can give you the objective feedback and encouragement you need to deal with your emotions in a constructive manner.

If you don't already have a counsellor that you like and respect, your family doctor should be able to recommend someone, possibly attached to the practice. Contact your local Relate office. Relate offers individual divorce counselling as well as couple counselling. Your solicitor, mediator or a trusted friend or relative may also be able to give you the name of a local counsellor. Or try the British Association of Counselling and Psychotherapy website at www.bacp.co.uk to find a counsellor in your area. (See Chapter 2 for more information about counselling.)

Fighting the Urge to Return to Your Ex

If you feel desperately lonely after your divorce, which happens to many people, stay away from your ex-spouse except when necessary – such as when making arrangements for children. Endings should remain as endings. Don't attempt to look for comfort in those old, familiar arms no matter how much you want to. It's time to move on. You may feel that reconciling is the only way to stop the heartbreak and ease your loneliness, but don't be fooled. None of your old problems are likely to be solved that way unless you both have very serious doubts about the decisions you've taken.

Focusing on Your Work

Your work or professional life may have suffered while you were going through your divorce. You may have used every ounce of your energy and concentration just to accomplish the most basic tasks of your job and to get through each day. Now that you're divorced, re-focusing your energies on your work can provide the ordered routine that you need in your life. In addition, your professional accomplishments can make you feel good about yourself and may even land you a pay rise or a promotion. If you've been out of the workforce for a while and want to re-start your working life, Chapter 19 offers some useful advice.

Don't look to your colleagues to provide you with the physical closeness or the emotional understanding that you crave – dating or sleeping with colleagues is always dangerous territory. What you want is security, not uncertainty, in your job.

Getting in Touch with Your Spiritual Side

If you believe in God or some other higher power, don't be ashamed to pray for guidance and understanding. You may also want to try meditation or yoga, which can give you a renewed sense of calmness and added self-awareness. Mary Kirk's book *Divorce: Living through the Agony* (Lion Hudson plc) draws on the spiritual aspects of divorce, including a chapter on forgiveness. Or try *Divorce – a Challenge to the Church* (Bible Reading Fellowship) published in 2008. Written by Bob Mayo, an Anglican priest, himself divorced and now working in a cosmopolitan area of London, he likens being no longer married to living 'in exile'. For him Christianity 'is not about forgetting but about remembering well. Forgiveness does not mean pretending that nothing bad has happened. It means acknowledging, understanding and then forgiving.' This book can help anyone of faith who wishes to make sense of his divorce experience.

Cleaning Up Your Debts

Try to get debt-free as quickly as possible. Just now, you don't need the extra worry of dealing with unpaid bills and debt collectors. Plus, the sooner you can wipe out your debts, the sooner you can start saving money for the things you really need or want. If you don't have a spending plan or budget, develop one now. A plan can help you determine if your monthly income is sufficient to meet your monthly outgoings. If your living expenses and debts exceed your income, consider ways of earning extra income, or carefully analyse your expenditures to see which ones you can reduce or eliminate. Chapter 3 provides detailed instructions for developing a personal budget.

If you have enough income to cover your monthly expenditures and debts, focus on paying off the debts carrying the highest interest rates and service charges. These debts usually include credit card debt, store cards and finance company loans.

Trying Something Entirely New

Seek out activities that you think you may enjoy as a newly single person – join a gym or take a dancing or cookery class where you can meet other people who are also looking for new activities. Dare to try something alone that your ex-spouse never wanted to do with you – go skydiving or back-packing, or go on that cross-country drive you've always dreamed about. (A change of scenery may be just what the doctor ordered!) If outdoor activities don't sound appealing, discover the artist within you. Singing in a choir concentrates your mind, and painting, sculpting or photography keep your hands and mind busy, and you have something to show for your efforts.

Sharing Your Space to Save Money

If you're financially strapped, you may consider getting a lodger. By sharing your home with another adult, you can reduce some of your monthly expenses and your living space may seem less lonely. Another option may be to move back in with your parents temporarily. Returning to familiar surroundings where you're around loved ones can provide you with a safe place to regroup and save money until you're back on your feet. However, make sure that this arrangement doesn't last too long, otherwise you and your parents may begin to lose the independence gained from each other.

If your children live with you full- or part-time, try to put their needs first whenever you can. Although a lodger, particularly a student, may work out well with your children, they may equally not welcome sharing their home or you with anyone else – at least, not too soon. Make sure that you consult them thoroughly to find out how they feel before making any decisions (see Chapter 10).

Re-starting Your Social Life

Get out of the house and meet new people. Join a support group or a singles club for the formerly married. Meeting other divorced people and doing fun things together is good therapy, not to mention a way to meet people with whom you may want to make friends or new relationships.

At some point you want to get back into the social swim. But don't begin dating as soon as the ink has dried on your divorce decree. Statistically, the majority of divorced men and women remarry within a few years of getting divorced. Most counsellors suggest not dating anyone seriously until you've been divorced for at least a year.

When you decide that you're ready to date, you may be in a quandary about how to meet new people, especially if you've been away from the social scene for some time or didn't socialise or go to clubs much before you were married. Meeting potential partners may require some resourcefulness:

- ✔ **Tell your friends that you want to start making new relationships.** They may be eager to introduce you to someone, perhaps by inviting both of you to a dinner party or to join them in some other low-stress group activity.

- ✔ **Attend a class.** A car repair or language class is usually a good place to meet both men and women.

- ✔ **Take up a sport.** Joining a volleyball team, tennis club or bowling league that attracts both sexes can be a healthy, relaxed way to meet people you may want to get to know better.

- ✔ **Do some voluntary work.** Giving your time and energy to a cause you care about can put you in touch with like-minded men and women.

- ✔ **Join a singles group.** Contact One-Parent Families/Gingerbread in your area. You may find some groups listed in your *Yellow Pages* or local newspaper. Your place of worship may also have an organised singles group.

- ✔ **Try a dating agency, online dating, placing a personals ad, or answering one.** Read the sidebar 'Tips on using dating agencies' below to see if one of these methods is right for you.

If you use personal ads to meet potential dates, for safety reasons always choose a public place for your initial meetings and steer clear of bars. A meeting at a lunch place, coffee shop or bookshop is usually a good choice. Don't give anyone you meet your home phone number or address until you feel comfortable and safe with that person.

Tips on using dating agencies

If you've been out of the dating scene for a while or have difficulty meeting people of the opposite sex, using a dating service can be a worthwhile option. But watch out: These services are in business to make a profit, and so choose a service carefully. Make sure that you're comfortable with the service's approach to matchmaking.

If you decide to try your luck, you need a sense of humour and an open mind. The Association of British Introduction Agencies (take a look at www.abia.org.uk) recommends that you ask the agency how many introductions you can reasonably expect given your parameters, and that you remember that a successful introduction may not happen right away. Sometimes it takes a few tries before you meet the right person, and if you're not happy with the way things are going, tell the agency sooner rather than later. They may be able to redefine the criteria they're using to match you with someone else for a more successful introduction. Introduction agencies operate in a number of different ways:

✔ **Dating agencies:** These take your details and attempt to match you with another person. They vary enormously in their methods and effectiveness. Some use hunches, others computerised matching. Agencies' client lists and the number of appointments they offer you can also vary greatly, and they differ in their fees as well. For example, one woman we know paid £900 and had only one introduction. Another friend did rather better for £250 with a different agency and met her new partner after a few introductions.

✔ **Supper clubs:** Some agencies set up supper clubs where six or so people are booked to a table in a restaurant or the pub. Sitting down to supper with six strangers can test your conversational skills and is a great way to meet new people of both sexes.

✔ **Online dating:** Many dating agencies, such as Match.com or Udate.com, are based solely on the Internet. You can upload your picture, a description of yourself, and what you're looking for in a partner, and then scan through as many other people's profiles as you like. Usually you pay a monthly fee for the service, which allows you unlimited access to the site's database of profiles as well as a contact email address within the site. You then decide whether to take the next step of giving an email address outside the site to someone you've met and 'talked' to, or moving up to a phone call, meeting, and so on.

✔ **Speed dating:** This low-risk, low-cost, and highly social method gives you anywhere from three to eight minutes to talk with one person and at the ding of a bell move on to the next person. By the end of the evening, you hand over a list of all the people you'd like to meet again. The agency then compares all the lists and sends you email addresses for all the people you've chosen who have also chosen you. At the very least, you have a good laugh trying to figure out which questions to ask to find out what you need to know – all in the space of a few minutes.

Chapter 24

Ten Strategies for Next Time

In This Chapter

▶ Making a point of communicating

▶ Spending more time together

▶ Trying creative problem solving

▶ Maintaining a sense of humour

▶ Keeping things in perspective

▶ Encouraging your spouse to have outside interests

*B*efore you can get behind the wheel of a car, you must pass a test on your driving skills and knowledge of the rules of the road. But no such test exists to determine your fitness for marriage. Many couples fail to realise that a good marriage doesn't just *happen* – it takes work.

Both parties to a marriage must nurture and care for that relationship. People often come to this realisation the hard way – through trial and error, living through failed marriages, going through a divorce, and trying again. With that in mind, this chapter offers you several key ingredients that relationship specialists have found in just about every successful marriage.

Communicating, Not Just Talking

Failure to communicate is at the root of many marriages gone sour. Poor communication manifests itself in many ways. You may have a tough time speaking your mind or broaching uncomfortable subjects with your spouse, or you may have assumptions and expectations that are completely unknown to your marriage partner.

If you want to talk with your spouse about something that you know is a sensitive or difficult issue, carefully choose the time and place for the discussion. You may also want to rehearse what you're going to say to avoid inadvertently using words that may make your spouse angry or defensive.

When you tell your spouse about something that's bothering you, avoid using statements that begin with 'you' and asking 'why' questions, both of which are almost certain to put your spouse on the defensive. Many relationship educators and couple counsellors suggest writing down a three-part statement that begins with how you feel, followed by what you would like changed, and ending with what you would like your spouse to do instead. For example: 'I feel frustrated when you tell me that we're going to the cinema and then you don't get home from work until 10 pm. I wish you would phone me if your plans change.' Men and women tend to differ in their communication styles, which can sometimes cause problems in relationships. If you want help with understanding what your spouse is really saying, pick up a copy of *Men are from Mars; Women are from Venus* by John Gray (available on www.amazon.co.uk).

Making Time for Each Other

Maybe you and your ex-spouse were inseparable at the start of your marriage. But over time, as you got caught up in the day-to-day details of your lives and struggled to balance career and family, you began to have less and less time for each other. Some studies show that people talk for longer in the day to their work colleagues than they do to their spouses. Gradually, couples can drift apart, emotionally and physically.

You may feel that in our time-deprived, high-pressure culture, you have too little time for yourself, much less for your spouse. Yet, if you want your marriage to stay healthy, you must create regular opportunities to be together, show that you care for each other, and demonstrate how much you appreciate your spouse's company. Here are some suggestions for showing your spouse how you feel:

- **Say 'I love you'.** Don't assume that after you marry your spouse doesn't need to hear those words any more. A woman once accused her partner of never telling her that he loved her, to which he responded 'But I buy you flowers every week'. Sometimes, your different ways of expressing yourselves pass each other by.

- **Eat at least one meal together each day.** Talk to one another during your meal and don't watch TV while you're eating.

- **Go on a date together at least once a month.** Mark the day on your calendar like you would any important meeting or appointment. Your date doesn't need to be expensive – it can involve a walk in the woods, a film, a picnic or a drive in the country. What you do is less important than taking the time to be alone and to enjoy one another.

✔ **Don't sit in front of the TV every night.** Instead, have a conversation with your spouse. Do a puzzle together, play a game, or just share the silence of reading and enjoy simply being with one another.

✔ **Don't assume that the way you like your spouse to demonstrate her love for you is also what your spouse desires.** Ask your spouse to make a list of the caring behaviours she would welcome in order to feel loved. Give your spouse a list of your own preferences. You may be surprised at how the two lists compare.

Fighting Fair

Arguing is a healthy way for you to clear the air and resolve problems. Good fighting is fair fighting. When you fight fair, you avoid personal attacks, insulting language, finger pointing, recriminations and threats. Any one of those things is likely to put your spouse on the defensive, increase the emotional level of your argument, and make your spouse less willing to listen to what you're saying and less open to compromise. The goal of a fair fight is not to have a winner or a loser, but to resolve your disagreement in a way that makes you both feel good about the outcome. If your tempers are flaring, take time out and cool down. Fix a time to discuss the subject later when you both feel more calm and collected.

Trying New Ways of Resolving Old Problems

In every relationship, certain problems seem to occur time after time. Even if the problems that keep repeating themselves are quite minor, over months and years they can create a considerable amount of anger and resentment in your marriage. Often, the solution to recurring problems, both big and small, is to find a new way of dealing with them. For example, you like the tube of toothpaste to be squeezed from the bottom and rolled tight as it's used up. Your wife drives you crazy because she's a free-form tube squeezer. You have had countless arguments over the toothpaste tube – you don't know why she can't remember to do what you ask, and she can't understand why you're making such a big deal out of what she considers to be a very petty issue. The solution? Buy two tubes of toothpaste – one for her and one for you.

Although the solution to every recurring problem may not be quite as easy as resolving the toothpaste debate, creative problem solving can work wonders for a marriage.

Maintaining Your Sense of Humour

Laughing together is one of the best experiences you can have in a marriage and you can find ways to make it happen. Tell jokes, look for the humour in everyday situations, go to a comedy film, recount amusing situations from home or work, or simply smile more often whether you feel like it or not. In addition, making light of a problem can be a gentle way of letting your spouse know that something she is saying or doing (or *not* saying or doing) is bugging you and the time's come to talk about it.

Forgiving and Forgetting

In a relationship as close as marriage, occasionally you're going to get on each other's nerves. Although these minor irritations don't usually signal the end of your marriage, if you overreact by making them more significant than they really are you can damage your relationship over time.

When your spouse's behaviour irritates or angers you, try to understand why. Is it because you had a bad day at work or because you're really worried about one of your children? Does your spouse's behaviour remind you of something your ex-spouse used to do or remind you of the way one of your parents used to treat you?

Try to keep your spouse's behaviour in perspective. Ask yourself: 'Is what my spouse said or did *really* that important?' Try to remember all the good things about your spouse. Also, consider the things you do that drive your spouse crazy and how much you've appreciated a forgiving attitude. If your spouse's behaviour is really a problem for you, try talking about it together. If the problem is serious, get professional help (see Chapter 2 for more on relationship counselling).

Resolving Problems Quickly

If you and your spouse have had a big row, you may have to swallow your pride and say 'Let's talk' or 'I'm sorry', even if you still feel hurt, vulnerable or angry. Resolving your marital differences sooner, and not later, minimises the likelihood of your relationship becoming infected by hurt feelings, festering anger and unresolved conflict.

Attending Pre-marriage Counselling to Avoid Surprises

Too often, the euphoric pleasure of falling in love and planning a marriage overshadows the truly important preliminary work you should be doing – ensuring that your new relationship is the real thing and that you both have what's needed to make it work. That means getting to know one another, warts and all, making certain that you share the same basic values and priorities, and building the relationship skills necessary to weather love's slings and arrows when the newness and excitement of your relationship wears off.

A growing number of marriage or couple counselling agencies offer help in this area. For example, Relate provides pre-commitment workshops called 'Couples' at many of their centres. Look at the website www.relate.org.uk for details of courses in your area.

Attending a Marriage Enrichment Course

You can attend a marriage enrichment course with your new partner in a relaxed setting over a weekend in company with other couples and the guidance of course leaders. Marriage enrichment is a process of education about the improvement of close relationships in general and marriage in particular. It involves discovering things through experience in couple groups, with the aim of achieving changes in attitudes and behaviour to increase the couple's sense of satisfaction with the relationship.

The main emphasis in marriage enrichment courses is on commitment to growth, communication and constructive resolution of conflict. As a couple, you're shown how to work through your own problems and conflicts more effectively and set your own goals for your marriage realistically. Some of the courses are faith based, such as the Roman Catholic courses *Marriage Preparation*, *Marriage Enrichment* and *Initiatives to Support Family Life* run by the Diocese of Westminster (take a look at www.rcdow.org.uk).

Supporting Your Spouse's Outside Interests

Some newly marrieds, including those marrying for the second time round, assume that after they become a couple they have to do everything together. Although 'being joined at the hip' with your new husband or wife may be fun at first, after a while at least one of you is going to want to do things on your own, or spend time with your own friends. If your spouse suddenly wants to do her own thing, don't assume that your spouse loves you any less. And, don't be resentful over your spouse's new-found interest or hobby. Instead, support your spouse in pursuing new interests, maintaining old friendships and making new ones. Those things that make your spouse happier and more satisfied produce positive feelings that transfer to your marriage. You may find that your conversations are more interesting and you're laughing more often. You may even discover new things to appreciate about your spouse, which can deepen your love for the person you married. Don't let fear of another marriage failure make you restrict the freedom of either of you.

Attempting to control how your spouse spends every waking hour can make a once-happy marriage feel suffocating and create needless anger and resentment in your relationship. If you're feeling threatened by the changes taking place in your relationship, try to understand why they bother you or make an appointment to talk with a counsellor about it (see Chapter 2 on how to find a relationship counsellor).

If you sense that your spouse feels saddened or threatened by the activities you want to do by yourself, talk with your spouse about your interests, make sure that your spouse meets your new friends, and reassure her with your love and affection that everything is fine in your relationship.

Part VII
Appendixes

'Hey! – I'm supposed to be leaving you!'

In this part . . .

Appendixes aren't usually the first part of the book that readers head for. For most people, the first and only time they notice a book's appendix is when they're standing in the bookshop flipping through the book to see if it meets their requirements. With this book, though, the two appendixes are collections of vital information.

The first appendix is a glossary of terms that we use throughout this book. Legal lingo can be complicated and daunting if you're not used to it. We've tried to keep technical terms to a minimum, but where we've not been able to get by without using them, this is the place to turn to for short, snappy definitions.

The second appendix is an indispensable collection of the most useful websites we know of to help you with your divorce. Obviously, we've included as much as we possibly can within the covers of this book, but this appendix is for when you need a quick overview and a starting point.

Appendix A

Glossary of Terms

• •

Abduction: The removal of a child from the parent with care without his permission.

Acknowledgment of Service: The form that the **respondent** returns to the court to confirm receipt of the divorce petition.

Actuary: A professional who estimates the current or future value of an **asset** such as a pension.

Adultery: Voluntary sexual intercourse between people of the opposite sex, one of whom is already married to someone else.

Affidavit: A statement of facts, sworn on oath or affirmed to be true by the person making it. Mostly used in court proceedings, for example in relation to financial matters. Sometimes called a **sworn statement**.

Alimony: See **Maintenance**.

Ancillary relief: The range of financial orders the court can make on divorce (including **maintenance** (or **periodical payments**), lump sums, transfer of property, and pensions) for you and transfer of property or lump sums for your children.

Annuity: A payment of a certain sum of money made every year.

Annulment: The legal end to a marriage that is void or voidable (in other words not valid in some respect). A religious annulment doesn't have the force of law whereas a legal one does.

Answer: A response to a petition for divorce, separation or **annulment**. Only necessary when the person served with the petition is defending it.

Ante-nuptial agreement: See **Pre-Marital Agreement**.

Appeal: When a party in a court action asks a higher court to review the decision of a lower court in order to determine whether a legal reason exists to order a new hearing or to change some aspect of the lower court's decision.

Assets: Things of value. Depending on the type of asset, you can use it to purchase something else, you can sell it, or you can use the asset as collateral for a loan. An asset can be tangible – such as cash, property, vehicles, antiques, fine jewellery or art; or intangible – such as stocks and shares, bonds or pension benefits.

Assurance: Insurance on someone's life.

Attachment: A court order instructing pension trustees or administrators to pay a lump sum or income to a former spouse when the pension matures. Used to be called **earmarking.**

Attachment of Earnings Order: An order that requires an employer to deduct **maintenance** regularly from wages or salary in order that it can be sent to a spouse or former spouse (known as an *arrestment* of earnings in Scotland).

Barrister: Also known as **counsel**; a lawyer instructed by solicitors to give an opinion or to represent solicitors' clients in court.

Cafcass officer: Also known as Family Court Adviser; a person who assists the court in deciding what arrangements are in the best interests of the children, where a disputed issue relating to them exists. He normally meets both parties and the children themselves. He can conciliate between the parents at court and if the parents still disagree the Cafcass officer will be asked by the judge for a written report.

Capital Gains Tax: A tax payable on any profit made on the disposal or transfer of an **asset**.

Capitalising maintenance: Paying a lump sum or other capital **asset** in return for a final dismissal of spousal maintenance claims.

Cash Equivalent Transfer Value (CETV): The cash value given to the benefits accrued in a pension fund at any time, based on the value of the fund if it were to be transferred from one scheme to another.

Chambers: When a court sits 'in chambers' the proceedings are heard in private, so that only you, your legal representatives and the judge are allowed to be present. Witnesses are allowed to be present only while giving their evidence. 'Chambers' can also refer to the workplace where barristers are based.

Charging order: A court order to enforce the payment of a debt against an **asset**, usually **real property**, which may lead to an order for sale of the asset.

Child support or maintenance: Money paid by one parent to the other parent to help meet the financial needs of their children. Ordinarily, the support continues until a child completes full-time secondary education, although a parent may have to provide support while a child is a full-time college student or attending a further education course.

Child Maintenance and Enforcement Commission (CMEC): A new organisation gradually replacing the **CSA** over the period 2008–2011.

Child Support Agency (CSA): A government agency with statutory powers set up to calculate, collect and enforce child support payments from the non-resident parent to the parent with care of the child. See **CMEC**.

Children's Guardian: A court-appointed trained social worker who represents the interests of children (or occasionally vulnerable adults) in divorce or child proceedings. This person is a Cafcass officer operating in this particular role.

Civil Partnership: A relationship between two people of the same sex when they register as civil partners of each other.

Class F: The formal means by which a non-owning spouse's rights of occupation of the matrimonial home are protected in a property that isn't registered at the Land Registry.

Clean break: A financial arrangement where it's agreed or ordered that the husband and wife will make no further financial claims against each other. A clean break may be expressed to relate to claims for income, capital, property and/or pensions.

Common law marriage: A popular expression for the relationship between couples who are living together without being married. This term has no legal status in England and Wales, although it's commonly used and does have some legal status in Scotland.

Community Legal Service: The service set up by the government to deal with the provision of legal aid and legal services.

Consent Order: The order made by a judge confirming arrangements that the parties have agreed and settled.

Contact: The right of a child to keep in touch with another person, usually a parent, and the arrangements made for him to do so. The word replaces the previous term 'access', although the general public and the media still regularly use the old terminology.

Contempt of court: A wilful and deliberate violation or breach of a court order, judgement or decree (for example, breach of a **non-molestation order**). Spouses in contempt of court may be punished by the court.

Co-respondent: A person with whom the **respondent** is alleged to have committed adultery. The law no longer requires that person to be named in the divorce proceedings.

Costs: Legal expenses and fees.

Counsel: An alternative term for **barrister**, describing the role of a particular kind of lawyer rather than a title. A barrister or counsel is usually engaged to act as the advocate in court or to advise on the law.

Court order: A legally binding written document issued by a court and made by a judge.

Cross-examination: The questioning of a witness by the solicitor or barrister representing the opposing party to ascertain the truthfulness of what the witness said or to further develop the witness's testimony. Witnesses are cross-examined during a trial or court hearing.

Current market value: The amount an **asset** is worth if you sell it at the present time on the open market.

Custody: This term is no longer used in UK courts. It has been replaced by the concept of **parental responsibility**, whereby the parent with parental responsibility continues to be legally responsible for his child after divorce, and by *residence*, which is where the child lives. The term 'custody' is still used by the media and in the international context.

Decree absolute: The final legal stage of a divorce.

Decree nisi: The first stage of a divorce, when you prove your ground for divorce.

Deduction from earnings: An order or power at the disposal of the **CSA** or **CMEC** requiring an employer to deduct child support from a non-resident parent's wages and pay it direct to the CSA/CMEC.

Deed: A legal document signed by the maker, and sealed.

Default judgement: An order or judgement made on the basis of the claimant's information only because the **defendant** or **respondent** failed to respond, didn't respond on time, or didn't appear in court.

Defendant: The person being sued; usually known in family and divorce proceedings as the **respondent**.

Diligence: The Scottish term for enforcing **maintenance** orders.

Directions: Instructions from the court about what the parties or their solicitors must do before the next court hearing.

Directions appointment: A preliminary meeting at court to decide the way forward.

Disbursements: Usually, the out-of-pocket expenses a solicitor incurs on your behalf.

Disclosure: Providing the other person with information or documents relevant to the case.

Dissolution: The end of a marriage or civil partnership (in other words, a *divorce*); the term doesn't include **annulments**.

Domestic abuse or violence: Domestic abuse or domestic violence includes emotional and verbal abuse between couples as well as physical harm.

Domicile: The country that a person regards as his home country whether or not that person currently lives there.

Duxbury calculation: The formula for working out the lump sum appropriate for a clean break, based on the amount of **maintenance** payable and life expectancy of the recipient.

Earmarking: See **Attachment**.

Emergency applications: Applications that are urgent, such as applications for injunctions; can be *ex parte*.

Equitable distribution: A legal system of dividing up the value of a divorcing couple's property based on what's fair to both of them.

Evidence: Relevant testimony, documents, videos, tape recordings and other information offered to and accepted by the court to prove or disprove an allegation.

Examination: The questioning of a witness on the stand by the solicitor or barrister representing the spouse on whose behalf the witness is testifying (including the spouse himself).

Ex parte: old but still used phrase for an application to the court made without the other party being present, being notified or having an opportunity to participate in the action. Now often called a 'without notice' application.

Financial Dispute Resolution Appointment (FDR): An appointment with a judge to try to resolve financial disputes without a full hearing. The appointment is on a *without prejudice* basis, so that a different judge deals with the final hearing without being privy to offers disclosed in the FDR.

First Directions Appointment (FDA): The first appointment with a judge in financial proceedings to assess the issues and what needs to be done before the final hearing. The judge gives directions for the future conduct of the case.

Form E: The form used by the courts and also by solicitors and many mediators to collect financial information for or within divorce proceedings.

Freezing order: A special court order preventing the disposal of **assets,** such as money in a bank account.

Garnishee order: An order allowing money to be taken from a spouse's bank or building society account in order to pay a debt, typically arrears of **maintenance** (known as an *arrestment* of the account in Scotland).

Get: A Jewish religious divorce.

Ground: The legal basis or reason for a divorce.

Hague Convention: An international convention whose philosophy is that decisions about child custody or residence should be made in the jurisdiction in which the child was habitually resident prior to an abduction.

Hearing: A proceeding before the court that attempts to resolve an issue through testimony, legal arguments and the introduction of evidence.

Injunction: A court order prohibiting someone from acting in a way that's likely to harm someone else, for example by causing a financial loss for that person or hurting that individual emotionally or physically, or requiring a person to do something such as allow a spouse back into the home.

Intangible property: An **asset** with no intrinsic or marketable value in and of itself but that instead represents or has evidence of value (for example, stocks and shares, bonds or pension benefits).

Interim hearings: Hearings for a judge to hear applications for interim court orders, for example for personal protection, child contact or spousal **maintenance**. Decisions are for the short term.

Intestacy: Where no will has been made.

Joint custody: See **Parental responsibility**.

Joint property: Property legally owned by two or more persons, a husband and wife for example.

Joint tenancy: A form of joint ownership of property under which the survivor automatically inherits the whole property. Contrast to **tenancy in common**, below

Judgement summons: An application for an order for committal, for example if arrears of **maintenance** aren't paid. Committal to prison is likely only if *wilful refusal* to pay is evident.

Judicial separation: A formal separation sanctioned by the court, which releases the spouses from the duty to cohabit and enables the courts to make orders about money and property. The marriage isn't dissolved. In Scotland, only orders for **maintenance** can be made.

Jurisdiction: The authority of a court to rule on a particular legal matter. Different types of court have different jurisdictions. For example, certain county courts can deal with divorce but Family Proceedings Courts can't.

Land Registry: The office where the ownership of property is registered.

Legal aid: See **Public funding**

Legal separation: A legal agreement or court judgement formally authorising a couple to live apart and spelling out the terms for their living apart. The couple are still married to one another.

Lump sum: A capital payment that may be ordered between a husband and wife on or after their decree of divorce, judicial separation or annulled marriage. Can also be ordered in favour of a child in divorce and certain Children Act 1989 proceedings.

Maintenance: The regular payment of money by one spouse to another for his financial support or for the children. Maintenance may be provided for only a limited period of time or can last until the payee spouse dies or remarries. Also known as spousal support or **periodical payments**. Child maintenance is payable normally until the child/young person reaches 18 years of age or ceases full-time education.

Maintenance pending suit: A court order for temporary financial support while a couple's divorce is pending.

Matrimonial home: Any property in which a married couple live together, whether or not they own or rent it.

Mediation: A non-legal means of resolving a divorce-related dispute with the assistance of a neutral third party. Decisions made in a mediation session are arrived at by mutual agreement and not ordered by a judge. The issues discussed in mediation can be about children, finance, property, communication or other practicalities.

Memorandum of Understanding: A non-legally binding statement of proposals, used in mediation and agreed upon by the parties.

Mesher Order: The matrimonial home stays in joint names with a provision for sale at a future date when an agreed event occurs, for example, child or children finishing education, or remarriage of the occupying spouse.

Money purchase or defined contribution scheme: A type of retirement pension scheme. The final amount you receive depends on how much is contributed to your scheme and how much the value of the **assets** in the scheme appreciates over time.

Nikah: Muslim marriage contract.

No-fault divorce: A divorce granted with no requirement to prove that one of the spouses was guilty of some marital misconduct. The UK doesn't grant a divorce without fault, except for a two-year separation with consent to divorce or a five-year separation without (in Scotland one year with consent and two years without consent).

Non-molestation order: An order forbidding a person to abuse, harass, threaten or molest another person.

Non-resident parent: The parent who doesn't live with his children most of the time. Ordinarily, this parent is obliged to pay child support.

Nullity decree: A decree that the marriage has been declared voidable or null and void. Also called annulment.

Occupation Order (or ouster order or injunction): A court order that can force your spouse to leave your home, allow you to return, forbid your spouse to enter or come within a certain distance of your home, or restrict his rights within the home.

Order: A ruling by the court on an application that requires the parties to do something or not do something, or that establishes the parties' rights and responsibilities.

Parental responsibility: All the rights, duties and responsibilities that by law a parent of a child has in relation to that child. If you are or have been married, you both have joint parental responsibility for your children before, during and after divorce or separation.

Pension sharing: Division of a pension fund between two spouses on divorce.

Periodical payments: Regular **maintenance** for a spouse or child.

Petition: The legal document filed to initiate a divorce.

Petitioner: The person who files a **petition** or initiates a couple's divorce proceedings.

Pleading: Formal written application to the court for relief and the written response to it. Among other things, pleadings can include petitions, answers and replies.

Post-marital agreement: Sometimes called a post-nuptial agreement. A legal agreement made between spouses after marriage that spells out their present and future rights and responsibilities towards one another if they divorce or one spouse dies. Rarely used and not always enforceable in the UK.

Power of Arrest: A power allowing a police officer to arrest your spouse if he breaches or violates the terms of an injunction.

Pre-marital agreement: A legal agreement between a couple made before they marry that spells out their rights and responsibilities towards one another in the event that they later divorce or one of them dies during their marriage. Not automatically enforceable in most of the UK but generally thought to be enforceable in Scotland. Sometimes called a pre-nuptial agreement.

Pre-trial hearings: Pre-trial hearings are held by the judge before the final hearing to settle issues or give final directions, for example relating to the arrangements for the children following receipt of the Cafcass report.

Privilege: The court can't enquire into the content of your **without prejudice** negotiations or mediation discussions nor can you quote each other without each other's consent.

Prohibited Steps Order: An order prohibiting specific steps in relation to a child, for example, a change of surname or removal from the jurisdiction.

Property Adjustment Order: An order that a husband or wife transfer property to the other, that a property be sold, or that the spouses' shares in a property be adjusted.

Public funding: Financial help available to assist parties with the costs of a legal dispute. Currently administered by the Legal Services Commission in England, Wales and Northern Ireland, and by the Scottish Legal Aid Board in Scotland.

Real property: Homes, other buildings and land and any attachments to those **assets**.

Redemption: Paying off a mortgage.

Request for Directions: An application to the court for a decree nisi.

Residence Order: An order stating the arrangements about with whom a child is to live.

Respondent: The **defendant** in a divorce.

Restraining order: An order made by a judge or magistrate in the criminal courts to protect a person from the following: being followed, waiting outside a person's home, making threatening or harassing phone calls, or displaying other sorts of behaviour in order to harass, intimidate or frighten.

Rule 2.61 Statement: See **Statement of Information**.

Secured debt: Debt that you have collateralised or secured with an **asset**. If you don't pay the debt, the creditor can take the asset that you put up as loan collateral.

Secured Periodical Payments Order: An order that ensures that your **maintenance** payments continue on the death of your ex-spouse. Such orders are very rare, only occurring when the paying spouse has capital **assets** against which the maintenance can be secured.

Separation Agreement: A document setting out the terms agreed for separation, usually before divorce proceedings commence.

SERPS: State Earnings Related Pension (now replaced by the State Second Pension).

Service: A term for delivering a legal document, for example by post or in person.

Settlement: An agreement between spouses resolving the financial issues in their divorce. Also sometimes used to refer to the final financial order made by a judge in court proceedings.

Sharia: A system of Muslim law. The Muslim Law (Sharia) Council can deal with Muslim divorces in the UK.

Specific Issue Order: An order determining a specific issue relating to a child, such as where he should go to school.

Statement of Arrangements: The form that has to be sent to the court with the petition if there are children of the family, setting out the current arrangements and the arrangements proposed for the children when the divorce takes place.

Statement of Information: The statement that accompanies a draft financial consent order to the court, in the form of a simple agreed summary of your respective finances and intentions.

Statutory Charge: The means by which the Legal Services Commission recoups any costs that you have incurred under the legal aid scheme.

Stay: Bringing an end to proceedings before the court has given a final judgement.

Subpoena: A legal document served on a witness requiring that he appear in court. Ignoring a subpoena can result in punishment by the court. Sometimes referred to as a witness summons.

Summons: A written notification to the **defendant** or witness in a lawsuit that the lawsuit has been filed and that a response is needed.

Sworn Statement: Same as **Affidavit**.

Talaq: Muslim divorce. A bare talaq is a single unilateral declaration of divorce by a husband.

Tangible property: Property that has value in and of itself, such as a house or a car.

Tenancy in Common: A form of joint ownership, sometimes used by cohabiting couples, in which each owner has a distinct share. If the size of the share isn't defined, it's usually assumed to be 50 per cent. Either joint owner can leave his share by will or intestacy.

Testamentary guardian: A person appointed to hold parental responsibility in the event of both parents' deaths.

Testimony: Statements or evidence provided by a witness under oath in court.

Transcript: A typed record of the trial or court hearing.

Trial: A formal court hearing presided over by a judge to resolve the issues. Sometimes referred to in this book as a final or fully contested hearing.

Trust: A legal entity established to hold and manage **assets** for one or more beneficiaries.

Undertaking: A solemn promise to the court to do or not to do something. Breach of an undertaking is punishable as a contempt of court.

Unsecured debt: Debt that isn't secured against an **asset** (see **secured debt**), such as credit card debt.

Without prejudice: An opportunity afforded by the courts to make offers or proposals that aren't revealed to the court without the maker's consent or taken account of by (that is, will not prejudice) a court if agreement isn't reached.

Appendix B
Useful Divorce Websites

The Internet is no substitute for solid legal advice, but you can quickly get hold of basic information about divorce-related issues online. This appendix lists some of the most useful websites for people who are contemplating, are going through, or have been through a divorce, plus some sites for children.

Divorce and Procedure

Many family law firms of solicitors and many barristers have websites. The following three aren't necessarily 'the best' or recommended by us to act for you, but they make a good starting point for information.

- **www.divorce.co.uk:** This practical and user-friendly site has been compiled by one of the largest family law practices in the UK and provides guidelines to help you plan what you want to do about your divorce and how to do it. As well as legal issues, proceedings and forms, the website covers emotional matters and alternatives to court such as mediation.

- **www.divorce-online.co.uk:** You can download here just about any legal form you need for a divorce. Costs are anywhere from £65 for a DIY divorce to £180 for an application to vary maintenance. You can even pay £125 for a missing persons trace or £24.99 for a change of name deed. The site gives general advice and links to solicitors and mediators in your area.

- **www.divorceaid.co.uk:** This site is run by an independent group of solicitors and mediators who volunteer to provide divorce advice, support and information. The website contains online advice for children (www.divorceaid.co.uk/child/teenagers) and parents (www.divorceaid.co.uk/child/parents) in divorce, with extensive sections of information such as www.divorceaid.co.uk/child/help/others, www.divorceaid.co.uk/child/teenshelplines/247helplines, and www.divorceaid.co.uk/child/help/books.

Advice, Information, and Support

Sometimes you may need some quick guidance about being a separated or separating parent, or about what to do in an emergency. The following sites are a starting point, and some also have helplines that are particularly useful.

✔ www.advicenow.org.uk: This site gives a range of general advice on many family issues, welfare benefits and rights. It has especially good advice and information about the law and consequences of living together and how to avoid the financial pitfalls. Another site – www.direct.gov.uk – gives advice on welfare benefits, finding work and much more and is also well worth a look.

✔ www.relate.org.uk: Relate offers advice, relationship counselling, sex therapy, workshops, mediation, consultations, and support face to face, by phone and online. Here, you can find your nearest Relate location, book yourself on a course, buy books and consult their experts online.

✔ www.oneplusone.org.uk: One Plus One gives information on both marriage and couple relationships, explaining the different legal effects of living together and being married.

✔ www.parentlineplus.org.uk: Parentline Plus is for parents who need information, support or advice about parenting. It doesn't give legal advice but the website provides confidential advice by email and an advice helpline on 0808 800 2222.

✔ www.fnf.org.uk: The Families Need Fathers website aims to ensure that fathers can gain access to a range of information about family courts, including court forms and other information. You can find contact details for local FNF groups for even more information and support. A helpline is available on 0870 760 7496.

✔ www.matchmothers.org: MATCH offers non-judgemental emotional support to mothers after their children have been abducted abroad or alienated from them after high-conflict divorce. Many mothers become non-resident parents and lose contact with their children.

✔ www.fatherhoodinstitute.org: The Fatherhood Institute provides information for fathers about all aspects of parenting, including pregnancy, domestic violence and parenting after separation.

✔ www.womensaid.org.uk: The Women's Aid site outlines research and development on domestic violence and abuse, including updates on government policy and initiatives on domestic violence. (You can also access government policy information on domestic violence directly at www.homeoffice.org.uk.) The site allows you to use it privately without leaving any evidence on your computer that you visited.

✔ **www.refuge.org.uk:** Refuge provides help and advice about domestic violence and abuse. It has links and telephone numbers for organisations providing support for men, women and children. It runs a freephone 24 hour National Domestic Violence helpline in partnership with Women's Aid: 0808 200 0247.

Solicitors and Mediators

Personal recommendation is often the best way to find practitioners. These websites don't just list practitioners, but give general information as well.

✔ **www.resolution.org.uk:** Resolution is the country's leading organisation of family solicitors. It has lots of useful information on its website, including fact sheets on a range of topics such as financial arrangements on divorce, mediation, cohabitation and arrangements for children after divorce or separation. The website can also help you find a solicitor in your local area.

✔ **www.lawsociety.org.uk:** The Law Society site contains a searchable database to help you find a solicitor, advice on what to expect, guides to common legal problems, and what to do if things go wrong. Further guidance covers paying for legal services, specialist solicitors, complaints, directories, protocols and frequently asked questions.

✔ **www.nfm.org.uk:** National Family Mediation (NFM) is a network of local not-for-profit Family Mediation Services in England and Wales, offering help to couples, married or unmarried, who are in the process of separation and divorce. This website not only has information about mediation but also has videos, case studies, links to other websites and a directory of services near you. I list other mediation organisation websites in Chapter 16.

Five Government Help Websites

These websites can be really useful resources but again, do also remember to seek proper advice.

✔ **www.hmcourts-service.gov.uk:** Download all the court forms you need for divorce and for children applications absolutely free. Also gives guidance on filling in the forms and how to apply. The site lists all the courts and how to contact them.

✔ **www.familymediationhelpline.co.uk:** The Family Mediation Helpline is staffed by specially trained operators who provide general information on family mediation, advice on whether your case may be suitable for mediation, information about eligibility for public funding, and contact details for mediation services in your local area.

✔ **www.csa.gov.uk:** When you need to know more about the Child Support Agency (CSA)/Child Maintenance Enforcement Commission (CMEC), try this website. The CMEC site (www.cmoptions.gov.uk) helps you make your own child maintenance agreements.

✔ **www.communitylegaladvice.org.uk:** This site is for when you need to know more about public funding/legal aid. The multilingual site gives you the largest available directory of names and addresses in your area for community legal service-approved solicitors, mediators and divorce information providers, plus other national organisations and professional bodies to contact for further information.

The thousands of professionals in the directory have all been awarded the Legal Services Commission Quality Mark, which means that they have been given a stamp of approval by the Community Legal Service. You can also find a legal aid calculator to work out if you're likely to be eligible for legal aid, as well as definitions and descriptions of the types of aid available. You can download Consumer Association leaflets on divorce-associated topics, including legal help, mediation and buying and selling a house.

✔ **www.dcsf.gov.uk:** The Department for Children Schools and Families (DCSF) is responsible for government policy on supporting family relationships and services for children. The website has lots of useful information about caring for children, schooling, day care, and so on.

Four Websites for You and Your Children

No matter how much we love our children, at stressful times their feelings can get overlooked. These websites act as a reminder to keep their best interests to the forefront.

✔ **www.cafcass.org.uk:** Cafcass looks after the interests of children involved in family proceedings. It works with children and their families, and then advises the courts on what it considers to be in the children's best interests. Cafcass only works in the family courts. This useful website has information specially designed for children and young people as well as information for parents – especially for devising parenting plans.

✔ **www.itsnotyourfault.org**: One of the best things about this website is that your children can use it. The site is run by NCH (formally called National Children's Homes), a charity that provides mediation and children's counselling services. The colourful, engaging material and resources, including a diary where children can record their thoughts and feelings, can help your children feel normal and not alone while you're going through a divorce. Information on how to cope with the experience of separation is directed to three groups of people – parents, teenagers and children.

✔ **www.family-justice-council.org.uk**: This website has advice and information including websites, helplines, leaflets and booklets about families and children and what can happen if courts become involved. Download the excellent 40-page booklet especially designed for parents and young children in words and pictures: *The Court and your Child: when mum and dad split up.*

✔ **www.childrenslegalcentre.com**: The Children's Legal Centre provides general information and signposting on legal advice for children and parents, legal fact sheets on child and family law and numbers for a Young People's freephone line and a Child Law advice line.

Children's Commissioners Websites

The four Children's Commissioners around the UK promote and safeguard the rights of children and young people to whom the websites are geared. The sites are clear and interactive, and help to give children a say in how they experience life – especially with their parents!

✔ **England:** www.11million.org.uk

✔ **Northern Ireland:** www.niccy.org

✔ **Scotland:** www.sccyp.org.uk

✔ **Wales:** www.childcom.org.uk

Ten Websites in Scotland

Following is a list of websites with information specific to getting a divorce in Scotland. As the laws are slightly different, these websites can help if you need information on what steps to take if you're Scots.

✔ **www.relationships-scotland.org.uk** (previously www.family mediationscotland.org.uk and www.relatescotland.org.uk): Family Mediation Scotland and Couple Counselling Scotland have combined to form a tremendous one-stop shop for family services relating to separation, divorce and counselling. Here you can find information about family mediation services, contact centres and counselling services, along with useful links to other related sites.

✔ **www.calmscotland.org.uk:** This site gives you information on mediation and how to find a solicitor mediator, and also contains a video clip of mediation to let you see what mediation is like.

✔ **www.parentingacrossscotland.org.uk:** A partnership of adult relationship organisations and children's charities, which deals with issues affecting parents and children: contains details of various resources for parents.

✔ **www.fla-scotland.co.uk:** The Family Law Association in Scotland site provides details of its member solicitors specialising in family law.

✔ **www.slab.org.uk:** The Scottish Legal Aid Board website provides general information about Scottish law. You can find info on how to find a solicitor specialising in family law, getting legal aid, and general information about navigating through various legal issues.

✔ **www.sclc.org.uk:** This site for the Scottish Child Law Centre provides specialist information on the law relating to children and young people.

✔ **www.opfs.org.uk:** The One Parent Family Scotland website is useful if you want information, help or support on being a single parent.

✔ **www.children1st.org.uk:** This site is the Scottish equivalent of Parentline, with information on parenting – whatever your family situation.

✔ **www.scottishwomensaid.co.uk:** The Scottish Women's Aid website is extremely helpful if you're considering a divorce, or need help in an abusive situation.

✔ **www.cas.org.uk:** The Citizens Advice Scotland website has details of Citizens Advice Bureaux throughout Scotland.

Ten Websites in Northern Ireland

Here's a list of websites with information specific to Northern Ireland:

✔ **www.familymediationni.org.uk:** This site gives details of how to contact the mediation service in Belfast. The service has outposts elsewhere too.

✔ **www.afriendlydivorce.co.uk:** The Collaborative Law Association of Northern Ireland is a solicitor organisation that offers an alternative to court.

✔ **www.relateni.org:** Relate Northern Ireland provides a confidential relationship counselling service for those who have relationship or marital problems.

✔ **www.niwaf.org:** The Northern Ireland Women's Aid Federation gives information and help on domestic violence.

✔ **www.barnardos.org.uk:** In over 45 services, Barnardos (Northern Ireland) helps 11,000 children, young people and their families every year.

✔ **www.gingerbreadni.org:** Gingerbread (Northern Ireland) provides a wide variety of services to lone parents including advice, child care, membership and training.

✔ **www.parentsadvicecentre.org:** The Parents Advice Centre (Northern Ireland), sometimes known simply as PAC, provides help and support to parents facing any family difficulty.

✔ **www.themii.ie:** The Mediators Institute of Ireland, (the MII) is the professional association for Mediators in the Republic of Ireland and Northern Ireland.

✔ **www.irish-counselling.ie:** The Irish Association for Counselling and Psychotherapy acts as a link between those who are looking for counselling/psychotherapy and those who provide it.

✔ **www.mensproject.org:** The Men's Project aims to increase awareness of the issues facing men and boys in Northern Ireland including those experiencing domestic violence.

Index

• A •

abduction, of children, 344–346, 369
abuse, spousal. *See* domestic violence
acceptance, of divorce, 139
accountant
  division of assets, 176, 187
  initiation of divorce, 109
  negotiations with spouse, 229
  pension information, 187
acknowledgement of service, 78–79, 369
active listening, 133
actual property, 175
actuary, 369
additional voluntary contribution, 39
adult children, 130
adultery
  annulment criteria, 28
  behaviour during separation, 99
  civil partnerships, 60
  dating while separated, 27
  defined, 369
  described, 68
  divorce petition, 76, 78
  divorce rate, 70
  formal separation tips, 98
  irretrievably broken down marriage, 68
  legal grounds for divorce, 11
  shared financial responsibilities, 35
  signs of troubled marriage, 22
affidavit
  defined, 369
  maintenance changes, 204–205
  in support of petition, 80
age, person's
  children's living arrangements, 62
  civil partnership, 60
  contact with children, 63
  conversations with children, 129–130, 131
  division of assets, 178
  end of child support, 220
  marriage licence, 57

pre-marital agreements, 342
spousal support considerations, 202
agenda, written, 228, 270
aggressive legal strategy, 300
agreement. *See specific types*
alcoholism, 68–69, 162–163
aliment, 179, 180, 198
ancillary relief, 76, 83–84, 302
anger
  asking for divorce, 105–108
  children's living arrangements, 157
  contested divorce, 121, 122
  coping of children, 134
  domestic violence, 23, 30
  effects of troubled marriage, 22
  final hearing, 306
  negotiations with spouse, 224, 227
  range of emotions, 137
  stage of grief, 138–139
annuity, 369
annulment, 27–28, 369
answer, to petition, 78, 369
anti-stalking order, 31
anxiety, 124, 133
appeal, legal, 72, 90, 309–310, 369
applicant, 307
argument
  asking for divorce, 106
  break from troubled marriage, 23
  contact with children, 160, 161
  contested divorce, 75
  decree nisi, 81
  emergency orders, 83
  formal applications to court, 83–92
  formal separation tips, 98
  informal separation, 96
  involvement of children, 128–129
  remarriage tips, 363
  signs of troubled marriage, 22
arrears, 331
arrestment of earnings, 201, 370

asset. *See also specific types*
  charge on property, 259
  contested divorce, 120–122
  cost of divorce, 116
  defined, 36, 370
  drawbacks of separation, 95
  emergency order, 83
  financial assessment, 36–37, 109–112
  first actions after finalised divorce, 316–317
  formal separation tips, 100
  informal separation tips, 97
  information for solicitor, 288, 289
  initiation of divorce, 109–112
  need for solicitor, 240
  pre-marital agreements, 345
  spousal support considerations, 202
  statement of means, 85
assets, dividing. *See also* finances, dividing
  business ownership, 191–194
  described, 173–174
  house, 181–185
  insurance/endowments, 194–195
  legal guidelines, 177–178
  mediation process, 271–272
  negotiations with spouse, 235–238
  post-divorce conflicts, 336
  professional advice, 181
  retirement benefits, 185–191
  Scotland, 175–176, 179–180
  types of property, 174–176
  value of asset, 176–177, 180
Association of British Introduction
    Agencies, 360
Association of Independent Financial
    Advisers, 181
assurance, 370
attachment
  defined, 370
  of earnings, 201, 219, 332
  pension, 190
authorised user, 51
automatic payment deduction, 219

• *B* •

bailiff, 78, 332, 334
balance statement, 37, 113, 193

bank account
  budget tips, 37
  contested divorce, 120–121
  financial assessment, 36
  informal separation tips, 97
  initiation of divorce, 109–110
  mediation process, 271
  post-divorce conflicts, 333
  statement of means, 85
bankruptcy, 332, 339–340
bargaining, 139
barrister
  children's living arrangements, 168
  defined, 370
  described, 64
  final hearing, 300
  selection, 247
behaviour, of spouse
  court costs, 90
  division of assets, 178
  irretrievably broken down marriage, 68–69
  negotiations with spouse, 224–225, 227
  separation tips, 99
  spousal support considerations, 202–203
beneficiary, 319, 321
bereavement benefit, 59
Bien, Melanie (*Buying and Selling a Home For
    Dummies*), 183
bigamy, 57
biographical information, 287
birthday party, children's, 160
blame, 54, 69, 106
bookshop, 47
British Association for Counselling and
    Psychotherapy, 22, 24
Brown, Marc and Laurence Krasny
    (*Dinosaurs Divorce: A Guide for
    Changing Families*), 135
budget
  basic concepts, 43
  creation, 37–40
  information for solicitor, 289
  initiation of divorce, 113–114
  mediation process, 273–274
  post-divorce life, 321–322, 357–358
bundle, 304
Burrett, Jill (*But I Want to Stay With You*), 136

business ownership
  disability insurance, 215
  division of assets, 191–194
  information for solicitor, 288
  need for solicitor, 240
  pre-marital agreement, 343
But I Want to Stay With You (Burrett), 136
Buying and Selling a Home For Dummies
      (Bien), 183
buyout, business, 192, 193

• *C* •

CAB (Citizens Advice Bureau), 46, 47
Cafcass officer. *See* Children and Family
      Court Advisory and Support Service
      officer
CallCredit (credit reference agency), 48, 50
calm behaviour, 105–108
capital asset, 203
capital gains tax (CGT), 185
capital settlement, 338
capital sum, 180
capitalising the maintenance, 203, 370
career plan
  job training, 323–324
  pension benefits, 191
  post-divorce life, 357
  spousal support considerations, 202
cash, 122
Cash Equivalent Transfer Value (CETV),
      187, 370
celebrity divorce, 59, 342
certificate, marriage, 57, 77
CGT (capital gains tax), 185
chambers, 307, 370
charge on property, 259, 317
charging order, 201, 332, 334, 370
chartered financial planner, 322
Chartered Insurance Institution, 322
child abuse. *See* domestic violence
Child Benefit, 119, 212, 220
Child Maintenance and Enforcement
      Commission (CMEC)
  calculations of liability, 208, 210–211
  defined, 371
  described, 54
  importance of child support, 217

living arrangements of children, 156
post-divorce conflicts, 330, 331–334
recent changes in, 210
resolution of divorce issues, 71
role of, 208
website, 208
Child Support Act 1991, 54
Child Support Agency (CSA), 54, 71, 208, 371
child support/maintenance
  age of ending payment, 220
  agreement, 217, 218, 234
  calculations of liability, 208
  changes to, 218
  children's living arrangement, 209
  court orders, 84
  defined, 371
  extra expenses, 214–216
  family law history, 54
  Internet resources, 384
  judge's decisions, 213–214
  lack of payment, 218–220
  link to parent-child contact, 217
  mediation process, 273–274
  negotiations with spouse, 216–218, 232–234
  post-divorce conflicts, 330–334, 338–340
  rates of, 210–211
  resolution of divorce issues, 71
  role of CMEC, 208
  state benefits, 211–212
  taxes, 211–212, 220
Child Tax Credit, 119, 212, 220
child welfare hearing, 169
children. *See also* parental rights/
      responsibilities
  abduction by ex-spouse, 334–336
  arguments, 128–129
  behaviour during separation, 99
  changes to final settlement, 337–338
  communication tips, 125–132, 134–136
  confidentiality issues, 92
  contested divorce, 76
  co-operative divorce, 75
  coping tips, 123–124, 126
  cost of divorce, 116, 118, 119, 120
  division of assets, 177
  divorce from parents, 172
  domestic violence, 30, 31, 32
  drawbacks of separation, 95

children *(continued)*
  emergency orders, 83, 285–286
  emotional effects of divorce, 13, 15, 16
  estate planning, 319–321
  fair division of property, 45
  families' response to divorce, 141–142
  Family Help scheme, 257–258
  family law history, 54
  family law specifics, 11, 61–63
  foreign divorce, 66
  formal applications to court, 91–92
  healing process, 140
  importance of, 147
  information for solicitor, 289
  manipulating, 353
  marriage rights, 58
  mediation benefits, 17, 262
  mediation process, 270, 274–275
  name change, 171
  need for solicitor, 240
  nullity decree, 28
  petition process, 77
  post-divorce life, 327–336, 351–354
  pre-trial hearing, 299
  print resources, 135, 136
  reasons to stay in marriage, 22
  refusal to visit parent, 132
  resolution of divorce issues, 70, 71
  Scotland's divorce petitions, 79
  spousal support considerations, 202
  support groups, 15, 325
  types of contact with, 62–63
  types of courts, 64–65
  welfare officers, 17
Children Act 1989, 11, 54, 167
Children and Family Court Advisory and
    Support Service (Cafcass) officer
  children's living arrangements, 168, 170–171
  contact with children, 161, 162, 163
  defined, 370
  described, 17, 91
children, contact with
  contact centres, 161, 162, 267
  court hearing, 170
  criteria for, 63
  defined, 149, 158, 371
  described, 158
  divorce law, 11
  domestic violence, 162–163
  effects of living arrangement, 150–152
  forms of, 158–159
  good versus poor relationships, 152–153
  link to child support, 217
  parenting plan, 164–166
  possible problems, 161–164
  post-divorce conflicts, 329–330
  refusal to visit parent, 132
  tips for success, 159–161
  types of, 62–63
Children Order 1995, 61
Children's Commissioners (children's rights
    organisations), 385
children's guardian, 171, 320, 371
children's living arrangement. *See also* house
  child support, 209
  children's opinions of, 130, 155–158
  criteria for, 63
  described, 62
  divorce law, 11
  issues to consider, 150
  negotiation options, 167–172
  parenting plan, 164–166
  parents' versus court's decision, 148
  petition process, 77
  primary parent arrangement, 150–152, 209
  resolution of divorce issues, 70, 71
  shared residence, 153–155
Church of England, 57
Citizens Advice Bureau (CAB), 46, 47
civil divorce, 74
civil partnership, 1, 12, 60, 371
claw-back, 118
clean break, 201, 371
client care code, 250
closing argument, 308
clothing, 215, 305
CMEC. *See* Child Maintenance and
    Enforcement Commission
cohabiting couple, 11, 13, 55–56
Cole, Julia (*How Do I Feel About My Parent's
    Divorce*), 135
collaborative law
  cost of, 294
  described, 73, 293
  process, 293–294
  solicitor selection, 248

college education, 323–324
committal to prison, 334
common law marriage, 11, 13, 55–56
communication
  asking for divorce, 105–108
  behaviour during separation, 99
  children's living arrangements, 155–157
  conversations with children, 125–132,
    134–136
  coping tips for children, 124
  final hearing, 305–306
  formal separation tips, 98
  importance of, 24
  negotiations with spouse, 224
  parenting plan, 165
  pre-marital agreements, 343–344
  remarriage tips, 361–363
  response of family/friends, 143
  signs of troubled marriage, 22
  with solicitor, 283–284, 287
  solicitor's skills, 241, 243
Community Legal Service (legal aid), 244,
  251, 371
compromise
  asking for divorce, 107
  cost of divorce, 116
  formal separation tips, 99
  negotiations with spouse, 224
computer skill, 47
conciliation, 91, 168
C1 form (application to court), 91
confidentiality
  cases involving children, 92
  counselling session, 25
  mediation process, 273, 279
  negotiations with spouse, 224
conflict of interest, 249
consent order, 254, 255, 290, 371
consultation, with solicitor, 245
Consumer Credit Counselling Service, 47, 322
Contact Order, 170
contact, with children
  contact centres, 161, 162, 267
  court hearing, 170
  criteria for, 63
  defined, 149, 158, 371
  described, 158
  divorce law, 11

domestic violence, 162–163
  effects of living arrangement, 150–152
  forms of, 158–159
  good versus poor relationships, 152–153
  link to child support, 217
  parenting plan, 164–166
  possible problems, 161–164
  post-divorce conflicts, 329–330
  refusal to visit parent, 132
  tips for success, 159–161
  types of, 62–63
contempt of court, 31, 330, 372
contested divorce
  cost of, 117–118, 120–122
  defined, 82
  described, 73, 75–76
  disclosure process, 87–89
  emergency orders, 83
  hearing basics, 90
  solicitor's skills, 241
contract, with solicitor, 250, 282
co-operative divorce, 73, 74–75, 89
co-respondent, 76, 372
co-signer, 51
Council Tax Benefit, 120
counsel. See barrister
counsellor
  confidentiality, 25
  effects of troubled marriage, 22
  function of, 16
  healing process, 141
  personal finance issues, 47
  post-divorce feelings, 356
  pre-marital agreements, 344
  reconciliation after separation, 102
  remarriage tips, 365
  selection, 22, 24–25
  solicitor as, 285
  stages of grief, 139
  visit without spouse, 25
counter-claim, 79
County Court, 64, 65
court. See also judge
  changes in maintenance, 204
  children's living arrangements, 148, 168–172
  confidential negotiations, 224
  consent order, 291
  decree nisi, 80–81

court *(continued)*
emergency orders, 83
fees, 76, 77, 90, 116
flexibility of, 72
formal applications, 83–92
hearing basics, 90
irretrievably broken down marriage, 68–70
main financial orders, 84
marriage rights, 58
petitioning process, 76–79
post-divorce conflicts, 330–331
Scotland's financial orders, 180
types of, 64–65
view of maintenance, 200–203
Court of Session, 65
court order. *See also specific orders*
child support, 213–214, 217–219
defined, 372, 376
domestic violence, 83 30–31, 285
final judgement, 308–309
post-divorce conflicts, 330–334, 338–340
urgent/interim orders, 285–286
Court Welfare Officer (Northern Ireland), 17
courtesy, 225
Courts Service (website), 259
credit card
authorised users, 51
budget tips, 37
contested divorce, 121, 122
credit-building tips, 50–51
divorce initiation, 112
first action after finalised divorce, 317
formal separation tips, 98, 100
importance of positive credit report, 49
late payments, 50, 51
credit record
contested divorce, 122
credit-building tips, 50–51
defined, 48
financial assessment, 37
importance of positive report, 48–49
informal separation tips, 97
review of, 49–50
criminal charge, 30, 31, 65
cross-examination, 307, 372
cross-petition, 78
Crown Court, 65
CSA (Child Support Agency), 54, 71, 208, 371

current market value, 109
Curtis, Jill (*Where's Daddy?*), 136
custody, of children. *See* parental rights/
responsibilities

dating
remarriage tips, 362
responsibility to children, 354
return to social life, 359–360
during separation, 27, 94, 99
deadlock, in negotiations, 225
death
children's benefits, 214
estate planning, 319–320
marriage rights, 58, 59
shared pension, 191
spousal support, 205
debt
communication with solicitor, 284
cost of divorce, 116
defined, 36
division of, 195–196, 235–238
drawbacks of separation, 95
financial assessment, 36–37, 45, 112–113
first actions after finalised divorce, 317
formal separation tips, 98
importance of positive credit report, 49
matrimonial property, 176
mediation process, 272
need for solicitor, 240
post-divorce budget, 322, 357–358
resolution of divorce issues, 71
statement of means, 85
decree absolute
application, 292
defined, 292, 372
described, 81
filing for, 81–82
order for ancillary relief, 84
reconciliation, 82
decree nisi
decree absolute application, 292
defined, 372
described, 80–81
reconciliation, 82
decree of judicial separation, 101

deduction from earnings order, 219, 333, 372
deed of charge, 184
deed of trust, 184, 372
deed transfer, 316
default judgement, 372
defendant, 373
defender, 79
defined benefit scheme, 38
defined contribution scheme, 38, 376
denial, 138
Department for Work and Pensions, 186, 187
depression
  coping tips for children, 124
  effects of troubled marriage, 22
  range of emotions, 138
  stages of grief, 139
desertion, by spouse, 11, 69
diary, 140, 356
diligence, 373
Dinosaurs Divorce: A Guide for Changing Families (Brown and Brown), 135
direct contact, with children, 62, 161
Directory of Solicitors and Barristers (Law Society), 244
Disability Benefit, 120
disability insurance, 215
disappointment, feelings of, 138
disapproving friend/family, 141–142
disbursement, 242, 247, 373
disclosure process
  Cafcass involvement, 92
  defined, 373
  described, 87
  final hearing, 301–302
  initiation of divorce, 113
  mediators, 264
  pre-marital agreements, 346
  shared financial responsibilities, 35
  types of disclosure, 88–89
disease, 28, 178
dismissed claim, 200, 201
dispute. *See* argument; contested divorce
dissolution, 1, 60, 373
distress action, 334
divorce
  agreement, 100
  cost of, 116–120
  defined, 9
  goal of, 72
  grounds for, 11
  issues to consider, 13–14
  options for, 73–76
  petition, 73–79, 106
  preparations, 33–34
  process, 13, 80–83
  rate of, 11, 33, 70
Divorce – a Challenge to the Church (Mayo), 357
Divorce Act 1976, 10–11, 67
Divorce is Not the End of the World (Evan and Stern), 135
divorce law. *See* family law
Divorce: Living through the Agony (Kirk), 357
Divorce Recovery Workshop (support group), 326
do-it-yourself divorce, 79, 259
domestic violence
  children's living arrangements, 171–172
  contact with children, 162–163
  cost of divorce, 120–122
  criminal charges, 30–31, 65
  defined, 373
  described, 29
  effects of divorce, 13
  emergency orders, 30–31, 83, 285
  helplines, 23
  injunction against spouse, 30–31
  irretrievably broken down marriage, 68–69
  mediation safety, 262
  need for solicitor, 240
  police involvement, 29
  reasons for separation, 94
  refuge, 31–32
  safety actions, 32
  spousal support considerations, 202–203
  types of courts, 65
domicile, 68, 373
driving licence, 334

• E •

education
  job training, 323–324
  personal finance courses, 46, 47
  return to social life, 359
embarrassment, 137

emergency situation
  abduction of children by ex-spouse, 335–336
  court orders, 30–31, 285–286
  defined, 373
  solicitor affordability, 247, 256, 258
emotion. *See also specific emotions*
  arguments around children, 128–129
  asking for divorce, 105–108
  break from troubled marriage, 23
  children's feelings, 13, 15, 16, 135
  children's living arrangements, 167–168
  common feelings, 1
  contested divorce, 75
  conversations with children, 126, 131–132
  coping tips for children, 123–124
  cost of divorce, 116
  domestic violence, 13
  final hearing, 305
  limitations of law, 72
  mediation issues, 262
  post-divorce life, 325–328
  range of, 137–138
  reconciliation after separation, 101–102
  responses of friends/family, 141–143
  responsibilities to children, 352
  signs of troubled marriage, 22
  tips for handling, 140–141, 356
employability
  financial responsibility, 47–48
  job search, 323–325
  spousal support considerations, 202
endowment, 194–195
enforcement, by court, 330–331
England
  contact centres, 161
  divorce law basics, 10–11, 12, 68–71
  divorce petitions, 77
  divorce rate, 11
  endowments, 194
  home ownership, 42
  judicial separation, 101
  key laws, 67
  pre-marital agreements, 59, 342
Equifax (credit reference agency), 48, 50
equity, 182
estate agent, 182, 229
estate planning, 319–321

Evan, Zoe (*Divorce is Not the End of the World*), 135
evidence, for hearing, 302, 303, 373
ex parte order, 286, 374
examination, 307, 373
exclusion order, 30
execution against goods, 332
executor, 319
exercise, 140
expense
  budget basics, 43
  budget worksheet, 39–40
  child support rates, 210, 211
  children's extra expenses, 214–216
  court hearing, 299
  division of assets, 178
  formal separation tips, 100
  informal separation tips, 97
  mediation process, 271
  negotiations with spouse, 229
  solicitor affordability, 242, 247, 252, 284
Experian (credit reference agency), 48, 50
expert witness, 302–303, 308
external transfer, 190

• **F** •

failure, sense of, 138
fair market value, 176
fairness, 108, 125
faith community
  civil divorce, 74
  counselling, 25
  judicial separation, 101
  legal marriages, 57, 59
  marriage enrichment, 365
  parenting plan, 165
  post-divorce coping, 357
  reasons for separation, 94
family
  break from troubled marriage, 24
  children's living arrangements, 148
  conversations with children, 127
  counsellor referral, 25
  domestic violence, 32
  healing process, 140–141
  marriage within family, 57
  mediation process, 275–276

reasons to stay in marriage, 22
rebuilding after divorce, 327–328
response to divorce, 141–143
Family Care Centre (court), 65
Family Court Advisor, 91
Family Help scheme (legal aid), 253–258
family law. *See* law, family
Family Law (Scotland) Act 1985, 179
Family Mediation Council, 266
Family Mediation Helpline, 267
Family Mediation Northern Ireland, 265
Family Mediation Scotland, 265, 267, 278
Family Mediation Service, 15
family mediator. *See* mediator
Family Proceedings Court, 64
Family Proceedings Officer, 91
father
    contact with children, 163
    divorce petition, 76
    non-resident types, 152
    parenting plan, 164–166
    primary care of children, 150
    rights of cohabiting couples, 56
fatigue, 140
FDA (first directions appointment), 86, 374
FDR (financial dispute resolution)
    appointment, 86–87, 299, 374
fear, 22, 124, 138
feelings. *See* emotions
fighting. *See* argument
final financial order, 70, 75, 84
final hearing, 300–309
finalised divorce. *See also* post-divorce life
    decree absolute application, 292
    divorce stages, 81–82
    final judgement, 308–309
    first actions after, 316–319
    interest in home, 185
    post-divorce conflicts, 337–339
    resolution of basic issues, 70–71
    Scotland's law, 82, 108
    settlement out of court, 297–298
    solicitor's tasks, 289–292
finances, dividing. *See also* assets, dividing
    cohabiting couples, 55
    debts, 195–196, 235–236
    described, 14
    divorce preparations, 33–34

emergency orders, 83
fair distribution, 45–46
financial effects of divorce, 34
first directions appointment, 86
formal applications to court, 83–90
home ownership, 41–45
issues to consider, 14
mediation process, 270–274
pension benefits, 14
positive credit report, 49
pre-trial hearing, 299
resolution of divorce issues, 71
financial advisor
    division of assets, 181
    initiation of divorce, 109
    negotiations with spouse, 229
    personal finance courses, 46
    post-divorce budget, 322
financial dispute resolution (FDR)
    appointment, 86–87, 299, 374
financial responsibility
    benefits of mediation, 265
    children's living arrangements, 154, 156
    credit record, 48–51
    drawbacks of separation, 95
    employability, 47–48
    financial assessment, 36–37, 46–47, 108–114
    first actions after finalised divorce, 316–319
    household income sheet, 41–42
    informal separation tips, 97
    information gathering, 288–289
    initiation of divorce, 108–114
    Internet resources, 47
    irretrievably broken down marriage, 68–69
    marriage rights, 58
    mortgage information, 45
    personal finance courses, 46, 47
    pre-marital agreements, 344–345
    resolution of divorce issues, 70–71
    shared between spouses, 34–35
    spending plan, 37–40
Financial Services Authority, 181
financial statement, 113, 193, 248, 280
financial support. *See also specific types*
    cohabiting couple's legal rights, 13
    divorce initiation proceedings, 76
    government support, 15
    separation agreement, 26

first directions appointment (FDA), 86, 374
fixed expense, 43
flat fee, 242
foreign divorce, 66
foreign wedding, 59, 66
forgiveness, 364
Form A (application to court), 83
Form E (statement of means), 84, 270, 374
Form G (guidance request), 85, 87
formal disclosure, 88–89
formal separation, 97–100
four-way meeting, 293–294
freezing order, 374
friends
    healing process, 140–141
    post-divorce life, 328, 359
    response to divorce, 141–143
frustration, 283
full and frank disclosure, 301
full-time student, 210, 213
furniture, 110, 237

• *G* •

gambling, excessive, 68–69, 289
garnishee, 201, 332, 374
get, 74, 374
gift, 175, 215
giving judgement, 90
goal setting
    mediation process, 273
    negotiations with spouse, 226
    solicitor's information, 289
goodwill value, 193
grandparent, 127, 142, 275
Gray, John (*Men are from Mars; Women are from Venus*), 362
grief, 137, 138–139
gross income, 43
Guarantee State Pension Credit, 255
guardian, 171, 320, 371
guilt, 107, 129, 138, 157

• *H* •

Hague Convention, 374
Hall, Jerry (celebrity), 59
head hunter, 324

health insurance, 98, 214–215
hearing
    Cafcass involvement, 92
    children's living arrangements, 168–172
    contested divorce, 75–76
    cost of divorce, 116
    defined, 64, 374
    described, 90
    final hearing process, 300–306, 307–309
    judge's role, 306–307
    out-of-court settlement, 297–298
    pre-trial review, 298–300
    recent legal changes, 295
    types of courts, 64–65
    weighing options, 296
High Court, 65
HM Revenue and Customs, 212, 220
hobby, 327, 358, 359, 366
holiday
    break from troubled marriage, 23
    children's extra expenses, 215
    contact with children, 160
    parenting plan, 165
honesty, 89, 125, 157
hourly fee, 242
house. *See also* children's living arrangement
    children's comfort, 353
    cohabiting couples, 55
    cost of divorce, 120
    division of property, 181–185, 237–238
    first action after finalised divorce, 316–317
    informal separation tips, 97
    initiation of divorce, 109
    initiation of separation, 96
    marriage rights, 59
    mediation process, 271, 274
    negotiations in, 226
    ownership law, 42
    registered interest, 42–44
    resolution of divorce issues, 70
    statement of means, 85
    types of ownership, 44
household budget. *See* budget
household chore, 326–327
household income
    budget basics, 43
    budget creation, 40
    child support, 209, 210
    clean break, 201, 371

deduction of earnings order, 219
division of assets, 177
Family Help scheme, 254, 255, 257–258
financial assessment, 36
information for solicitor, 288
initiation of divorce, 113–114
mediation process, 271
spousal support considerations, 202
statement of means, 85
support, 119–120, 211, 255
women versus men, 203
worksheet, 41–42, 113–114
household spending plan. *See* budget
Housing Benefit, 120
How Do I Feel About My Parent's Divorce
    (Cole), 135
humour, sense of, 364
husband
    contact with children, 163
    divorce petition, 76
    non-resident fathers, 152
    parenting plan, 164–166
    primary care of children, 150
    rights of cohabiting couples, 56
    support systems, 141

• *I* •

IFS School of Finance, 47
illness, 133
immigrant, 66
income. *See* household income
income tax. *See* tax
indemnity, 183, 316
indirect contact, with children, 63, 158,
    162–163
individual voluntary arrangement (IVA), 340
inflation rate, 217
informal separation, 96–97
inheritance
    death of spouse, 205
    division of, 46, 175, 178
    pre-marital agreement, 343
Inheritance (Provision for Family and
    Dependents) Act 1975, 205
initial writ, 175
injunction, 30, 285, 374
Institute of Financial Planning, 322
insurance. *See specific types*

intake appointment, 262
intangible property, 174, 374
interdict order, 30, 285
interest rate, 51
interest-only mortgage, 194, 195
interim aliment, 179, 198
interim appointment, 85
interim hearing, 374
interim order, 285–286
interim periodical payment, 198
internal transfer, 190
International Child Abduction and Contact
    Unit, 335
Internet resources
    child support, 208, 385
    children's books, 136
    children's support groups, 15, 126, 385
    collaborative law, 73
    contact centres, 161
    conversations with children, 126, 127
    counsellor selection, 22, 24–25
    dating agencies, 360
    debt advice, 322
    divorce procedures, 381
    do-it-yourself divorce, 79, 259
    domestic abuse helplines, 23
    family law, 53
    financial advice, 47, 181, 322
    foreign divorce, 66
    government agencies, 383–384
    home ownership registration, 42–43
    job search, 323, 325
    legal aid, 118, 251
    marriage enrichment, 365
    mediation, 383
    negotiations with spouse, 229
    Northern Ireland, 386–387
    parenting plans, 164, 165
    pension information, 186–187
    professional advice, 382–383
    Scotland, 385–386
    single parenting, 151, 152
    solicitor complaints, 250
    solicitor referrals, 244, 383
    state benefits, 212
    tax credits, 119
    valuation of vehicles, 177
    youth advocacy, 172
intimidation, 224

inventory, asset, 97
investment
  budget tips, 37
  division of assets, 183–184
  initiation of divorce, 110, 111, 113
  mediation process, 271, 272
  pre-marital agreements, 345
irretrievably broken down marriage, 68–70
irrevocable trust, 320
IVA (individual voluntary arrangement), 340

Jagger, Mick (celebrity), 59
jargon, 311
Jewish faith, 74, 374
job
  change, 219
  pension benefits, 191
  post-divorce life, 357
  search, 120, 211, 255
  training, 323–325
Jobcentre Plus (job search agency), 324
Jobseeker's Allowance, 120, 211, 255
joint asset
  contested divorce, 120–122
  defined, 36, 375
  fair division, 45–46
  financial assessment, 36
  types of, 44
joint credit, 48–50
joint tenancy, 44, 59, 375
joint/shared residence, 62
judge. *See also* court
  Cafcass involvement, 91–92
  child support, 213–214
  children's living arrangements, 148, 167
  contact with children, 63, 162
  decree nisi, 80–81
  disclosure process, 89
  emergency orders, 83
  fair division of property, 45–46
  final dispute resolution appointment, 86–87
  final hearing, 306–307
  first directions appointment, 86
  flexibility of, 72
  formal separation process, 98
  function of, 17

grant of single status, 10
hearing basics, 90
occupation order, 30
pre-trial hearing, 298–299
separation agreements, 26
types of courts, 65
judgement, of hearing, 308–309, 316–319
judgement summons, 201, 333, 375
judicial separation, 27, 101, 375
jurisdiction, 375

• K •

Kirk, Mary (*Divorce: Living through the Agony*), 357

• L •

Land Registry, 42–44, 316, 375
late payment, 50, 51
law, family
  basics of, 68–71
  child support payments, 218–219
  children's concerns, 11, 169–172
  children's living arrangements, 167
  civil partnerships, 60
  cohabiting couples, 13
  collaborative law, 73
  confusing language, 2
  debts, 196
  defined, 53
  division of assets, 177–180
  fair division of property, 45–46
  flexibility of, 72
  history of, 53–56
  home ownership, 42
  importance of children, 147
  international citizens, 66
  Internet resources, 53
  legal marriages, 56–59
  maintenance, 179, 198, 205
  mediation outcomes, 264, 277
  parental rights/responsibilities, 149
  pension benefits, 38
  pre-marital agreements, 342, 345–347
  purpose of, 10
  regional differences, 12

terminology changes, 311
types of courts, 64–65
Law Society, 244, 250
Law Society of Scotland, 79, 267
legal aid
  defined, 247
  described, 118, 247
  mediation, 117, 262, 278–279
  qualifications, 251–258
legal annulment, 27
legal capacity, 342
Legal Complaints Service (LCS), 250
Legal Representation (Family Help
    scheme), 256
Legal Services Commission, 118, 251, 252, 258
legal strategy, 300–301
letter, agreement, 292
liability order, 334
licence, marriage, 56–57
life insurance
  benefits for children, 214
  divorce initiation, 110, 111, 113
  estate planning, 321
liquid asset, 100, 122
listening
  conversations with children, 132–133
  negotiations with spouse, 224
  solicitor's skills, 243
living arrangement. *See* children's living
    arrangement
loan
  credit review, 49–50
  credit-building tips, 50–51
  division of assets, 236
  divorce initiation, 109–110, 111
  mediation process, 272
  solicitor payments, 259
lodger, 358
lottery prize, 178
lump sum order, 84, 203, 375

• M •

magistrate, 17, 64
Magistrates Court, 65, 201, 333
maintenance. *See* child support/maintenance;
    spousal support/maintenance
maintenance pending suit, 84, 375

MALE (Men's Advice Line Enquiries)
    Helpline, 23
manipulation, 353
marital property, 174–175
marketable asset, 192
marriage
  annulment criteria, 28
  enrichment classes, 365
  foreign weddings, 66
  international citizen, 66
  legal requirements for marriage, 56–59
  mini-break from, 23–24
  minimum divorce requirements, 68
  reasons to stay married, 22–23
  relationship counselling, 23–25
  signs of trouble, 21–22
MATCH (Mothers living Apart from Their
    Children) (support group), 152
Matrimonial Causes Act 1973/1978, 10–11, 67
matrimonial fee funding scheme, 259
matrimonial home, 376
matrimonial property, 175–176, 179–180
Mayo, Bob (*Divorce - a Challenge to the
    Church*), 357
means test, 257–258
mediation
  agreement to mediate, 269
  benefits of, 17, 262, 265–266
  children's living arrangements, 168
  confidentiality, 273, 279
  cost of, 117
  defined, 74, 261, 376
  described, 261–262
  divorce initiation, 113
  divorce options, 73, 75
  emotional participants, 262
  Internet resources, 383
  lack of agreement, 279–280
  legal aid, 118, 257, 262, 278, 279
  legalities of outcome, 264
  mediator's role, 263
  Northern Ireland, 265, 267
  post-divorce conflicts, 330
  process, 268–277
  purpose of, 17
  safety of, 262
  Scotland, 265, 267–268, 278
  solicitor's help, 277–278

mediation *(continued)*
  solicitor's skills, 243
  successful negotiations, 81
  when to avoid, 264
mediator
  described, 17
  pre-marital agreements, 344
  qualifications and background, 263–264
  role of, 263
  safety of mediation, 262
  selection, 266–267
  solicitor recommendation, 264
Mediators' Institute of Ireland, 267
medical expense, 35
Memorandum of Understanding (mediation
    form), 276–277, 376
Men are from Mars; Women are from Venus
    (Gray), 362
Men's Advice Line Enquiries (MALE)
    Helpline, 23
minor, 320
Money Advice Scotland, 47
money management. *See* financial
    responsibility
money purchase, 38
mortgage
  division of assets, 177, 181–185, 236, 237
  divorce initiation, 109–110, 112
  endowments, 194
  financial assessment, 45, 109–110
  first actions after finalised divorce, 316
  mediation process, 272
  post-divorce money management, 321
  statement of means, 85
mother. *See also* wife
  child support negotiations, 216
  contact with children, 163
  divorce petition, 76
  financial effects of divorce, 34
  non-resident types, 152
  parenting plan, 164–166
  rights of cohabiting couples, 56
  spousal maintenance issues, 200
Mothers living Apart from Their Children
    (MATCH) (support group), 152
Muslim faith, 23, 74, 376, 379
Muslim Women's Helpline, 23

• *N* •

name change, 171
National Debtline, 47
National Insurance Contribution, 186
National Youth Advocacy Service, 172
negative statement, 128
negotiating with spouse
  anger, 224, 227
  asking for divorce, 107
  benefits of, 223
  child support payments, 216–218, 232–234
  children's living arrangements, 148, 155,
      167–172
  confidentiality, 224
  contact with children, 161, 162, 164
  court costs, 90
  deadlock, 225
  division of assets/debt, 235–238
  drawbacks of, 223–224
  effective behaviour, 224–225, 227
  expert advice, 229–230
  final agreement, 231–232, 238
  frustration with solicitor, 283
  Internet resources, 229
  mediation benefits, 262
  mediation process, 269–276
  method of, 225–226
  note taking, 230
  order of business, 227–229
  parenting plan, 164–166, 232
  preliminary stage, 225
  pre-marital agreement, 343–345
  session schedules, 227
  setting for negotiations, 226
  settlement details, 290–292
  shared financial responsibilities, 35
  solicitor's attendance, 230–232
  solicitor's skills, 241
  spousal support, 234–235
  taxes, 238
  tips for, 81, 228
net income, 43, 210
net value, of property, 176
New Deal (support program), 120
nightmare, 133
no order principle, 63

no-fault divorce, 376
nominal maintenance order, 200
non-aggressive strategy, 300
non-molestation order, 30, 31, 376
non-resident parent
　child support, 209, 210
　effects of living arrangements, 152
　post-divorce conflicts, 329–334
　post-divorce life, 327
Northern Ireland
　child support, 54, 212
　children's welfare officer, 17
　court systems, 65
　divorce law basics, 10–11, 12, 68–71
　divorce petitions, 80
　divorce rate, 11
　financial applications, 83
　helpful resources, 386–387
　home ownership, 42
　key laws, 67
　legal aid, 118, 252, 253
　mediation, 265, 267
　pre-marital agreements, 59
　statement of means, 85
note taking, 230, 246
nullity decree, 27, 28, 376

occupation order, 30, 31, 376
occupational pension scheme, 38, 187
offsetting assets, 189
older couple, 343
One Parent Families/Gingerbread Helpline,
　151, 212, 326
online dating, 359, 360
Open Financial Statement, 280
Open University, 47
opening speech, 307
order. *See* court order
ouster order, 30, 31
Outcome Statement (mediation form), 276–277

paid up policy, 194
parent with care, 209

parental rights/responsibilities. *See also*
　children
　children's divorce of parents, 172
　cohabiting couples, 55, 56
　criteria for contact, 63
　defined, 372, 377
　described, 61–62, 149
　family law, 11, 54, 55
　parenting plan, 164–166
　resolution of divorce issues, 70, 71
　support groups, 325
　types of contact with children, 62–63
parenting plan
　child support agreement, 217
　described, 164–166
　mediation process, 273, 274, 275
　negotiating with spouse, 228, 232
parenting skill, 155, 325, 352
Parentline Plus Helpline, 152
parent-teacher event, 160
part-time work, 48
party litigant, 79
patience, 107
payment plan, 258
Payplan (financial helpline), 47, 322
The Pension Advisory Service, 187
pension benefit
　cohabiting couple, 38, 55
　described, 38–39
　division of, 14, 178, 185–191
　divorce initiation, 112, 113
　first actions after finalised divorce, 318
　Internet resources, 186–187
　main benefits, 188
　main court orders, 84
　marriage rights, 59
　mediation process, 272, 274
　recent laws, 38
　resolution of divorce issues, 70, 71
　separation, 38, 98, 100
　statement of means, 85
Pension Credit, 119
periodic expense, 43
periodical allowance, 179, 180, 198, 205
periodical payment
　death of spouse, 205
　defined, 76, 84, 377
　described, 198
　formal applications to court, 83

personal finance course, 46
Personal Finance Society, 322
personal information, 287–288
personal injury settlement, 46, 178
personal need, 48, 63, 85
personal pension scheme, 38–39
petition, divorce, 73–79, 106
petitioner, 76, 82
pets, 165, 237
phone
  call to parent, 160
  expense, 97
police, 29–31, 335
portable information, 270
positive attitude, 128, 159
post-divorce life. *See also* finalised divorce
  bankruptcy filing, 339–340
  budget, 321–322, 357–358
  changes to settlement, 337–339
  conflicts with non-resident parent, 329–336
  considerations before divorce, 114–115
  debts, 195, 196
  described, 18
  division of assets, 176
  emotional response, 325–328
  estate planning, 319–321
  first actions after divorce, 316–319
  information for solicitor, 289
  job search, 323–325
  money management advice, 181
  parenting plan, 164–166
  property transfer conflicts, 336
  responsibilities to children, 351–354
  shared financial responsibilities, 35
  social life, 328, 355, 359–360
  spousal support conflicts, 336
  spousal support negotiations, 234–235
  stages of grief, 138–139
  tips for moving on, 355–360
post-marital agreement, 347–348, 377
power of arrest, 377
pregnancy, 28
pre-marital/pre-nuptial agreement
  child support agreement, 218
  defined, 341, 377
  described, 59, 341–343
  hearing process, 301
  initiation of divorce, 113
  legal agreements, 342, 345–347

marital property, 174
national differences in laws, 342
negotiations with spouse, 343–345
solicitor selection, 248
solicitor's help, 347
pre-mediation interview, 262
pre-trial hearing/review, 298–300, 377
primary school children, 130, 133, 135
principal private residence, 185
priority setting, 226, 273
prison, commitment to, 334
prisoner, child support from, 210
private insurance, 214–215
private investigator, 335
private process server, 78
privileged information, 273, 280, 377
problem solving, 22, 363, 364
process server, 78
profit-and-loss statement, 113
Prohibited Steps Order (court action), 171
promise, to children, 353
property. *See* asset
property adjustment order, 84, 378
property settlement, 183, 338
protective order, 30
publicly funded mediation, 257–258
publicly funded solicitor, 251
pursuer, 76, 79

questionnaire, 88

rebellion, 134
reconciliation
  after separation, 101–102
  during divorce process, 82
  irretrievably broken down marriage, 69
  post-divorce urge for, 356
redemption, 378
re-examination, 308
refuge, local, 31–32
register office wedding, 57, 60
rejection, 137
Relate (support group), 15, 24
Relationship Counselling for London, 25

relationship counsellor. *See* counsellor
relevant date, 113, 175, 187
religious annulment, 27, 28
religious wedding ceremony, 57, 59
reluctant witness, 303
remarriage
  civil divorce, 74
  decree absolute, 81
  spousal maintenance, 198, 204
  tips for success, 361–366
  trap, 70
remorse, 107
resentment, 23, 35
residence, of children. *See* children's living
    arrangement
Residence Order, 170, 378
Resolution (law organisation), 244
respondent, 76, 307, 308, 373
restraining order, 378
restriction, property, 44
retirement annuity contract, 38
retirement benefit, 185–187
Reunite (child-find organisation), 336
revenge, 122, 155
revocable trust, 320
Roman Catholic faith, 25, 27, 74
routine, daily, 129, 155, 164, 354
rules of intestacy, 319

• *S* •

safe deposit box, 121
salary scheme, 38
sale of business, 192
sale of home, 182–185
Samaritans (support group), 326
same-sex marriage, 57, 58
school performance, 133, 160
Scotland
  advocate's role, 64
  child support, 212
  children's living arrangements, 156, 167, 168
  civil partnerships, 60
  cohabiting couples' rights, 56
  confidentiality, 92
  contact centres, 161
  court systems, 65
  credit report error, 50

division of assets, 184, 187, 191
divorce law basics, 10–11, 12, 68–71
divorce petitions, 76, 79, 80
divorce rate, 11
exclusion order, 30
finalised divorce, 82, 108
financial applications, 83, 84
helpful websites, 385–386
key laws, 67
legal aid, 118, 252, 253
maintenance laws, 179, 198, 205, 285
matrimonial property, 175–176, 179–180
mediation, 265, 267–268, 278
pre-marital agreements, 59, 342
single parent support, 151
urgent orders, 285
waiting period, 54
Scottish Family Law Association, 79
Scottish Legal Aid Board (SLAB), 252, 265
Scottish Marriage Care (counselling), 25
Scottish Women's Aid, 23
sealed order, 277
secondary school age children, 129–130,
    133–135
second-hand news, 106
Section 41 certificate (children's living
    arrangement), 167
Section 32 buy-out policy (pension
    arrangement), 39
Section 28 bar (maintenance order), 201
secured debt, 195, 378
secured periodical payments order, 205, 378
self-esteem, 123–124, 128
self-invested personal pension (SIPP), 39
self-pity, 108
separation
  agreement, 26–27, 96–100, 290, 378
  behaviour during, 99
  dating during, 27, 94
  deed, 96
  defined, 375
  described, 25–26, 93
  discussion with spouse, 95
  divorce petition, 80
  drawbacks of, 94–95
  formal versus informal, 96
  initiation of, 96
  irretrievably broken down marriage, 69

separation *(continued)*
  judicial, 101
  legal grounds for divorce, 11
  pension benefits, 38
  permanent without divorce, 27
  process, 97
  reasons for, 94
  reconciliation, 101–102
  types of, 26
  waiting periods, 54, 69
service, 378
settlement. *See* finalised divorce
sex, 28
shared pension, 190–191, 377
shared residence, 152–155, 209
Sharia law, 74, 379
Sheriff Court, 65
shock, sense of, 138
sibling, 154
signing agreements, 100
single adult
  emotional adjustments, 325–328
  judge's role, 10
  support for parents, 151, 325, 359
SIPP (self-invested personal pension), 39
SLAB (Scottish Legal Aid Board), 252, 265
sliding scale payment, 255
small self-administered scheme (SSAS), 39
social housing, 184
social worker, 91, 92
sole residence, 62
solicitor
  affidavit in support of petition, 80, 284
  affordability, 242, 251–259
  appeal, 309–310
  children's living arrangements, 168
  client instructions, 283–285
  collaborative law, 73, 248, 293–294
  communication tips, 283–284, 287
  cost of divorce, 116–118
  defined, 63
  described, 16–17, 64
  disclosure process, 87
  dismissal of, 250–251
  divorce initiation, 113
  divorce options, 73–76
  divorce preparations, 37
  domestic violence, 30–31
  Family Help scheme, 254–258

  final hearing, 304–308
  foreign divorce, 66
  frustration during negotiations, 283
  informal separation tips, 97
  information collection, 286–289
  Internet resources, 383
  legal strategy, 300–301
  mediation help, 277–278
  mediator's recommendation, 264
  negotiations with spouse, 230–232
  payment alternatives, 203, 254–259
  poor mediation outcome, 279–280
  post-marital agreement, 348
  pre-marital agreement, 248, 347
  refusing to work with, 18
  role of, 243, 281–283
  Scotland's divorce petitions, 79
  selection, 240–242, 245–250
  separation process, 26, 27
  settlement details, 289–292
  specialists, 244
  successful negotiations, 81
  terms/conditions of business, 250
  tips for locating, 243–244
  types to avoid, 245
  urgent/interim orders, 285–286
  when to hire, 239–240
sorrow, 139
specialist, legal, 244
Specific Issue Order (court action), 171, 379
speed dating, 360
spending plan. *See* budget
spirituality, 357
sports, 359
spousal support/maintenance
  capital versus maintenance, 203–204
  changes in, 198–199, 204–205
  cohabiting couples, 56
  court's view, 200–203
  defined, 198, 375
  described, 197
  employability, 48
  factors affecting, 199–200
  family law history, 55
  lack of payment, 201
  negotiations with spouse, 234–235
  post-divorce conflicts, 336
  pre-marital agreement, 347
  remarriage, 198, 204

resolution of divorce issues, 71
Scotland, 179, 285
tax concerns, 206
urgent need, 85
SSAS (small self-administered scheme), 39
stakeholder plan, 39
stalking, 31
standard security, 184
state benefit. _See also specific benefits_
child support, 211–212
children's living arrangements, 156
cost of divorce, 119
Family Help scheme, 255
first actions after finalised divorce, 318
Internet resources, 186
mediation process, 271
State Retirement Pension, 38
statement
arrangements, 77, 379
means, 84–85, 270
support of application, 80
witness, 88
statutory charge, 118, 203, 252–253, 279
statutory scheme, 190
stay, of proceedings, 379
staying contact, 158
stepfamily, 124, 275
Stern, Sue Ellen (_Divorce is Not the End of the World_), 135
stress, 133–134, 325
subpoena, 379
substituted service, 78
summary annual report, 187
summons
defined, 379
division of assets, 175
divorce petition, 80
witness, 88, 303
supercession, 220
supervised contact, 158, 161, 162
supper club, 360
support group
children's, 15, 126
divorced singles, 326
domestic violence, 32
grandparent's, 127
healing process, 141
mediation in Scotland, 268
single parents, 151, 152, 325, 359

surname, 171
surrender value, 194
surveyor, 176, 182
sworn statement. _See_ affidavit

• _T_ •

talaq, 74, 379
tangible property, 174, 379
tax
budget basics, 43
child support, 211–212, 220
children's living arrangements, 156
cost of divorce, 119
division of assets, 185, 193
divorce initiation, 113
first actions after finalised divorce, 318
maintenance payments, 206
negotiations with spouse, 238
tenancy in common, 44, 59, 379
testamentary guardian, 320, 380
testimony, 308, 380
third party, 76
third party debt order, 334
timing
asking for divorce, 107
Cafcass involvement, 92
conversations with children, 129–130
decree absolute, 81
division of pension, 188
first directions appointment, 86
formal applications to court, 83–84, 91
hearing considerations, 296
initiation of separation, 96
legal appeals, 90
matrimonial property, 175
negotiations with spouse, 227
petition service, 78–79
pre-marital agreements, 346
resolution of divorce issues, 70–71
start of mediation, 262
waiting periods, 54, 69
toddler, 130, 133, 135
tradition, family, 328
training, job, 323–324
transcript, 380
transfer of ownership, 180, 316–317, 336
trial. _See_ hearing

trust, 157, 320–321, 380
trustee, 214, 320

• U •

undertaking, 31, 183, 380
unsecured debt, 195, 380
utilities, 97

• V •

variable expense, 43
vehicle, 111, 177, 272, 317
verification of statements, 272
violent behaviour. *See* domestic violence
visiting contact, 158
vocational course, 323–324
voluntary contribution, 39
voluntary disclosure, 88
voluntary work, 359

• W •

Wales
    Cafcass officer, 91
    contact centres, 161

divorce law basics, 10–11, 12, 68–71
divorce petitions, 77
endowments, 194
home ownership, 42
judicial separation, 101
key laws, 67
pre-marital agreements, 59, 342
wedding, 57, 59
Where's Daddy? (Curtis), 136
wife. *See also* mother
    divorce petition, 76
    family law history, 53
    financial effects of divorce, 34
    household income, 203
    pension benefits, 191
    spousal support changes, 55
    support systems, 141
will, 319–320
without prejudice basis, 86
witness, 88, 302–304, 308
Women's Aid Helpline, 23
Women's Aid in Northern Ireland, 23
Working Tax Credit, 119, 211, 212
writ, 80
written agenda, 228, 270

FOR

DUMMIES®

Do Anything. Just Add Dummies

UK editions

BUSINESS

Starting a Business For Dummies
978-0-470-51806-9

Understanding Business Accounting For Dummies
978-0-470-99245-6

Lean Six Sigma For Dummies
978-0-470-75626-3

FINANCE

Investing For Dummies
978-0-470-99280-7

Tax For Dummies
978-0-470-99811-3

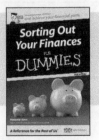

Sorting Out Your Finances For Dummies
978-0-470-69515-9

PROPERTY

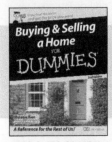

Buying & Selling a Home For Dummies
978-0-470-99448-1

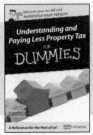

Understanding and Paying Less Property Tax For Dummies
978-0-470-75872-4

DIY & Home Maintenance For Dummies
978-0-7645-7054-4

Backgammon For Dummies
978-0-470-77085-6

Body Language For Dummies
978-0-470-51291-3

British Sign Language
For Dummies
978-0-470-69477-0

Business NLP For Dummies
978-0-470-69757-3

Children's Health For Dummies
978-0-470-02735-6

Cognitive Behavioural Coaching
For Dummies
978-0-470-71379-2

Counselling Skills For Dummies
978-0-470-51190-9

Digital Marketing For Dummies
978-0-470-05793-3

eBay.co.uk For Dummies,
2nd Edition
978-0-470-51807-6

English Grammar For Dummies
978-0-470-05752-0

Fertility & Infertility For Dummies
978-0-470-05750-6

Genealogy Online For Dummies
978-0-7645-7061-2

Golf For Dummies
978-0-470-01811-8

Green Living For Dummies
978-0-470-06038-4

Hypnotherapy For Dummies
978-0-470-01930-6

FOR DUMMIES®

A world of resources to help you grow

UK editions

SELF-HELP

978-0-470-01838-5

978-0-7645-7028-5

978-0-470-75876-2

HEALTH

978-0-470-69430-5

978-0-470-51737-6

978-0-470-71401-0

HISTORY

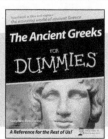

978-0-470-99468-9

978-0-470-51015-5

978-0-470-98787-2

Inventing For Dummies
978-0-470-51996-7

Job Hunting and Career Change
All-In-One For Dummies
978-0-470-51611-9

Motivation For Dummies
978-0-470-76035-2

Origami Kit For Dummies
978-0-470-75857-1

Personal Development All-In-One
For Dummies
978-0-470-51501-3

PRINCE2 For Dummies
978-0-470-51919-6

Psychometric Tests For Dummies
978-0-470-75366-8

Raising Happy Children For
Dummies
978-0-470-05978-4

Starting and Running a Business
All-in-One For Dummies
978-0-470-51648-5

Sudoku for Dummies
978-0-470-01892-7

The British Citizenship Test
For Dummies, 2nd Edition
978-0-470-72339-5

Time Management For Dummies
978-0-470-77765-7

Wills, Probate, & Inheritance Tax
For Dummies, 2nd Edition
978-0-470-75629-4

Winning on Betfair For Dummies,
2nd Edition
978-0-470-72336-4

13902_p2

FOR
DUMMIES®

The easy way to get more done and have more fun

LANGUAGES

978-0-7645-5194-9

978-0-7645-5193-2

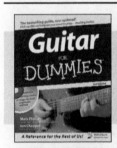

978-0-471-77270-5

MUSIC

978-0-7645-9904-0

978-0-470-03275-6
UK Edition

978-0-7645-5105-5

SCIENCE & MATHS

978-0-7645-5326-4

978-0-7645-5430-8

978-0-7645-5325-7

Art For Dummies
978-0-7645-5104-8

Baby & Toddler Sleep Solutions For
Dummies
978-0-470-11794-1

Bass Guitar For Dummies
978-0-7645-2487-5

Brain Games For Dummies
978-0-470-37378-1

Christianity For Dummies
978-0-7645-4482-8

Filmmaking For Dummies, 2nd
Edition
978-0-470-38694-1

Forensics For Dummies
978-0-7645-5580-0

German For Dummies
978-0-7645-5195-6

Hobby Farming For Dummies
978-0-470-28172-7

Jewelry Making & Beading For
Dummies
978-0-7645-2571-1

Knitting for Dummies, 2nd Edition
978-0-470-28747-7

Music Composition For Dummies
978-0-470-22421-2

Physics For Dummies
978-0-7645-5433-9

Sex For Dummies, 3rd Edition
978-0-470-04523-7

Solar Power Your Home For Dummies
978-0-470-17569-9

Tennis For Dummies
978-0-7645-5087-4

The Koran For Dummies
978-0-7645-5581-7

U.S. History For Dummies
978-0-7645-5249-6

Wine For Dummies, 4th Edition
978-0-470-04579-4

**Available wherever books are sold. For more information or to order direct go to
www.wiley.com or call +44 (0) 1243 843291**

13902_p3

FOR DUMMIES®

Helping you expand your horizons and achieve your potential

COMPUTER BASICS

978-0-470-27759-1

978-0-470-13728-4

978-0-471-75421-3

DIGITAL LIFESTYLE

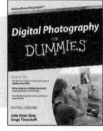

978-0-470-25074-7

978-0-470-39062-7

978-0-470-17469-2

WEB & DESIGN

978-0-470-19238-2

978-0-470-32725-8

978-0-470-34502-3

Access 2007 For Dummies
978-0-470-04612-8

Adobe Creative Suite 3 Design Premium
All-in-One Desk Reference For Dummies
978-0-470-11724-8

AutoCAD 2009 For Dummies
978-0-470-22977-4

C++ For Dummies, 5th Edition
978-0-7645-6852-7

Computers For Seniors For Dummies
978-0-470-24055-7

Excel 2007 All-In-One Desk Reference F
or Dummies
978-0-470-03738-6

Flash CS3 For Dummies
978-0-470-12100-9

Mac OS X Leopard For Dummies
978-0-470-05433-8

Macs For Dummies, 10th Edition
978-0-470-27817-8

Networking All-in-One Desk Reference
For Dummies, 3rd Edition
978-0-470-17915-4

Office 2007 All-in-One Desk Reference
For Dummies
978-0-471-78279-7

Search Engine Optimization For
Dummies, 2nd Edition
978-0-471-97998-2

Second Life For Dummies
978-0-470-18025-9

The Internet For Dummies, 11th Edition
978-0-470-12174-0

Visual Studio 2008 All-In-One Desk
Reference For Dummies
978-0-470-19108-8

Web Analytics For Dummies
978-0-470-09824-0

Windows XP For Dummies, 2nd Edition
978-0-7645-7326-2

Printed and bound by CPI Group (UK) Ltd, Croydon, CR0 4YY